Petru Popescu was Romania's most provocative young author before defecting from Ceausescu's brutal regime to make his home in Los Angeles, where he writes books and films. He is best known in Britain for his thrillers *Burial of the Vine* and *Before and After Edith*.

Amazon Beaming is his first work of non-fiction.

AMAZON
BEAMING

'A truly remarkable book that bears comparison to Bruce Chatwin's *The Songlines* as an exploration of native ways of thought, a journey at once through space, time and consciousness.' *Outside*

'If you thought *Dances With Wolves* was a good civilized/savage story, this one will amaze you. It's the non-fiction equivalent of *At Play in the Fields of the Lord*.' *Booktalk*

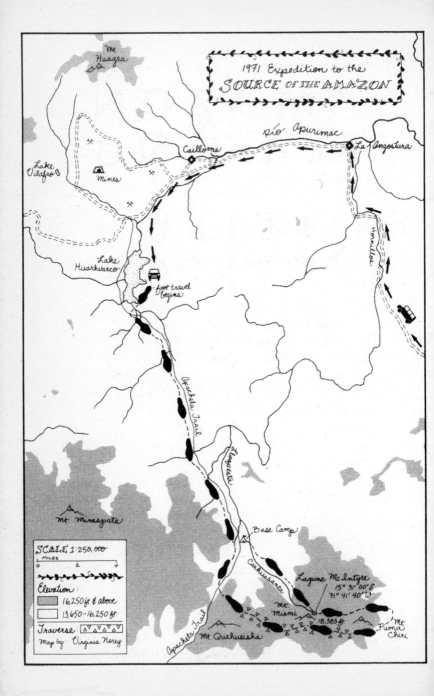

1971 Expedition to the
SOURCE OF THE AMAZON

Mt Huagra

Río Apurimac

Cailloma

La Angostura

Lake Vilafro B

Mines

Lake Huarhuarco

foot travel begins

Homillos

Apacheta Trail

Huaquista

Mt Minaspata

Base Camp

Carhuasanta

Laguna McIntyre
15° 31' 00" S
71° 41' 40" W

SCALE 1:250,000
MILES
0   2   4
Elevation:
16,250 ft & above
13,650–16,250 ft.
Traverse: △▽△▽△▽
Map by Virginia Norey

Mt Mismi
18,383 ft.

Mt Quehuisha

Mt Puma Chiri

Apacheta Trail

AMAZON
BEAMING

PETRU
POPESCU

AN ABACUS BOOK

First published in Great Britain by Macdonald & Co Publishers (Ltd) 1991
This edition published by Abacus 1993

A CIP catalogue record for this book is available from the British
Library.

ISBN 0 349 10453 0

Printed in England by Clays Ltd, St Ives plc

Abacus
A Division of
Little, Brown and Company (UK) Limited
165 Great Dover Street
London SE1 4YA

"The river now widened, so that in places it looked like a long lake; it wound in every direction through the endless marshy plain, whose surface was broken here and there by low mountains. The splendour of the sunset I never saw surpassed. We were steaming east toward clouds of storm. The river ran, a broad highway of molten gold, into the flaming sky; the far-off mountains loomed purple across the marshes; belts of rich green, the river-banks stood out on either side against the rose hues of the rippling water; in front, as we forged steadily onward, hung the tropic night, dim and vast."

THEODORE ROOSEVELT,
Through the Brazilian Wilderness

For Iris, Adam and Chloe

Preface

As the reader will notice, *Amazon Beaming*'s narrative style alternates between the third person and the first. That may seem unusual, but the book really wrote itself that way.

When I started researching the story of Loren McIntyre's quest for the Amazon's source, and of his unusual relationship with a branch of the Mayoruna tribe, I was faced with a global difficulty. Most of the events to be narrated were twenty years old. Despite the integrity of McIntyre's own memory, the documentation was fragmented into personal notes (some were intended to become part of a regular diary, yet never did), as well as letters, photographs and their captions, books and articles, stories published in the *National Geographic*, and testimonies of friends and colborators. Altogether, I started telling McIntyre's story by pulling it out of that overpowering mass of material, as a third person narrative.

But through the writing, as I came to passages that needed expanding or simply peeked my curiosity, I asked Loren new questions, recorded his answers on tape, and re-recorded older first person accounts of this or that incident. At that point, the fact that it all had happened in the past became an advantage. Loren could comment with all the acumen provided by verified references and hindsight. We were both able to speculate and to add new data. And in recounting the most suspenseful moments, I could use a pace and wealth of description that no diary can afford.

Thus the recordings, enlarged and rewritten, became the book's first person sections. They are the best I could do to recreate McIntyre's own voice. I thought about converting them back to the third person, but that seemed more artificial than using two narrative modes, because it robbed the book of a naturalness and sincerity that only made the story more poignant.

So I left them in the first person. I hope that the readers will forgive the trick, and enjoy the immediacy of an adventure happening here and now.

PETRU POPESCU   *Los Angeles, March 1991*

Contents

The Ritual

The Source

Introduction

by Loren McIntyre

We were embarked on the greatest mass of flowing fresh water on earth. Yet in the comfort of my cabin, amid a clutter of cameras and conversation, we were conscious of sailing down to the sea at eighteen knots only when our six hundred passenger vessel heeled a little to port or starboard in answer to the rudder that urged it to follow the river's sinuosities.

We were three. Petru Popescu, Jean-Michel Cousteau, and I. Although Petru's native tongue was Romanian and Jean-Michel's was French, we chatted in the relaxed Californian English that suited us best. And we gesticulated in silent languages, as when we lifted our glasses to some of the bold ones who had made this transcontinental voyage in dugout canoes: Friar Brieva in 1637, Madame Godin in 1769, and John Schultz in 1947. And we saluted the Amazons, whoever they might be, who had showered Orellana with arrows in 1542 and lent this river their name.

On our own voyage down the River of the Amazons, Petru wondered aloud how explorers communicated with remote forest Indians in the absence of interpreters. "Among the Achuara, how did you deal with it?" he asked Jean-Michel, son of oceanographer Jacques.

Jean-Michel raised his hand chest-high, palm outward, as if to put a stop to something. "Like this. Or with grunts and grimaces that transcend cultural and even species differences. Body English that even wild animals understand."

"Well, that's fine for showing anger or sorrow or asking for something to eat," said Petru. "But how would you advise a creature of the forest about a plot against his life? Or ask him the reason for worshipping the wind? Abstract things . . ."

"There may be a way." I spoke without thinking. Maybe the champagne had loosened my tongue. All these years I had kept from mentioning a strange case of apparent thought transference I experienced among the Mayoruna Indians because it seemed preposterous. Now all of a sudden, I brought it up.

I didn't mean to make a big thing out of it, but evidently I told just enough about my Mayoruna experiences to whet the literary appetite of Petru Popescu and to leave Jean-Michel Cousteau vowing to join me on a headwater expedition as soon as he and his father finished the long sojourn they called "the rediscovery of the world." Jean-Michel pocketed the wire hood of the champagne bottle, saying, "This is a cage." He handed the cork to Petru. "You keep the bird. When we meet again, whoever fails to produce either bird or cage must buy the bottle."

Verbal communication is Petru's occupation. He speaks four languages, reads a couple more, and wrote books in Romanian and then in English before settling in Hollywood, where he divides his time between writing books and screenplays. Even so, Petru has long been fascinated with non-verbal communication. He asked me to tell him more about the Mayorunas, peppering me with questions all the way down the Amazon. I now believe that somewhere in the back of his head Petru had already begun to write *Amazon Beaming*, while in the bottom of my brain lay the conviction that the story would never be told.

Since he works in a medium and in a locality – Hollywood – where high visibility is the stuff of success, Petru was puzzled by the lack of hullabaloo about my expedition to the most distant Amazon headwaters in 1971. The *National Geographic* published an account of it. But not until 1987, the year of our shipboard conversation, did my name and picture appear in *The Guinness Book of World Records* as discoverer of the source. Petru had long been fascinated by Burton and Speke's tales of their search for the source of the Nile. Though we had only known each other for a few days, he told me that he would drop everything and write the full story of the discovery of the ultimate source of the Amazon, if I would participate.

Doubtful that anything would come of it, I agreed, never imagining how drastically it would interfere with other plans and change my directions. For four years, since that day on the river when we shared a bottle of champagne with Jean-Michel Cousteau, Petru's thoughts and mine have lunged and parried as in a duel until, at last, to my amazement, *Amazon Beaming* has become pinioned between two hard covers.

Petru Popescu wrote this book with enormous enthusiasm, but he had the devil's own time with it because of my inaccessibility. There was a burst of note-taking while we descended the Amazon and cruised the Caribbean. Petru is a swift writer, but I ran off to Brazil for the *Geographic* and a year went by before he cornered me with a tape recorder in Washington D.C. I had assignments and my own books to write and illustrate, but there was no backing away, despite distances and time differences. For the next three years we both wrote bulky letters. I narrated episodes into tapes and mailed Petru clippings, photographs and other pieces of research. We spent hundreds of hours on the phone, met twice in Washington and twice in California, and talked into the night, arguing about literary renditions of events or thoughts that had been intimate or minuscule at the time, yet were creating now a sort of philosophy of the places and people I had encountered during some forty years.

For a good part of the process, I felt reluctant. Things I had lived but rarely talked about would be exposed to an unseen audience. I feared readers would think I'd gone around the bend. Petru was drawing upon his considerable research on time and early man to lend logic to something that was never logical in the first place: communication that was so direct that no poet could find words for it.

And I was torn by the usual dilemma of a lensman who aims at unknown and unknowing targets. He wants to bring back a great picture that makes the viewer say "Wow!" yet he's morally uneasy about exposing innocents to alien societies and possible future intrusion by aliens, by us. But maybe that's just an excuse to mask a yen for exclusivity, as in the case of some anthropologists who try to keep their subjects pristine by excluding all contact with outsiders – except, of course, themselves.

Because he no longer writes in his own tongue but in English, Petru Popescu reminds me of Joseph Conrad. Conrad's masterful novels about South America, Africa, and other hearts of darkness were largely autobiographical and ridden with visions of despair, whereas Popescu dares to tackle themes beyond his personal experience that require enormous research, and he is optimistic about the human condition. A *joie de vivre* that blossomed with his escape fifteen years ago from Romania and its multiple censorship has not withered. While Conrad viewed writing as an illness, Popescu is that rare writer who really likes to write in his adopted language. His pairing of themes in this book strikes me as just right for telling about my concurrent journeys through psychological and physical time, on the Rio Javari and to the Apurímac source.

Someday, I'd like to take Petru to a certain Shangri-La in Amazon headwater country. He would find it overflowing with material for an autobiographical novel which would release the cry of freedom that has been swelling in his chest ever since his defection from Romania. I'd ask Jean-Michel Cousteau to join us. If Jean-Michel brings along the small wire cage and Petru remembers the champagne cork, it would fall to my lot to buy the bottle.

LOREN MCINTYRE *Arlington, Virginia, April 1991*

THE VANISHING TRIBE

"For forty-eight days we saw no human being. In passing these rapids we lost five of the seven canoes with which we started and had to build others. One of our best men lost his life in the rapids. Under the strain one of the men went completely mad . . . murdered the sergeant and fled into the wilderness."

THEODORE ROOSEVELT
Through the Brazilian Wilderness

"The first explorers of South America were Indians who hunted in forests, erected stone shrines on snowy peaks, and buried treasure in desert tombs."

LOREN McINTYRE
Exploring South America

1

Over the Ocean Forest

Upper Amazonia, October 1969

"I am afraid," said the pilot, "that we won't be able to land anywhere."

"Where is the village?" asked the explorer. "If this is the area where you saw the village, let's go on as long as we can. Make sure at least that it's still there."

They were hurtling at a hundred miles an hour over jungle treetops in a Cessna 206 floatplane. The clouds were hanging low, less than three hundred feet above the jungle, and in order to reconnoiter the terrain the plane had to fly beneath them. Carrying extra containers of gasoline, their limit of flying time was nine hours, of which four had elapsed. To be safe, they should turn back now and arrive at base with an hour's worth of fuel still in the tanks. If they didn't find what they were looking for within minutes, they would have to give up.

Even so, the return would not be without risk. They might meet a thunderstorm which they would have to bypass, depleting the reserve fuel even more. A Cessna was hard to glide down, and it could only be put down on the river, since landing on wheels in a jungle without clearings is practically impossible. But this Cessna had no wheels anyway. Rivers were the highways out here—you flew along them and landed in them. They were the entries into the Amazon Basin, the routes for trading, the front lines of population growth and development.

The rivers were also the main feature on maps: ever since man had begun to record his exploration, the hydrography, the "blue stuff," had been marked on his maps first. It was the same with the maps aboard the Cessna: the most reliable contours on them were the rivers. The forest was a giant green mask, hiding most other variations of terrain. As for the tributary the plane was now following, at its lowest level in the month of October, it looked like a trench filled with the skeleton of a giant fish. The tree trunks fallen across the brown stream were its bones, the sandbars and mudbanks its rotting flesh.

"There were plenty of good stretches to land on just two months ago," lamented the pilot.

He swooped down deeper into the trench. Suddenly the flight became a struggle to keep the Cessna's wingtips between the treetops flashing past on both sides. As the pilot was flying too low now to anticipate the curves of the river, all he could do was expect one every few seconds and brace himself to stay with it.

The Rio Javari, a south bank tributary of the Amazon and possibly its most tortuous due to the extremely mild incline of the terrain, meandered some nine hundred miles from its birth to where it flowed into the Amazon proper. By cutting curves in flight, however, there were only some five hundred miles from source to confluence, practically the distance flown by the Cessna in the last four hours. Which meant that the muddy stream below was soon to disappear. The Cessna was struggling for a clear stretch of water to land on only minutes from the source of the Javari.

For the last half hour, the pilot had been marking down on his chart the exact location of every *estirón* ("straight stretch of river") that he could land on, timing his progress almost to the second. If he found no landing place by the Javari's source and had to turn back, he knew exactly how far he had to go. But turning back would mean giving up on the Indian village which, as the pilot had explained to the explorer, lay minutes from the source, on the Brazilian bank of the Javari.

The Javari's banks were built of soft earth, without rocks or stones. As the river lowered from May through October, the flow's failing pressure no longer held up the banks and they frittered, letting a generation of trees fall across the riverbed. Some were over a hundred feet tall.

The curves were unpredictable, the map of no specific usefulness. The Javari's path had been shifting every year since long before man had appeared in the Americas, following the dictates of its changing volume. The soil of its banks was soft: the billions of root ramifications weaving through it failed to give it a lasting structure. The river kept reshaping the banks, abandoning old beds and cutting new ones, sometimes bisecting itself. The history of that shifting was absorbed by the facelessness of the jungle. And now this small plane, an object of puffing pistons and grinding gears, flew above this vast primordial space, searching for one short stretch of clear flow to land on.

"Logs," the pilot called over the sound of the engine. "Fallen trees everywhere."

Three minutes later, they were still hugging the river's curves. In the seat next to the pilot, a half-Indian guide kept a tense silence; the pilot noticed him mop a tear of sweat from his temple with his brown thumb.

"In two minutes, I'm going back," the pilot shouted over his shoulder. He turned his head to check on the explorer, who flew strapped in the seat by the Cessna's starboard doorway. The door had been removed to enable him to take pictures, so Loren McIntyre sat in silhouette against the blur of the treetops zooming past the plane. He aimed the stubby cannon of a Minolta SR–101 at the jungle.

"First find that village," he shouted back. "Climb a little higher and see where we are."

With a shrug, the pilot thrust up and out of the river's trench, climbing as high as visibility permitted. They zoomed under the boiling edge of a planet of clouds seeming ready to crash down into the misty forest.

Suddenly a crater-shaped clearing opened below. All three fliers, one looking through the camera lens, saw a half circle of Indian huts, the space between them zigzagged by a handful of running figures. The half-Indian guide waved. Then the vision was harshly cut off by the jungle.

The plane banked sharply back to the river. The three men looked down anxiously. Fallen trees and sand bars snagged the flow upstream and down. A Cessna could land and come to a full stop in less than five hundred feet, but it needed three times that distance to get airborne again. And without a beach to unload the explorer's supplies and equipment and steady the plane for refilling the gas tanks from the plastic containers now cramping the cargo space, a clean stretch of water was useless.

Despite all that, a smile played on the pilot's stubbly face. "I think that's the village," he yelled.

That was the village he had told McIntyre about back in Iquitos, Peru, when they had met. The pilot thought it to be a village of Mayoruna Indians, the most enigmatic tribe of the region, until recently believed extinct.

McIntyre nodded back, aware that each moment, even the instant of his nodding, was taking them farther away, into jungle time. Jungle time is measured in days and weeks— their landing spot might be moments away by air but would turn out to be several days of paddling from the village. He looked at the mixed-blood bush guide; Carlitos, a half-Cahuapana Indian, had been hired only two days before in Leticia, Colombia, near the confluence of the Javari with the Amazon. He'd insisted that he knew the river and the sites of several Mayoruna villages. He also claimed that their dialect was related to his own, which neither McIntyre nor Mercier, the pilot, could confirm, since they didn't speak Mayoruna. At the moment, Carlitos was looking airsick.

McIntyre leaned toward the plane's open doorway. The treetops zipped by so fast that a good shot was out of the question. But he always got a bang out of sweeping thus over the jungle, and it helped keep his anxieties in a suspended state. The last four hours had been compact with risk. A storm could punch out of the clouds at any time, fracturing this flying toy. Engine failure could make them lose control and crash into the trees. A forced landing over fallen trunks could slam cargo and people forward with deadly force, tearing the plane apart, blowing the flammable gasoline vapors against the exposed hot engine and turning fuselage and bodies into a pyre. But zooming like this kept his anxieties abstract; just a few more inches of leaning toward the slipstream, and the air roaring past the plane would slap his face and peel his eyelids back. What he felt now was a frantic urge to see enough, to *be* enough to comprehend the forest underneath. It looked planetary. It was an ocean of forest. It was fitting that the Amazon River had been baptized "O Rio Mar" by the first Portuguese explorers: the River Sea.

This was also the easiest, most pleasant part of exploration, when the wilderness was spread at his feet. Once down, the walking and paddling began, and with them came the sweat, the stickiness, the strange food. And then the insects, the jungle's first line of defense: gnats and mosquitoes, *piums* and *isula* ants, *chicharra machacuys*, or viper locusts, and so many others named and unnamed. Everything that stung, bit, pricked, or slipped its eggs into human skin for delayed invasion, wrapping a human in a cloud of insect activities, the least aggressive of which was the buzzing.

He heard his own grunt of relief: he'd just glimpsed a clean stretch of water, running past a brown riverbank. The riverbank sloped gently out of the water, then rose steeply and vanished under the forest that covered the whole Brazilian shore. McIntyre checked his watch. Only two minutes had passed since they had been above the village.

Two minutes of air time. Maybe two days of jungle time.

Yelling over the throb of the engine, they discussed a way of alerting the Indians in the village that they would be landing not too far upstream. They agreed to turn back and fly over

7

the village wagging the plane's wings. "Let's do it twice," McIntyre suggested. Even for uncontacted tribes, aircraft were becoming familiar, and that sort of aerial body language was the closest to an explicit message they could think of.

The pilot turned the Cessna. For a whole minute, the clearing seemed lost. But then a crenellation of treetops announced the empty space beyond, and the village reappeared. More tribesmen had spilled out of their huts; McIntyre estimated there were at least three dozen. They made no hostile gestures and didn't attempt to hide, surprising for a tribe that had been in virtual hiding for seventy years. Were they really Mayoruna?

As if reading McIntyre's mind, the guide turned and ran his brown thumb over his upper lip, indicating the Mayorunas' specific tattoo, which McIntyre knew from drawings and a single recent photograph: a broad dark blue line hemming in both lips and continuing back across the cheeks. Men, women, and children wore it, also puncturing their lips and the outer sides of their nostrils and sticking in the holes five- to seven-inch-long palm spines, the same kind of thin straight spines they used as sewing needles. Primitively but hauntingly, the tattoo and spines made them resemble jaguars, which they believed themselves to be descended from. For that reason they were also known as cat-people.

Yes, the guide was saying. Those were cat-people down there.

After circling above the village, the Cessna flew upstream and descended toward the river. Float planes usually land against the current and take off heading downstream. Mercier touched down on the water and almost came to a stop, then proceeded to dock by the mudbank by revving against the current while the cargo rattled like a crateful of chickens waking up. McIntyre stepped out and onto one of the floats with a rope and a long oar in his hands. As soon as the propeller stopped and the floats grated against the brown sand, McIntyre stuck the oar down into the sand, threw the rope around the oar, and fastened it. They would look around later for a strong tree trunk, to provide better mooring for the plane's twelve hundred pounds. The guide had already started to move McIntyre's gear toward the open doorway.

McIntyre jumped ashore. The Indian guide jumped out after him, landed in the brown shallow ripples, and shivered. It was eleven in the morning. Even without sunlight, the heat wrapped them possessively, and McIntyre immediately felt his collar go limp with sweat.

After three hours of engine roar, their dulled hearing barely perceived other sounds. But soon the gurgle of the river and the jaggedness of bird calls, the sound of one's own breathing, words, every kind of natural noise became audible. McIntyre's equipment and supplies were stashed in flour sacks which had been rubberized—dipped into liquid latex to make them waterproof—and strung three feet apart on a long rope. If they were washed from a canoe while running rapids or otherwise dumped into the river, he stood a good chance not only to save his equipment but also to save himself, as the buoyant sacks would catch a low branch and stop both man and gear from drifting away or sinking.

As the guide and the pilot helped McIntyre with the sacks, the guide shivered again, then suddenly shook so hard that he dropped his load. McIntyre heard the clinking of a sack of presents: little mirrors, combs, knives, and other trinkets easy to hang on bushes and trees. He had bought them in a riverfront store in Leticia, to help seduce the uncontacted Mayoruna into contact.

Both he and the pilot rushed over. Mercier, who was French and a Catholic missionary, had a training in tropical diseases. It took him one look to guess what the trouble was.

"Malaria?" he inquired.

Carlitos murmured confusedly that he'd had malaria once. But he had been cured of it for years.

McIntyre and Mercier exchanged a glance. Their friendship was less than a week old. They had met in Iquitos, the Amazon's last big port, twenty-three hundred miles upstream from the mouth, three hundred miles from Leticia.

Iquitos, a sprawl of tin-roofed houses looking from the air like corrugated turtles, is the capital of Peru's largest Amazonian state, Loreto, selling to the world timber, zoo articles like snakes, caimans, and monkeys, and, more recently, drugs. A lavish metropolis by bush standards, it flaunts paved streets and licensed dentists.

Mercier and McIntyre had met the way civilizados usually meet at these latitudes, chancing their trust in each other within minutes without asking for credentials. They had grown friendly over the topic of the cat-people's reappearance. At Yarinacocha, Peru, a team from the Summer Institute of Linguistics, the best organized of all the evangelizing breeds active in Amazonia, had contacted the Mayoruna several times in the last three years; they were the ones who announced that the Mayoruna, believed exterminated at the time of the rubber boom, had survived in the depth of the jungle. No one had officially attempted a contact on the Brazilian side, though the tribe had traditionally straddled the border, but Mercier told McIntyre how he had landed next to a village on the Javari that summer and deemed the inhabitants to be Mayoruna.

Mercier had spent a few hours among naked men and women with cat whiskers, found them intelligent and friendly, and decided that they were good material for a mission. Mercier spoke no Mayoruna and had never met Mayorunas before, but what convinced him of their identity were the cat whiskers, worn by no other tribe in the area. By his estimate, the village lay close to the Javari's source.

Anthropologically speaking, that constituted the beginning of a first contact with an unacculturated tribe, so McIntyre listened to him with fascination. Though he was not an anthropologist, McIntyre had a passion for visiting tribes and had done it repeatedly since 1953, being even part of a first contact once, with a branch of the Chacobo tribe of Bolivia. The chance of another first encounter and perhaps of taking some sensational photographs excited him. Thinly financed from home, Mercier often rented his services as a pilot, so McIntyre hired man and plane at $120 an hour plus an hour's rate for each overnight. From Iquitos they flew to Leticia, where the already mile-wide Amazon received the muddy flow of the Javari, and from there they had headed upstream.

Now here they were, hoping that the village they had glimpsed from the plane was the one Mercier remembered.

"What are we going to do if Carlitos is sick?" Mercier wondered aloud.

McIntyre pondered. "Postpone the expedition and take him back."

Carlitos suppressed a chatter of teeth and said that he was all right. Then he needed to sit down: in the last fifteen minutes his cheeks had sunk. Contritely, Mercier delayed the refueling of the plane and they sat down on the brown sand for a lunch of sandwiches and Cokes still cool from the plane's ice chest.

Carlitos had scouted the Amazonian bush both for missionaries and geologic prospectors and planned to become a one-man tourist agency specializing in Indians. Both he and Mercier were quite typical of the Amazon's cast of characters. The exception was the *yanqui*, the photographer. In his early fifties, five-ten but looking taller from the tautness of his lanky body, McIntyre was now pulling out of his kit some chloroquine tablets, his straight strong profile cutting the hot air. He had hazel eyes that trained themselves on things and people with some initial fixedness, as if eager to observe them exactly. His voice sounded like he'd never been angry in his life, and his gestures were efficient and uncomplicated, all actually part of the self-discipline taught by ten years of naval service. After handing Carlitos the tablets, he rose and prowled back and forth on the mudbank, taking pictures of the plane, of the location, and of the two other men, documenting the already doubtful expedition.

He stopped once, to instruct Carlitos to drink more liquid.

Camera clicking, he noticed that the shore, some ten feet high, dropped in one spot, becoming almost level with the strip of mud they had landed on. There the trees rose from the waterline, making for a spectacular shot, so McIntyre headed for the trees.

He kneeled, getting his camera ready, then got up slowly and made his way back to the others.

"Indians, in the forest," he whispered, and reached to pull over a bag of gifts. He broke out of it a cardboard box with six cheap pocket mirrors and walked back with it and with the camera toward the unseen Indians.

Mercier jumped as if struck by an electric shock. The village they had overflown seemed unwary of strangers, and if it was the same Mercier had visited in summer he had reason to expect a friendly reception. But two minutes of flight upstream meant that they were now at least two days of paddling away from it, so these had to be other Indians, their intentions as yet unknown. Historically, the Mayoruna were a numerous enough tribe to spread over thousands of square miles and had developed dialects sometimes as dissimilar as separate languages. The Javari, marking the border between Peru and Brazil, was sparsely dotted by civilizado settlements of a few houses, none deserving to be called a town. Instead, its beaches invited the sunbathing of caimans fourteen to eighteen feet long while its swamps bubbled with piranha. Two years before, oil prospectors forcing their way into this dereliction had been porcupined with arrows by unidentified tribesmen. The Mayoruna, never successfully acculturated, had always been at war with both civilizados and the neighboring tribes that sold other Indians for slaves. In fact, their relation with the outer world had become so adverse that at the turn of the century, as the rubber boom brought more intrusion and conflict to upper Amazonia, they had simply plunged into the forest and disappeared.

And now they were reappearing, undoubtedly still carrying memories of strife and bloodshed.

All that was suddenly thrown at Mercier, like an ominous background to Loren's sparse communication. He had no weapons within reach, though there was a rifle in the Cessna.

Yet that didn't hold him back. He moved to follow McIntyre, and Carlitos shuffled behind. Mercier's plan to start a mission here received an inspirational boost from what he saw: inside a pattern of spiky leaves shone several small brown faces. One showed a blue tattoo or streak of paint over the upper lip—or maybe it was just the shadow of a leaf. But staring at McIntyre's camera, the faces conveyed the innocence of children everywhere.

2

Gifts on the Riverbank

McIntyre had first read about the Mayoruna in the chronicles of the conquistadors. The Spaniards had first entered the area in 1541, coming down the Andes after subduing the Incas. They were looking for El Dorado, a quest that saw many expeditions return to their bases in Peru and Ecuador decimated and empty-handed. Especially gruesome was the story of Don Pedro de Ursúa's expedition. Ursúa was betrayed and killed by his lieutenant Lope de Aguirre, who ended up rising against the crown and pillaging the Spanish settlements on the Caribbean. So demented was Aguirre that his own soldiers had preferred to desert and take their chances with the cannibal-infested jungle.

Legend had it that some Spanish soldiers joined the Mayoruna tribe, a scattered confederation who claimed descent from jaguars. Travelers who met the Mayoruna later described them as having thick beards and white skins ("more like English than Spaniards," one noted). Other accounts, more likely correct, explained the nickname *barbudos*, "bearded," by the labrets of palm wood they wore in their lips. The Mayoruna's first major contact with civilization set the pattern for subsequent encounters: no commerce with the white world, but a measure of pity for its stragglers. Later, as their numbers were depleted in intertribal wars, the Mayoruna resorted more and more to capturing Europeans, especially females, which explained their occasional light pigmentation.

Like their jaguar fathers, the Mayoruna were described as impossible to "tame" (which meant to convert). They had always been semi-nomadic. For a long time they even lacked the blowgun, which is standard in the area, and fought with only arrows and clubs. They fought neighbors and civilizados, fought the slave-trading Conibo and Puna, who raided them over and over until and particularly during the rubber boom. Never strong in numbers (a 1940s report guessed three thousand), they were a constant target, but would respond fiercely to attacks before drawing deeper into the forest. Thus by 1910 they had disappeared, remaining totally unheard from until the sightings reported in 1966 by the Summer Institute of Linguistics.

Yet they had managed to create quite an impression, more memorable than that of bigger and more stable tribes. With their spines sticking out of noses, lips, and even earlobes, they seemed like a spirit of the place, elusive yet haunting like the felines of their totem.

Very little was known about them, and some of it may have been just hearsay. They wore no clothing except an occasional penis sheath for the men, and they put their young through severe puberty rites (for the girls, that included the excision of the clitoris). They spoke Panoan lingoes of extreme complexity. Their marriages were polygamous. About marriage particularly, they had interesting regulations, one being that parallel cousins (the children of two brothers or of two sisters) could not marry each other, while cross-cousins (the offspring of a brother and sister) could marry and were encouraged to do so. Since Mayoruna families were numerous, cross-cousin marriages occurred constantly. Maybe that practice reflected a sense of vulnerability to which was opposed the strength of common blood, but it also allowed for a lot of inbreeding. To correct the effects of inbreeding, the Mayoruna were known to strangle their defective infants or cast them into animal holes, and to replenish their blood by capturing females from outside. Their close sense of kinship could be observed in other attitudes, including that toward death. The Mayoruna were endocannibals: rather than leave a relative's dead body to the worms, they roasted it and ate it; they kept the head until it filled with maggots, then spiced the brain with wild herbs before eating it, and even ground the skull into an edible powder. In that way, by putting the loved one inside their own bodies, they symbolically reinforced their tribal cohesiveness.

The information about Mayoruna marriages and funerals, interesting and unusual, had caught the attention of earlier visitors. Their resistance to acculturation was established. But many other things about them were not known. They had been roaming for several centuries, but where was their origin? If they came from outside Amazonia, when had they arrived here, and following what route? Their folklore had not been recorded and studied; their religion was superficially understood (they were rumored to be "superstitious," killing members of the tribe, even children, if suspected of sorcery). Only recently had the Summer Institute of Linguistics begun to compile a Mayoruna dictionary.

And there were more unanswered questions regarding their social structures, manufacture of their artifacts, techniques of hunting and fishing, agriculture, diet, festivals, their own beliefs about their origin and ancestry.

As for the kidnapping of civilizados, both infants and adults, it was documented; yet there was no history of prisoners escaping back to civilization, and no tradition of horror stories about their captivity. Which could mean that the prisoners were never many, or that they received a tolerably decent treatment.

What was known with certainty was that they were largely unknown, and probably still unsullied by the contact with the modern world. It was precisely that unsullied state that McIntyre hoped to record with his camera, before the Mayoruna would be dragged, like so many before them, into the basement of Western culture.

McIntyre snapped a few shots as he advanced towards the little brown faces. A tremor of apprehension seemed to seize the children; the branches around their faces vibrated, as if from the tension of bodies ready to jump back. Letting his camera hang on his chest, McIntyre set the mirrors on the hardened mud several yards from the edge of the vegetation, then backed away. He signaled the other men to turn, and all three retreated toward the remains of their lunch.

They moved slowly and talked at normal volume. Slowness is key with natives. So is noise. Enemies, not friends, steal in quickly and silently. They had to show that they were not enemies.

They talked, excitedly and interrupting each other. They had seen no adults, but there was undoubtedly a tribal group of some size nearby. By the children's stance, glimpsed so briefly, they could be unacculturated Indians. They belonged not to the village they had overflown but to another one, closer, whose clearing they hadn't spotted from the air. Clearings abandoned by a semi-nomadic tribe (which the Mayorunas typically were) succumbed to secondary growth in a matter of months. If these were Mayoruna, they were related to the ones first sighted in 1966 in Peru, doggedly pursued since by a missionary pair from the Summer Institute of Linguistics known as the two Harriets. Harriet Fields and Harriet Kneeland kept flying over the Peruvian jungle, calling in Mayoruna through an airborne loudspeaker the way an alien ship would call to the earth race in a science fiction movie.

Five months earlier, intrigued by the two Harriets' reports, McIntyre had flown to their base at Yarinacocha and asked to join their flights. He was turned down: their plane could barely carry their weight, their pilot's, and their interpreter's. McIntyre handed two fresh rolls of film to the pilot, Ralph Borthwick, himself a missionary. Borthwick later sent McIntyre a shot of a contact climaxing three years of efforts: in it, Loren saw tribesmen with labrets in their lips and noses standing against the silvery body of the plane. The labrets, extremely thin and straight, at least five inches long, were clearly visible against their hairless cheeks. Their eyes peered at the camera with quiet intelligence, their bodies were svelte, gracefully smooth and fawn as if from a light tan. One wore the gift of a T-shirt, the first sign of the change his nation would undergo if it accepted permanent contact with the missionaries.

The photograph had reached McIntyre just weeks before he met Mercier and hired his floatplane. It made the idea of a first contact on the Javari's Brazilian shore seem eminently possible. McIntyre had made a feverish string of preparations, including wholesale purchases of objects to be used for the gift–exchange process. Then came the flight from Iquitos to Leticia, the spontaneous hiring of Carlitos, and this morning's exciting thrust out into the unknown.

Now this unknown looked populated. Contact had already begun, though now, scanning the edge of the trees, McIntyre no longer saw the little faces. They had melted back into the bush.

The mirrors had not been picked up, which wasn't surprising: gifts were not accepted at once. In some cases months passed from the first laying down of the gifts to the first tenuous face-to-face encounter. Slowly, McIntyre walked up to the mirrors, and past them. He stepped through the screen of bushes, whose tops mixed with the parasite plants hanging from the towering trees. He could detect no movement and saw no discernible trails through the vegetation carpeting the inner edge of the forest. Just as he was about to turn back, he tripped on an object lying on the forest floor, looked down, and found sure proof that the children had not been an illusion. It was a bird snare of the spring pole type, a thin and flexible young sapling bent down and attached to a toggle connected to a vine looking like any old vine dragging on the forest floor. Any creature that tripped the vine pulled out the toggle and released the sapling, whose end was fitted with a noose like a lariat. The lariat tightened around the creature's feet and snatched it up in the air. The Mayoruna used the same mechanics to power much larger snares set in the paths of their human enemies.

This snare looked new and no bird fluttered about in it. All it said was that the children knew this shore's abundant game, and that could mean a relatively stable community. A portrait of the unseen tribe was beginning to draft itself in Loren's mind.

He called Mercier and showed him the snare. Mercier nodded. "This might be easier than we thought," he reflected aloud, even more reluctant to abandon the expedition; yet for a few days, at least, Carlitos would be no good for hacking his way through obstinate undergrowth, and they could give him no proper medical care.

They backtracked to the mudbank. "*Estoy bien*," Carlitos kept saying, "I feel fine," yet he looked anything but fine, and his pulse pounded under Mercier's fingers. They would have to fly him back to Leticia.

"Or I could set up camp here, and you could pick me up in a few days," suggested McIntyre.

"But that's too risky. You don't even have a weapon," mumbled Mercier, though he knew that a firearm was dubious protection against a determined Indian attack.

"I've never taken a weapon into an Indian territory. As for risks, they might be slighter if I'm completely alone. The Indians won't feel threatened."

Mercier pondered. He didn't lack personal courage: he had left the safety of a European seminary for the life of a bush aviator. But if he stayed with McIntyre he would not be much use to him; if the explorer decided to advance without Carlitos into the jungle's interior, the pilot would be grounded on the mudbank guarding his plane. A few years earlier in the Curaray Forest of Ecuador, five missionaries, one of them a pilot, had been speared to death by Auca warriors, who also bashed in the *wood bee*, their landed plane. The pilot's sister, a celebrity in the evangelical community appropriately named Rachel Saint, later converted and turned into personal bodyguards the very warriors who had killed her brother.

In any case, McIntyre's solo success in starting a relationship with the tribe would be an indication of Mercier's own chances to build a mission among them.

McIntyre had already started to move his sacks toward the edge of the trees, where he would have to sling his hammock if he set up camp on the mudbank. He was not afraid to stay here alone—he felt less safe crossing a street in Rio de Janeiro, where motorists seemed to deliberately aim their cars at pedestrians. Since the early fifties he had been roaming the jungle and had visited tribes in the Andes, in the Xingu, in Venezuela, in the cloud forests lining the headwaters of Bolivia and Ecuador. One particular tribe, the Aguaruna, had even initiated him. Like the Mayoruna, the Aguaruna had a history of cannibalism and attacks on intruders.

Carlitos felt cold, so cold that they made him lie down under the closest tree and covered him with a blanket. McIntyre helped Mercier filter the gasoline from the latch-down canisters through a chamois skin into the plane's tanks—with no water in the fuel, at least one risk of engine failure was eliminated. Halfway through the operation, they saw a brown shadow streak out from the bushes: an Indian child grabbed the mirrors and raced back into the jungle.

"It's going to be easier than we expected," Mercier repeated with discernible envy.

Any hesitation McIntyre had about staying vanished. He would not give the erratic Mayoruna a chance to disappear. Mercier would return for him in three days, or a week at the most if the plane was beset with unforeseen delays. If McIntyre decided to head inland, he would not stay away from the river shore more than forty-eight hours. And he would leave at his camp on the shore a written message for the pilot.

The day was October 18, 1969.

Even before the Cessna took off, the forest that loomed

beyond its aluminum spine seemed to project an air of distrusting watchfulness. There were mahoganies and cedars in it, and *palo sangres*, their wood so heavy that it refused to float and so red it justified the name of "blood trees." There were *huacapus* so hard that nails wouldn't penetrate them, giant *sumaumas*, and tall *lupunas*, known as "river lighthouses" because boatmen used them as landmarks (one rose not far from where the floatplane was moored, an excellent memory aid for Mercier's return). There were rubber trees, chonta palms producing long hardwood shafts popular for making bows and arrows, and scores of others, each species with its particular use and story. All those and their retinues of bromeliads, vines, parasites, mosses, and bark mushrooms seemed to exude a tense stillness, like that of a beast ambushing its prey.

Modern man had always been a transient here, coming and going irritatingly, unlike the aboriginal man, who was nothing more to the forest than were the howler monkeys or the *sauva* leaf-cutting ants. The forest tolerated tribal man but fought the European intruder, and in that lay its current triumph. What surrounded the floatplane was forest of the wildest type, entirely dependent on its laws alone and ignoring all symbiosis with civilized man. In it resided and evolved in an ancient rhythm half the natural inventions of the planet. No one knew for sure how many plants and animals lived on earth and the estimates were continuously revised upward, but Amazonia kept adding to the list more new species than any other part of the world. The concentration of unknown species was naturally assumed to be where the forest had been invaded least. This "total forest" fascinated McIntyre, and so did the tribes living in it. Least known, least harmful to the habitat—*homo inconspicuus*, an attribute modern man had completely lost.

That kind of forest had an interesting effect on the minds of the *civilizados* prowling its edges. There was nothing to be found in the forest but more forest, thicker and more tangled and matted and less witnessed and understood, but the *civilizados* kept assuming that something else lay in its depth, as hard to reach as it was rewarding to look for. Since the earliest conquistador forays, the jungle was expected to be a protective shell snuggling a treasure in its midst. That treasure was variously imagined as a mythical realm on the shores of a fabulous lake, an inexhaustible mother lode of gold or diamonds, a race of prosperous and gullibly hospitable half men, half beasts, even a giant deposit of petroleum. It was baptized in turns El Dorado, the Kingdom of the Omagua, Sevilla del Oro, Beni, Mojo, or Gran Para. With it in mind, conquistadors started on treks trumpeted as "civilizing missions" but ended up dead, insane, or captured by Indians.

Those who returned sick and crippled kept the myth up. The treasure was there. Right before crawling back, half mad with exhaustion and hunger, they had glimpsed those fabulous towers looming above the treetops. They had met the proud envoys of that kingdom, their clothes and weapons adorned with gems and gold. They had sipped water from the fabulous lake. The myth survived and grew. Such was the density of biota on nearly three million square miles that it could cover, conceal, disguise, and keep ready for unleashing any beast of the imagination. In 1925, when McIntyre was a schoolboy, the much publicized Colonel Fawcett had vanished in the jungle somewhere near the headwaters of the Xingu River, looking for a city of crystal. And who was to say that he hadn't found it, and perhaps turned into crystal himself, succumbing to the place's supernatural exudations?

The banks of the Javari had sporadically attracted visitors. Three hundred years earlier, a *bandeira*, as the Portuguese called their exploring parties, had reached this area led by the son of the governor of Rio de Janeiro. Their goal was to find slaves for Brazil's east coast sugar plantations, and jewels reputed to lie in the forest in mounds twenty feet high. Paddling upriver for weeks, going crazy from heat, hunger, bugs, and Indian attacks, the Portuguese finally discarded weapons too heavy to carry, ate their clothes, revolted against their commander, stabbed each other, and left a trail of 180 unmarked graves. The survivors reached an Indian village, where they were fed manioc, but they were so insatiate after weeks of starving that some ate "till their bellies burst." They quarreled with their saviors, attempted to take them into slavery, were captured themselves, and some were eaten. Those who escaped eventually returned to the coast, a few bringing back children sired with native women. They found their wives remarried and caring for new families. This expedition, a classic of wilderness disaster, in no way discouraged further ambitions.

In 1750, the Treaty of Madrid redrew the boundary between New Portugal and New Spain along the Javari River, bestowing status upon the otherwise forsaken backwater. Both the Spaniards, anxious to stop the Portuguese from claiming more territory, and the Portuguese, eager to establish credible outposts, announced grand plans for settlement. Viceroys and governors waved the lucre of virgin land and abundant Indian slave labor. In fact, there were no roads, cutting trees and starting plantations were exhausting and dangerous labors (snakebites always took their toll), and floods could wipe out the work of a year in hours. The Indians were indifferent to the Word or downright hostile. Development started and always petered out.

The region seemed almost supernaturally protected against exploration. Even today, its maps remained poorly drawn and its settlements small and unsophisticated. Puerto Carmen was a town of four huts, Concepción a city of fifteen houses, Puerto Amelia, a district capital, still had no radio station. As for Leticia, the base for McIntyre's current trip, the annually published *South American Handbook* described its Hotel Victoria Regia as "primitive and just possible. People are often stranded for a week in Leticia. It is not worth it."

For some travelers that misery itself was the attraction. The unknown was the enticement and the doggedness in pursuing it the story to bring home. River steamers still sank out there in unsuspected rapids, making their oxidized hulks homes for turtles and turkey vultures, or got lost on dead ends where hanging branches ripped away their bridges, tore off their capstans and stanchions, and ruined their paint. The region seemed equipped to disable anything that didn't belong to it: it demolished, rotted and unhinged, clogged up pipes, ducts, and hoses, blocked cylinders and all other types of machinery, corroded metal, gnawed at fabric, unbalanced wheels, tilted buildings, bloated walls and floors with its insidious humidity, short-circuited, spoiled, bacterized, and liquefied. Food and drink soured and bittered, turning from nourishment to poison. Human bodies lost their tautness and puffed up. Livers swelled, eyes clouded with glaucoma, sores festered, lungs plugged up with the fluids of colds and allergies. Nothingness itself seemed able to mushroom here, to become alive and contagious.

In such wicked circumstances myth flourished and invariably included the Indians, Amazonia's other commodity. The mysterious natural man who vexed the civilizado's self-proclaimed superiority by surviving in any conditions, slinking through the bush soundlessly, swimming untouched in piranha-infested rivers, staring death in the face every day of his life. Accused of laziness and a mind that couldn't figure out the clock, the Indian nevertheless was in everyone's conscience the superman of endurance and adaptation. Overtly, the civilizado feared and despised him; secretly, he admired him and yearned to best him.

The Cessna taxied back upstream to the stretch of log-free river, then turned and revved its engine. Racing downstream on its liquid runway, it lifted, floats trailing shiny garlands of drops, and barely cleared the treetops.

In seconds it became a cross shining painfully in the sky, reflecting sunlight filtered through the clouds. Like a spaceship, it returned to its own galaxy while McIntyre was left to voyage on here, into the unknown. The explorer watched the plane until its fieriness melted in the sky. The drone of the engine faded. The man on the mudbank selected from the bag of presents another item, a box of comb and brush kits of plastic, sold for a few cruzeiros in every Brazilian drugstore. To the Javari's tribal natives they would be a fascinating novelty. McIntyre set them down on the shore, this time right by the edge of the forest.

This was the traditional process of *trocar presentes*, the exchange of gifts, which started with a phase called *atracção*, literally meaning "attraction" in Portuguese. A more accurate translation would be "luring." During the luring stage the civilizados would leave in the bush gifts of all kinds, some useful, like knives, machetes, and matches, others decorative, like bracelets and rings, others just entertaining, like babies' whistles and rattles. That was to convince a formerly wronged or simply suspicious Indian community to come out of its savage safety and attempt commerce with the white man.

The gifts were placed successively closer to where the tribe was believed to have its communal house or its scattering of huts. If things went well, the tribe would remove one gift after another, allowing the guests deeper and deeper into tribal territory, so the luring in fact worked both ways. The process took days, months, on occasion even years. Sometimes the tribe took the gifts but wouldn't establish a relationship. In a few cases, Indians had thus lured civilizados in and then killed them.

Most often, however, a gift accepted was an encouraging sign. At some point tribesmen started responding with gifts of their own, which meant that the attraction stage was over and the regular exchange was on, almost guaranteeing a contact. Sometimes the natives' gifts were of lesser craftsmanship or purely symbolic, like a feather or clay figure, and sometimes they were prized tools or adornments—once McIntyre had swapped a nylon jacket, a bowie knife, a Swiss army knife, and a pair of reading glasses for an elaborate toucan headdress. Sometimes the Indians offered finely made arrows, which signified friendship. Sometimes they offered nothing but their enigmatic presence, coming closer and closer until the relieved civilizados and their interpreter (an indispensable member of the contacting party, even if he or she was just a child) stepped into a village, engaged in a dialogue, and stated their purpose.

Despite the tortuousness of the welcoming process (often outsiders were guided to a village over a complicated map of twisting pathways), the natives seemed both interested in outsiders and willing to engage in an exchange. For the civilizados, the wait was suspenseful and exciting. The natives experienced their own excitement, laced however with deeper apprehensions and perhaps with grim memories. The real fun was for the whites. The process was, in the words of a romantic Brazilian novelist, "all for the moment when the tribe would demand one more expression of trust, and then, like a reluctant but curious bride, accept the newcomer."

The tradition of *trocar presentes* was not inherited from the Europeans, though its practice went back to Columbus's first trip. The Indians had always exchanged gifts among themselves and insisted on receiving gifts from outsiders even if they didn't really want them. Repeatedly, McIntyre had seen them at FUNAI* posts accepting quite useful pots and pans, utterly serviceable utensils or adornments; but later, trailing an Indian group back to their village, he would spot the gifts tossed aside by the path. It was the giving they valued; when it came to possessing, to holding, they were loose and inconsistent. "An Indian giver," far from meaning as in English someone who gave only to take back, defined an Indian's attitude to possession. The act of giving could never be forsaken or taken back; the gift itself could and often was.

Now the gift of comb and brush kits lay at the edge of the green, waiting. The children had not reappeared, and they might not reappear until tomorrow. Chances were that they had taken the mirrors to the village and shown them to an assembly of adults who forbade them to hurry back for more. The adults themselves would approach the shore soon,

*Fundaçao Nacional dos Indios, or National Indian Foundation, Brazil's government agency for Indian affairs.

to catch a glimpse of the visitor. For them, McIntyre got up and prepared a separate plastic bag of adult presents. It included a sheathed machete, a pair of scissors, several necklaces of colored beads made in Czechoslovakia (for a number of years, that country had held the monopoly on such glass goods in Amazonia), nylon fishing line, which an Indian could use for a hundred other things, colored yarn which required little space to pack and weighed nothing but was appreciated by tribeswomen, and a flashlight.

He still had plenty of time to finish setting camp and sling his hammock between two trees. McIntyre pulled the cases with his photographic equipment into the shade and opened them. The cameras, lenses and light meter, flashes and rolls of film were all in order. The only arsenal he had ever taken into the wilderness stood at the ready. Another thing he always carried—besides the picture caption report forms which every professional photographer must keep—were little books in which he took down notes for his diary. He jotted them full during his trips, intending to expand on them later, but unless they got lost or stolen with some other luggage as he kept winging around South America, they usually ended up in the smooth dust of his Arlington, Virginia, attic. Once back home he always found them lacking, not important enough to complete, and just too pale compared to those bright frames of reality that spoke so clearly to everyone, his photographs.

But the idea of that expanded diary remained alive in his mind, a project he would properly address one day. Meanwhile, note-taking itself was always a good companion and antidote to empty hours. Sitting against a pile of rubberized sacks, McIntyre opened a virgin book, found a virgin pen, and started to write in an efficient, slightly slanting hand.

3

The Cat-People

Sixty-five years ago, perhaps on this spot, an American traveler witnessed Peruvian *caucheros*, or "rubber tappers," sailing up the Javari in search not just of rubber, but also of Mayoruna women. Such incidents were common at the time—these rugged men thought nothing of dragging native girls out of raided villages, which they then set on fire. In that 1904 incident, the *caucheros* landed, confident of the strength of their rifles and pistols, close to a fairly large village. Suddenly they were attacked by Mayoruna armed with cudgels studded with jaguar teeth, and five-foot arrows dipped in stingray poison. The cudgels cracked heads, the jaguar teeth bit into human brains. The *caucheros* managed to shoot four Mayoruna before being massacred to the last man.

Around the same time a tribe of Aguaruna were credited with attacking rubber tappers and eating them. They were the same Aguaruna who initiated me into their tribe in 1953, on the upper Marañón. But the Aguaruna's experience with the white man was not as tragic as the Mayoruna's. At all times, the Mayorunas were *the* fleeing, vanishing tribe. Until the Harriets talked to them from the air, they were believed dead, a fossil culture, a certified victim of encroachment.

And now here I am, trying to meet them. In fact, I've

already met them.

He looked up from his notes. His pen on the filling page seemed as incongruous as the plane had seemed against the backdrop of forest, but it was real. He clutched the pen with damp fingers and wrote more, enduring the assault of the heat.

The Mayoruna. What mystery there is in names. How does a tribe come to name itself? How did such words become formed; how were they thought up, combining certain sounds and not others? Did they occur at random, an utterance from one tribesman spontaneously adopted by the tribe? Or were they played with, rehearsed till habit and general acceptance confirmed them into the vocabulary? How did all that come about?

Who are these people?

His thoughts were interrupted by the bushes beginning to stir not far from where he had left the gift. He waited but no one appeared, and the bushes grew still. He rose and walked along the shore's irregular tree line, stepped into the trees, listened, peered. In some places the visibility was as deep as fifty feet, yet he saw no one. It was three in the afternoon and the horned screamers and macaws shrieked and squawked only now and then. The heat had slowed down most processes except for the transpiration of leaves, putting back into the air humidity that would come down in more rain and go out again in more evaporation, endlessly.

He walked back and sat down again, closed his notes, put the pen in his pocket and let his thoughts wander. Man had settled this area long before the Conquest, but the forest's density, the heat and humidity, the abundance of beasts of prey and parasites and the thin soil had never allowed him to develop more than subsistence agriculture, precluding the food surpluses needed for urban development. Now as always, tribes were small and divided by fierce stretches of wilderness and their languages were surprisingly dissimilar and varied.

He smiled, alone on the bank of the uncharted river, realizing how close his thought process might be to that of the conquistadors before him. Despite his training, despite the dislike of bombast that made him rewrite his books and articles over and over, he was vulnerable to myth just like the conquistadors. The cat-people had become his great obsession. He expected insights from this encounter superior to his other contacts with unacculturated tribes.

A dose of activity was what was needed. McIntyre macheteed the lower branches of a tree that would be visible from the river, then tied his rubberized bags as high up as he could reach. The height precaution was twofold, against animals or a sudden rise in the water level, which a torrential rainfall could always bring about. The visibility was also important, for the rubber bags would act as a landmark on Mercier's return. He covered his belongings with a couple of shower curtains, easier to handle or replace than a tarp. The camp was thus protected from rain and ground animals, though not from ants.

He selected two trees strong enough to support his hammock—if the Indians didn't reappear, this was where he would spend the night—then stepped back into the forest, where he tied several knives onto bushes and discovered a pathway sunken under floor leaves; he couldn't tell whether it was from animals or humans. He spun some colored yarn across branches, cautious not to make it cross the path. Indians lay arrows across paths to mark off limits for civilizados, and he had to be careful not to give them an ambiguous message. Finally he walked back and inspected his little camp. Perhaps a hundred yards down the beach stood that "river lighthouse," the *lupuna* tree, whose tall shape would provide another valuable landmark.

He drank a bottle of Coke, as warm now as the surrounding jungle, built a fire, and prepared for the night.

Just before six P.M., nightfall at this latitude, the foliage came alive with activity anticipating the night's coolness. For breathing, hunting, mating, the darkness and lowered temperature meant friendly conditions, and the night, far from being a realm of fear, was greeted with excitement. The red howler monkeys dilated their monstrous larynxes and chorused discordantly. The rain forest prepared to double or triple its activity, which was already many times more than that in any colder climate.

In its midst, Loren McIntyre tested the ropes of his hammock, ran the golden beam of his flashlight over their whole length, and swept the hammock's belly with it. Then he scanned the hammock's supporting trunks for ants. Socks on to discourage bites to his feet (he'd had some rubs of that sort with bloodsucking bats on the Caquetá, an Amazonian headwater flushing the southern regions of Colombia), he lay in slantwise and tried to fill his mind with the gurgle of the river, isolating it from all other sounds.

Soon he slept.

A few hours later he awoke to a monstrous croaking of bullfrogs, and wondered vaguely where that swamp was, the location of their throaty minstrelsy. It was cold. He pulled a cotton blanket over himself and slept again.

4

The Encounter

At daybreak, he was awakened as if by a silent clock. Without a second of confusion he remembered where he was, and why. He breathed the morning air and smelled the coolness that had accumulated during the night: it gave the river a scent momentarily fresh.

Then he looked up and spotted a large animal hanging almost above his hammock, claws locked around a branch. A three-toed sloth, one of the few creatures who slept in. Looking around he saw another, hanging from a neighboring branch. Both motionless, prisoners to sleep. Sleep was their labor and pastime, and was comparatively safe. Greenish algae grew in the furrows of their coats, camouflaging them from the sharp eyes of harpy eagles and jaguars. They couldn't walk well on their long curved claws adapted to hanging, so they spent almost their entire lives in the trees and even died there, sometimes in sleep, hanging upside down.

He swung his legs over the side of the hammock and put his feet on the ground, wondering whether the sloths' sleeping position had inspired the Indians with the invention of the hammock, the world's only sleeping contrivance that doesn't touch the ground. With well-disciplined movements—discipline is critical for survival in the wild, and in solo situations even more so—Loren untied his hammock and rolled it up. He had a snack of instant coffee made with bottled water, and a few cheese crackers.

He bathed in the river, put his clothes back on, washed the T-shirt he had slept in, and spread it on a low branch. Then he cooked some oatmeal, dusted it with powdered milk, and ate it while the sun was rising behind the same blanket of clouds the plane had flown under yesterday. He finished his breakfast and decided to check on the *presentes* and make sure that they hadn't been disturbed by some animal's nightly foraging.

With the same quiet routine he loaded one of his cameras and hung it around his neck. He was going to stray only a short distance from the camp; no sense in hauling along other cameras or his three-pouch belt with his lenses and light meter. Yet just in case, remembering past experiences, he slipped three rolls of film into his pocket. Moving with ease, still feeling the relaxation of sleep in his limbs, he almost reached the trees, then backtracked and picked up the bag of presents he had put together the day before. It bulged with the sheathed machete, the scissors, the nylon fishing line, the clinking heap of colored beads, the colored yarn, the flashlight. Had the other presents been picked up, he could replace them.

Somehow, on the screen of his mind, the image of yesterday's children had dimmed and the vaguely glimpsed blue tattoo around their lips seemed abstract now, improbable.

He broke in between two trees and recognized the sunken path. It stretched ahead about ten yards; then a curtain of parasitic vines fell across it like streamers, hanging from a thick lintel of foliage about five feet from the ground. He advanced till he had to bend low, grinding brown leaves under his feet. Dead, they should have crumbled or scattered, but they stood right where he trampled them, anchored invisibly to the tentacular roots of a muscular tree. Not finding enough nourishment in the soil's thin top layer, the roots shot out a secondary army of rootlets called hyphae, literally hyphenating the litter on the forest floor into an extra soil, and sucking its residual minerals and liquids.

The mighty tree depended on the trash of the forest floor and even more so on the air, invisibly loaded with minerals. McIntyre passed the tentacular tree. He could see the colored yarn swaying where he had left it yesterday, undisturbed.

You are not alone, said another part of his mind, as if autonomous.

He had a sensation of presence and almost instantaneously saw a young Indian, naked, five feet or a little over—his shiny black hair just touched the foliage under which McIntyre had to bend. He was skinny but robust: the first impression was of the muscles of his neck, chest, and arms contrasting with a face that looked emaciated under a band of palm leaf tied around his forehead. Two plots of red urucú paint on his cheeks didn't relieve that look of famished hollowness. Hanging from his shoulder, he carried a slain howler monkey, its hands and feet trussed up with vegetal fiber.

Remembering to move naturally and make noise, Loren trampled over the forest floor toward the red-cheeked native, just as another naked tribesman stepped out from behind the first. Behind the bushes lining the path on the left, Loren saw the tip of a long bow; there was another native there. And yet another one appeared now on the path, his brown hand spooling the brightly colored yarn off the bushes. Four young Indian warriors. Loren felt the weight of the bag of gifts in his right palm, and raised it briefly as a declaration of good intent.

The Indian with the red cheeks faced him now full front, firm pectoral muscles under a loose necklace of peccary teeth, ropes of muscle lining his hips and thighs. His calves bulged from ligatures of palm fiber tied under his knees, the same type of kneelets Columbus had reported after his first voyage to the New World. He had a club in his hand. The others held six-foot-long bows and arrows. Three of them carried slain howler monkeys hanging from shoulder sashes, and the fourth a deer of the pigmy rain forest variety. All stared at McIntyre with eyes like black bullets while he stared at the wide blue tattoo lines hemming the mouth of the red-cheeked warrior. The lines went back all the way to his earlobes. Spines bristled out of his lips and nose, and they looked eight inches long. There was no doubt, these warriors were Mayoruna. Cat-people.

The Indian behind Red Cheeks wore no paint and his tattoo was thinner, but the same spines stuck out of his lips; he watched the explorer with his mouth slightly open, showing teeth sharpened by filing. The look of his teeth added to the animal air of his whiskers, making him really seem like a big cat.

McIntyre cleared his throat. "*Hola!*" he called out. Then again: "*Bom dia!*" "Good day," in Portuguese. Once more he raised the bag of gifts, an explanation of his presence. He saw a knife in one brown hand, one of the knives he had hung on the low branches. *They're taking the presents, good*, said that autonomous part of his mind. "Good day," he repeated, passing the bag of gifts from his right hand to the left. Equipped with a 28–85mm zoom lens, his camera weighed on his chest. He wasn't afraid—the way he hadn't been the day before, leaning into the plane's open doorway while flying over the treetops.

"*Bom dia!*" for the third time. His right hand went to his camera; his thumb groped for the shutter release. *From the hip; I could shoot from the hip*. The moment was wonderful, and unrepeatable. The distance to the Indians was under ten yards. Maybe they had never been so close to a civilizado before. *Click*. First contact. Ideal first contact.

"*Escúchen me*," he said, in Spanish this time. "*Soy de Leticia*." His hand quit the camera to gesture back toward the river.

This was the instant when things could go either way, toward friendliness or hostility, depending on how his voice and appearance registered on the inner graphs of these tribesmen's minds. They didn't react. They probably didn't know where Leticia was. "*Leticia es un lugar aguas abajo*," he explained. "Leticia is a place downstream." "*Amigos. Soy un amigo.*" "Friends. I am a friend." "*Soy norteamericano*," he added. "I am from North America."

No reaction. Maybe they spoke no Spanish either. Loren's thoughts crackled in frantic succession, while his eyes kept recording more details. None of them wore any clothing. Strings of twisted fiber reached down from their waists to the tips of their penes, catching the foreskin in a little knot and keeping the penis suspended. This practice was not confined to the Mayoruna; Loren had seen it in other tribes. It was dropped when tribes entered regular contacts with civilizados and started trading manioc and bananas for T-shirts, shorts and baseball caps. But these men seemed as untouched by civilization as could be. They had perhaps sighted civilizados: their faces displayed no utter bewilderment at the explorer's presence. Maybe aircraft too, though there were damn few planes on the upper Javari. Most likely, though, they hadn't been contacted.

An upswell of excitement filled McIntyre's chest. Here they were, in their natural state, the legendary Mayoruna. His plan was to photograph them and then withdraw, affecting them as little as possible.

He stepped closer, let the bag of presents drop to his feet, and raised the camera. No reaction. *Click*. At least Red Cheeks would turn out clearly, with the other three massed tightly behind him. *Click*. Just a second, fellows — they were starting to turn — *Click, Click*.

They turned and it seemed all right to follow. He picked up the bag, suspended it from his wrist, trained the camera at the game bouncing on the Indians' backs. *Click*, a howler monkey's red tussocks of hair against a muscular back. Very effective. The foliage above, the bushes and vines right and left, sifting the hesitant light caught in the canopy. The heat of the day was already building.

An abundance of vines clogged the path, snaking away in all directions. The warriors' feet padded them carelessly, used to them. Loren snapped some shots of the vines and almost lost the Indians when the path twisted. He hurried after them, hoping for a little clearing where he could entice them again with the gifts, and perhaps get them to talk. He stopped to aim a shot at the thinning canopy, filtering down a golden haze of light.

The path was exceedingly tortuous: ten minutes earlier, the river had been straight behind him. Now he didn't remember where it was. He hurried on, caught up with them again. They talked in low voices. He managed a profile shot as they walked past a bush, Red Cheeks's headband looking almost white against the shades of green.

He decided not to burn a whole roll on four silhouettes and a piece of pathway. He would also need both hands to change rolls and, the way the Indians were hurrying, if he stopped to put down his bag and open the camera he would lose them.

And he was far too busy to break off twigs and mark the trail.

In his head the jangle of optimistic, excited thoughts continued. The gamble with hiring Mercier and flying down here practically on a hunch had paid off. He had met Mercier at the end of a *National Geographic* assignment to create a photo-portrait of the whole Amazon ecosystem from mouth to headwaters. During three months of sailing, flying, and hacking paths across the forest he had shot hundreds of rolls of film which had already been shipped back to the States. The Mayoruna, not specifically part of the assignment, had emerged at the end of it like a crowning experience. Their existence, so utterly untouched by Western ways, promised an additional understanding of all the wilderness he had already encountered.

Those thoughts were to be elaborated on later. In immediate terms, the Mayoruna were terrific photographic material, and it was in pictures that their relationship with the wilderness would first be captured.

He expected a village to appear any minute. He was surprised not to hear the sharp voices of children and noted that yesterday's little hunters had walked a long way to set up their bird snares.

He still had not heard the children, nor glimpsed the village five, ten, twenty minutes later.

He was now walking a few feet behind the warriors, watching the warm play of their shoulders and arms against the narrow limits of the footpath. Red Cheeks turned once as if to make sure that they hadn't lost their visitor. The path narrowed more, becoming a twisting tunnel through the brush. By following the Indians so closely McIntyre was sure not to fall into a pit with sticks of hard palmwood pointing up, or step in a snare and be hoisted up by an ankle and banged against a tree trunk. The gifts in the bag rattled with each of his steps. Ahead, the warriors moved faster, and he hurried on. Indians could sustain such a pace through the bushes for a day or longer, hottest hours included.

All of a sudden, freed from the narrow path, the men stepped into a tree-enclosed swamp and Loren splashed into murky water. The canopy above was punctured, and he verified that the clouds had not lifted. But the heat was here. Familiarly oppressive, it stuck to his face while the back of his neck leaked sweat loaded with dissolved body minerals. Dropping the game and their hunting gear, the Indians trampled into the swamp and started to splash water on themselves. Loren caught his breath, saw a broken branch jutting out of a fallen tree, suspended the bag of gifts from it, and finally raised his camera with both hands.

"*Hola,*" he tried again. "*Soy escritor norteamericano,*" he continued, smiling, clicking the camera, lowering it.

They looked at him and went on splashing and beginning to laugh playfully. Great shot. Loren kneeled in the swamp water, aimed the camera, clicked. "*Hablan español?*" he asked rising, dripping muddy water. Another group shot— shiny squirts of water scooped up by brown hands. "*Falan português?*"

They looked at him doubtfully.

"These are presents," explained the explorer. "For you." He grabbed the bag, opened it, and pulled out the machete. He demonstrated it by slashing at the fallen tree, then offered it handle forward. Red Cheeks reached out to take it. As the group huddled to examine it, Loren tried for another shot, discovered that he was at the end of a roll. He wasted thirty seconds changing rolls, then snapped another group shot. Expecting to glimpse that village through the trees, his eyes scanned around the swamp, seeing only more green. Wondering how far they were from the river, he glanced at his wristwatch. It was five to nine.

He put his ear to the watch, straining until he heard the ticking against the sounds of the bathing men. Under the digit 12, through a round little slot, the date peered out: October 19. He hardly ever checked his watch in the bush, as there was no reason to do it. The light and the heat, especially the heat, divided the day in time zones regulating the activity of both animals and people. There were no appointments to keep in the bush, no deadlines to meet, and hardly any activities that could not be rescheduled for the afternoon or the next day or the next week. In the midst of the world's most intricate system of life-forms, where the survival of so many living units depended on the speed of their reactions and escape from predators on the accuracy of their timing, time itself was amorphous and plentiful, and Loren seldom felt compelled to think of it.

He had left the camp to check on the presents around seven-thirty. He had been walking with the Indians for more than an hour. *I may not be able to retrace my steps to the river*, he realized abruptly.

They had followed a twisting trail, deviating right or left practically every few steps. There were probably as many twists now between himself and his camp as there were lapsed minutes, and he had left his compass in the camp, sealed in one of the pockets of his three-pouch belt. He would have found it hard to break twigs with his hands full of camera and presents, but the truth was that being so fascinated with the Indians he had simply forgotten to mark his passage. A wing of anxiety fluttered over him and over the peaceful scene in the swamp. He was utterly alone with four tribesmen, a totally unusual circumstance. He ordinarily visited a tribe accompanied by a local guide, by missionaries, or, in Brazil, by an agent of FUNAI. The least he could have done was remember how to return to his own camp, which he had left without taking any supplies or orientation devices. He felt almost amused by this breach in the rigorousness of his habits. *Bad performance. Very bad performance.*

It's all right, he reassured himself. *They'll just have to give me a guide to take me back.*

Meanwhile, satisfied by the machete, the Mayoruna waded over to McIntyre, who opened the bag again. He handed out the kettle, the knives, a length of fishing line, the flashlight. Hitting the flashlight's button to turn on the light was a big success with the four. They laughed loud and crowded tightly around the explorer. "I have more on the shore," he announced. If they understood him, they might backtrack with him, unaware that he was lost. He pointed at the presents, then described with his hands the height of a whole other pile of gifts. By the river, he insisted, pointing at the swamp's water and gesturing to indicate flow. Then he beckoned the group to come back with him: if they did, the presents were theirs.

Silence. Then a rapid rattle of Indian words, as clear as they were incomprehensible. The closest tribesman raised his hand to adjust a spine in his lower lip, in a sort of cogitative reflex action. Another cat-man opined something to which Red Cheeks countered negatively, then he grabbed the machete and splashed out of the swamp to pick up his game and his weapons. The others instantly did the same and McIntyre saw all four brown bodies recoagulate into a column, ready to weave back into the forest. He became convinced that they spoke neither Spanish nor Portuguese. Which in terms of the value of the contact was excellent.

He assumed that they had been moving in a general southwesterly direction; he could of course decide to head back alone. He would ultimately break out onto the Javari's shore. But unless he was extremely lucky he would find himself either upstream or downstream from the camp, which would be even more perplexing. Following the shoreline, where the jungle was most overgrown, required a machete, and he had given away the one in the bag of gifts.

He made a quick decision: better follow the tribesmen. Maybe there would be someone who understood Spanish or Portuguese in that village.

With the camera around his neck, he followed them, moving easier now without the presents. The Indians moved just a couple of yards ahead of him, feet stepping full force onto the bed of decomposing forest litter. Soles and toes over-layered with desensitized cells, they broke every root and twig they stepped on. Their legs were thin yet sinewy, their shoulder blades wide, their chests convex, but beneath that parade of strength there was emaciation. And where the hell was the village? *Maybe the children belong to another village*, he told himself. *Maybe a whole nation abides close by*. He checked his watch again: it was almost ten, and the path had straightened. The Indians advanced fast, showing no signs of fatigue. The howler monkeys and the deer hanging on the warriors' backs were fully grown—Loren knew the monkeys to weigh as much as thirty pounds and the deer twice that much—but those weights didn't slow down the hunters any more than the heat did.

The distance back to his camp was increasing with every step.

A whitish twisting creeper known as *erva de espinha*, "spine grass," covered the forest floor, as if fallen from some giant skeleton suspended under the canopy. It alternated with the live carpet of selaginellas, acanthi, and thalias, while the trees carried at various heights the baroque clumps of amaryllis, begonias, orchids. It was always springtime for some species in the rain forest: where one bloomed, another shed its petals. The sight of the Indians, successfully integrated in this organized chaos, gave Loren a secret sense of optimism.

That village can't be far, he reassured himself.

He carried in his pockets two more rolls of film, a Swiss army knife, his watch, a pen, and in a back pocket one of his notebooks. Sometimes in the past he'd torn pages from a notebook and stuck them on bushes to mark his passage, but that wouldn't make much difference now: at least an hour of unmarked trail separated him from the camp. He had no food with him, no medicine, and no more presents to exchange; but he was confident in his ability to make himself understood. He had found himself among strangers before, though never entirely alone.

He hurried on, letting his mind wander about the pictures he'd be taking once he was in the village.

Since 1953 he'd been photographing Indians, sometimes leaving his Halliburton case unlocked in the tribal men's house, and never having any trouble except for greasy fingerprints on his equipment. They often opened his case, took its contents out, and almost always put everything back exactly in reverse order from how they took it out. They were the best subjects to photograph, the Indians, apart from an occasional fear that cameras steal souls— but that usually happened up in the Andes. More often than not they went about their business, letting him run around freely, dropping to his knees, leaning on trees, doing everything to secure a good angle, a dramatic backdrop, an inspired foreground of twigs or blades of grass for composition, and then bang—just when he was all focused they cleared the scene and he had to start all over again. Which he did; again and again he went through photography's ritual like a computer through its programmed motions, all for *the big one*—photographers are so momentary and fickle, their aim is always *the big one*, the superlative shot, the image crowning a whole career. Of course there was no such big one, he was experienced enough to know that by now, but the frantic quest for it was the key to a photographer's untiring enthusiasm. During that quest, time got broken, moments were torn out of its continuous flow and rearranged and offered as the whole, and the result was always just a shot, attempting to define a whole reality. What lurked behind that frenzy—it seemed to Loren as he panted, camera about his neck, behind the Indians' naked shoulder blades and backsides—was fear of the future. Among man's inventions, photography seemed the most capable to fixate the ephemeral present. So the present was compressed into increasingly smaller units of duration, clocked by the camera's eye.

Totally unlike the Indians, he thought. A forest Indian's sense of the future was so remarkably unpressuring that jungle tribes never made any provisions, never saved or hoarded; they were puzzled when they saw heaps of hammocks or rows of canned food kept in stock at a FUNAI store. Those who lived close to civilizados and got used to their planning and preparedness for emergencies acquired a completely new concept of time. And it was time they found hardest to adapt to, once forced into urban living, for it implied pressures unheard of in forest life, such as precision, competitiveness, a constant delay of gratification, and a sense of the best moment.

Somehow, it all tied back into time. For the Indians, time was an ingredient of life, comfortable and unseen, like the air. For the civilizados, time was a possession, an increasingly more efficient machine.

The trees suddenly pulled back. A roofed structure sailed into view, just four poles holding up a thatch of palm leaves dropping at the back into a slanted wall. The front was open, the palm leaves green as if freshly cut; a woman and a child perched on the roof, weaving the ends of leaves over wooden shafts stuck in the forked ends of the sustaining poles. Staring in surprise, Loren stumbled: a narrow horizon of huts, perhaps eight or nine, jolted upwards and then down before his eyes. All their roofs were green, and some were still unfinished. They rimmed a narrowly oval space with a huge *sumauma* tree collapsed in its midst.

The canopy above the village had been torn open by the fall of the *sumauma*. Loren wondered if this was the village he'd seen from the plane.

His nose registered the proximity of humans. Odors of smoldering fires and cooked food (though not of human waste, since forest Indians use the bush as a lavatory, and their feces and urine get quickly washed away by the afternoon rain showers). He heard yelps of dogs and screeches of pet macaws. Before his eyes, a tide of bodies rolled out of the huts or splashed down from the unfinished roofs. Loren straightened himself and was surrounded by tribespeople with cat whiskers sticking out of their faces. Like most forest Indians, they showed their surprise by silence and an almost solemn expression. A number of children rushed ahead of the adults but stopped, keeping a careful fleeing distance.

Loren saw one of his mirrors in the little brown hand of a boy perhaps seven years old. The mirror was dirty and already cracked, and the boy was cross-eyed. He alone of the bunch of kids came as close as four feet, inspected Loren briefly, then stepped back and smiled with shiny white teeth.

The children he'd seen on the shore were here. But the village looked brand-new, as if built in the last few hours.

5

Man's Fragile World

At a glance, it looked as if this community had just chosen its new location.

There were more than eight or nine huts: Loren scanned the clearing and counted fourteen in all, most of them still being worked on. He knew that Indians could whip up temporary shelters in under an hour. The ground surrounding the collapsed sumauma tree was a mess of broken branches and bushes razed by the giant's collapse. Youngsters with sticks of chonta palm thrashed at the bushes and at clusters of parasites still clinging to the broken branches, chasing the remaining wildlife out of them. Baskets and rolled-up fiber hammocks lay on the ground by the huts, looking barely unloaded; rectangular babracots had been set up before the huts; the explorer saw narrow strips of fish being fried on them, one of the few types of food a forest tribe could store. A general air of improvisation hung over the place.

There were plenty of children, walking about stark naked except for adornments like necklaces and bracelets. The men were naked too, except for adornments and a cincture of fiber around their middles, from which hung the strings knotted up around their pulled-out foreskins. Tying and untying those strings each time they needed to pass water was reflex action for them, suggesting how serious they were about tribal etiquette (in other tribes Loren had observed males stuff their penes inside their scrotal sacs, making them all but invisible). The women were also naked, but a few wore a sort of apron of palm leaves, or cinctures of fiber. Their pubic hair and eyebrows had been plucked out meticulously, while the men showed no bodily hair, beards, or mustaches. To pluck off their hair they probably used empty river shells, their valves snapped shut like tweezers, which was rough cosmetics, but Loren had seen Indians suffer such operations and hardly blink. Some of the faces around him had filed teeth. Some noses were perforated by shell and wood ornaments. The cat-whiskers gave all of them that eerily feline appearance.

They were small and powerfully built. The epicanthic folds of their eyes were very pronounced. But the thinness of their faces and bodies was general; they looked starved. McIntyre was used to tribal children being taut and trim, but these particular ones showed not even a memory of baby fat. And though they ran and jumped with the zest of children everywhere, their eyes were ringed and their faces had an unhealthy sallowness.

Simultaneous with the smells and images, the community's noises invaded him. After their initial silence, the adults talked now all at once against a background of crying infants and squawking pet macaws. Red Cheeks passed around Loren's gifts and spoke loudly and animatedly, pointing frequently at him. Then he pointed up at the thin canopy. Then again at Loren. He was interrupted and asked questions. He answered referring to the bag of presents, and again to Loren and the canopy. It seemed to Loren that he was embellishing the story of this morning's encounter or perhaps editing it. The young warrior with filed teeth stood nearby with eyes narrowed and brow wrinkled, as if somewhat miffed by Red Cheeks's account. Of the words that were said, Loren identified not one word of Portuguese or Spanish, though over the years even marginal tribes had borrowed from those languages.

He waited, erect, resisting the tired impulse to let himself fall down on the ground. At one time Red Cheeks seemed to run into an argument with other tribesmen; he broke free and walked around on the outer perimeter of the crowd with an irritated expression, then joined the group again, arguing on and gesturing toward the canopy. The explorer saw other natives look up at the canopy and then at him, and wondered whether they had established a link between him and some passing plane. Then a small empty space grew around him, and in it advanced a short character with a conical hat of leaves. Red Cheeks kept arguing and gesturing at the sky that had evidently produced Loren. Other tribesmen smiled at him, the labrets and tattoos around their lips turning their smiles into those feline grins, which even when friendly seemed to have a subtext of warning. Only on the children's faces did the tattoos not look threatening.

The cat-man with the hat of leaves conferred quickly with Red Cheeks, then turned and asked Loren a question in an Indian language. The explorer shook his head apologetically:

"*Não falo*," he explained. "*Fala português?*" he asked the man with the hat, then he raised his voice to repeat the question for the whole community.

Men's and women's eyes lifted up from the presents, which were now circulating freely; children and adults had fun seeing their faces distorted by the spherical mirror of an aluminum kettle, and the flashlight was an unqualified success. The machete was being handed back and forth, its efficiency demonstrated and redemonstrated. The colored yarn had been torn up in countless pieces: bits of it resurfaced throughout the crowd. But the people listened attentively to Loren's words, some wrinkling their foreheads. None seemed to understand him.

Well, I'm either in a jam or starting a great experience, he thought.

By now some adults were bold enough to stare closely at Loren's camera, but as long as it hung about his neck he didn't worry. There was still half a roll of unexposed film in it, and two more rolls in his pocket. He had burned so many shots on the trail following the hunters' backs, and now there was so much humanity here, all to be fitted into less than a hundred shots. *They'll take me back to the camp, and I'll get more film.*

Red Cheeks was explaining to the man in the leaf hat (*He could be a shaman*, thought Loren, remembering the shamans' attire in other Amazonian tribes) how they had found the explorer, putting his hands, squared up expressively, before his eye and imitating the taking of photographs. The shaman nodded without much bewilderment. Loren was almost sure that they had sighted civilizados, but sighting is not contacting, and the contact's major transfer, that of words from one language to another, had apparently not happened to these natives.

The shaman pointed to Loren, then assumed a curious pose, leaning sideways. He rotated his right arm while twirling his left hand from the wrist. All of a sudden, the explorer found himself in front of a helicopter, mimed so convincingly that the art of a Marcel Marceau looked rudimentary in comparison. His lips bubbling like an engine while the big rotor and the little rotor churned, the shaman bent his knees toward the brown floor of forest litter, conveying a slow, vibrating landing. It was so perfectly essentialized that the explorer felt like stepping back from the powerful whirl of the blades.

For a few seconds the shaman *lived* the image, then gestured inquiringly and Loren nodded yes, he recognized the helicopter, then shook his head energetically no, no, that wasn't the way he had arrived. He threw his arms wide open and banked right and left with palms stretched to suggest a plane. A quick conversation followed between the shaman and other tribesmen, and an air of confusion swept the shaman's face. While the crowd still surrounded him tightly, Loren noticed that all of them had orbited away, almost halfway along the fallen sumauma tree.

I must have some liquids, or I'll pass out. He gestured,

imitating drinking, and was instantly understood; a calabash with water dancing in it was quickly paraded over by
helpful hands. He put his face into it and ordered himself to
drink slowly. Inside the calabash, light sifted in through the
thinned walls of the dried-out shell, and the shape had the
reassuring roundness of a womb.

Somehow that sense of roundness persisted when he lifted
his face and took a breath. The area on which the village
was built was elongated, following the linearity of the fallen
tree. However, immediately around it reality organized itself
into a sphere, equally deep wherever the eye tested it. A tiny
planet of space wrenched from the forest, into which the
natives had arranged their belongings, their abodes, and
themselves—it took just so little for them to exist.

Another shaman with a conical hat of leaves hurried over;
the shamans and the Indians who had brought him in
parleyed animatedly. Then, without being physically
pushed, the explorer was made to advance along the fallen
tree toward a hut as unassuming as all the others. A man
with a headdress of white egret feathers sat before it on a
stool of a single piece of carved wood, saddle-shaped,
characteristic of forest cultures. Assuming that he was the
village's highest authority, Loren examined him closely. He
was a bulky individual, with scraggly filaments of hair
sprouting from his chin, to which his labrets added an
impression of almost full beard. The bridge of his nose was
high, and his eyes were narrowly set against it. His cheeks
sagged with a tiredness not devoid of majesty. A strong set
of ears pushed out of the thick columns of his black hair,
while a swarthy scattering of spots on his face made him
look even more jaguar-like. As the group approached, he did
not stand, just sat up straight, and the explorer saw his big
hands with dark and chipped fingernails pause from
working on an arrow. On the ground next to him there were
several other arrows, heads still unfastened, and some palm
fiber thread, and a pile of perforated nuts. Tied under the
arrowheads, the nuts produced a whistling noise when

sailing through the air—whistling arrows were popular in Amazonia.

Glancing from the unfinished arrows to the man, the explorer noticed something crawling on his legs: it looked like a rash of creatures with shells spreading up to under his knees, but after an instant he realized that they were not moving. The headman, if headman he was, had dry crusty warts on his ankles and calves, resembling barnacles.

Around the seated man, the controversy about the guest grew to its loudest and most confused. Red Cheeks retold the story, brandishing the machete. The shamans kept cutting in, and so did the other tribesmen. The man with barnacles on his legs pursed his lips, making his mouth into a ball of tattooed blue, then parted his lips in a smile. He had a mouthful of teeth, but they were eroded and cracked, some of them black like chips of obsidian.

"*Bom dia*," McIntyre tried again in Portuguese, "Good day. I'm coming from downriver. I got lost. I have a camp on the shore and I need to get back to it."

The headman listened patiently.

"I need someone to take me back to the river," said Loren. The headman was silent. Loren crouched, grabbed one of the unfinished arrows. He looked up; the headman made no forbidding gesture. With his hand, Loren brushed aside the rotted brown leaves, uncovering a stretch of humid soil. Using the arrow, he drew a map of the river.

"I came from downriver and landed here," he explained. He made a cross where the shore might have been; at this arbitrary scale he would only be off by some fifty miles each way. He drew up next to it a semblance of plane fuselage supported by pontoons, and three sack-shaped human silhouettes with dashes for limbs and little circles for faces. Two of them—he erased them—had flown back—he mimicked the plane taking off, pointed to where he thought was east, realized that he had no notion of where the cardinal points were. He wondered whether the other two's departure had to be justified. One got sick—he mimicked a man throwing up, shaking—so the other had to take him back. Only he—he jabbed a finger at his own chest—had stayed on that shore where the camp was.

He waited.

They talked all at once again, all but the headman, who turned and vibrated in his chair, seemingly trying to get up but not making it. Was he a cripple? *Of course, they're wondering why I stayed back, since the other two left.* To explain that appeared like a major challenge. The camp, he insisted, tapping the arrow at the camp's presumed location. He had to return to the camp.

He knew how Indians indicated time. They raised an arm and pointed to a certain position of the sun in the sky, after sunrise: thus, though having no concept of hours, they signified the equivalent of one hour away, or three, or six, and if they rotated their arm full circle it meant a whole day. Simple and clear, with errors that didn't count out here. If they did it repeatedly it meant as many days as rotations, and they rarely went over three. In most tribes, after one, two, three there was just "many."

Like an Indian, Loren raised his arm to an angle indicating at least four hours away. That was how far his camp was. Obviously, too far to reach it by himself. But it was on the bank of the Javari. He repeated the name, Javari, and pointed at the map of clayey soil. Maybe they called it something else, he thought momentarily, and cursed his lack of anticipation; he could have at least asked the malaria-stricken guide whether he knew the Indian names to the region's main features, particularly the rivers.

"Javari," he repeated.

"*Ateahwah?*" asked one of the shamans.

Several others repeated the question: "*Ateahwah? Ateahwah?*" Loren looked at the chief, who pointed at the map of clay with his own arrow.

Is he mute? he wondered.

"*Ateahwah? Ateahwah?*" they kept prattling. He shrugged, realizing that he couldn't tell what *ateahwah* was. Red Cheeks broke in again, raising his voice, almost haranguing the others, the chief included. Whatever *ateahwah* meant, he seemed to say, that wasn't it.

With that, the debate fragmented into practically each Indian taking one or two others for witnesses and demonstrating something, while the chief looked at Loren and smiled with teeth like black shards of obsidian. He seemed to be in his midlife. He made no gesture, but it seemed that an interview had just come to its conclusion. His expression was patient, almost detached.

Again, without pushing, most of the onlookers gravitated away and Loren had no choice but to continue along the big tree, the axis of that community. He was extremely hot, still thirsty, and very tired. Hungry for hours, he had forgotten the pangs in his stomach. He was frustrated by such a failure in communication and uncharacteristically angry with himself.

This was dumb. The dumbest thing I've done in half a lifetime of roaming.

But it was not in his nature to remain angry for long at anything. Anger never provided solutions; what he needed to do was optimally employ his time among the Mayoruna while planning a sensible way out.

Loud calls announced another party of hunters appearing from the forest, and half of the explorer's congregation left him to welcome them. The hunters singlefiled in from the bush, some eight or nine men, bringing more howler monkeys, a couple of peccaries, and some turtles.

6

Beiju

As most of the villagers rushed to meet the hunters, Loren was left with a dozen followers, including the two shamans, who escorted him back around the top of the fallen tree still decorated with bromeliads turned brown from lack of sunlight. He thought of photographing them later; but he didn't have enough film to waste on plants.

He kept glancing at people as he passed them. Women and men sat before their huts, on the ground or on mats and fallen branches. Some of the eyes staring back at him looked almost round, their epicanthic folds depleted by emaciation. *These people are hungry. They usually open a clearing when they plan on a more permanent settlement, but they didn't do it this time. They just used the space around the fallen tree. They are hiding.*

But if they were hiding, why had the young warriors allowed him to follow them? And what was the tribe's reason for moving the village—that morning, apparently, since the huts were still being built? Doubting that yesterday's children had trekked hours to the shore just to try their bird snare, he wondered whether the previous location was closer to the shore. Had the tribe moved away from *him*? But in that case, why would the young warriors lead him back to the tribe?

He had no answer for any of these questions. Meanwhile,

the hunters, joined by a group of males from the village, sat on a log in an inverted pattern, one facing out to one side of the log, the next to the other. Heads held straight up but eyes aimed down, each man brought a cupped hand to his mouth and chanted with the others, a ceremony Loren had witnessed in other tribes, and knew it to be called a "reacquaintance." Each tribesman chanted to a neighbor, then switched hands and chanted to the neighbor on his other side. All said the same thing: *It is good, it is good to be back in the village; it is good, it is good to be again together.* Those who had faced the perils of the forest and those who had waited for their return became thus one family again (when the separations were longer those who stayed behind would provide information about births and deaths, in the same impersonal simultaneous fashion). The anxiety of sailing the wild or of waiting for the sailors to return was thus turned into a ritual while all of them together built confidence for the next hunt and waiting.

Meanwhile, the women had taken charge of the fresh game. The young girls eagerly helped and Loren saw two girls of about thirteen grabbing a clobbered howler, which, though smeared with blood from the crown of its head to its belly, was not dead yet, for it woke up at the touch and tried to fight its captors. One of the girls picked it up by its tied legs, swung it in the air, then slammed it hard against the ground. Squirts of blood shot up through the howler's nostrils and its limbs twitched. The girl had uniquely shiny eyes, a short nose and wide lips, and exuded energy. The other girl stood at the ready with a club, but it wasn't necessary: the monkey was dead at last. The two tied one hind leg to the tail and used the natural hook to hang the animal facedown over a fire. Some vital reflex still operating, the monkey's face cringed and a remnant of air bellowed out of its extraordinary larynx. Loren raised his camera and clicked.

There was soon to be a meal, maybe the community's first in a while—Loren heard gurgles from the stomachs of passing tribesmen. The cooking would take perhaps an hour.

In the interim, one of the shamans used gestures to ask to look through the camera's lens, and the explorer had no choice but to let him. Trailed by a group of adults and children, they stepped together toward the trees, where Loren photographed a colubrid snake, the green paradise variety, no fangs, not poisonous, its sinuous shape sliding down from a low branch to strike at a caterpillar twice as long as a man's finger. Instants later, the shaman showed him a harlequin beetle crawling on a leaf. Mature specimens reached thirty centimeters and came complete with their personal pseudoscorpions, just four millimeters long, living in the beetle's crevices and cleaning it of mites. The harlequin flew away and Loren showed the shaman how to take a photograph, then posed while the shaman snapped an unfocused shot, his brown face solemn with shyness. Finally, it was all right for Loren to photograph the shaman, then another shaman, then the children again, then the village. He finished a roll of film, took it out, and allowed several more Indians to peer through the lens of the unloaded camera. Then he reloaded and was soon halfway through the next roll, and there was only one more left in his pocket. But he had plenty of unexposed film at the camp.

It was three in the afternoon. Three more hours before nightfall.

He was exhausted and for a while had not given a thought to the camp he had left on the shore. The Mayoruna were not hostile, but finding a guide to take him back would be a problem, since none spoke Spanish or Portuguese. "*Hola, me llamo Loren*," the explorer kept repeating, and by now they had learned his name: *Lowen, Lowen*, they repeated, not able to duplicate his *r*, while the kids grinned and tittered.

They didn't understand. They were not pretending, because they had no reason to. Had any of them spoken a civilizado language they would have come forward by now. He was not overly concerned. He would find a way to explain what he needed. Staying longer with them only increased his chances of being trusted.

He was elated about the photographs. Deciding to save the last film for tomorrow, he let the camera hang on his chest, and without anything to do allowed himself to enjoy his unusual company. Now his hosts were preparing to eat all at once. Fires under the babracots roasted swatches of peccary meat, which Loren had tasted before and knew to be good. Clay plates two feet in diameter laid directly over flames had been loaded with coarse grains of manioc powder, which the women flattened with wooden spatulas into quarter-inch-thick pancakes before letting them cook. The pancakes were called *beiju*. Loren had eaten beiju before (it was flat, thick, tasteless, and yet satisfyingly filling), and also photographed it.

The girls who hung the howler over the fire let the flames singe its hair off, roasting the meat superficially, then judged it ready to eat and unhooked it, its face still fixed in a cruel grimace. The girl with the shiny eyes held up a roasted paw and offered it to Loren. He made a gesture of refusal. He'd never been able to eat monkey like that, *crispado*—especially the paw, considered a delicacy, reminded him too much of a child's hand. He looked at the girl, her forehead sweaty from the fire, every hair on her plucked out from pubis to eyebrows. Lifting the paw to her own mouth, she turned to a group of other girls. Other youngsters, lean and fast-bodied, moved among the older Mayoruna, contrasting their tautness against breasts tired of motherhood, stooped backs, and flaccid stomachs.

All were famished, though. On the clay plates, the big wheels of beiju were flipped onto the other side. In a few minutes they were done, copiously stained with soot from the fire. Fish, pounded into a gray paste with the heads and bones in it, was spread on the beiju, and eager hands tore pieces, folded the pancakes over the fish, jammed them into avid mouths. The explorer was offered a fish-laden slice by a woman whose features reminded him of the girl with the monkey paw. She could well be her mother or her aunt. The blood that flowed in these people's veins was being poured back from one individual to another, on and on, remixing a base material old yet always new. Like the silts of the Amazon itself.

He sat down, taking bites from his folded slice of beiju, heavy and filling. He was being bombarded with stimuli by people whose existence had been in doubt till yesterday, and most of those stimuli were raw and primal. Their total quality registered inside him as a sound sensation, a buzzing or some other continuous noise, though he wasn't quite sure that he was experiencing it. For an instant, the loud voices around him seemed to fade, replaced by that amorphous murmur. Loren sat up and fought the heat, listened hard, and the sounds of the village came back.

The heat was oppressive and he was very tired. His senses, at peak alertness for a number of hours, were now relaxing while his hunger and thirst were being appeased. That produced the sensation, the inner hum. Trying to clear his mind, he stood up again. Seen from several feet higher, the world looked more organized and controllable. But the unusual sensation didn't diminish.

As if to test reality, he looked around. The girl with strikingly shiny eyes had torn a big slice of beiju in two and laid one half down on a large leaf while eating the other. The cross-eyed boy, on all fours on the ground, tried to sneak a brown little hand toward the half she was saving. "*Tuti! Tuti!*" she called out, a name or an interdiction, and then pretended to swat him with her palm; nevertheless, he grabbed the piece. She jumped up to chase him, her body shaking in one healthy mass of flesh, her thighs and shoulders and brown arms going into a subtle throb. Youth saved her from that sad look of emaciation.

Loren watched the village. Every cooking fire shone on a ring of warm nudity, while the Mayoruna tribespeople bit and tore at the food. They ate hungrily, food uncooked and unchewed forced down in big gobs. Among so many pumping cheeks, he noticed an older man slowly chewing a piece of meat, eyes almost closed, as if eating in prayer. The intimation of sensuousness was so rare among Indians. He wanted to photograph him, then suddenly decided to let the chance pass and enjoy the moment for what it was. An instant later, he saw the naked girl holding the cross-eyed boy in her lap. Faces smeared with fat, they ate together, reconciled.

The obscure murmur coming from all of them was just his response to being alone in their midst.

7

The Dream

An hour before dusk, he was adopted by a family of four who offered him the use of a hammock in their hut. Nothing like the sophisticated article he had left in the camp, this hammock was made of knotted palm twine which would leave marks on his skin. All five hammocks in that particular hut were tied to the hut's central post, so he would have to retire simultaneously with at least one other member of the family, otherwise his loaded hammock would pull down the post and the hut with it. Tomorrow, if he was still here, he would hang the hammock out among the trees.

No Indian village turns in all at once. For the next ten hours the din of the village would repeatedly peak and decrease, as people went to sleep and woke up, rolled out of hammocks and fed the fires again, fed children if they woke up, got hungry themselves and munched on some leftovers, and then went back to sleep, all at will.

That buzzing sensation was still with him.

Of course, there was no other civilizado around, he kept telling himself, so he experienced a special type of loneliness in the midst of an active, sociable community. He climbed into his hammock in sync with another member of his new family, and lay the camera down next to him. He pulled out his notebook and pen and tried to write but could not gather his thoughts, so he leaned back letting the indirect reflection of a fire play on the blank page. Indian voices were speaking right outside the hut, and Loren thought he recognized the young cat-man whom in his mind he called Red Cheeks. Red Cheeks and several other young males were striding across the village ground, talking hurriedly. A somewhat skeptical male voice interrupted Red Cheeks, who interrupted back, angry at the contradiction. Ego was present here in the wild; ambition and leadership were characters in this primal play, the same as in the world Loren had left behind.

The little sphere of voices sailed into the general hum, faded. Soon after it did, the notebook fell by Loren McIntyre's side. He was breathing quietly and regularly, asleep.

He dreamed that he was airborne—not in a plane but hovering by himself, like a balloon, above a vision of jungle and mountains looking like an oversized map. It was a dream, and in his dream he knew it. A vast stretch of jungle spread out beneath him, emanating a rich phosphorescence, as if lit from underneath. That phosphorescence was the jungle's own richness. The intricacy of its life-forms. That was why Pizarro and Orellana and so many others had feverishly searched here. It was all here, that treasure. Generations of predecessors had simply misnamed it, but in his dream McIntyre recognized it instantly. It suffused the greenness of the jungle, while the distant mountains blew their godlike breath on it. An invisible force swelled up the mountains from within, making them pregnant with a captive message.

Then he was back standing in the middle of the tribal ground. He found himself in front of the headman. Somehow, the dream's camera lens focused itself first on the man's legs with their big warts, before it lifted to his face.

He woke up. Someone was fueling a fire next to his hut and the crackling flames roared, lighting brightly the ceiling of cane and leaves. On Loren's wrist the watch ticked on, its digits less luminous against the increased light of the fire. The pen was still clutched in his fingers.

The bush was full of the frolic of nightlife. Unseen predators chased unseen victims while thoughts scurried inside McIntyre's mind, anxious and unfocused. He had always been interested in dreams, though he gave them no premonitory value. What he found fascinating was the way they mixed together pieces of the past, thus playing with time. As a young man he had been fascinated with time, time of all kinds, chronometric, psychologic, terrestrial, sidereal; he had read avidly about relativity; he had imagined the dimension of time rebelling, changing its properties, announcing a major restructuring of the known cosmos. But he was scientific-minded, and of Scottish origin to boot. The Scots in his family, proverbially practical (his maternal grandfather, George Nell Alexander, veteran of the Civil War and the Klondike, had been Seattle's city engineer), had always applied their genius to building; bridges and road-ways, contraptions and motors had satisfied their imaginations better than speculation or poetry. Loren McIntyre, interested in time as a youthful exercise, had soon decided that it was flexible only in his mind.

Dream was interesting, though, because its material was time. Dream reversed it or made it run on parallel tracks, brought back memories with frightening realism, and sailed into the future like a space probe. All this was not of much consequence for a civilizado who sweated out reference and verification when writing his books and articles, except that dream was always relevant to the natives he visited. Dream was their explanation of everything beyond the physical and tested. For them, dream wasn't even dream.

Always, when among Indians, McIntyre allowed himself to play with that side of himself he ignored or kept shuttered in the civilizado world. He remembered his dreams and analyzed them in terms of what he had experienced. The headman with barnacles on his legs had smiled and listened through their encounter, but had not uttered one word. It made sense that his dream had brought him face-to-face with the headman, perhaps trying to compensate for that silence.

He could write by the bright glare of the fire. His notes

might not be legible tomorrow, but he would remember their general drift. He was doing it less to record his experience than to bring himself to a calm appraisal of his situation.

October the twentieth. Somewhere near the eastern bank of the Javari River. Seems not to be known by this name among the Mayoruna natives. Took good pictures of the group I contacted, and stand good chance to take pictures out of here.

I wonder what I'm starting by photographing these people. I'm not keen on seeing them inundated by government agents and scientists. They have no defenses against germs from the outside, which are invariably brought in through regular contact. I also wouldn't want them to become dependent on outsiders, which is the saddest effect of acculturation. Unfortunately, the best safeguard for leaving Indian life unadulterated is really *not to contact them*; every presence from outside, even that of one guest alone, potentially threatens their future.

But I'm alone and won't be here for more than a few days. My effect on them will be limited and hopefully unlasting.

He stopped. Writing in the hammock was awkward and slow. He lay down and let his mind pick up the unfinished lines. Not contacting such a tribe while suspecting that it was retreating from settlers created other moral dilemmas. To leave them alone added to their hardship because it held back help and protection. At first glance, the people around him had great need for needles, thread, better fire-making devices (he'd seen them use a most primitive fire drill), knives, and pots. Despite their muscularity, some would develop tuberculosis; the changes of temperature between daytime and nighttime were drastic here, and McIntyre was shivering in his hammock. For those with frail lungs, even T-shirts and shorts could save lives.

They all needed doctors and medicine, and their best chance of medical attention were the missionaries, who would certainly attempt to modify their culture, no matter how amicably. They could use the knowledge that not all of the outside was their enemy, to make better decisions about their future; but by the time they acquired some detailed knowledge of who in Brazil was their friend, the victim again would be their culture.

There was always the same question when opening the unknown: What to do with it?

Thoughts, thoughts. Like spaceships, whirling somewhere in a sort of suborbital space. Lying in his hammock, shivering from the cold and hearing the sounds made by the tribespeople who were still awake, McIntyre was aware of a subsphere of his mind in which a different species of mental processes, less explicit and formal, were forever meeting, colliding, mixing. The tribe he had just encountered was part of them. And among the tribespeople—curiously expressive and eloquent, though he had not said a word to his guest— loomed the headman with warts on his legs.

As always when he thought of Indians, a quick film from childhood started to unreel in the subspace of McIntyre's mind. Seattle in the late twenties. The streets of childhood. All he knew about Indians then was that there were some unusual people living at the foot of Cherry Street who were Indian and wove baskets and were descendants of Chief Sealth, after whom Seattle was named (few people know how young Seattle is: its first settler arrived there in 1852). As a girl, Loren's mother saw Chief Sealth's daughter, Princess Angeline, selling her baskets at the foot of Cherry Street.

Chief Sealth was a Siwash. Across the street from where the McIntyres lived there was a retirement home named after Caroline Kline Gallan, a Jewish lady who had turned her house into a shelter for the old and ailing. Neighborhood kids, Loren included, used to run off with apples stolen from the large orchard open to Seward Park Avenue. One of the few residents to ever emerge from the house was an erudite old Jew nicknamed Siwash Davis, because among a score of other languages he also spoke Siwash, and probably could understand Chief Sealth and Angeline.

He was an old man who walked around wearing a skullcap and aiding himself with a cane, and gave Loren a Siwash Indian nickname, "Little Bright Eyes"—Loren had long forgotten its Indian equivalent but remembered that his mother had translated it to him. He became "Little Bright Eyes" for Siwash Davis, and for himself too. That was the age when in every ditch, behind every tree, lurked the romantic shadow of one of his storybook heroes, and most often that hero was an Indian. Whenever he played cowboys and Indians, in woods or around the house, Loren wanted to be an Indian. Because the Indian moved silently and mysteriously, his shadow one of the many shadows of the forest. The mystery of that movement fascinated Loren. The thought of that life, which an Indian would be content to live all unto himself, without the contact that the palefaces forced on him, simply awed the seven-year-old.

Childhood imaginings, long dispelled by experience. But in the mind's subspace they remained alive, like the rolled-up history of a genetic trait, ready to unfold and transmit itself.

This scene from Loren's past always lit up in connection with two experiences: Indians and time, any form of time. Like now, the anonymous succession of seconds, while he waited for sleep to settle back in, waited for his thoughts to melt back into dream, building from dream's ephemeral material a home for what he was now: a tired civilizado, alone and lost in prehistory.

Being alone among these people put him in touch with that subspace of his mind where everything was; the present in its hidden implications, the past distilled to what was important and lasting, and even the future, obscure but nevertheless evident. And where fresh adventures, no matter how unsettling, were always welcome . . . .

On the planet's other side, a satellite-swirl away, the next day had already started. To the east, where the ocean hugged the jutting green coast of Brazil, complete with the two-hundred-mile-wide mouth of the giant Amazon River, morning was breaking. Clouds, millions of tons of water vapor, hung in the sky above Amazonia, trickling humidity into the air breathed by the Mayoruna tribe in its inconspicuous niche of forest. Inhaling the same air, the explorer fell asleep, connected.

He was rudely awakened.

A pair of hands was shaking the hut's central post. They belonged to one of the shamans. Like big ripe fruits, the brown bodies of Loren's hosts plopped out of their suspended beds, and the explorer groggily grabbed his camera and other possessions and touched down only seconds after his hosts.

Mist boiled over the village ground and the fallen tree. Above it, as if knitted into the canopy, the dark looked all-powerful, yet the jagged screech of the macaws already trumpeted the start of a new day. The hammocks were being rolled up and the head of the household motioned Loren to do the same with his. He obeyed with numb fingers, saw his pen bounce on the hut's ground, and picked it up. He stepped out into the tribal village plaza while the head of the household thrashed powerfully at the central post with a club of chonta palm. The post broke. The roof came down.

The rest of his adoptive family were outside, arms filled with baskets, drinking gourds, a bamboo spike with some sun-dried fish impaled on it, bows and arrows, a fishnet. They gathered off the forest floor things they had not packed up yet, threw them into the baskets. All around Loren, other natives did the same: into baskets went hatchets, skulls and locks of time-bleached hair (trophies, he noted), forked utensils for thatching roofs, necklaces of jaguar claws, junior-sized bows and arrows and other toys. On his right and left, other huts were coming down. With baskets and bundles full of their belongings, men and women joined a crowd assembling noisily between the huts. Suddenly the barnacled headman himself walked alongside the crowd, as if passing it in review. He was asked a question by Red Cheeks, which he answered in a surprisingly high-pitched voice. So he could move, and speak too.

A harsh grayish light spread where the canopy was thinnest. Macaws, matched in pairs of the same color, flapped out of the foliage, flying from tree to tree. The tribespeople were demolishing their huts and lean-tos quickly and without any apparent regret. Baskets went up and were balanced on heads, and little children were strapped on women's backs, secured with tumplines passed around their mothers' foreheads. The six-foot bows and arrows, the hurling clubs, the spears and harpoons were clutched in tribesmen's palms. The squirrel monkeys, on leashes of twine, were hitched to wrists and forearms, and the pet birds were made to perch on shoulders and even on thick manes of hair. All of a sudden, the Indians looked ripe, loaded with the fruits of their life in the forest. The barnacled headman passed them in review, puffing on a green cigar of wild tobacco. He found the explorer standing among the people he had spent the night with and graced him with no special greeting.

As if listening to an unspoken command, the column broke forward as soon as it was fully formed. *Where the hell are they going again?* was all that Loren's mind could articulate.

He decided on a symbolic rebellion. He rushed out of the ranks, stood by the edge of the trees. Right past him, the column headed into the bush, and all the characters by now familiar to him paraded by with their relatives and valuables. The girl who swatted the cross-eyed boy walked behind the older woman she so closely resembled. The cross-eyed boy himself followed, carrying a toy bow and a load of arrows. The shamans appeared, and filed past. No one seemed to be paying any attention to him.

Even in the uncertain light and with everyone passing him quickly, it was clear to his experienced eye that this tribe had an impressive arsenal of belongings. Each family had calabashes and drinking gourds. In the baskets bobbed all sorts of objects attesting to the people's ingenious use of the habitat. They had arrows of diverse manufacture, with points serrated, barbed, or knobbed. The bow staves were of different woods, and the featherings varied. Headdresses were made of collections of multicolored hummingbirds, sewed by their beaks into headbands of fiber, and necklaces were of monkey or jaguar teeth strung together, or of dried seeds and nuts. Earlobes were stretched by all manner of earrings. Some children held rattles of baby turtle shells. McIntyre noticed a woman carrying a bag of knitted palm fiber, with a fancy lid from an armadillo shell.

The forest, having offered man the best of its husk, fin, or fang, opened now to give him harbor. McIntyre watched the Mayoruna head into the trees. Quickly, they were swallowed up by the forest.

He couldn't stay here alone.

He rushed to catch up with the column. Room was made for him, almost indifferently. The path was soon as narrow as a tribesman's hips.

Damn it, he thought, *what is this, and where are they going?*

He was part of "they." He walked swiftly along like a Mayoruna whose possessions happened to be a pen, a notebook, a camera.

Half an hour later (he knew it was half an hour; he kept looking at his wristwatch as if trying to stay in contact with his clock-operated world), they crossed a muddy stream, using a fallen log as a catwalk. He was always apprehensive of such passages. The bark underfoot was mossy and slippery and one could easily fall and impale oneself on snags. The Indians seemed unaware of the risk; the whole column danced across almost without slowing down, but as Loren stepped across and faltered, a hand from behind caught his elbow and steadied him.

Much slower than the Indians, he negotiated the passage.

Once on the other bank, he thought of abandoning the tribe right there. This little subtributary, if he followed it, would take him to the main stream, to the Javari.

But would it? Not only was there no telling where it joined

the main stream in relation to his camp, but maybe it didn't flow into the Javari at all. Maybe it meandered eastward, eventually running into one of the next tributary systems, the Itui, or even the Jandiatuba. That was not out of the question. The maps of the region were sketchy, following the chartings of the Brazilian and Peruvian navies. Where gunboats couldn't cruise, the cartographers didn't venture and the mapping stopped. Just recently aerial photography had added to the maps a host of new tributary systems, including some that appeared and disappeared, segments of their courses being forever sealed under the canopy. No one could tell where those little rivers connected, and at times not even in which direction they flowed. At the peak of the dry season they bogged down in their own silt and almost stopped moving, but at floodtime they erupted out of stagnated beds and meandered freely in new directions. Occasionally a flood or freshet backed up a river and reversed its course: that happened frequently here because the gradient of the forested plain was so very gentle. Since not even the direction of a flow was entirely reliable, there was no guarantee that this narrow subtributary, possibly still unnamed, would take him where he wanted to go.

Yet Loren knew upper Amazonia. He had sailed it, walked across it, and surveyed it from planes again and again, and had examined generations of its maps. As for the giant river, he had been obsessed with it for more than three decades. He was all the more amazed to feel like a prisoner in a territory where he'd always felt comfortable and free.

He remembered well his first time on the giant river, for it was an encounter full of brightness and energy, the brightness and energy of youth. He was eighteen, a deckhand on a merchant ship, the SS *West Notus* putting in at Belém. The hot steel deck burned sailor McIntyre's naked feet, while the Para River ran past the ship, enormous, sea-sized. The Para wasn't even all of it; all the arms hugging that monstrous delta added up to a flow sixty times the Nile's, pushing into the Atlantic eight trillion gallons of sweet water daily—

twenty times the daily water needs of the United States for power, industry, farming, and all household use combined.

The year was 1935. The SS *West Notus* chugged upstream as deckhand McIntyre stared into an estuary wider than anything he had imagined. At that time he was not fully aware of the giant's dimensions, and many of them had not been firmly established yet. Anything that big couldn't fail to excite man's statistical curiosity, so attempts to measure the Amazon were as old as its earliest explorations. But how reliably could one measure such a monster, particularly since the seasons made it shrink and grow so wildly? At Manaus, capital of the state of Amazonas, a scale built into the harbor's escarpment showed variations of water level of fifty feet between June and November, between the dry and the wet seasons. At all times a thousand other factors modified the flow, making the biggest river also the least predictable. In the records of the Amazon's hydrography, the variance of data was overpowering, but that was just the outer shell of its complication. To describe its behavior at all, stream geometry, water level, rainfall-runoff relationship, velocity of flood wave, slope of gradient were just a few of the specifics. The river could not be defined by exact figures but rather by generations of figures with their distinct histories, and by aggregates of data merging survey with projection and fact with theory.

And among them were those by which a river is considered to be extra large: the discharge at the mouth, the area of basin drained by the stream (*thousands* of streams in the Amazon's case), and the total length from farthest source to mouth.

In discharge and drainage, the Amazon easily surpassed all other rivers. Its average of seven million cubic feet per second at the mouth exceeded the Mississippi's tenfold and equaled the total yield of the world's next eight largest rivers. Along the lower course of the main stream its colossal volume required a riverbed many miles wide. The Amazon's area of drainage, conservatively estimated at 2,230,000 square miles, was twice that of the Nile. As for length, supposedly only a hundred miles made it inferior to the Nile, yet that had never been truly confirmed, since the Amazon had never been properly measured.

Besides, the source, the farthest source, had never been convincingly identified.

Of so many fabulous mysteries, it was the source that sparked the sailor's imagination. Young McIntyre's mind shot up along the unseen length of the Amazon to where its source, the spew of water most distant from the giant mouth, lay hidden somewhere in the Andes. It was still assumed at the time that the giant started in Lake Lauricocha, source of one of its main headwaters, the Marañón. There was no clear picture of that source in the public mind; while Burton and Speke's trek to Lake Victoria conjured up relatively familiar images of Africa, Amazonia in 1935 was *terra viridis incognita*, the green unknown, starting frigidly way out west, in a range of snowcapped mountains of interest to no one.

Yet McIntyre's mind coursed uninhibitedly into that bleakness, looking for a beginning as tiny as the end result was colossal. He found it: not the image of what the source would be like, but the *feeling* of such a discovery.

The instant was brief. But its impact lasted through the morning, and the next day, and the whole week that the *West Notus* spent on the Para before she aimed her rusty prow back toward the monotonous ocean. It persisted, ramified, and became a direction in a man's life. As is normal with crucial moments, McIntyre remembered it fairly often. Its meaning was resurfacing now, as he walked single file through the Amazonian jungle behind the nude shoulders of a Mayoruna native.

Things had changed since 1935. Amazonia in October 1969 was better known than ever before. Aerial photography had spectacularly improved its cartography despite vast areas that remained veiled by persistent cloud cover; thanks to it, the headwaters leading to the source could be measured for the first time with road gauges on wide maps spread on well-lit desks, in the fully appointed comfort of professional offices. Thus the longest headwater, leading to the most distant source, had been identified as the Apurímac-Ucayali rather than the Marañón, the Huallaga, or the Mamoré-Madeira. The Apurímac-Ucayali twisted some eight hundred miles through the tall canyons of the Andes before escaping into the plain and meeting the main stream above Iquitos, the city where McIntyre and Mercier had planned their trip to Mayoruna land.

Fifteen months earlier, in mid-1968, an American expedition sponsored by the *National Geographic* had traveled to a frozen plateau in the high Andes and confirmed the most distant source to be on the western slope of Mount Huagra, a snowcapped massif in the Andean continental divide, right at the edge of the Apurímac's highest feedbasin. The expedition was made up of Helen and Frank Schreider, a husband-and-wife team with some spectacular trips to their credit. Since they wanted to be the first to sail down the whole length of the Amazon in a motorboat, their goal was not specifically the source, yet they had to start at the source. As source, they accepted a trickle of water already pinpointed in 1953 by French explorer Michel Perrin, who had climbed Mount Huagra before setting out on an ill-fated kayak journey down the river—his kayak sank and his companion lost her life just days after they started. Wiser, the Schreiders accomplished their trip in a 30-foot vessel of cedar wood, with a 12-horsepower gasoline engine.

Mount Huagra rose more than a hundred miles south of Cuzco, former imperial capital of the Incas. The trickle of water bubbling from its side became a little brook, the Huaraco (or Huarajo), fed by the melting of the snow on Huagra's twin peaks. Down in the valley below Huagra, near Cailloma, a little mining town at more than fifteen thousand feet of altitude, the Apurímac received the Huaraco and then twisted away on its pilgrimage to the plains. Huagra was thus one of the most distant peaks in the Andes linked by an uninterrupted flow of water with the Amazon's mouth.

As for the Amazon's length, calculated from the slopes of the Huagra to the intricate mouth with half a dozen big islands in it (one, Marajó, was as large as Switzerland), Frank and Helen Schreider put it at just over 4,000 miles measuring by the northern exit, the Canal do Norte, or at just under 4,200 measuring by the southeastern exit, the Para, the mouth's busiest shipping lane, also cradling the port of Belém. Last surveyed by a Belgian hydrologist, M. Devroey, the Nile boasted 4,145 miles minus a few lost to the construction of the Aswan Dam. After dwarfing the Nile in both flow and drainage area, the Amazon, if measured by the Para, also proved to be longer by some fifty miles.

But the decision that the source was on Mount Huagra raised doubts with a veteran of cartography like McIntyre. Huagra had already been designated as the site of the source in 1934 by Colonel Gerardo Dianderas, a Peruvian geodesic specialist who based his search on even earlier estimates. His position was unorthodox because it questioned the traditional source, the one in Lake Lauricocha, but it confirmed what some geographers already knew, that the headwaters coming from the south coursed longer through the Andes than the Marañón did.

Although Dianderas had put "his" source on the map with the precise latitude and longitude, he wasn't credited for it by Perrin in 1953, when the Frenchman reasserted the source to be on Mount Huagra. Almost certainly, Perrin knew about Dianderas. The tragic cancellation of Perrin's expedition brought a lot of attention to the concept of the most distant source and created some awareness of it among the inhabitants of the Cailloma Basin. Those who didn't much care were the local Indians, whose ancestors had scaled all those peaks and peered at all the sources without ever recording their deeds on maps or in history books. The others were mining specialists, mostly from Europe and the United States. They were excited about Huagra's and the Huaraco's claim to fame, and started to act as "source guides" to the infrequent guests from the outside.

Such a guide was Siegfried Stephan, engineer in charge at

one of the local mines, who assured Helen and Frank Schreider that the most distant source lay just nearby, then had a mine foreman drive them up to Mount Huagra. The Schreiders reported that they had been guided up the Huagra by a local, and justified their belief that this was the most distant source by quoting Perrin and Siegfried Stephan rather than by carrying out a verification of the Huaraco's length against the other headwaters in the area.

Aerial photography was critical for verifying the length of headwaters and the whimsical complexity of the tributary system, of which Loren was getting a fresh taste down here, in the steaming forested plain. That legendary "ultimate source of the Amazon" had often been found only to be disputed later, so McIntyre approached all fresh reports with skepticism. A few months after the Schreiders had climbed Mount Huagra, McIntyre had flown over the Apurímac's feedbasin himself, comparing the maps with the terrain below and concluding that the Huaraco might not be the longest flow of water running into the Apurímac. The area contained several other candidates, other little rivers joining the Apurímac, and for a definitive identification each had to be examined and measured. In fact, despite the authority of the *Geographic* and the report of the Schreider team, McIntyre had started to plan his own verification trip during that very flight. It was the only thing to do after the Schreiders had camped on the iced-up bank of that little brook and proclaimed it to be *the source*.

All that seemed so futile now. With or without an established most distant source, the Amazon held him captive in its exasperating net. Aerial photography, the study of maps, exchanging information and opinions with fellow geographers and travelers had given him a false sense of knowledge. He had felt in control, able to rise above the enigma, and then appraise it aided by science's latest gadgets.

Of that control, nothing was left now. He was being swallowed by the Amazonian growth, on its own terms. So were the other humans surrounding him; yet they had never attempted to master such a system and were at peace with its dangers. They found in its most frightening depth relief from that other world, to which their visitor hoped to return.

Maybe the new day was overcast, and maybe it was not: advancing under thick foliage, Loren couldn't tell. Taking the sun as a point of reference he could have used his wristwatch as a compass, but the clouds blocked off the sun just like the canopy blocked off the sky, so there was no way to achieve any orientation. Still, he could follow practically any flow of water in Amazonia confident that he would finally end up on the master river and encounter boat traffic. But he had no food, no medicine, and no weapons. A sprained ankle could immobilize him. An infected cut could kill him. Despite the fact that the Amazonian jungle harbored no mega-fauna of the African type, its jaguars and snakes, caimans and wild boars (from those in particular, when met in a pack, escape lay only up a robust tree), not to speak of its poisonous insects, arachnids, frogs, slugs, and plants, made for enough danger to challenge any man, no matter how well prepared. Fungi, bacteria, intestinal parasites, radical fluctuations in temperature, and lack of cooked food or purified water interwove their menace around him like a macabre aura, and against them all, apart from relying on his captors, the explorer had only his better judgment, his resolution, and his experience.

"Goddamn it," he kept muttering, realizing that the appearance of yesterday's four hunters and now the whole tribe's exodus had restricted his moves and decisions more effectively than if he had been kidnapped. Bound hand and foot. Trussed up like a peccary and hung upside down from a spear. This was capture of the most definitive sort, it was bondage to the big green wild, and undoubtedly the tribesmen around him were as deep in bondage to the stuffy, dense, reliefless green as he was. But they didn't mind. That green pit within which they so deliberately plunged was their goal, their liberation.

He thought of Mercier. The arrangements he had made

with the pilot suddenly seemed ridiculous in light of the area's perils. McIntyre's rescue depended on Mercier, yet the pilot had no idea where McIntyre was and what had happened to him. Moreover, to conceal from the river authorities his intentions about founding a mission, Mercier had not filed a flight plan with the Direccion de Aeronautica Civil in Leticia and was in no hurry to mention the *norteamericano* deposited on that muddy beach. Except for the landmark lupuna tree, the beach would be hard to locate again, while a rainstorm or freshet might destroy the camp and obliterate any record of where they had landed. Mercier depended on customers for his bush-hopping, and a bad record with the DAC was not what he needed. Still, he would report the disappearance sooner or later, unless he was detained in Peru before returning to rendezvous with McIntyre. His machine could break down, or the authorities might not act on the report—not only regulations, but civic duty was lax out here. All in all, there was a host of reasons why McIntyre's rescue, if it came to that, could be late or ineffective.

He concluded that for the present he only had himself and his enigmatic hosts to rely on.

He decided to try to walk closer to the headman. If he needed help, he might as well ask for it from someone of stature. Slowly, forcing himself past little clusters of tribespeople, he made it to the vanguard of the column.

The cat-man with barnacles walked escorted by the shamans. Loren slowed down and kept himself right behind their little group.

By now, he realized that some of these men and women would help decide his fate. They might as well have names. In his mind, he baptized the headman Barnacle. The girl and her aunt walked not far behind the headman. He named the girl Zonia, short for Amazonia, and for the aunt he chose Tia, meaning "aunt" in Spanish. The cross-eyed little boy became Tuti (he remembered Zonia calling it out to him, and maybe that was the boy's real name), and Red Cheeks stayed Red Cheeks. As for the shamans, he decided to call them *huaca*, after the Inca concept of something holy (from gods and their temples to places and people and domestic charms, anything magical was *huaca*), and to distinguish them by numbers. Thus the men in conical hats of leaves became Huaca One, Two, Three, and Four.

The new path was less labyrinthian than the one the day before. Several young warriors walked in front, breaking some of the hanging creepers and jutting branches, yet it was amazing how little destruction the tribe left in its wake. This time, the explorer made mental notes of the turns. His trained sense of orientation told him that they were describing a half circle. Getting away from the river, but then circling back toward it.

Late in the afternoon, the column broke into what had once been a clearing. Secondary growth had invaded it, and a lower canopy, thirty feet high instead of eighty or a hundred, already obstructed the sunlight. As they entered the clearing, a sudden rainstorm lashed the secondary growth leaves, wider and belonging to far fewer species, making them reverberate like brass plates. This time, instead of the usual low fraction, almost half of the water from the sky made it down to the ground. Barnacle stopped, making everyone stop; chonta sticks and hatchets and Loren's machete started to slash for the huts' posts and branches for the roofs. Before the rain was over the huts were half raised.

As soon as the clouds dispersed, the thinner canopy allowed some late afternoon sunlight to filter through. A golden haze seeped through the strainer of leaves, gathering unevenly in the clearing. Pieces of pure yellow seemed to melt inside the canopy and slip down the tree trunks. In some places it was thick like honey, and Loren photographed Tuti and other Mayoruna children rushing cheerfully through it, as if taking a bath of gold.

He found two trees between which he could hang his hammock. He laid it down still rolled up, and spotted a nest of paper wasps damaged by the rain. The surviving adults had divided their number between two tasks: some sucked the raindrops off the surface of the nest and then spat them out in transparent gobs of water as big as their heads, others pulled out of the nest their larvae, little whitish bundles like wrapped newborns, then sat right next to them vibrating their wings hard and loud, to dry out the tribe's next generation. They would make great pictures, but he had no macro lens for extreme close-ups and was also saving his shots.

He couldn't understand the purpose of destroying last night's village and of rebuilding it just a few hours later, just a few miles farther. It seemed to accomplish nothing but contribute to everyone's exhaustion and hunger. He walked among the huts being readied around a central plaza invaded by grass specific to secondary growth—as long as bigger trees did not shut sunlight off completely, floor vegetation still found enough sustenance. Various lengths of palm twine lay coiled up on the grass, left over from the building of the huts. He saw Barnacle sitting on his carved stool, his cheeks gaunt. The headman's eyelids were at half-mast, but his hands moved with precision, making another arrow. Out of a pouch, he pulled wild boar hairs, using them to seal the feathering to the arrow's shaft. Around the shaft his fingers went as if dancing, weaving hairs of different colors, from different parts of the boar's body: whiskers, mane, spine.

McIntyre had an idea. He picked up several feet of palm twine, tough and flexible like machine-made cordage, and walked up to Barnacle. The cat-man didn't blink when the explorer sat cross-ankled next to him, with the palm cordage in his lap. He divided it into eighteen strips of the same length, and his hands started to move too, first slowly, remembering an almost forgotten trade. Then they moved faster and more confidently. He was braiding an eighteen-strand belt.

He'd learned to make belts in his first year with the merchant marine; during off-duty hours on the SS *President Jackson* steaming toward Japan, able seaman Frank Glahe showed him the technique and taught him that handicraft was the best way to fight boredom at sea. Braiding a truly good belt took days, but the manic ballet of the fingers gave structure to the amorphous flow of time and created a welcome sensation of control. Loren still kept some of those belts at his home in Arlington, Virginia, but the best benefit from the craft had been learning how to approach other men. The most untalkative sailors opened up after such shared exercises, buffeted together in the narrow crew quarters of a freighter. In thirteen voyages to the Far East and South America between 1934 and 1941, McIntyre had learned how to get along with any sort of enigmatic or hostile male. Other men did it by hunting, but Loren liked animals too much to enjoy killing them. After the war, out of the navy and deciding to put his energies into exploration, belt-weaving had come in handy with Andean mountain men, or with river people. Particularly with Indians.

Trusting the old trick, he started to braid the sinuous coils of jungle twine into the familiar pattern of a Turk's head. Barnacle's eyelids fluttered—he had noticed the civilizado next to him, and his activity. Loren knew it could be more effective than conversation, because Indian men, though given to passionate group dialogues, spoke little when in pairs. Talk would be useless anyway, since neither spoke the other's language. He let himself be carried by the dance of the fingers. Instants later he remembered how Barnacle had mentioned that some of the Indians were friends. But the headman had not spoken. Or had he? No, he hadn't spoken. Not in English and in fact not at all.

He stopped braiding the twine, struggling with a sensation of memory gradually coming into focus. *Some of us are friends*, that was the headman's message. Without words, not opening his whiskered lips, uttering no sound at all. Stunned, McIntyre considered the thought in his mind. It felt like a message. Though the headman had not spoken, though McIntyre spoke no Mayoruna, and none of the Mayoruna, he was utterly convinced, spoke English.

He looked at the headman: the Indian wasn't even

smiling. Loren was close enough to hear him breathe slowly through his nose; he could see his lips closed, his labrets immobile, all but his hands inactive. He remembered hearing no sound in Panoan, the headman's language, or in any other language. But he found the content of the message echoing in his brain.

He shook his head. The heat was at its peak. At this time of the day his drowsy senses slipped into that sensation of hum.

Some of us are friends.

He moved his hands again, pondering whether he was listening to his own thoughts. Maybe being so near to the cat-man explained the sensation of message, unobtrusive and wordless, to which his mind unconsciously added words in English: Some of us are friends. Was it an attempt to reassure him, or a warning?

The cat-man was working on. His fingers passed the boar hairs around the tip of a palm-wood shaft, sewing in a punctured nut to make another whistling arrow. McIntyre looked at the hands, at the arrow, and rewarded the headman's work with a smile. The headman looked for the first time directly at the Turk's head braided into Loren's belt and smiled back. The meaning of both smiles equaled something like "Good work." But there was no beamed message about the belt or the arrow. The appreciation of each other's work didn't need it.

Slowly, trying to gather his thoughts, Loren watched the beamed message fade. He thought of the Panoan dialect he didn't speak, of the fact that the Indian knew no English. He strained his mind to focus not on the words of his next thought, but on their content. And instead of thinking *I'm also a friend; you can trust me*, he tried to fill himself with the feelings of that thought. Then he waited. *I know*, somehow appeared in his mind. Maybe it was just the feeling of that answer, with words in English hurrying in to illustrate it.

This time he was so attentive that he leaned tensely toward the headman. The pores in the man's face were like craters in a lunar landscape, his eyes had a tired black luster, and his lips were shut. There was nothing hypnotic in his appearance. The headman rose and held out the almost finished arrow. After an instant the explorer realized that he was being offered a gift, and took it.

Feeling that he had been allowed into a sort of intimate space, he remained seated in front of the headman's hut, ankles crossed next to the pouch with the boar's hairs and the finished and unfinished arrows. He watched the headman walk across the grass-filled plaza, as if checking the construction of the huts. As soon as Barnacle was several yards away, Loren reached into his memory tracks: the sensations of the two messages were there. He stiffened suddenly, realizing that if there had been some declaration of friendship from him to the chief, the chief had received it and responded by offering the arrow. He searched his memory again. No, he had not spoken out loud. And Barnacle understood no English.

He rose too, fascinated with what he felt. After almost two days with this tribe, he had been given a hint of communication between himself and this preliterate man. The communications, though short, had seemed anything but primitive. He strained his ears, remembering yesterday's buzzing, curious to hear it again, wondering whether he was going insane. He meaninglessly checked his watch, as if that single piece of Western machinery could provide some valuable counterbalance to what he was experiencing. He recognized that sensation of background hum, and it was not words, just a hum. A global sound that he couldn't describe, extrasensory though made of all the senses. He stepped across the overgrown clearing, staring at random at tribespeople's faces—for the last two days he had seen them over and over, and very few struck him as still unknown.

It was that unique ambience, he told himself. Stimuli he was not even aware of, hard to distinguish from that continuous bombardment with colors, sounds, and smells, yet real. Like the taste of the beiju—it was so easy to call it tasteless because civilizado palates were used to an abundance of taste, while the beiju was nothing but manioc with a smoky flavor from the fire it was cooked on. But its very blandness was essential and heavy, like the tuber it was made from. No, beiju was not tasteless. It tasted like pure nutrient. And there were so many other things here in their pure state. Why not thought too? Why not the simplest form of human contact, mind to mind?

He started, hearing something concrete and real: huge coins seemed to drum onto the bottom of a leather bag. Heavy drops of rain made their way down again, slapping at the foliage.

He had the time to tear a large leaf and hold it over his head like an umbrella, while naked tribesmen streaked across the plaza going for the shelter of the brand-new huts. (Some of these people were friends—did it follow that *others* were enemies?) Meanwhile, children splashed out of the huts in reverse direction, exhilarated to play in the rain. Loren noticed Tuti the cross-eyed boy prance wildly in the rain, then stop and stand panting under a corniche of leaves. Raindrops collected at their spiked tips, and one leaf, funnel-shaped, trickled down the drops in separate sets of three. Drop drop drop. Then a pause. Then again, drop drop drop. The cross-eyed boy studied the phenomenon, his unaligned glances joining over the bridge of his nose.

Then he started to pound the ground with his little feet. Step step step. Pause. Step step step. Pause. Drop drop drop. Step step step. Perfectly in sync with the rain.

Loren watched, arrested by the symbolism of the scene. Early man had gained the concept of succession, the earliest symbol of the passing of time, by observing natural phenomena. The dripping of water from natural faucets, the repeated call of birds, man's own heartbeat, his own footsteps. They had been man's first clues that time existed as a pulsing vein, invisibly uniting all life. From such early rhythms of nature, dance was born, to stay with man forever.

Perplexed, he felt again that it all had to do with time, though he wasn't sure how time explained, or challenged, the communication he thought he had experienced. He felt, however, that everything was an expression of time, including his dreams, which were nothing but time liberated to jump back and forth at memory's command.

He watched Tuti dancing the dance of the rain. Devising a game and an interpretation of reality out of three drops of rain. The boy and early man were now the same. Meanwhile, downriver, men from Loren's world were busy elaborating plans that would deliver Tuti, so close to the Stone Age that his brain contained almost no abstract imprints, to the world of machinery and televised news, soft drinks and government welfare.

Tuti danced on, unsuspectingly. The explorer stood watching the Mayoruna boy, finding himself at the center of an amazing web of connections. He couldn't tell what the contact with Barnacle meant, or even if it had happened, yet it had left him with a satisfying sensation of causality. Much had occurred in his life before he could share that instant with the Mayoruna headman, and then watch one of the tribal sons deal with perhaps his first abstraction.

A while later, the fires were restarted. Beiju was cooked again. Loren noticed that Barnacle, back at making his whistling arrows, was not eating.

8

Around the Face of Time

This is the third day of my strange captivity. I woke up feeling fingers on my left wrist, but when I reached with my other hand, I found my watch already gone. I blinked and saw several faces above me, one of them belonging to the shaman I baptized Huaca One. I breathed nauseating smoke and an odor of melting rubber. Glancing over the side of my hammock I realized where it came from: my Adidas running shoes, smoldering on a fire. I bolted, swung out of my hammock, and landed on the ground in one motion.

I was still wearing my pants and my shirt. I had fallen asleep with my camera against my hip, but now it wasn't in the hammock and I couldn't see it anywhere. About a dozen Indian males, among whom I recognized some of Red Cheeks's young toughs, watched me with curiosity; I almost fought my way through them to get to the fire. Huaca Two and several other males were gathered around the fire and my first impression was that they held hands. I broke through, pulled my running shoes off the flames, and rolled with them on the grass.

I got up, smoking shoes in hand. Some of the gathered tribesmen started to laugh, but Huaca One admonished them loudly and the laughing stopped.

Now, as I remember this scene, I wish I could've

witnessed it for the value of all its symbols cramped together in a two-minute action. My Adidas shoes were parched, but I could still put them on. I did, scorching the soles of my feet, feeling that my only defensible territory was my body.

Gritting my teeth, I walked back to my auto-da-fé and found Huaca Two in my way. Without thinking of the consequences, I shoved him aside and stared at the little crowd as fixedly as I could, making some of the tribesmen avert their eyes. My real concern was my camera. I tore the hammock open and searched its whole length, then threw myself under it and lunged out on the other side, into the grass. I saw nothing rectangular and black anywhere. I rose, pivoted around in my hot sneakers, rushed back to the crowd. But the camera was not in their hands. Their expressions were not aggressive, and my frustration was too evident. They parted to let me walk through. I zigzagged back and forth, almost ready to grab them and open their clenched fists to see if they clutched pieces of my camera. But these people were so disarmingly naked, they couldn't hide my camera anywhere on their bodies. I angled back across the clearing, wondering whether to storm the huts and knock open the household baskets. *Slow down. SLOW DOWN.* In such a situation, calm, coolheadedness were critical. I could hear my heart pounding furiously, and I felt my blood racing.

I suddenly found myself facing Barnacle, who was lumbering over, starting to smile with his blackened teeth. Somehow, he looked innocent of all this. I glimpsed Red Cheeks standing between two huts, seeming very uninvolved. Zonia was sitting on the forest floor right beside him, legs stretched, some palm fiber knotted around her big toe: she was weaving a basket.

I strode back, very determined yet not knowing what exactly I was going to do, and Barnacle stepped in my way again. I had been awake perhaps twenty minutes. A thought flashed up in my mind. *I need to know.* It felt like my own thought but an instant later I wondered whether that was the headman thinking it. *I need to know.* Its meaning in English felt somewhat post-added, as if I myself had provided the words, but I had no time to speculate now, things were happening too fast. Barnacle seemed angry; he was flashing dark looks at the tribesmen but also at me, as if ready to mete out some punishments. I looked at his eyes and thought I deciphered in them a gamut of emotions and calculations. What to do with me. What to do with his own people. Not acting would be a loss of face. Acting would add to the confusion and perhaps backfire. From behind all that, he informed me of a bigger emergency. *He had to know.* I almost started to laugh: So? I had to know too.

He turned his head and walked away from me, and the crowd gravitated after him. I wondered if I was being ostracized. (I've had adverse situations with tribal people before. I know how effectively they can ignore a guest. They let you eat, walk around, sleep, relieve yourself, even watch them, without paying any attention to you whatsoever. They make you feel utterly invisible. Of course, such hours of invisibility are the best for observing a native culture.)

I was in no mood to be cut off from them more than I already was. I had to do something about this *now*. I had an advantage, the advantage of having been the subject of aggression, and I wanted to act before it eroded. I quickly tied up the laces of my sneakers, frilled by the fire, and started jogging in a circle around the inner perimeter of the village.

I watched my feet pound the grass. The shamans had reassembled by the fire they had tried to hex me with (burning personal belongings is almost always a hex). Two laps. Three laps. Four laps. Now everyone was outside, even the pet squirrel monkeys and macaws. I passed Zonia and Red Cheeks again, fleetingly wondered whether they were lovers—one can hardly ever guess the Indians' relationships; newlyweds are very undemonstrative and couples display little conjugal behavior. Seventh, eighth, ninth lap. I felt as if my heart was racing ahead of me.

Now it was impossible to tell any buzzing sensation from the actual noise of the crowd. I was looping around the clearing, wanting them to think I was making a spell of my own. Barnacle returned and stood next to the track I was pounding across the grass. Every time I passed him, I lowered my forehead and exploded into a furious hammering of feet and fists, almost in a parody of intent. I could think of no other way to jolt the situation out of where it was. We had to communicate. We were communicating.

There was a jangle of thoughts in my mind. Orlando Villas Boas, a Brazilian anthropologist and fighter for the rights of native tribes, used to tell me such stories. How the true *sertanista*, the really insightful frontiersman, develops a sense about the forest people and learns to equal them in riddles, charades, symbolic gestures, improving his chances of surviving his encounters with them. I wanted to survive, and wanted them to survive too. Running felt good. Being alone among them had distorted my senses to such an extent that I had started to hear my own thoughts, projected right back at me. Running felt wonderful. It was active, mind-cleaning, definite.

Twentieth lap. I passed Zonia, noticed that she had tied in her hair some of the yarn I had brought with me. Blue yarn. She seemed overpowered by the situation. I looked for Tuti and didn't see him. Barnacle was now scanning his crowd, trying to interpret their reactions. I saw hands convulsing on clubs, but also foreheads wrinkled with attention. I became aware of a physical voice, discoursing nervously behind the circle of tribesmen. It was Red Cheeks. He broke into the circle and stood, arms crossed, muscles naturally flexed. I wondered whether he was ready to put an end to my nonsense yet felt restricted by the headman's presence.

I slowed down, walked a lap, and stopped a few yards from Barnacle. I was drenched in sweat. Then Barnacle turned and started jogging. Just the way I had, following my trail of trampled grass, but in the opposite direction: I had done it clockwise; he was doing it counterclockwise. He's a big ox of a man, and when he ended the first lap and passed me, I felt the air displaced by his massive body, while the ground's vibration reached into my cheeks. He went into the second lap, pumping harder when he passed me, and seemed careful not to deviate outside the trail. He was undoing my spell. I felt I was inside Barnacle's head, literally thinking his thoughts. Put plainly, they ran something like this: *I don't know if this will work. It's supposed to, it did before. But everything is so different now.*

That was "beamed" to me, superimposed on my own train of thought. I've never been able to read someone else's thoughts, I know myself to be not in the least psychic, as for intuition I'm probably just average. Still, I received it: it felt like my mind had allowed another person to "come in" on a second track. At no point did I feel confused about who I was. For a moment I just experienced the novelty. I tried to tune Barnacle out, and managed: the second track grew faint. But my curiosity had been so heightened that I immediately called him back, anxious that I'd lost him. I got him back, and received some personal stuff, like the strain of the run plus a sort of abandonment to fate. As he kept running, I experimented by raising and lowering the "volume," and realized that I could really tune him out at will. Which meant that I hadn't been invaded.

Now, as I review the events of that morning, I remember that at the time I wasn't overly surprised. I wondered if I was losing my mind, and whether the lack of surprise itself was a symptom. To test my perceptions, I focused on a roof thatch a few feet to my left: palm leaves lined up like ribs were affixed to a central beam by pulling the split ends of their stems around the beam and tying them into a row of clumpy, hairy buttons. They crawled with large black caterpillars. For a few seconds I watched them attentively.

My senses seemed to function normally.

But if I focused back on the tribespeople I felt that I was getting fragments of beaming which seemed personal, and an overall rumor of beaming, like the blurred sound produced by a crowd. In the main, the tribespeople seemed to share Barnacle's anxiety, though some, the younger ones, seemed excited. This was a threshold of some kind in their tribal life. The outcome was suspensefully uncertain.

As a final test, that of pain, I sank my teeth into my lower lip. The pain contradicted none of my other perceptions.

Other features of the experience, analyzed later: all throughout I was quite aware that it was nonverbal. I didn't hear a voice, or words; the words in English were a translation to myself, so to speak; they felt post-added, and I was worried that they diminished the acuity of the communication. I felt that I couldn't tell exactly when a communication started, but it probably built to the point when I "found it" at the surface of my mind and was forced to apply my own words to it. The timing of the process seemed so fascinating that I wondered again whether I hadn't lost my mind. I was perhaps defining and taking apart something that wasn't happening at all.

But no. Something was happening; something was traveling between them and me. I wondered what I was putting out to those people. At that moment, I felt capable of some beaming of my own.

Thinking back on the circumstances, some of these developments seem explicable. I woke up surrounded by a ritual-performing community, inside a continuum of symbolic activities, in a space probably valued as inspiring and magical. The combined awareness of all that could play on my heightened senses and create impressions of mental contact.

Carefully, trying to distance myself from the buzz of the community, I summed up what I had learned: Barnacle was anxious that his magic might not work anymore, on me or on the world as he knew it. Yet he had no alternative but to revive the magic and try to make it work again. To achieve that, all he could use was strength of character.

I was nervous, yet felt a measure of perplexed sympathy for the headman. Barnacle kept running, while his message no longer glowed in my mind. Rather, it had dissolved and was being digested. A residual beaming, a sort of leftover, persisted and it had to do with time. It crystalized as I watched the headman run: it was the face of time that both I and the headman had circled, running around the village.

The face of time. That didn't seem too strange: the space Barnacle was circling was, after all, round like a dial. The face of time seemed like an appropriate metaphor for it. There was no further explanation, and I had to accept it as such.

Apparently determined to match me lap for lap, Barnacle ran till his chest became a mirror of sweat. I noticed Zonia, standing now: her feet were shuffling excitedly in place, and every time Barnacle passed her, she let out a soft whoop of respect. The other tribespeople uttered rough encouragements: "*Ay-yah, ay-yah*," they rasped, bending their torsos out into Barnacle's trajectory and pulling back one second before he hurtled past, as if wanting to instill him with their own energy. Behind this ring of enthusiasts, I noticed Red Cheeks: somewhat disoriented, he prowled among his young warriors. He ranted about something, and they listened, immobile and grim. Then they started to scatter into the crowd.

Barnacle slowed into his last lap, and everyone hailed the chief.

Barnacle stopped in front of me, raised a knotty finger, and uttered something solemn. When he was finished, Huaca One and then all the other shamans hurried to surround him (there was a note of servility in the shamans' haste). They walked off together, leaving the spell and counterspell open to debate and expectation.

Red Cheeks waited for Barnacle to reach his hut, then

mixed in the crowd and I heard his voice again, hoarse, screechy. The other tribespeople didn't seem to want to listen: they pulled away and dispersed.

I was left alone. Monitored, for sure, but left alone, free to move as I pleased. I paced undecidedly and came to the dying little fire.

Here was my watch, or what was left of it. Using a leaf, I lifted it off a warm pile of ashes: the face was burned to a blackened disc, the glass cover broken and smoky, the hands oxidized and twisted. I dropped it on the ashes and looked back to the space Barnacle and I had circled performing our competing spells.

The face of time. Maybe that message of concern was in direct response to the destruction of my watch. Maybe I had put out to the headman a message about my watch and about the anxiety its loss kindled in me. The face of time was his attempt to respond, and reassure me. If anything, that enhanced the sort of comradeship I was beginning to feel for him.

But at the same time, unless everything was just a product of my mind, unusually impressionable in this solitude, this confirmed a contact, even a dialogue.

Meanwhile, everyone had returned to their chores or their hammocks. I felt, however, that we were all waiting. Whatever happened would be interpreted as the result of the spells Barnacle and I had traded. Filled with that anticipation as much as anyone in the clearing, I stepped toward the trees and stopped dead, seeing a black strip of film hanging from a branch. I slammed my hand to the side pocket I kept the exposed film in, and felt only two rolls of film through the fabric. I had lost one, in my hammock or while running around the village. The last one, still unexposed, was in my camera.

Simultaneously, I saw my camera: a pet woolly monkey, the kind called *barrigudo*, "potbellied," since they eat themselves to death in captivity, had it clutched to his chest with one hand while climbing with the other. He reached a safe height, sat on a branch, held the camera with his toes, pulled the rewind knob . . . and the camera back flew open.

The tree's trunk was lean and free of branches to a height of at least a dozen feet. I looked on the ground, found a fallen branch, grabbed it and snapped it against my knee, and threw a piece at the barrigudo. He clutched the camera in the palms of his feet and used his arms to climb higher. Then he sat again with a kind of smirk on his face, played with the camera, swung the door again, tore it off. They are powerful little animals and can stand three feet tall. I threw another piece of branch at him, but there was a screen of twigs and foliage right under the monkey—the branch hit it and fell back down. The barrigudo clutched the camera in his feet and pulled the film out. Hand over hand, he tore out the film and threw it away; the film floated just a few inches, then got tangled in the foliage. The monkey put his palm inside the camera, broke a twig, poked at the lens. Something popped out of the camera, probably the little take-up spool. It tumbled down through the branches and was lost.

I stood and watched my camera being destroyed. Finally the monkey tossed it away; the little black box fell bumping against the branches. The two strips of 35mm film swayed from the foliage, looking like long black creepers.

9
The Witnesses

Loren McIntyre's knees sagged. He sat on the forest floor.

For an instant he felt more defeated by losing his film than by his unwitting capture, and more stunned now than by the morning's bizarre occurrences. He was now without a camera, a situation almost as unfamiliar to him as losing knowledge of who he was—photography had been his constant companion since 1937, when, armed with a 35mm Argus anyone could buy for $10, he had first sailed around the world. His navy years, university studies, marriage in 1942 to Sue Shelton days before sailing off to the Pacific war theater, his postwar transfer to Lima as a gunnery advisor to the Peruvian Navy, his fatherhood, finally the choice of that hard-to-define true métier of his life, exploration, all had been greeted by Loren McIntyre camera in hand. His passion was to probe reality through the camera's eye, recording it obsessively and to the detriment of his other activities: books due to be edited were turned in late, articles were interrupted, lectures and tours were turned down or canceled, while the stacks and stacks of prints and slides from his wanderings filled his Arlington office to capacity, growing over the years to almost a million images— probably the largest one-man visual library on South America. The sheer number of the shots and the uncounted hours used to take them matched the immensity of McIntyre's subject.

Lately his passion had found a market. As the world awakened to the Amazon rain forest like a child to an amazing toy, a wilderness industry sprouted, in the United States and other industrialized nations, demanding a regular ration of pictures. Books by geographers, anthropologists and ethnographers, social scientists and political analysts, both American and foreign, owed some of their attraction to McIntyre's rain forest photography. To keep scientists and publishers satiated, it was necessary for McIntyre and a few others like him to fly planes and sail dugout canoes, hang their hammocks in trees crawling with deadly *barba amarellas* and excruciating *utusi* ants, and share quarters with a bizarre assortment of humanity, from Indian warriors to the lepers that make up one per cent of Amazonia's population. In short, a subculture, not new but renovated by new interests and attitudes, required as supporting evidence exactly what McIntyre had lost in the films hanging now among jungle creepers.

He kept touching the exposed rolls of film in his pocket.

The blow registered as particularly painful because it had occurred while he fought to make sense of where he was and what he was experiencing. Enduring thirst, hunger, fatigue, and pain came with the territory. But not knowing and not being able to bring back a sample of that knowledge ... that, that was a defeat.

He sat on the forest floor inches from his damaged camera, reduced, he felt, to an id he didn't know. Loren McIntyre was now a tourist here. If he lost the other rolls of film, arresting time and sharing its images with an audience would not be the fruit of this trip at all. And even though the trip's most unusual feature consisted of new thoughts, invisible and unprovable, the reality of the people that provoked the thoughts was documentable. Whether their headman possessed a method of communicating nonverbally, or whether their ritual pointed to what was most essential in man, his sense of occupying a niche in time, this tribe was precious. Documenting its presence had been the impulse that brought him here. Documenting its presence was now reduced to two rolls of film.

He felt disoriented. He felt disconnected, useless, reduced to an epidermal existence. He had opted for the wilderness, suffered the cold of high altitudes and the sticky heat of the bush, hacked his way through jungle and clung from craggy peaks because he believed that the world should become better known to its own residents. In that way, he was as dedicated as a missionary and completely unused to being purposeless. Now he was forced to be purposeless, or at least inactive. He would live by nature's clock. He would be like the Indians.

In a way he had already become like this unusual headman, who seemed to be growing surreptitiously and improbably into his naked alter ego. Barnacle too wanted to know, though Loren couldn't tell exactly what, and Barnacle also lacked the means and devices. Distilling the morning's "beaming session," Loren remembered that time was the headman's concern also, though why and what sort of time wasn't clear. The tribe seemed to be on some kind of quest, but he didn't know what they were seeking—in fact, now, facing the damaged camera, he felt he hardly knew anything. The camera had been such a support of his sense of reality, such a marvelous authenticator, that with it gone he doubted everything that happened.

Or everything that he felt right this instant. Which was a sudden, robust conviction (his own? transmitted to him by others?) that he was connected to these people and that their quest had to do with time.

Again he told himself that his senses were inflated. He was alone, without any testing devices, all his standard ways of corroboration absent or useless, including his language. Nothing had happened this morning, or the day before. Fighting to break down a wall of cultural difference, he had been projecting, daydreaming, making things up.

He called logic to the rescue.

He got up and began to pace. Stop imagining things, he

muttered. Just fall back on truths that you can actually document.

He corraled the facts that made him an individual, and put them in order. Born Loren Alexander McIntyre in Seattle, Washington, 1917. Eldest son of Mellie Alexander, who graduated from the University of Washington in 1908 with a degree in library science, and married Loren Smith McIntyre, in 1915. Together they raised four children on his pay as Traffic Manager of the Seattle Chamber of Commerce. Born in Michigan, Loren senior had come to Seattle at twenty, following a spell in Mississippi—after a couple of drinks, he talked like a Southerner. The children arrived in even succession, every two years, Loren, then Neil, then Mary Jean, and finally Roger. In grade school, Loren was too shy for team sports, but never Absent or Tardy. He built a boat when he was twelve, sailed it out on Lake Washington and almost capsized in a gale, nearly drowning himself and the other little McIntyres. Upon graduation from Franklin High School in 1934, four years into the Great Depression, Loren joined the Sailors' Union of the Pacific. Three months later, he shipped out for Japan, China, Manchuria, and the Philippines.

Many other trips followed, including South America. Seagoing and longshoring paid his way through the University of California at Berkeley. He earned the first AB that Cal ever granted in Latin American Culture. After four years of Naval Reserve Officer Training Corps, he was commissioned into the navy. With the war looming, reserves were called to active duty, so ensign McIntyre was ordered to the USS *Charleston* four months before Pearl Harbor. A four-year ordeal in the Pacific followed. At the Battle of Attu in the Aleutian Islands, he directed the *Charleston's* main battery gunfire on the Japanese, the first foreign troops to occupy US soil since the war of 1812.

He hadn't chosen the sea because he liked it, but because during the Great Depression, sailing was the only way to travel. So he went to sea and stood wheel watches and holystoned decks for a dollar a day. During World War II, all nine merchant ships he'd sailed on were sunk. In 1942, on shoreleave, Lieutenant McIntyre found the time to get married. In 1947, McIntyre was transferred—with his wife Sue and two sons, Lance and Scott—to Lima as gunnery advisor to the Peruvian navy.

Thus a childhood passion came full circle. As a teenager, he had read avidly about South America; visiting it for the first time in 1935, he'd found it spellbinding; finally, he was posted to it. In 1950, he resigned from active duty to stay in Lima and learn how to become a freelance writer-photographer.

The learning took eighteen years, during which he had to provide a livelihood for a family of four. He raised funds in Peru to form a film company, partnering with Hollywood film technician Edward Movius. They produced a feature starring Pilar Pallette, who married John Wayne after the superstar visited McIntyre's upper Amazon location. For five more years, McIntyre and his partner went on producing dozens of lesser films, mostly documentaries. Meanwhile, he explored Peru, and studied ethnology at the University of San Marcos.

Moving in 1957 to Bolivia to become a communications media specialist with the US foreign aid program, McIntyre set up the La Paz Audiovisual Center with a film studio, printing presses, photolabs, radio programs—and even puppet shows—to help technicians spread information about agriculture, public health, and education. He was gaining a reputation as a specialist in the field, and his opinion was valued. In 1961, after the "Bay of Pigs" fiasco, the US ambassador to Bolivia encouraged McIntyre to create a "battle plan" for winning the War of Ideas in Latin America. Laying it out like a War College exercise, McIntyre's plan argued that emotions shape political environment more than money. FDR's Good Neighbor policy towards South America was all but forgotten, and a fresh burst of good will was needed to thwart Castro's influence. One Sunday in August, McIntyre called on Dean Rusk at his home in Washington, audaciously proposing to the Secretary of State that President Kennedy make a flying visit to South America. Rusk pored over the proposal for hours, asking about the hazards of a weekend trip to either Colombia or Venezuela, and ordered all copies of the War of Ideas to be stamped "confidential" and earmarked for immediate action. A few months later, JFK and Jackie blazed through both countries, and Latin Americans were won over by the charisma of the *presidente católico*.

By then, McIntyre was back in La Paz, running his audiovisual center and taking pictures for a *National Geographic* story about Bolivia, with tireless attention to detail, the mark of an obsessive perfectionist. Soon, his photography would start paying for itself. Soon, another trip would start, the one that would finally take him to this perplexing end of the world, and of the mind.

He plunged into his memories again.

At one time or another, he had dreamed of contributing something worthwhile to mankind. He didn't know what, but he thought he knew how: with a typewriter, or with a camera. At twelve, he'd written a short story whose opening line was "Pink flashes of gunfire blossomed from the forest along the Amazon shore." He wanted to see the world—and to record faithfully what he saw, not so much for himself as in answer to that vague idealist urge. Early on he learned he would need a notebook, since his camera couldn't catch the click of Mah-Jongg tiles in Kowloon, or the smell of the Bombay waterfront.

To force himself to become a professional, he staked his family's future on the risky chance of earning a living freelancing. For two years after resigning his navy commission, he traveled, meditated, sharpened pencils, and sold nothing except worn-out belongings. Then he learned cinematography from Ed Movius. Mastering motion pictures led to shooting better still photographs. Producing films, he became sensitized to the demands of the market place, and learned how to write for others instead of himself—mostly in Spanish. Film-making led him all over the continent, to adventures among highland and forest Indians, rubbing elbows with campesinos and presidents, diamond seekers and farmers, missionaries and lepers. He witnessed a lot of the continent's turmoil and caught it on celluloid. He even filmed for CBS the fall of Peron in 1955.

None of that prepared him for what he was experiencing now. The cornerstone of his career was communication. Precision was his bible, and science his philosophy. He just couldn't accept that *this* was happening.

Who the hell were these cat-people?

He knew who the cat-people were.

Right before his trip, he had reread the Mayoruna entry in the *Handbook of South American Indians*, a seven-tome compendium about the continent's aborigines published by the Smithsonian in 1946. The Mayoruna were described as anomalous by virtue of their history. Semi-nomadic, warring with their neighbors, constantly retreating into the bush, which kept their culture undeveloped, their numbers low, and their whole existence problematic. Many times they had been reportedly wiped out by the Conibos or by other tribes who raided their neighbors for slaves to be used in mines or on coca plantations. The rubber boom finally made them disappear for good. Back into the bush, and into prehistory.

Their inability to jump into the present was all the more interesting when compared to the adaptability of their notoriously prosperous neighbors, the Omagua. In 1542, Francisco de Orellana had entered an Omagua village and found huge jars of glazed pottery, some reportedly able to hold a hundred gallons of chicha, the native maize beer. Orellana's soldiers ate to satiety and partook of the native women. The friendliness of the savages, unaware of what sort of relationship lay ahead, astounded them. The myth of the unspeakably rich kingdom of the Omagua was instantly born. They wore gold apparel, while their villages stock-piled food—maize, yucca, sweet potatoes, beans, and dried fish. El Dorado was deemed found, and the Omagua started the typical curriculum of deception at the hands of the civilizados. Living off the fertile forest, exhausting work was unknown to them and toiling for others all the more so. They made terrible slaves. But the peak of their suffering came three centuries later, when rubber became a hot commodity. They were beaten to work harder, had ears and fingers cut off for laziness or insubordination, were shot, hanged, and even fed to alligators to entertain the civilizados on slow afternoons. In short, they were treated as if their extermination, not the exploitation of rubber or other natural wealth, was the purpose of the civilizados' expansion.

It was hard to explain why the Omagua initially appeared so overdeveloped while their Mayoruna neighbors were so poor, but the Omagua were more or less stable, the Mayoruna always on the go. The Omagua's wealth promoted them for slavery. The Mayoruna's roughness did not save them from isolation or hardship, yet definitely reduced their toll of humiliation. While "softer" tribes accepted acculturation and gradually died from it, the Mayoruna survived by hiding deeper and deeper and surfacing less and less, till they were finally declared extinct.

Then in 1966 and 1967 word of their reappearance filtered out from among the missionaries of the Summer Institute of Linguistics.

That period coincided with McIntyre's first contributions to the *National Geographic*. In Washington, Florence Thomason, backstop officer for the U.S. Operations Mission in Bolivia, sent a package of McIntyre's photographs to a friend in the brick building on 17th Street. Suddenly, America's most venerable exploration magazine asked him for a story and photographs about Bolivia. It was published in the *Geographic*'s February 1966 issue, and McIntyre had the pleasure of seeing on the magazine's cover his shot of a felt-hatted Bolivian woman selling grapes. Next he was asked to write a story about Ecuador. Spirited, Loren McIntyre suggested a triple project to the *National Geographic*: a magazine article, a book, and a film about what was becoming his bailiwick, the Amazon. He also decided to quit government service for an existence scarier than the jungle, that of a free-lance writer-photographer.

The book and film materialized, but not under his authorship. McIntyre's credits were documentary and educational films no one had seen apart from Indians and South American government officials. The film seemed important enough to be assigned to a Hollywood producer, and David Wolper was hired. Asked to join the film crew as a still photographer, McIntyre declined, suspecting that he was wanted mainly as an interpreter and advisor on bush trivia. For seven weeks, the men sent by David Wolper shot footage in various parts of Amazonia, only to come up with a rough cut which, David Wolper decided, lacked drama. To supplement that, an episode with piranha fish was ordered, but since underwater photography never could capture more than a few seconds of a piranha feast because the prey's spurting blood instantly fouled the water, the film-makers resorted to a trick: captured piranhas were held in glass tanks of clear water for five days without food. Then a live capybara was tossed into the first tank and cameramen started filming through the glass sides. As soon as spurting blood fouled the water, the capybara was hooked out and thrown into the next clean tank, for photography to resume until the bare bones were filmed in the final tank, with piranhas still darting at them.

Completed, the film sported in its midst the piranha feast with added sound effects of bubbling river water. Another episode in the film were the two Harriets flying out of their operational base at Yarinacocha, Peru, dropping gifts for the Mayorunas and talking to them on the loudspeaker in a Panoan dialect (whether the dialect was actually intelligible for the Indians below was not certain, since the Mayoruna had been scattered over an area vast enough to develop dialects as divergent as separate languages). All throughout, McIntyre had followed the two Harriets' progress, and even requested to accompany them. After being turned down because the Helio Courier used for those sorties was overloaded, he had given a fresh roll of film to pilot Ralph Borthwick, who brought him back that shot of natives with labrets silhouetted against the landed plane.

There was no actual encounter with the Mayoruna in the final cut of the *National Geographic* film. Watching the film, McIntyre saw only the Helio Courier flying over dense jungle, into which the two missionaries dropped gifts wrapped in plastic. That episode was several minutes long, and when it was over the Mayorunas still hadn't been enticed into appearing. But the two Harriets, always going out unarmed and alone except for one guide and the pilot, continued their attempts, and finally reported contacts. The shot snapped by Borthwick on McIntyre's film ended up on page 85 of the *National Geographic*'s Amazon book suggested by McIntyre in his three-pronged Amazon proposal. The book, however, had not been assigned to McIntyre, but to Helen and Frank Schreider, who were both *National Geographic* staffers.

The Schreiders had just returned from a trip to Taiwan and needed an assignment. A few years earlier they had completed an acclaimed drive down the whole length of the Pan American Highway in an amphibious jeep. They seemed right for the task of sailing the Amazon from source to mouth, the final 3,000 miles in a 30-foot-long diesel-powered boat. The quest for the source was a limited part of their goal, but no one had recertified the source since 1953, when Michel Perrin had pointed out the superior length of the Apurímac-Ucayali over the traditional source tributaries, targeting Mount Huagra as the source area, and then following the Huaraco down to where it joined the Apurímac.

The Schreider expedition started with a repeat of Perrin's achievement, with the difference that they encountered right by the source a competent advisor in the person of Siegfried Stephan, the mining engineer. Quite likely, someone like Siegfried Stephan would also know of the geodetic surveys of Colonel Gerardo Dianderas, who claimed that Huagra was the Amazon's birthplace as far back as 1934.

But whether Dianderas, or Perrin, or the Schreiders, or all of them had discovered that the Amazon's birthplace was on Mount Huagra, what mattered was that the source had been discovered.

The Schreiders' book was quickly written, its text and photographs were evaluated by the *National Geographic* staff, and the photographs were judged short on how varied the Amazon was in terrain, climate, life-forms, and population. Loren McIntyre, who was now shooting the entire country of Colombia for the *Geographic*, had sent back some shots of its diversity to support his three-pronged proposal. Suddenly he was reapproached to supply the photographs missing from the Schreiders' book, enough of which were needed to keep him out in the field for three months.

He accepted the assignment with an interesting feeling of superfluity. The exploit of climbing to where the Andean snow turned into an uninterrupted flow of water which, tantalizing expectation, might prove longer than the Nile's had been completed. The source had been authenticated. The controversy was over; the time when as many as seven apocryphal sources battled each other on the maps was history.

And—dared he say it—so was his own dream of being the one to achieve all that. He had carried it inside him for years, though not quite acknowledging it to himself. He could trace its beginning to that morning of August 1935 when the *West Notus* carried him up the Para River toward Belém. That dream accounted for many hours of poring over maps drawn from aerial photography, trying to assess the comparative length of the shifty water trails dressing in a loose liquid net the eastern slope of the Peruvian Andes. Now, after reading the Schreiders' account of their discovery, he could put aside his maps and the road gauge he used to determine distances on them. One of the last major explorations of the planet except for the underseas had been accomplished.

But he didn't put aside his maps. In fact, even on this trip he had brought along several, printed by Peru's Instituto Geografico Militar, just stuff to fill a lonely hour with. He wished he had them with him now, but they were on that shore where Mercier's plane had landed, along with everything else he had brought: his food and supplies and his other cameras, the stuff he could record his experiences with, his silent witnesses.

He had never traveled without his witnesses. The last three months especially, while taking pictures for the Schreiders' *National Geographic* book. He had started in Belém, where he had wondered years before about the giant's source, now apparently established. From Belém to Santarém, a hot outpost of progress 450 miles upstream from the mouth, where the Amazon's brown flow received the bluish injection of the Tapajós, pouring out of Mato Grosso, whose name meant "Thick Forest." In Santarém's cemetery slept Brazilians with names like Riker and Jennings and Vaughn, sired by Dixie farmers who fled the South after the Civil War, fearing a local black administration; they hadn't reckoned with Brazil's impudent mixture of races. Then four hundred miles south by plane and boat to the Tapajós gold camps, mined by trigger-happy *garimpeiros* who worked waist deep in mud and inhaled deadly vapors from the mercury purifying their gold dust. Back to the main river and another seventy miles upstream to Óbidos where the river narrowed for the first time into a single channel between green jungle walls, inviting easier measurements of its volume. Then on to Manaus, heart of Brazil's Amazonas state, larger than Alaska. Here the Río Negro, three miles wide, mixed the darkness of its billions of decaying leaves into the main stream's muddy brown, like black tea poured into coffee and cream. At the turn of the century the Manaus rubber barons had built stately mansions, given their city the first streetcars in Latin America, and taken their wives sweating in mink coats to listen to European opera at the Teatro Amazonas. Today, the Teatro Amazonas' dome of French tiles, green, red, blue, and yellow, could no longer be seen from all parts of town, as an aggressive generation of highrises was now mounting into the steamy sky. Also here, in the harbor, was that giant scale of the Amazon's rise and fall through dry and rainy months, for which inevitable emergency the harbor's floating dock was built on hollow iron tanks twenty-five feet in diameter, to seesaw high and low with the flood. Upstream from Manaus, the waterways grew more and more confusing, there were no cities, just villages and hamlets, and the real Amazonia, the land of frightening isolation and lawlessness began.

Clicking along with his Minolta, McIntyre flew to the Beni, Bolivia's northern province, to photograph his old friends the Chacobo tribesmen in a flooded forest. Then to San Pablo de Loreto, a leper colony run by nuns and priests from New Brunswick, Canada; there some of the lepers making up one percent of Amazonia's population worked tiny plots of land by tying machetes to the stumps of their arms and gave birth to children who lived safely in the colony for years, leprosy being neither hereditary nor easily contagious. McIntyre photographed them working and eating and reading books and dancing on a Saturday night, an existence made normal by their amazing acceptance and selflessness. He zigzagged on, from San Pablo de Loreto to Acre, to Xingu, and to Rondônia, named after Marshal Cândido Mariano de Silva Rondon, Roosevelt's companion in the 1913 expedition up the River of Doubt, now the Roosevelt River. Rondon, founder of Brazil's first Indian Service, was himself part Indian. From Rondônia McIntyre flew some fifteen hundred miles northwest for a shot of the erupting Sangay volcano. Sixty million years earlier such eruptions had started shaping the Andes, whose snows gave birth to the river. The Sangay towered above the Curaray tributary and forest, where missionary Nate Saint had been killed by Auca warriors now evangelized by his sister Rachel. Speaking with Rachel Saint, McIntyre heard again of the reported reappearance of the Mayoruna. From Yarinacocha, in the Peruvian jungle, missionaries busily flew out in Cessnas and Helio Couriers, to find and bring into the fold the Amazon's most elusive natives.

By this time, his feeling of superfluity had abated. There was always something to see on the river, there was always a lesson to learn, be it just the lesson of humanity pursuing its goals against nature's most formidable obstacles. Indian and mestizo, civilizado and savage, fisherman and tribes-man and settler and prospector and missionary, these people were building together the river's society, connected like everything here by that incessant flow of water. It felt as if the river flowed inside the people's blood systems; their very fates were determined by it, which made traveling among them an unending tale, and traveling was McIntyre's calling, with or without a prize awaiting him at the destination. The Amazon's source had supposedly been found; as for the river in its totality, it was too vast and fabulous to be conquered by any one man. So McIntyre accepted becoming, his eye glued to the camera, one of its many quiet worshipers.

In Yarinacocha and later in Iquitos, McIntyre thought of the possibility of a contact with the Mayoruna on the Brazilian side. The flight wasn't a problem: a Catholic missionary, thinly funded from home, was accepting passengers to pay for his gasoline and other supplies. McIntyre's assignment was over; the additional photography for the Schreiders' book was in the can. It had been such a temptation to pack his cameras and fly up the Javari.

He had done it.

And now he was a virtual prisoner in this clearing bustling with Mayorunas building a new village. He didn't know why they had abandoned their old one, and wondered whether they were building a new one only to abandon it again; their previous village was well concealed and as far as he could tell no immediate threat forced them to an exodus. But if moving about was part of a ritual, he had no choice but to follow them wherever they went, perplexed.

Not able to communicate with them other than by the bizarre telepathy he had shared with the headman, he wondered what they thought of him. He no longer carried any proof of who he was, except his clothes and the few possessions in his pockets. He emptied his pockets, dropped their contents on the grass, stared at the little pile of things, each connecting him with his past. The two rolls of film that had eluded the shaman's hands and the monkey's forage.

10

What Was in the Dark

Some three hours before dusk: now I only have the daylight and the canopy's activity by which to estimate time.

I bathed in the stream, washed my clothes, and headed back wearing them still wet (best way to dry them up quickly). I walked back inside the perimeter of huts and surprise: Barnacle was there, as if waiting for me; as soon as I stepped close enough, he offered me a finished, beautiful arrow.

I reciprocated with the belt: I pulled it out of my back pocket and gave it to him as it was, unfinished. Then I saw that Huaca One had gathered some children and teenagers and was leading them toward the forest. Barnacle started after them, looked back, and, another surprise, he pointed his clutch of bow and arrows at me, then at the forest, signaling that I should join him.

I did. I followed his barnacled legs into the bush. I could watch comfortably his shoulders, the pattern of his shoulder blades in very clear relief, as if he'd recently lost a good amount of weight. I wonder if he's been fasting. Still, he is a bulky and powerful male. When he walks, the ground vibrates, and his broad torso displaces the air.

I reasoned that, after all, if I'm immersed in this, I might as well plunge to the bottom.

Later

We just got back. What I learned is what I expected. I feel
that in a sense I knew it already. Which makes me
conjecture: if the beaming is allowing me to share so much
with this man, yet I have no notion of this tribe's future, it
may be because the headman himself has no idea of what
lies ahead.

As soon as we were together, the contact started again,
and it was smooth and implicit. Each time, I found a
thought in my mind that belonged there quite naturally,
yet seemed to come from him. After a while, there was
another thought, and it felt like an answer to some
thought of mine. The only way to accurately render what
was transmitted is to transcribe it as dialogue, so this is
what I'm going to do despite the fact that no words were
exchanged—except for an attempt of mine to address him
in Portuguese—and lengthy pauses between the wordless
communications. He transmitted something like, *You are
sad because what was in the dark should've remained in
the dark*. I looked at him and he looked back at me, as if
confirming the message.

I had almost convinced myself that this morning's
happenings were a projection of my own thoughts;
therefore, accepting that *this was happening again* felt like
a serious jolt. I controlled myself somehow, did not jump
up and down, did not grab him or shake him, but opened
my mouth and declared loud to his face (these were the
only words that were uttered) that I thought he
understood Portuguese. He was silent, attentive, as if
intrigued. Then he leaked into my mind somehow that he
didn't understand my words.

I managed to calm down. Even if he didn't spy on me,
he was the headman, aware of everything that happened
in his little realm. Even a dimwit could notice my distress
at finding my film ripped out of its box. What had been in
the dark had been ripped out and strung all over the
bushes. There was nothing deeply meaningful to

Barnacle's message: quite simply, he had observed an incident, and my reaction to it, and he was offering his sympathy.

Analyzed that way, the message became acceptable. What was less acceptable was my conviction that we were in contact, unless again it was just projection. A simple defense mechanism against my overpowering loneliness.

So, back to where we were before. Either I accepted that it was happening, or had to assume I was hallucinating. The more so since if he knew nothing about cameras, then I, I, was the one somehow putting out messages (which confirmed the notion of a dialogue of sorts). But when had I done it? Was he spying on me earlier, while I sat, despondent, by my broken Minolta? I know that I don't go around thinking elementary truths about film emulsions and the results of their exposure to light. But that, of course, is stored up in my memory. It's in a fold of my mind, silent, rarely referred to, but available. Then—what? Was he culling stuff straight out of my brain?

Then that was over, and we were together in the forest, and Huaca One, who walked ahead of us leading the children farther into the trees, pointed at all sorts of insects and talked seriously in Mayoruna as if instructing the youngsters. The children seemed to look for honey combs because they inspected every hole in the tree trunks. They didn't find honey, but instead they found larvae and pupae of other species, and plenty of caterpillars. At one point I stopped behind a pack of youngsters scattered in the bushes and found myself next to Barnacle again.

I thought I heard Barnacle tell me that I should run away. Here was the forest; if I did it right now, he wasn't going to stop me.

I said nothing. I didn't even think of the compass and other things necessary to make it.

For a while, nothing happened. Then Barnacle transmitted that other white people had been here before me. They brought death. So, Barnacle explained, his tribesmen were dying now to avoid *that* death.

MCINTYRE (just to make sure): *What death? The death brought by those white people?*

BARNACLE: An eloquent silence.

I thought I detected an emotion that accompanied the notion of death: it was like a brief and violent inner struggle. I remembered the huts they had destroyed. I wondered whether, according to some ritual developed through centuries of flight from encroachment, they didn't perhaps start by destroying their homes only to work up to killing themselves.

Instantly, the vision of the tribe munching on beiju, just a few hours after my arrival, flashed up in my mind as if he had projected it there. No, they were not killing themselves. But dying, yes. Not eating enough, not hunting enough, while walking back to the beginning.

MCINTYRE: *The beginning?*

Another eloquent silence. I was pretty convinced that he, Barnacle, was fasting—through all our meals together I'd never seen him put any food in his mouth. Which made sense: most cultures prescribe fasting for the liberation of mental powers of all sorts, including clairvoyance and divination. I don't know what exactly I "responded." I suppose I might've expressed some inquiry about their makeshift village, made to be abandoned again. He transmitted that they had been moving around.

MCINTYRE: *How often?*

He didn't answer, just shrugged. What did it matter? When it got to this sort of moving, all hope was lost.

I asked him if they had been attacked. *Yes*, he answered, *by strange people that came down from the sky*.

Several times he looked me in the eyes—tribesmen very rarely do, direct stares being considered both impolite and hostile. His stare was brief and opaque, and there seemed to be nothing hypnotic about it.

I burst back with a host of thoughts, not the least being, *What will happen with these children?* We both could hear their sounds in the forest.

They're coming with us to the beginning, he beamed

back peacefully. And after a pause: *What are you doing?*
When I realized whom he meant, my hair pricked up. *Are
you coming with us?*

I stood, mentally inert. I didn't know what to say.

He repeated. Since I was with them now, was I joining
them in their trip to the beginning?

I suppose I answered something, about not knowing
where they were going. *The beginning*, he kept repeating.

MCINTYRE: *What beginning?*

He beamed something about it again. This time it felt
less like death, and more like a sort of deliverance, or
disclosure.

So it went, for a length of time I couldn't determine
(how provident that my watch had been destroyed that
very morning!). Of course, many of those could've been
my own thoughts.

Meanwhile, Huaca One was yelling at the children to
stay close together: they had fanned out of our sight, and
their warbling voices could be heard echoing back from all
directions. They cantered back, mouths smeared with all
sorts of gooey pastes of crushed caterpillars, worms, ant
eggs, and other such delicacies. A few of them focused on
a bush crawling with insects, giggling and pointing at a
few wingless bugs marching out from under a leaf: dark
brown, and military in the way they kept a tight
formation, approaching some other species. "*Tica-tica!*"
said Huaca One with a chuckle, perhaps identifying it.
The closest bug (I don't recall seeing it in any insect book)
stopped next to a gathering of mites and sprayed a pink
halo from a tubular gland which I mistook for its head (it
wasn't; the head, peculiarly elongated, was placed *under*
that tube). The mites reacted with a few seconds of
twitching, then were still, and the tica-ticas ate them, and
went on to the next bunch of bugs. In under a minute,
with good discipline and taking turns at shooting their
paralyzing gas, they cleaned up the whole top of the bush,
showing a remarkably eclectic taste: whatever came their
way, they sprayed and gobbled. The children didn't eat

this natural exterminator, because it smelled foul, like its spray, but they enjoyed watching it.

I did too, and couldn't help fantasizing about the potential uses of such a natural biopesticide. Here it was, just waiting for agrobiologists to collect it, breed it, and let it patrol the fields, putting DDT manufacturers out of business.

Then we all headed back toward the village. Barnacle let me pass in front of him, and while I did that he scanned me with his eyes. The question they spelled was clear, no beaming necessary: what was I going to do?

I was asking myself the same question.

Returning along a shallow, sluggish tributary, we heard voices and splashes and suddenly came upon many of the villagers, engaged in their evening rinse in the river. Men and women swam together, and as I looked at their bodies I felt a disturbing anticipation of death, as if the nudity were a preparation for a mass sacrifice.

Zonia was here, swimming close to that older woman, Tia. I noticed Red Cheeks, watching while Tia helped wash Zonia's hair with a sort of vegetal shampoo that produced a lot of bright green foam. Tia's breasts are maternally floppy, she's taller than the average Mayoruna woman, and her belly is scarred on one side. Her belly is generous, classically shaped, with a high and well-buried navel. Her legs are round and muscular, and her feet are broad, with straight, symmetrical toes that were never deformed by shoes.

I watched Red Cheeks watch Tia come out of the water. She combed her wet hair with a comb of palm spines and retied a string of palm fiber around her waist, letting a free end hang down her belly. With a well-versed push of her finger she tucked the loose end inside her crotch; thus protected against temptation, she stepped back into society.

As for the men present, they wore only those genital strings tied around their foreskins, pushing the member back inside and shrinking it till its tied-up tip looks like the knotted end of a balloon. The string keeps the penis at half-mast, giving the men an unconsciously priapic allure. I wonder if the custom originated as protection against scratches and cuts while running through the bush. Now it's a social requirement; boys learn it before puberty and then put up with it year after year, the way they do with the labrets in their lips. The men from the Kabano branch of the Cintas Largas nation have an even stranger custom: they push their penes inside their scrotums, making them practically invisible through whole days of hunting, dancing, or playing with children.

That makes me think of the tribal learning process in general. Undoubtedly, the learning of customs and skills comprises pains, limits on freedom, and all sorts of frustrations. However, compared to our learning process, the tribal way is almost totally imitative and hardly competitive at all. Excellence is not required; Indian children are not given abstract problems to solve, just actions to repeat and roles to emulate. Education is on-the-job training, indistinguishable from tribal life itself. The lesson and its practical application are inseparable.

Later in the Evening

I am back lying in my hammock. In the clearing, the fires crackle, the village echoes with voices, the monkeys utter a sleepy squeak now and then and the pet birds a dreamy cluck. They, the animals, are the only ones to follow night's discipline. The village will sleep in shifts, each person to his fancy. The odds that I could slip away are slim; someone would see me or notice my absence and weave through the thicket in pursuit and catch me, for Indians can move through the forest much faster than any civilizado.

My thought wanders back to those children hunting for

bugs and to how much they already know about the
forest, even the little ones. Shamans and headmen know
the usages of hundreds of plants and animals. There's a
whole natural science in every routine of daily tribal life,
based on centuries of unwritten practice. If one lives by
the river, one knows a lot about the river's cycles. If
one uses vegetal dye, vegetal poison for arrow points,
vegetal emetics, vegetal contraceptives, herbs that induce
perspiration and reduce fevers or perform some other
medical relief, saps and bark infusions good for all kinds
of purposes from dressing wounds to gluing pieces of clay
together, one knows the time when all those plants flower,
become ripe or wither, and how to find them.

That gets lost with the arrival of "civilization." Fathers
stop transmitting secrets to their sons, not after some
conscious decision but purely because the surroundings
change in such a fashion that the lore no longer applies. If
a family lives in a house on a reservation and depends on
government or missionary stores for needs formerly
satisfied by the forest, why would a father instruct a child
in how to get from the forest what he already has from
the store?

Meanwhile, tribal ways become embarrassing. Body
painting and adornment are abandoned. Some integrated
Indians work at menial tasks in towns or on someone
else's farm, but many live on drink and in poverty, and
die early. The general consequence of integration is that
the need to align oneself with the seasons and the natural
forces disappears. Urban walls deny the integrated Indian
the total horizon of forest life and force him into a
fragmented identity, in which the dominant feeling is that
of nonbelonging.

But the Indian who can still live in the forest has
minimal identity conflicts. Death is all right. He is never
pressured by time.

I am pressured by time every instant of my conscious
existence. While the Indian lives in a vertical time, where
the present is a sort of unseen territory wrapped around

each individual's life and drifting along with it, my present, at least in the urban environment, gets reduced to its narrowest form, the second, the nanosecond. I strive to do as much as possible in that second, and do it not just once. Trying to fit more and more into less and less, trying to stuff the genie back into the lamp. Why do I take pictures? Because my camera captures reality in segments of 1/60 to 1/1,000 of a second. No wonder that I am so fixated on my camera. In its click I seize time in the only form granted to me: the infra-present.

But now a woolly monkey has robbed me of my ability to catch the present, and in so doing has given me a gift of time as pressure-free as an Indian's. I wish I could feel thankful, instead of distraught.

Later Still

A few feet from my hammock, two older men are sitting on the ground by a dying fire. Naked, no protection, no barrier between them and the habitat. A psychological distance of twenty thousand years separates me from them, and yet I'm physically overlapping with them as the three of us watch the same fire. Despite their lack of technological advance, in their goals and practices these men are already divorced from nature, just like I am. No matter how close to nature they are still, they are no longer one with it.

Forever, the same issue: the separation from nature. What made us do it, of all species? Why did the universe produce a race now trying to master the universe, and why is man that race? Other creatures, intelligent, highly organized, social, didn't attempt it.

I think Red Cheeks is trying to foster a political crisis. His tough friends are entering the huts, sitting down with the men to discuss something I don't understand, canvassing.

Have to be careful about this diary—I might wake up

and find its pages lying like dark butterflies on a heap of ashes.

Later Still

I sleep for about an hour and get up without reason. I slip out of my hammock and walk among the huts, feeling the touch of the night on my face, cool but not uncomfortable. My body sails across the wilderness, mosquito-bitten, dirty, but one with the surroundings.

The only way in which mankind's progress would not appear absurd and potentially suicidal would be if . . . we were not from here. If we came from somewhere else, free of commitments to this planet, expecting to simply serve our time on it before we fly back to other worlds. Cosmic travelers, temporarily stationed on earth, leaving behind us other planets we inhabited, a slew of empty, burned-up shells.

What a tempting theory. Our responsibility would lie elsewhere. Our purpose, unknown to us, would be in alien hands. But then, whose envoys are we, and what is our message?

It's all contained in that initial stage, which none of us remember. Our birth as humans.

Funny, ridiculous, absurd, call it what you will, I feel a near certainty that Barnacle knows some of the answer. I start chuckling alone in the night. I'm going daffy.

My watch no longer loads my wrist, and I'm acutely aware of its absence—ridiculous, since a watch is useless out here. Since childhood I've owned dozens of watches. Among them, they've clocked the growth of world population from one and a half to four billion people, all in my lifetime. In a case of bizarre symmetry, as we multiplied down here, the stars up there multiplied, too. A century ago, astronomers thought the universe was not much larger than the Milky Way. The spiral nebulae were explained as balls of gas, all inside our galaxy. Now we know that they are separate galaxies, millions of them. The stretch that new concept forced on people's minds made their brain cells crack with strain. I suppose Columbus's mind would've cracked just as loud picturing *his earth* peopled by four billion bipeds in five centuries' time.

Every time I observe forest Indians, they reveal to me a multitude of implications which seem near infinite. As practical as their existence is, as global as their thinking is supposed to be, unspeculative, unanalytical, not counting over three, not distinguishing present from future, they are a walking, hunting, fighting, living *system of reference*, whose stimulative effect cannot be priced.

I walk back to my hut, missing stars over my head. Stars, sky, clarity of thought, instead of this oppressive, impenetrable mask of foliage.

I pass a hut, notice a hammock swaying gently, edges rolled up, like a giant pod come alive. A mass of tangled hair seems to hang out of the pod, and suddenly Red Cheeks's profile above Zonia's catches the glow of a fire, and their breathing is heard for just an instant, heavy and in sync. I pass the hut, and the vision closes and falls into my memory, round and whole like an acorn containing its own future germination. The tribe is alive. A child might result from that union.

I make it to my hammock and spend a few minutes beating the ants and other night bugs out of it. Red Cheeks and Zonia are making love undisturbed by their company.

11

Around the Face of Time II

A day passed. Another day passed. It rained, and we didn't switch locations again. As far as I can tell, Barnacle is still fasting.

I have nothing to do but lose myself in the routines of these people and let my life mesh with their lives. They no longer stare at me or follow me wherever I go, and I know what that means—I've been accepted. I've experienced that odd sense of adoption with other tribes. When the Indians stop staring at you (though they never stare very overtly anyway), it means that they are no longer suspicious or surprised and that life is back to its casualness and anonymity. That is the loneliest time one can spend with a tribe. Surrounded by people who treat you, at least outwardly, as one of their own.

I keep being obsessed with time in the midst of this timelessness. I try to guess the passing of an hour. Obviously, being free of time makes me so uncomfortable that I try to recreate mentally the frenzy of that other world, my own, where everyone lives on a deadline. But why am I doing that? I've always been doubtful of civilization's achievement ethos; yet now when I have a chance to live outside it, at least temporarily, I shrink back and crave my old world.

Later That Afternoon

My gut chooses to hit me with cramps. I've eaten some plantains this morning, and also some mash of caterpillar pupae, whose only real taste was its oiliness. I have the time to sprint out of the clearing, across the trees, and reach the shallow tributary's shore. My gut is a war zone. I spend minutes of torture squatting in the water, then the cramps relax a little and I can wash myself and get up.

In such a case keeping oneself supplied with liquids is imperative. The river water looks brown, but cupped up in my palms it is transparent and colorless. I drink till my stomach swells, have more cramps, drink more, and in the meantime the rain comes down again. I stagger up, drenched by sweat and rain, planning vaguely to talk to Barnacle. Which means to hunker next to him and braid another belt, perhaps, and beam or vibe or whatever the hell it is we're doing together, about a deal he could make with my world if he helped me go back to negotiate it for him. I'll champion with FUNAI the importance of this tribe's survival, the value of its culture, the intactness of its tribal grounds . . . . Halfway through my thought, I realize that I could never accomplish that with a big bureaucracy like FUNAI. I'd just catch hell for being here without official permission, and open the door to a bunch of strangers who would modify this tribe's life disastrously.

It's raining hard, so right now there's nothing to do but go back to my hammock and try to restore my energy by sleeping.

I doze off, wake by my reckoning around three. The rain keeps hitting, the moisture, smoke, and heat from naked bodies smother the little community in a woolly blanket of fog. My pants are wet and crumpled, ideal for fungus growth. More cramps. Out into the fog I go. I can smell my own body, distinct from the sweetish putrescence of the forest floor. Pungent, as if the burning of fat brought out caches of junk, unhealthy deposits that stagnated there for years. For a moment I'm ready to let go of my courage and just collapse.

No. The Portuguese and the Spaniards knew how to take it. They handled it. While Europe's print shops rolled out the *Malleus Maleficarum*, ascertaining the witches' consortium with Satan and empowering the Inquisition to lawfully burn, quarter, and hang, the conquistadors escaped that hell of holiness run amuck, and landed here, and handled it.

I might be in a situation similar to Hans Staden's, a German naval gunner in the employ of the Portuguese (ominous coincidence: my specialty in the navy was also gunnery!). Staden was captured in 1552 by the Tamoio, a branch of the Tupinamba inhabiting lands now moaning under the concrete canyons of Rio de Janeiro and São Paulo. He was alone hunting when a group of them appeared from the forest, surrounded him, and took him to their cannibal chief. Asked to partake in one of the chief's meals, Staden protested that even wild animals didn't eat their own kind; to which the chief laughed and explained that he was a jaguar, therefore different from humans and entitled to eat them.

Staden spent months with the Tamoio, who assigned women to their prisoners and reared the resulting children as Indians. The tribe reserved the right to club prisoners to death at any time and eat them (the *coup de grâce* was always struck humanely, from behind and bringing instant death). The victim's brains were mushed in, the body skinned, cut in small pieces, boiled, and eaten immediately from nose to toes. However, the brain was spiced up and eaten only after it spoiled, as a delicacy.

The chief thought of himself as a jaguar—like the Mayoruna, who also have a record as cannibals. The Tamoio kept skulls as trophies. From arm and thighbones they made flutes, and used human teeth in necklaces.

The Mayoruna haven't assigned me a woman, at least not yet. Instead, I shared some moments of absurd contact with their headman (we were of one mind, quite literally). In so many ways, my fate and Staden's seem the same.

I see how I could start sliding down a dangerous slope. I don't feel afraid of death, but I'm definitely afraid of losing my mind.

I remember a report from an expedition attempting to find Colonel Fawcett years after he vanished looking for his city of crystal. Advancing through the wilderness, they encountered a deranged white man who sat by the side of a rutted muddy road, dressed in rags, staring haggardly at the approaching civilizados. As they stopped before him and someone commented on the multitude of mosquitoes on his legs, he answered hoarsely in English that they had to live too, then stared into empty space. The expedition passed him and lost him. Later, after G. M. Dyott found in the bush a map case with Fawcett's initials, it was assumed that the stranger had been Fawcett, alive but crazy. His remains were never found.

Must do something physical. As soon as the rain stops, I'll go for a swim in the muddy river.

Later That Evening, by the Fire

This is the sixth day with this tribe, or is it the seventh? I must make myself some sort of calendar. In tribes as primitive as this one, counting devices and memory aids are very simple. Time is counted by drilling holes in a stick and filling them with pegs of wood, stone, or wax, which can then be removed one by one. Also by gathering wood chips or stones and dropping one from the pile each day: that way several tribes calculate the time separating them from a common holiday. By removing a stick or stone each day, they coordinate themselves and manage to join the gathering on the same day. Pretty effective for people with no formal calendars.

The successfully bureaucratic Inca used a variation of the same device. A string or a bunch of multicolored strings with knots—the knots signified quantity and the colors the kind of quantities tabulated. Those portable recorders were called quipus and contained data on crops, population, military conscription, food supplies, and the number of work days individuals owed to the empire for building roads or fortresses. They were obviously reliable: a complex and populous empire used them for years. The guardians of the quipus, the quipu camayocs, enjoyed status in society and passed the skill down to their offspring.

I could make myself a belt with notches. I settle on a piece of branch, which I whittle clean. I'll try to remember to add a nick on it each day with my Swiss army knife.

While I make my first such indentation, Red Cheeks notices and comes and stands close to me, then signals through gestures that he is very interested in my knife. I play a pantomime of how dear this knife is to me. I place it on my heart, then rotate my arm many times in that gesture that signifies a whole movement of the sun from sunrise to sunset. I've had the knife too many days. I'm too attached.

He understands and leaves, expressionless, though I can tell that he is irritated.

However, I cannot satisfy him. If I have to make it out of here on my own, this knife might save my life.

12

The Night Hunt

Through the afternoon and the evening my cramps
diminished. I slept intermittently till I thought I was
dreaming of a jaguar. When I woke up, my first
impression was that he was actually in the village: I could
hear his grunt not only in the darkness around me, I heard
it inside my head. The animal heaved the air out of its
lungs with short, powerful emissions, and it sounded like
an irritated *huh-huh*. Then again, *huh-huh*, as if the beast,
looking around, was finding reasons for discontent.

A jaguar in the village! I bolted upright in my
hammock. A jaguar in the village! My thoughts liquefied
into a paste of ancestral alarm: meeting with teeth in the
night. A jaguar can stand three feet tall and can stretch
more than six. A mature specimen can easily weigh 250
pounds, heavier than a leopard. Its power is concentrated
in the massive jaws (the whole head is large and square,
looking like a spotted rock), and in its short, herculean
legs. The Indians are fascinated with its ferocity and
strength; it features as ancestor or culture hero in so many
Indian cosmogonies (including the Mayoruna), it is taboo
to eat (though not to hunt), and to bag one is quite a
status symbol for a young warrior. However, as I listened
to its grunt I only thought of the jaws that could snap my
jugular vein like a pair of scissors. After that, I'd never

witness myself being portioned into edible pieces, chewed on and digested by this furry demon, and then excreted back into the jungle's next cycle.

In the nearest hut, Tuti released a miaowing cry, and like all the kids in the world, the tribe's offspring cried in panic with him. The beast kept grunting, sounding like it had gotten stuck in the passage between two huts—a fierce thrashing sound seemed to come from its tail, whipping at a bamboo wall. Hands, wakened from sleep before the brain commanding their motions, grabbed wood and threw it on the fires. I heard Red Cheeks screaming something, heard his naked feet pound the grass of the clearing. Then I saw him race along a bamboo wall, a firebrand in his clenched fist. I forced my feet into my sneakers and jumped to the ground.

The noise of the village tripled in volume in a few seconds. Red Cheeks kept shouting till six or seven young men brandishing spears and burning branches ganged up in the middle of the clearing. I found myself right in front of them, and Red Cheeks clearly gestured for me to join them. I was surprised by his friendliness, but too overwhelmed by the emergency to think about it. I had always wanted to see Indians pursue jaguars in the wild, and those hunts mostly happen at night. So I stepped closer to him and his group.

Red Cheeks glanced around to see how many tribespeople witnessed his civic bravura: most of them were awake, the huts' entrances were brown with faces and lit with eyes. He could be doing this for political purposes, possibly trying to unseat the old man (I'd become more and more convinced that there was an ongoing power struggle between them). In the pulsating light of the torches, Red Cheeks seemed to be very audience-conscious. Satisfied, he pointed with confidence to his right, and we all scrambled over the wet grass after him, into a solid wall of fogged-up vegetation.

We were immediately forced into a single file, but the Indians were still moving pretty quickly: the torches went into the darkness like flares, and the fog trailed their light like a memory. I heard the grunt again, but I was far back, the last runner in the party. I gritted my teeth and ran faster—the worst scenario was to lose them ahead of me and find myself alone in the dark. I glanced away from the torches dancing ahead and gained no impression of light whatsoever. Outside the forest, on the darkest moonless night, the human eye acclimates and perceives *something*. Here, away from the torches, there wasn't the tiniest dispersion of light waves, just *nada*, as if I had undergone an iridectomy.

The grunt rang out again and was interrupted by an almost humanlike cough; the beast apparently ran ahead of us, changing directions, but Red Cheeks seemed to guess the turns it was taking, for he kept the grunt straight ahead of us all the time.

"*Ayya, ayya!*" I heard him shout unexpectedly.

I got closer and found the young warriors stopped before a spiny thickness, which they were lighting with their torches: maybe the beast, growling and bristling, had crawled underneath. It was a cluster of thorny plants harbored between the aboveground secondary roots of a big tree, and I headed for it as fast as I could, so as not to miss the spectacle. Red Cheeks suddenly pushed me. Powered by my own run, I bull's-eyed into it.

Red Cheeks immediately dropped his torch and stepped on it with his hardened foot. The other burning branches vanished at the same instant. Total dark followed. I realized it before I could utter a sound. I was being scuttled here by the young radicals of the tribe! They turned and with a rustle of broken branches started back, and the rustle diminished quickly. I thought of the jaguar . . . and I realized that there wasn't one. Red Cheeks had imitated the grunt himself, which explained why the beast seemed to stay dead ahead of him all the time we zigzagged through the forest.

Of course, a well-imitated grunt could attract other jaguars. That was a common hunting practice.

I moved as gently as I could, to stir no animals if there were any around, and to invite as little contact as possible with the barbs on the branches I'd crashed through. I had a number of them lodged in my skin, on my upper arms and shoulders, in my back, in the nape of my neck. I used my hands to push two spiny masses aside, and I stepped out. Now my breathing sounded louder than the Indian party's exit. I wondered how far I was from the village, and if I'd hear the clamor of a fight, in case Red Cheeks chose to depose Barnacle tonight, or Barnacle himself took advantage of the situation to ambush his young rival.

There was no answer to that. I plucked the barbs out of my skin as best I could, wondering if they were poisonous—Red Cheeks's clever plan deserved an ingeniously cruel ending. I couldn't get all the barbs out; several were embedded right between my shoulder blades. I broke the stems but the tips stayed in my skin, and in the process I lacerated my right hand to bleeding. I moved it in the air to try to coagulate the blood, and took stock of my plight.

I was lost in the forest. I was imprisoned by the uncharted virgin growth, and if I didn't make it back to the village (assuming that my ingenious expulsion was not ordered by Barnacle), I could die ten times over before anyone even suspected my presence here.

I retraced in my mind Red Cheeks's attitude towards me, and found it clearly criminal. I became convinced of the poisonous content of the barbs. Then I decided that if they weren't deadly, it was only because, in the dark, Red Cheeks mistook a harmless plant for a lethal one. It happens all the time: viperine-looking snakes are not vipers; odorless bugs choose to look like other bugs who do exhale a repellent stench, and both imitator and model escape the hunger of birds.

I listened to the sounds of the forest, repeating to myself that unprovoked animals rarely attack humans, yet wondering how much room there was in that law for an accident. I was concerned about snakes. I was even more concerned about deadly insects. And then, reacting to the entire situation, I shook in place, wanting to race into the dark to where I felt, surely inaccurately, that Red Cheeks's party had disappeared.

I made an effort and remained where I was, wrapped in the night, touched by the cool air, lost.

In order to calm down and assess the situation better, I force myself to think about the forest. I muse randomly about species and their relation with the habitat, then concentrate on camouflage techniques and other survival mechanisms. I think of visually menacing appearances exhibited by the most innocuous animals, like the deceiving "pair of eyes" patterns on certain butterflies' wings. The "eyes" are dark and set in a surface of brown dotted or streaked with black, strikingly duplicating the look of a feline's face.

But how did butterflies, which ostensibly have nothing to do with felines, observe the performance of felines in the forest so as to draw the conclusion that imitating their appearance would have survival value? Simply put, butterflies can see ocelots and jaguars. One can assume that certain butterflies "observed" somehow the effect of an ocelot's or jaguar's presence on other mammals, but also on birds, who occasionally become a feline's meal. That kind of butterfly chose the feline pattern to frighten away birds, its prevalent enemies. From the felines' rapport with the rest of the fauna it extracted only what applied to itself and used it correctly.

The faultlessness of that logic is, for a species without mind as we know it, astounding. Yet the connection was established. A mechanism of genetic construction was set in motion, and through its own capacity of trial and error it blueprinted the enzymes, the pigments, all the organic chemicals necessary to create the appearance of an ocelot's eyes, staring out of an ocelot's face, duplicated on a butterfly's wings. The blueprints were judged satisfactory, and the species set out for mass production.

There are so many examples of that sort: bugs shaped like painful or poisonous thorns; corollas and leaves jagged like teeth and beaks; extra sets of organs that can be dispensed with. In one particular moth species, a vibratory extra pair of wings is calibrated to hum at such frequency that it attracts birds, who rip off the redundant wings and let the clever survivor get away on its conventional flying gear. There's so much of that, and it is so subtly interpenetrated, as if indeed a creator's hand put it all together at the same time, careful to protect all species and favor none.

But it wasn't all put together at the same time. There's where the true mystery lies. It took hundreds of thousands of years of "copying" and "memoing out" to the next generation. But how exactly were the copying and memoing achieved? How does a species observe, analyze, and draw conclusions for its own survival? The answer is "Over time," for only ample time allows for adaptation. But is it all a practical, empirical process, divided in so many anonymous occurrences, in so many inglorious, unnoticed yet necessary units of time? What about such sophisticated examples as the ocelot eyes?

We don't know how that is done. Despite our impressive tools, we haven't discovered the underlying essence of the process, and how could we do it in the brief time we've spent trying to figure life out? By observing butterflies for thirty-five years, the active spell of an entomologist's career? Perhaps four hundred thousand years were used to achieve that adaptation. We destroy every year uncounted numbers of marvels that took hundreds of thousands of years to bring up to optimal functioning.

Good therapy, rambling about such issues. It dissolves fear.

I stand in the dark, a few yards from the spines Red Cheeks threw me into, listening to the jungle's night sounds, thinking of nature's pace. Nature isn't slow, nature just *is*. Its thoroughness has a goal: optimal functioning. Things take the time they need to take, and nature has time. But we, nature's ultimate creation, do not.

Time, time is the key. What does that tell me about the importance of this tribe, still straddling the frontier between nature and modern technology? Facing disappearance yet living unpressured by deadlines, and certainly not anxious to fixate time through gadgets like photography.

I wonder how much my sense of the present has dilated in contact with this tribe's. I don't know what day this is, and the days have begun to fuse in my memory. Inside my old sense of time there is room for another kind of time, which I cannot define yet, though I feel its presence. It is abundant and crawling with unseen connections and causalities, like the forest.

About an Hour Later

I've gained control over myself, and know what I need to do. Remain here, quietly, until the light starts filtering back into the forest, and I can form some sense of direction. Which means basically finding the path the Indians cut through the forest. It might not be easy to tell it from the trail of some larger animal. How could I be so gullible as to follow them into the jungle in the middle of the night?

That adds an interesting aspect to the beaming. All through the last few days, I picked up messages from Barnacle and a sort of background hum from all the villagers (which makes sense: if these Indians have an unusually strong consciousness, why would they not be collectively hypnotic?), but nothing at all, whether menacing or malicious or just indifferent, from Red Cheeks. In fact, he moved in and out of the general hum like a strip of blank tape. As if the beaming had an off button in each individual, and his was shrewdly flicked off. Meanwhile, my dialogue with Barnacle never involved trivially objective messages like *Are you hungry?* or *Here's your hammock*. Obviously, for that there is the language of daily communication. So what is the beaming? A ritual type of contact?

If my assumption is correct and Red Cheeks and Barnacle are in conflict, why did Red Cheeks bring me in after we met in the bush? To create a diversion of some kind? And why did he push me out of the way just now? To deprive the chief of the choice of an outside alliance? The more I think about it, the more this youngster I saw in Zonia's hammock appears to me like a talented tribal politician, inexperienced but fully determined to use his opportunity.

The bugs have found me. They are a kind of gnat which I attract like a magnet, being no longer full of the B1 vitamin I took as a repellent when I had my supplies. Formations upon formations of gnats streak the air towards me, and I quiver in place, slapping my sides and my shoulders and reaching under my pants. It's useless. While I scratch an arm, they pucker my face. Called *jejenes* in Peru and *piums* in Brazil, they leave a black dot under the skin and their sting hurts for about an hour but isn't overly toxic—I've seen Indians who carried so many of their bites that they ran together, turning their skin black. From now on, trekking in the forest, I'll meet all my old acquaintances: the fire ants, whose sting feels like a cigarette burn but passes quickly, and the dreaded inch-long *tucanderos*, whose poison is so abundant it takes the body up to six hours to cleanse itself of it.

The way to shake them off is to move, but all I can do in the dark is creep away slowly, tentatively feeling the forest floor with my shoes, hoping not to shock some forest creature into a strike. But I have to do it; otherwise the assault of the bugs is too maddening. Luckily, I come close to some big emergents whose daytime shadow bans growth beneath their lower branches; all I have to expect is tripping over aerial roots, or creepers swaying right against my face.

I clench my teeth and advance. Maybe I'm getting away

from the path the Indians left through the underbrush, but I can't get away too far. I hope I'll recognize it in the morning. Cool, inert, a creeper hits my face. Then another. I tell myself that an animal would sense my approach. I notice suddenly that the *piums* have left me. I breathe. I stop.

They find me again. Again, I dance in place. This is a torture Dante left out of his inferno.

One way to distract myself is to listen to the forest's voices. Like an Indian village, the forest sleeps in pieces. When the spectacular howlers, macaws, and parrots are quiet, it's like an orchestra whose piano, bass, and tuba have quit, to leave room for flutes, violins, and violas. I hear frogs, whose sonorous variety is stupendous: it goes from a raspy belch to a sexual coo. A particular cricket makes me jump as she calls her mate, sounding like a knife being sharpened on a stone.

Then I *see* something: a spider whose four pairs of eyes are luminous. (It's the only moment of the night when, gaining some sort of orientation, I can relate to the space around me.) I lower my face toward a branch and bring my own eyes so close to the arachnid that its eyes are probably reflected in mine. Now I see it better: its legs have such long joints that the body hangs in the middle, lower than the knees, underslung like a carriage. It looks somewhat like a buggy, dwarfed by giant wheels. The furry body, almost spherical, is the source of light: it flicks on and off, on and off, regularly. When it's on, the light makes the body transparent and simply pours out of the little animal's eyes.

I edge closer still. The furry cornices hanging over the spider's lower eyes, which look almost like bushy eyebrows, are some sort of feeling organ (I overcome the fear that they are stingers, ready to extend and pinch my face). Through the eyes, I look into a palpitating mass of electric fire. I've never seen such a specimen, and I wonder if it's been collected and classified yet. In his day, Henry Walter Bates counted fourteen thousand Amazonian species, of which more than half were new to science. Later estimates increased that count tenfold. But while we keep discovering new species, scores of undiscovered ones go every year, sacrificed to development, their cry of protest unheard.

So goes this amazing fellow. After I peer into its body, wondering what sort of chemical compounds, rare and useful, it might contain, I see several other specimens like it, linked in pairs to different spiders, nonluminous ones. The dance of light is a wedding, the flashing a mating signal. Alas, it attracts not just mates, but also a paradise snake (I judge its species by its tiny size; glimpsed in the spider's glow, it looks like a sinuous twig suddenly come alive), who slithers along the branch and starts gobbling the newlyweds. Eaten, the victims utter some cry of distress on the spider frequency, because the lights of the others brusquely shut off, and we're all back in darkness.

I move away from where I danced, digging a hollow in the forest bed. Finally the *piums* lose me again. I stop and stand in the dark, and doze off standing.

13

In the Rain Forest

I slept on the forest floor and woke up scratching. The bugs had found me again and probably laid their eggs in the open cuts left by those thorns. Now I itch badly on my back, where I can't reach, and the itching feels suspiciously like screw-worms.

The day arrives with the kind of dark-to-light transition typical of the tropics: brusque, impetuous. That brief dawn always filled me with a feeling of perilous excitement. I know what the time is, with an error of maybe half an hour: it's six to six-thirty A.M. The light finds gray fog wrapped in thin strands around the trees. I immediately move, determined to find the village and take my chances with those desperadoes . . . if they haven't moved on already.

I can find some of my footsteps on the litter of the forest floor. I work my way back and spot the thorny growth under those aerial roots. Good. Let's look for a trail. I find a trail. I feel saved.

Then I find another trail, right next to it, but diverging considerably just a few yards down. Red Cheeks's party could've followed either one. The thrill of finding the first trail withers instantly.

Any trail can be deceptive. They all bifurcate sooner or later and without a compass you face the quandary again: which candidate to choose? I've heard so many accounts of exhausted travelers deciding erroneously to choose this path instead of that one. Either one could lead to life or to death. Many travelers chose death.

But death is here already, encrusted in the probability of so many other happenings. Death is always here, and its most perfect agent is being in the wilderness alone. A fall, a bird's screech stealing one's attention at the wrong instant, a toxic vine squeezed for water, a venomous insect. One can be killed by any of those. I keep thinking of a Frenchman who rafted down a tributary alone, doing quite well until he stopped on a shore to set up camp. The river rose unnoticed while he was making himself a meal. He looked up to see his raft almost disappear, jumped up and raced to catch it, and impaled himself on a broken branch jutting out of some driftwood lodged in the sand. The sharp end of the branch perforated his bowel. He lifted himself off that deadly snag, then sat on the shore for four days, dying a little bit with every passing minute, making notes in a diary. The diary was found next to his body, which had become swollen and black: in the tropical heat, body fat liquefies and seeps out of the skin like a dark ointment, and in a matter of days the body looks like it had crankcase oil poured over it. I've seen bodies in that condition, unloaded from rescue boats or planes. If they were not too mangled (the eyes get eaten off fast, and in three or four days the features become unrecognizable) their swollen faces seemed to carry, across their pumped-up lips and cheeks, a smile of lubricated complacency.

I have no choice. I must find my captors.

I wish I could walk in a spiral pattern, a "retiring search curve," as they call it in the navy when they try to locate a seaman fallen overboard and drifting away. Walk in a circle with an ever-increasing radius, alert for human refuse, for human smells or sounds, for anything that could be a clue to where Barnacle and his people are. But that's practically impossible: you can't follow a curved line in the forest any more than you can keep a straight one, because of buttresses, elevated roots, secondary trunks, lianas shooting down and sprouting little legs and sticking them in the ground, under your very eyes sometimes. All I can hope for is to find a rivulet and follow it until it merges with the main stream. I might stumble upon Barnacle en route, or if I reach the main stream I might find the camp I left on the beach, marked by that lupuna tree.

My other chance lies with Barnacle himself. He was friendly to me. It's not inconceivable that he'd send a search party after me.

Barnacle. Amazing how much a part of my life he has become. He and his bunch of Protopanoans with spines in their lips.

I walk.

Between six and eight-thirty (give or take half an hour), the temperature is bearable. I almost froze last night. I'm all right now. In an hour I'll be sweating and choking.

But I can't afford to stop, for fear that the tribe might weigh anchor again and move out of range. I have to budget my strength, move as fast as possible, and hope for some luck.

I see light ahead: the canopy is punctured. Sunlight pours into a clearing, making the air in it boil with humidity and higher temperature. I step into the clearing, look up, and glimpse, like the top of the Empire State Building fighting the clouds, a huge emergent tree, in bloom: masses of pink flowers float against sunlit strands of mist, at least thirty feet higher than the rest of the forest.

At this time, the air is still resonating with morning calls. Before the first sun ray, the howlers, the macaws, the oropendulas (a species of birds that hang meter-long nests from tree limbs) take up their instruments and go to it, *molto vivace*. There's a spasm of excitement in my heart as I notice that the clearing is littered with hacked-off branches: technologic man was here with his buzz saw, starting to clear a landing site.

I can't climb that huge tree without a rope or some other gear (the canopy is still the least explored part of the rain forest; lately, biologists have used crossbows to shoot lines up over high branches, then pull up bigger lines fitted with pulleys and all sorts of other equipment, to climb to the canopy and watch it on a more continuous basis). But a man-made clearing encourages me. It looks like it was abandoned just days ago. I'm close to my fellow modern man, the rapacious developer. As objectionable as he may be, I welcome the proof of his presence. He can't be far. I can survive on jungle liquids till I find him. I've torn vines before to wring water out of them. Most leaves that look at all fleshy store water, and most lianas do too. The toxicity of the juices some of them contain is a chance I have to take.

The area I'm in is the limit of how far the Incas journeyed out of their mountains to explore the jungle.

I leave the clearing, walk back into the trees, stop to consider a snack of fruits that look almost like blackberries. But they are sour and their nutritional value must be minimal, so I move on. Five minutes later, I glimpse another mass of light pouring through the torn roof of foliage. Out here, prospecting teams are lowered from hovering helicopters and *macheteiros* start hacking at branches, cutting a shaft downward through the many-storied foliage till they reach the ground; then they fell trees to make heliopads. I see a thick rope stretching on the forest floor, some cable, probably, abandoned. The dusk of the forest floor makes it shine and glitter, as if alive. I stop, realizing that it's not a cable but a two-lane traffic of army ants. Thousands of them parade in opposite directions, often scrambling over each other's backs, driven by an instinct that knows no confusion. They carry fragments of some unidentified matter toward (I follow the carriers) a multiple-cone anthill of mud and leaves, its tallest cone about four feet high. It looks like a busy downtown mall.

I follow the other lane away from the anthill and find a

shoe, reduced to its thick rubber sole and vestiges of its leather part. A rich crush of ants engulfs it, disintegrating it, carrying away particles of it. I watch it with almost morbid curiosity, as if I'm seeing a devoured corpse. Then I understand, but before I can fully articulate the thought, I start running along the freeway of ants.

And I find four bodies. I can tell they are human by their skulls: not much tissue is left on their bones. The swarming, teeming shoal of ants has reduced leather jackets to their zippers and metal buttons, and has shredded shirts, pants, underwear, everything. Piled on top of each other, the remains look like a gruesome work of art. The skulls have been cleaned thoroughly, except for patches of hair and one baseball cap. They show jaws without gums and teeth stained by tobacco, and they seem in subtle motion, as the ants, crawling tirelessly over them, give an imperceptible flutter to those sinister death grins. Little clouds of flies vibrate around the discarnate heads, like a film of busy, hungry life, but the ants don't give them much chance to break in.

Watching, morbidly curious, I notice an arrow coming out of a hulk of chest. Then I see another one, lying on the ground, loosened out of flesh that's not there anymore, and another. Their blackened ends could've been dipped in curare. They are whistling arrows; they sport the kind of boar bristles I saw Barnacle use to fasten the feathering onto the lean, graceful shafts.

I notice another column of ants, the leaf-cutting type. They look like hundreds of minuscule green umbrellas on a pilgrimage: en route to their anthill, each carries a piece of leaf, holding it above its head and body. Sauvas. Said to be so numerous that "if Brazil doesn't get rid of sauvas, the sauvas will get rid of Brazil." Their vanguard prudently avoids the horde that dispatched the macheteiros.

I move around the scene and identify a chain saw, the metal shell over its engine bashed in. Somewhere in this mess there might be wallets with the names of these people, but I can't bring myself to grope around with my hands in what's left of them. They probably belonged to some small prospecting operation, rather than to a government project; otherwise helicopters would've come back and evacuated their bodies.

Yet, out here, that isn't so sure. The most amazing foul-ups happen, because of faulty phone connections, inaccurate maps, or just because of the Brazilian way (or the Peruvian way). Search parties head in the wrong direction. People tire and decide they've done everything in their power. A letter to the family closes the case, while the bones rot out here, forever part of the wild.

Should I wait here? Will there be a rescue party?

Looking at the condition of the bodies, it seems silly to think so. I sweat heavily; the heat has risen to its highest level for the day, where it will hover till the brief, unsatisfying dusk. I decide to go on. I just can't linger near this hideous exhibit. I hope I won't look like this in a few days.

There's a serial number on the deformed shell of the chain saw, and I jot it down in my notebook. Maybe by reporting it, the missing men could be traced and identified.

I walk on, wondering if I haven't been moving in a circle. Where is the river? It couldn't've vanished. This underbrush should be crisscrossed by streams, brooks, subtributaries of all sizes, all pointing toward the main stream. I encounter not a trickle of water.

The itching has grown unbearable. In some sores on my back I feel the under-skin movement of what I'm sure is screw-worms. Sometime later, I notice a swelling on my left forearm. I pull out my knife, open the swelling, and pull out a white maggot. The larva of a flesh-eating fly. I remember its scientific name, *Calitroga hominivorax*. *Hominivorax* means "devourer of man." An infestation of calitroga can kill a full-grown steer in a week.

I keep walking, fantasizing every other instant that I hear the murmur of flowing water.

14

The Twin Waterfall

Sometime Around Noon

Where is the river?

I try to remember the map; I must be quite close to the Javari's source. In normal conditions that would excite me; I'm fascinated by sources and I traveled to the beginnings of many Amazonian headwaters, boating up in the flatlands or flying to the chilly slopes of the Andes. I don't know much about the source of the Javari, but it must be nearby, concealed somewhere in this green flatland.

It's no longer really a flatland: the forest floor under my feet is ascending—gently, but it is ascending. I don't remember elevations noted on the map, but finding one might be helpful; I could get a view of a larger area and understand where I am.

The heat is overbearing. Every twenty minutes or so I stop and break a segment from a vine resembling an extra-long cucumber and squeeze the juice out of it. It has a bitter after-taste, but I don't think it's toxic, and it's got more liquid in it than other vines. The forest's indirect luminosity has increased, and I walk without any feeling in my feet. After sucking on thirty or more of those vines, I reach an interesting state of inebriation.

The forest becomes my brain, and my brain the forest. I have the sensation of seeing my thoughts, and they're a mental version of this steaming matrix, exploding with complication and variety. All around and above me, birds, bats, and bugs zigzag in a complex of flight paths thousands of air traffic controllers couldn't keep track of. It's the same with my thoughts. God knows how they all find room in there, how my skull is not exploding from that incessant vibration.

I'm trying to find one river in a maze of some fifteen thousand. From the Javari's source, my thoughts jump to that other source, the most distant one. Just one, out of countless tributaries and subtributaries. Out of so many beginnings, one has to be *it*.

I keep moving.

I keep moving, and the slight hallucination (I don't know whether it's the juice of those vines or just the hunger and heat and exhaustion) changes. But it's still with me. I feel that my hand, groping around the universe, has torn a corner open. Now someone else's eyes follow me through the crack, slow and unwavering and sure like death. Soon there will be an encounter. I panic. Why did I tear that corner open, if I'm not prepared for the encounter?

That's true. I'm not prepared. Not like that spider dying on his wedding night. Death was a chance its species took, a variable it accepted. Feeding that snake, it flailed its limbs in agony, but that didn't communicate to its species a need to *change*. It was a loss, but no tragedy; nature contains no tragedies. No failures either, since no one in nature sets goals that cannot be attained. Except man. His motivational forces are no longer natural, survivalistic, and biotic. They are tragic, competitive, and intellectual, and above all obsessed with achievement. Maybe one should ask the question, how can modern, technological man understand a universe that isn't based on achievement?

I'm still climbing, unless I'm hallucinating.

I stop, for no particular reason. My feet land on an

obscure spot of the forest; my damp forehead stops level with the green blades of a parasite creeper, swaying down from a tall branch. Through the spaces between the blades, I see ahead perhaps a hundred yards. Farther, my eyes get absorbed into a visual swamp of green.

And then what I see in front of me changes. Though I keep watching a three-dimensional landscape of trees, secondary roots, and hanging parasites so dense that my eyes can't conquer more than a hundred yards of it, a rearrangement happens. Nothing disappears from the picture, and nothing is added, except an extra depth. The hundred yards of distance suddenly look as extended and spacious as a few hundred miles.

I watch, evaluating the distance: it is the same, yet it seems infinitely deeper.

That depth leads somewhere. What is behind it?

As if across a minefield, my imagination takes a step into the distance. Careful not to disturb the tiniest root, the narrowest branch, I travel across the depth, farther, farther, *farther*, while my breathing grows cavernously deep, and I expect to hear, like in my dreams, the tumbling of some shard torn from the bodywork of the cosmos.

When my mind gets close enough to the far end of the landscape, big drops of sweat roll down my forehead. I feel their wet streaks, harmonized with the vertical lines of the creepers hanging in front of me.

I hear the source, the most distant source of the river.

I hear it as a muffled trickle, thawed snow slipping over packed ice, meeting other trickles, growing into a veinlet of water. All of a sudden, the amazing new perspective plays a trick on me: I could stretch my arm, push through the branches and touch the bulky vastness of the Andes, feel around with my fingers and dip them in that most distant source.

That unsettles me more than anything. I'm losing myself. I don't have my camera, my watch, my compass, my maps, I don't have my mental latitude and longitude anymore. I have no tools to control reality and confirm my older understanding of it. Where am I? What am I?

I remember a trip I once took to the Grand Canyon. I descended into the chasm, a mile deep, some of its rocks so old that at one point every foot of descent corresponded to a million years of prehistory. It was like a slow tumble into the past.

I'm tumbling now. Amazed at this unknown depth.

All right. I'll stop and give myself a minute.

To gain some mental control, I think of the known dimensions. Length, width, depth. Time. Energy.

I seem to be experiencing another dimension. I want to think of its attributes, of what makes it real, but my mind blanks out, and for a while I have no words and no thoughts.

I resurface.

The beaming. It has to do with the beaming.

When I can think again, the connection makes sense. The source, the beaming, another dimension.

I breathe, and alter reality by bringing up an arm and wiping my forehead with it. I look ahead and still see an endless depth, stretching not just a hundred feet ahead, but much farther, into infinity.

I begin to walk again. Whether I keep my direction or not, I no longer know. Another thought gets formulated inside me, and when it's whole it howls savagely, and all the ramparts of knowledge I built in fifty years are blown to bits. I was never part of nature! None of us were! Not even the Indians! I, we, always belonged to a vaster space.

This upsets me more than anything. Bushes block my way, but I stagger on, no longer paying attention to branches, thorns, cutting edges. They prick, bite, sting me. I just stagger on; I don't care. Climbing the gentle slope, I begin to hear something. A flow of water.

I step closer to the sound and then, within seconds it seems, I'm on my knees with my face in fresh water, drinking from a clear, narrow brook.

*

After a minute of drinking, of dousing my face and arms and of drinking again, I know it isn't a hallucination. I stagger up and follow the brook downstream, lose it behind a line of bushes, break through them to find it again, and keep following it.

It becomes a shallow stream. Rather than trying to follow the shore without a machete, I walk in the water or on the shore when it's not too overgrown. There is the danger of stepping on a stingray, so I look mostly down, but I'm aware of sunbeams occasionally penetrating the trees. This is one of the few cloudless days since I've been here. When unexpectedly the stream opens into a river flowing narrowly but clearly, I lift my head, look up a long stretch, and there, at the end of the water, where perspective narrows the two forested banks into a point, there rises, like a green church cupola, a mountain.

Am I seeing things?

The sun sparkles on its slopes and at its bottom, as if it were set with precious stones.

I know that the river is real, for I'm wading in it right this instant, but what about that mountain? I shut my fist loosely, peer through the hole, and what looks like a tumble of jewels becomes two waterfalls, parallel and so close that I wonder if I'm seeing double from fatigue.

I advance while the mirage holds. It is a twin waterfall.

I find a beach of white sand, untainted by forest floor rot. I sit down on it, pick at the swellings on my arms and shoulders, extracting more maggots, and watch the wonder.

This can only be the source of the Javari.

Finding it like this, when I felt lost and exhausted beyond caring, has a wonderful effect. I sit and watch till the colors of the river and the mountain slope start changing, while the sun begins slanting over my right shoulder. So I must be looking south.

I don't know much about the Javari's source, but this elevation, if I'm not dreaming it, must be the end of the

Andes' reach into the plain. The last elevation, followed by two thousand miles of flatland. From the Andes to the Atlantic the altitude level drops only five hundred feet. Some three inches per mile, making all the tributaries meander sluggishly, like giant snakes.

The mountain looks fairly tall, its crest hovering maybe a thousand feet above the forest. Like a twin jet of pearls, the Javari cascades out of it, splashing into the stream that flows right past me.

The beauty of this Shangri-La is absolute, and in no way designed for human visitors. It's been here for thousands of years, seen only by tribal Indians, boundary surveyors, and maybe a rubber tapper or two. The crash of the waterfall blows mist into the heavy air, feeding a dependent cosmos of leaves, aerial roots, and creatures.

Now I can follow the river, staying on its right bank, the Brazilian shore (an odd and amusing notion at the moment).

But it's hard to leave this place. I finally do, still not sure whether the waterfall is real. I walk down, listening to its roar. I look over my shoulder and glimpse it back there, unchanged. Then the stream takes a turn. I follow it. The twin waterfall disappears. I have no more reason to turn and look back.

It would be untrue to say that I feel grief, but I feel something. A hard-to-define sadness, relating to that sight's perfection.

The hours pass, and I keep walking. Now the right bank is a string of pools and little bogs left after the seasonal lowering of the waters. I pause to rest next to a fallen tree and notice a little jaguar very occupied with something I can't figure out. It's a baby jaguar, under four feet long and very splattered with mud. He's using the tree trunk to hang above a muddy pool and dip a paw in it. The hair on his head is so frizzed up that I have trouble controlling a chuckle: he looks like some half-grown street urchin, totally in his own world.

I break a branch, betraying my presence. I need it to fight off the baby jaguar's mother, in case she's lurking nearby. He looks up. With yellow eyes bitten in the middle by a dark dash. He has that touch of intrigued attention in his stare, that how-can-I-get-you flicker of interest I've seen in other felines. I may be his first human.

I make no move. The water under him bubbles, recalling his attention, and two gray-green knobs surface, shining like a ceramic sculpture. A caiman's nostrils, followed by the whole snout. Its craggy skin is spotted almost like the jaguar's, and they're about the same size. Before the caiman can rise completely, the jaguar steadies his footing on the trunk, choosing his best angle of attack. Then he throws a foreleg around the caiman's neck, secures his grip, pulls the prey up, and tries to bite it behind the eye, where the neck is thinner and the scales more fragile. The caiman pulls down, and both splash into the water. They fight without any sounds except the thrashing and splashing. Then the jaguar sinks his teeth deep behind the caiman's neck and starts pulling it out of the water again. The reptile's left eye, wide open, stares straight at me without any expression, of pain or amazement. It knows who will win, and I know too.

Death in the forest is usually quiet, often undramatic; this time it fills me with an acute sense of loneliness. I feel so utterly alone that solitude's acidic taste cramps my bowels. Even the clammy heat feels like solitude of the saddest type. Forgotten, forgotten. Unneeded, useless.

I make it to the other shore. Suddenly I jackknife forward and fall on my stomach on rotting leaves. I order myself to crawl, but my body refuses to obey.

I remain lying, thinking of what will happen to me if I lose consciousness. There are jaguars in the area; I just sighted one. But jaguars rarely attack humans if unprovoked. Caimans are aggressive in the water, but not on land. Wild boars or even white-faced peccaries are what I fear. They're both carnivorous; when in packs of ten to twenty they unhesitatingly attack stragglers and can devour a human in minutes. Despite their prosaic appearance, they are the land piranhas of this region. Still more dangerous are the snakes and bugs, yet somehow I mind them less than the idea of being gobbled by pigs.

Well, I may never know. I manage to raise my face and see a lion marmoset, the smallest of all primates, observing me from a palm frond. With a humid little look in its eyes, as if ready to burst into tears. My last conscious impression is the marmoset's eyes. Death is a bank of klieg lights, being switched off. A vast theater in my head grows dim like a cavern, and then black.

They found him, and brought him back to the village.

He woke up in a hammock, sweating from high fever, under the hands of two shamans, who pulled gently at his limbs; finding no fracture, they turned him over and sucked out with their mouths the maggots and remaining thorns from his back.

Later, over a shaman's naked shoulder, he glimpsed the little pile of his belongings: pants, shirt, and notebook. His only links to the world he came from.

Then one of the shamans placed his mouth to McIntyre's forehead and "sucked out the demons." Then both shamans lit cigars of green tobacco and blew the smoke at his face and all over his torso. Then they stood on each side of the hammock and chanted, while he drifted back and forth between dream and reality.

THE RITUAL

"the mental attitude typical of archaic man: the exceptional value he attributes to *knowledge of origins.*"

MIRCEA ELIADE,
Myth and Reality

1

Burning the Past

The shamans kept him in the hut, fed him, sucked the demons out of his head several more times, and massaged his body. Once, as they turned him over, he glimpsed a face framed in the hut's entrance and thought it was the headman's.

He slept intermittently, woke up, slept again. Once, while awake, he tried by gestures to persuade the shamans to bring him his notched stick. They brought him a freshly cut branch instead.

When he reeled out of the hut, it was morning and he saw a mound of objects in the middle of the clearing. Tools, mostly: axes, manioc graters, calabashes for drinking and cooking. The shamans were walking from hut to hut, talking to the people in them, who later stepped out and threw more objects on the pile. It seemed to Loren that they did it contritely. He saw Tuti carrying a batch of arrows seven feet long, tips well sharpened, ends decorated with red parrot fluff. Onto the pile. Tuti seemed close to tears: maybe the beautiful arrows had been promised to him. Loren saw Zonia; she looked surprisingly unkempt and dazed and her eyes were puffy, the stare the explorer remembered as voraciously vital now dull and unfocused. He stumbled past an empty hut and stopped as if electrocuted.

Red Cheeks was here.

What Loren saw first was a sort of mummy: a body sewn inside a funeral basket, leaning against a supporting pole. Its head seemed to be smoldering, but when Loren looked closer the smoke became bugs swarming around the head, buzzing in and out through lattices of woven vines. Red Cheeks's face could be glimpsed inside, convulsed, *crispado* like the cooked howler monkey's. What held him up was the basket, and his own rigor mortis.

Loren stepped back into the plaza, too drained to be nauseated. He looked around, scanning the brown faces. He saw none of the youngsters who had lost him in the forest.

Quite likely, Barnacle had put down an insurrection.

Standing in the clearing, Loren closed his eyes, wanting to hear the normal sounds of an Indian community in peacetime—voices, barks, caws and cackles from pets, all in a random pattern. What he heard were hurried footfalls, the dragging of objects on the ground, thuds, slams. Inside that hub, he distinguished another sound: mechanical, monotonous, and uniform.

A low-flying plane.

He looked up, and the canopy's striations and fragmentations seemed to lash at his eyes. The jungle's green roof was compact and almost lightproof, unlike the one above the Indians' last village. They had changed locations again, and carried him with them.

Again, he was sealed under the canopy. The plane was sailing invisibly above it, sounding like a single-engine.

He leveled his face toward the village and scanned the Mayoruna's faces: their cheeks seemed pulled downward by an invisible weight. Their mouths were shut stubbornly. He looked again at Zonia: her body had lost its roundness, her lips were thinner, even the curve of her belly, which he remembered as voluptuous and fleshy, appeared shrunken now, as if dried up and bloodless.

The thought hit him like a punch in the solar plexus. Zonia wasn't just mourning for Red Cheeks. It was her own death that he saw chiseled in her flesh. It was everyone's death that carved the other faces. The actors on this stage were giving their last performance.

From across the plaza he saw Barnacle, whose face floated above the growing scrap heap of personal belongings. Watching Loren, as if making sure that he witnessed all this.

It seemed as though the shamans had gathered all the objects that could be gathered and that the little community was waiting. Loren wondered whether there was a connection between their waiting and the sound of the plane. The sound diminished and then faded. The plane was gone. His thoughts about being rescued faded like the sound of the plane.

The tribesmen continued to wait.

He sat by the pile of tools and weapons, his eyes reviewing it abstractly. He noticed several fishhooks scattered among other objects. He must get some of those, he told himself. Must sneak some fishhooks into his pockets and be alert for any other survival items. The tribe was not going to help him get out of here. He had to do it himself.

He saw several skulls on the pile, shiny, smeared with some protective ointment or perhaps just patinated by time. Trophies.

He was too exhausted to react with alarm. Yet if this pile was destined to be destroyed or left behind, the tribe was depriving itself of two commodities ordinarily too important to forsake. A tribe never abandoned its trophies: their pride and occult powers resided in them. Implements like fishhooks took skilled work to manufacture and were critical for physical survival. Neither would be destroyed or abandoned mindlessly.

What was happening?

People faded into their huts or straggled off to their daily duties, and McIntyre was left almost alone. He feverishly pulled the notebook out of his pocket. The pen stored inside the cover in a tiny sheath of plastic was still there, in functioning order, but the pages had turned brown like an Indian's skin, and the letters crawling across them looked like the hyphae of aerial roots struggling against a dark soil. Repeatedly the rain had soaked the little book and the midday heat had dried the moisture out of it, swelling the pages and then wrinkling them.

He promised himself to reread his notes before his book got completely destroyed. It was a little miracle it had survived so far. As soon as he reached Leticia or any other community, he would expand on them from memory, synthesizing them into some account of this contact.

Or maybe he wouldn't. He had no guarantee of surviving this, particularly since the tribe's preparations for the future included this ominous divestment of what tribes never got rid of.

He tried to write. The pen punctured the still-damp top of a page. He tried again. Squiggles of letters started to braid a text along the now almost invisible horizontal lines.

Maybe they were all close to death, and what mattered at such moments was understanding. He was simply trying to understand.

A couple of hours after the passing of the plane, Barnacle stepped out of his hut. His presence acted as an unspoken command on the men, who immediately started to build a fire next to the discarded weapons and tools. The flames rose, everyone came out, and under Barnacle's stare the men stepped over to the piled-up tools and weapons and started breaking them with their feet. What things they couldn't destroy with their hardened feet they picked up and bent with their hands or snapped against their knees, sometimes helping each other. They ground the pots with their feet, cracked the trophy skulls, snapped the bows and arrows, finally shattering the whole pile into bits of clay and wood, bones and feathers and husks, loose human teeth, and necklaces and other adornments which escaped, being too light and insignificant, that cool frenzy of breaking and splitting. If this was some kind of ritual, their gestures were not mystical and everything was done without chanting or dancing. Finally they were left with a mound of rubble. Into the fire it went, without a hesitation or a look of regret.

Fed with all that debris, the fire roared higher, beginning to singe the lower canopy. Barbecued twigs and vines started falling down, too moist to burn properly. Thick smoke wafted upward, some undoubtedly piercing through the foliage into the higher atmosphere. Just then, the headman stepped out from behind a compact mass of warriors.

He strode over and stopped right next to me.

I felt frankly hostile, and determined to be closed off to any sort of telepathy. I stared dead into the fire, but fought some anxiety as I waited to see whether anything unusual would appear in my mind.

I don't know how long I waited. Nothing was happening. I was hoping that Barnacle would go away, but he stood patiently right next to me. I thought of stepping away, but it seemed like a weakness. I stayed where I was. So did he.

I shot a glance sideways: smaller fires burned in front of some of the huts, while inside them the women and the men no longer occupied in the ceremony were packing the little that was left: the hammocks, a minimal number of bowls and gourds. At least we would be drinking. And if the hammocks were not destroyed, we could figure on some sort of shelter over our heads.

I stared at the fire. I filled my eyes with the broken spears and bows and arrows and bones. I felt that Barnacle would be leaving any instant and enjoyed a naive sense of male defiance. I wasn't going to be the one to move.

Then something came into my head. *They were holding them still*, or something to that effect. It became a clear, absorbable statement before I knew it. It wasn't obvious that it had originated with the chief. What *they* meant wasn't specified, but I knew. *They* were right in front of me; the tribe's possessions. Everything everyone had lumped onto the fire.

I wanted to turn and look at Barnacle, just to correlate that message with his expression. I needed my whole willpower not to do it. In a while the message faded, then grew in volume again, as if repeated: *They held us still.*

I was curious, and aware of being curious. Controlled lab conditions, I told myself, that's as close as I'll get to controlled lab conditions: standing here, awake, unintoxicated, staring away from this man, waiting, finding his messages in my brain, fitting them to the situation, and checking whether they were compatible.

To be sure that I was not abandoning my own thinking, I talked to myself on the first track of my mind. I noted our physical proximity; the fact that we were watching the same scene, the chance that my thoughts would've independently duplicated his sooner or later just by guessing the purpose of the ceremony; finally, my immersion into the existence of the tribe.

When they burn up, we move away, he went on.

Of course they were going to move away. After their objects, they were going to destroy their huts and then move off into the bush. I knew. I'd already witnessed the routine. Now I looked at the chief. He was looking at the fire. The sticks and bones in the fire cracked very loud, as if inside my head.

He seemed to say that the objects held them still. And by destroying them, they were able to set themselves in motion.

Of course, all that could've been my own thoughts.

Still in time, he seemed to say.

I made myself think: *Fine. So you're burning up all this, to get rid of its burden and be able to get going again. Very good. Heading where?*

To the beginning, he beamed.

What beginning?

The beginning, he beamed again, stubbornly, self-evidently.

All right, I made myself think again. *I don't care. Let's go. Let's go to your goddamn beginning. And what are we going to find, in that beginning?* Suddenly I realized that his answer might be "death." Death was awaiting us in the beginning.

This time I looked at him squarely. He gave me a swift glance and seemed to repress a smile, the smile of a modest success. Then he walked away, rolling his shoulders like an older man fighting stiffness; his shoulder blades looked enormous in his powerful but emaciated back.

I stayed where I was.

The scene oddly reminded me of a scene in Arlington, Virginia: the bonfire in Greenbrier Stadium, at the close of the Yorktown High School year. I kept watching it, playing with the notion of being held still in time by possessions. That seemed to be the logic of the ritual. Imagine *us*—I chuckled silently—burning *our* possessions not to remain still in time.

I pictured bonfires like this one on some affluent American street. Everyone dragging out paid-for belongings, furniture, appliances, toys, and feeding them to a purifying fire. All of a culture, the most materialistic and leisure-minded in the world, onto the fire. Spraying gasoline, dropping matches, watching it all burst in flames. In my mind, I saw flames spring up in a front yard, and another, and another. All along the street, all through the neighborhood and the next neighborhood. I pictured the town to be Washington. All of Foggy Bottom, on fire. Pennsylvania Avenue, the White House, on fire. All freeing itself, taking off, soaring, carried by the vehicle of sacrificial, purifying flames.

Carried where?

Maybe I'll live to find out the answer.

Soon after that, they set the huts on fire. Red Cheeks's body would go up in flames with them. Loaded with minimal utensils and carrying the children who couldn't keep the pace, the tribe formed another marching column. Barnacle watched me, maybe curious to see whether I'd join them or not. Why curious? Was he not aware of my plight?

I rolled up my hammock, packed knife and little book in the crumpled pockets of my stained and battered pants, and lined up with the tribesmen. Like a good civilizado without other choices.

We started.

We marched into the forest. (*March* is a manner of speaking: we advanced, twisting and turning, weaving through thickets, stopping and starting again sideways, climbing over trunks of fallen trees, wading across streams.) I kept straining my ears, trying to hear that plane or any other aircraft. I heard nothing.

We advanced all day. We stopped before sundown, rigged our hammocks. There was no evening meal. We slept in the forest.

We march on the next day, following a tributary. At least water is permanently available. No morning meal. I wonder if there will be an evening one.

But no hunters detach themselves from the ranks to spear or arrow something or catch some fish to cook it later. Barnacle walks on inexorably, like a brown-skinned, prehistoric robot.

The tribespeople follow him. By now most of the children are being carried. I see their faces, hanging over their parents' arms or shoulders, lolling about with vacant eyes, bouncing in the rhythm of the trek. So far no one has collapsed, but it won't take long, as we have among us a fair assortment of ages. The older people are already limping and our pace has slowed considerably.

I glimpse women breaking branches loaded with wild fruits, trying to feed their children. I look at the Indians I feel I know—Zonia, Huaca One and Two, Tia—as if they were friends from whom I could expect a will to survive, an insurrection against this madness. But their stares are so haggard; they drift past me, as if I were invisible.

Before sundown, we rig our hammocks again. There

is no food. And almost nothing to cook it in anyway. I wonder what would happen if I fell and passed out. Or if I woke up tomorrow morning unable to move.

I make a decision. Tomorrow I'll hunt something, somehow. All by myself. I don't care what happens, I might set a valuable example.

We drink water incessantly, all of us.

That night in my hammock I doze with interruptions, almost afraid to sleep. In the middle of the night I stay awake a seemingly long time, thinking of who I am and what I lived for, as if I could glean from that some physical strength. But I come back to the only issues that interest me. Where are we going? What will happen to us?

I haven't heard that plane again and have no way to find out whether it was Mercier looking for me. I know how rarely one hears planes out here; my missed chance appears painfully unique, and Barnacle's ignorance of my desire to leave almost criminal. On the other hand, the absence of any kind of civilizado sound (no boat engine, no plane, no report of firearms, no chopping of wood, nothing) is beginning to feel incredibly demoralizing. It feels as if we have moved into another time.

Alone, in my hammock, I start chuckling. Of course. After that old bastard freed us of our possessions, we left this century. Now we're hurtling away in time, toward his beginning.

All my life I've been obsessed with time. Physical, psychological, sidereal. Time of all kinds, measured in any possible fashion. I lived by the planet's forward clock, but was convinced that it tolled in tune with another one, a regressive clock, so to speak, which happened to be the clock of exploration. Exploration, while opening up new vistas, also brought back the past, untouched.

I always harbored a yearning for that kind of revelation, always felt that something was about to be unveiled, disclosed, and though demystified, it would be simultaneously raised upon a sort of eminence from which it could shine on everyone. I guess this is as close to it as I'll ever get.

Memory plays an interesting trick on me. It brings up scenes from Jack London's *Before Adam*, a book I read before I was twenty in the hiring hall of the Sailors' Union of the Pacific in San Francisco. Jack London's hero found himself back in time, running terrified on prehistory's plains of slaughter and superstition. That book fascinated me, for it captured a unique feeling of yearning to go forward yet somehow back, to a primal territory too quickly abandoned.

Maybe this "beaming" could awaken in me all sorts of atavistic memories, like those experienced by the protagonist of *Before Adam*. His dreams were so powerfully realistic that he hardly knew in which world he lived, the world of then or that of now. Then and now became one, and he moved back and forth inside them thanks to a sort of conviction that he belonged to both.

I think I understand that feeling now.

The time described in that book was not sequential, not unidirectional. It was flexible and reversible, just like the time of these people.

I wake up determined to take leave of Barnacle and his people. I decide that I'll only follow them in their march to the first navigable body of water, where we'll part company. I'll find a piece of log to use as a raft and drift down the river somehow. I'll take my own chances.

But we only march for an hour or so before my nostrils warn me of other humans ahead. I can't distinguish smoke or smell cooked meat or odors of decomposition. However, I recognize a human scent, made of all of those, so fine that if I try to focus on it I lose it. But it's there.

A village. A settlement. A camp of some sort. *Garimpeiros*, mining the muddy waters for gold. Poachers. Any sort of pirates of the wild, provided they have a plane, or a boat, or at least a radio.

I hear, however, no *civilizado* sounds.

Unexpectedly, over the wide leaves of an unknown ground creeper (my feet crash loudly through them, as if through a taut drum), a jabbering crowd of Indians storms forward through the trees and welcomes the vanguard of our column. Ahead is an Indian village.

They are Mayoruna—the same labrets stick out of their lips. They look in every respect similar to my companions, except that they appear less gaunt, less emaciated. They seem to have more energy too, as they rush to surround this and that newcomer, the children with a profusion of touching and jumping, the adults more restrained, but still smiling and exchanging loud greetings.

This makes me recover some of my strength, and suddenly I act as if a spell were broken. I no longer feel as narrowly dependent on my captors, and the immediate effect is that I straighten my back, hold my head higher, and look around to identify possible interlocutors. All in a welcome upsurge of faith in myself and in the future.

As I assume that new pose I notice Barnacle, just a few feet away and disappearing in a circle of women and youngsters of both sexes whose features strikingly resemble his—undoubtedly they are his family. I see the little boy, Tuti, struggling through that crowd and practically throwing himself on the old man. He is received with a tight hug and a glowing smile from the rotting teeth, after which Tuti is placed on the old man's shoulders, and I suddenly realize how similar they look. Tuti behaves like any son reunited with his father—except that they've been near each other a thousand times during the past week, and I never guessed their kinship. So why this discharge of feeling now? Was Tuti held back from his father by the awareness of the ritual? Was Barnacle required not just to fast, but to separate himself from all kin in order to achieve some purifying asceticism?

All that is possible. Meanwhile, Barnacle throws Tuti, who must weigh some fifty pounds, up in the air with the stamina of a vigorous man, only superficially depleted by the fasting and the long march. I'm pretty sure that Tuti is his son; tribesmen of Barnacle's age frequently have several wives, the last one almost always very young.

I can't help but enjoy the charm of the scene, and realize all of a sudden that my horizon has been cleared, at least partially, of a huge authoritative presence. Barnacle's presence. In his posture of inscrutable leader, determined and dominant, relating to me only through his enigmatic messages, whose content he limited to what he thought fit to impart, whose timing he controlled entirely. Of course, I was alone with him and his people, utterly alone. But now comes a stunning discovery: I don't feel alone with them anymore. As if this freshly appeared branch of the same tribe (more and more of them pour out of the trees every second, overpowering us) represented humanity as I know it, populous and diverse, and not submitted to the sovereignty, no matter how capable and charismatic, of one leader.

I wonder whether Barnacle has just relaxed his grip on my psyche.

I can't give myself an answer, and for the moment it doesn't really matter. I've forgotten my macerating hunger. My exhaustion. The pain diffusely felt in all my muscles, the maddening itching of my skin, the sweaty scratchiness of my beard. (I haven't shaved in a week, or is it ten days? Or have I been stranded in the jungle even longer than that?) Everything appears hopeful, everything feels possible. I am full of resolve and faith. Things are changing. Salvation is near.

In an outburst of independence, I start running around addressing my new fellow men. My name is Loren, I announce. I am a photographer . . . which has become irrelevant, as I no longer have a camera. I come from downriver, from a place called Leticia. . . . A circle forms around me, made of men, women, youngsters; some of my captors join it, apparently explaining my presence; not a word is said in Portuguese or Spanish. Some break out of the circle, more interested in their tribal reunion, while others step in, satisfy their curiosity by watching me for a few moments, then drop out again. . . . I keep addressing them in Portuguese or Spanish, receiving placid smiles and uncomprehending stares. I feel hot waves shooting up into my brain. Not that again, that candor of paradise dwellers, never confronted with an outsider. . . .

I spot a younger man with a hat of leaves almost identical to those worn by Huaca One, Two, Three, and Four. A shaman. But this shaman wears . . . a pair of tattered shorts.

I hold my breath, step closer to him. He is small, five feet maybe. He studies me patiently and attentively, but with an all-inclusive way of taking in my person that fills me with hope: I feel I'm not an alien to him. I take a breath, try to control myself—I don't want to be disappointed. But to find out, I have to try.

I stare at him. He stares back at me. There is definitely something of a different quality. Here goes, in Portuguese: "My name is Loren—"

"Lowen, uh-huh," replies the little man—impossible to tell in what language.

I start again: "My name is Loren—"

"*Lowen, sim*," he says suddenly, in Portuguese. "*Câmbio*."

I'm about to hug him, but his last word perplexes me, stops me. *Câmbio* means "change" or "exchange" in Portuguese.

"*Bem-vindo*, Lowen," the little man says in Portuguese, "Welcome, Loren." And then again, immediately: "*Câmbio*."

Câmbio also means "over," in radio parlance. The little man just greeted me with "Welcome, Loren, over," as if addressing me on the radio.

I babble something, I don't know how long I've been with these people . . . I point my chin toward the natives who brought me here, but they are no longer a group, they have been atomized into the new crowd. I lost count of the days, I say, I had a watch with a calendar, but that watch . . . it is too complicated to explain what happened to it. I ask questions. What's ahead, a village? "Yes, a village, over," in Portuguese.

The little man wears no labrets in his cat-whisker tattoo, which appears somewhat faded.

"So these people—" my chin points again to "my" natives, "are they relatives of yours?" Yes, they are relatives, close relatives, he explains in fairly fluent Portuguese, though mangling the *r*'s like an Indian, which makes him call me Lowen (as far as I can tell, this language has fewer consonants than English; but its vowels are richly utilized, resulting in a quite musical sound, especially when spoken by women).

"Your relatives told me that none of them speak Portuguese or Spanish," I say, anticipating a denial. I glance at Barnacle. I'll undoubtedly find out that the old clown pretended all the way.

"They don't speak Portuguese, over," confirms the shaman. "No one here speaks Portuguese or Spanish, over. Only I do, over."

"Only you?" I wonder out loud.

"*So eu, câmbio,*" he repeats gravely.

And he adds an almost cute gesture of "that's it," holding both of his palms up and out.

First I feel disappointment, having expected an acculturated tribe. But this one doesn't appear to be that. Then I'm back to excitement, it doesn't matter, one interpreter is enough, and if this tribe is unacculturated, then some study of their culture can be made possible, now or at a later date, hopefully after I get back my other cameras. And I won't be stranded among total strangers. Good. Then I am bewildered: why is it that he speaks Portuguese, while none of the others do?

Without giving each other a cue, we find ourselves ambling into the trees toward the village. Keeping up that habit of inserting *câmbio* after practically each line, the shaman explains that he learned Portuguese by spending three years with a Baptist mission in Peru. And how did he end up there? Six years ago (God, here's someone who reckons in sequential time!), *pistoleiros* appeared in the area, over, hired by a syndicate of developers, over. Clashes ensued, over, and he and two other Indians were chased into that mission, over, where he found asylum, worked as a basket maker, then waited personally on the man who operated the mission's radio. The operator, a Brazilian, used more Portuguese than Spanish on the radio waves, and the little man learned it from him as such, constantly punctuated with the Portuguese word for "over."

As he mentions the radio room, a Disneyland of memories lights up in the little shaman's eyes. The time spent at that mission was a high point in his life.

I ask him his name.

"They call me Câmbio," he says unself-consciously. Of course, Câmbio. Over. What else.

Good lord. I left my camp on a beach on the upper Javari, joined an uncontacted tribe, was accepted in their midst, and received strange messages. I almost lost my life a couple of times. I reached despair and was about to start alone across the wilderness. And all of a sudden, this new village, and Câmbio . . . . And now Câmbio and I are strolling leisurely, as if all this pressure on my life never happened, toward the still unseen village.

I smell food. Something roasted. I never smelled anything more wonderful.

Together, we pass Barnacle: now he's got a rich garland of naked kids hanging all over him; Tuti, carried on his shoulders, holds the place of honor. Barnacle looks at me as I walk by. With a slight pang of anxiety I ask Câmbio whether Barnacle is some sort of supreme chief to all the Indians in attendance. These villages are run either by a chief, often purely nominal, or by a council of elders; but sometimes, when several villages become loosely federated, one particular elder is designated as a sort of figurehead.

Câmbio tells me that Barnacle is not the supreme chief, but he is the "oldest one." There are older men around, so I realize that "the oldest one" is a title rather than a reference to age. It appears that among the chiefs in the area Barnacle is more widely respected and more frequently consulted than all the others. Câmbio adds that he is "the one who remembers." After a little groping, I understand that this is another title, apparently granted to an expert in rituals. While describing him that way, Câmbio gives Barnacle a look both casual and respectful.

The one who remembers follows us with an impenetrable gaze as we stroll on toward the village.

2

Câmbio

This village is on a slight elevation, a sort of rambling forested little plateau. It is also bigger than the makeshift villages we've moved in and out of: at least twenty huts ring a circular plaza only sixty or seventy yards across. But it takes a while to gain a complete sense of the layout because enough silk-cotton trees and rubber trees have been left standing among the huts and even in the center of the plaza to weave a decent roof of leaves over the community. This is the first time I've seen such an arrangement. The smaller trees and underbrush have been cut; the scrub is worn down from the come and go of feet. Still, only a plane banking very close to the treetops would allow an experienced eye to notice that the canopy is unusually thin. I suppose someone knowing that the village is here could find it. But who knows it is here?

"My" tribe is still in the process of being welcomed and escorted in and made to share the reacquaintance process with the hosts. I see now many of "my" warriors, not just Barnacle, being surrounded by their kin. Then the men sit on logs in the standard fashion, in preparation of the "it is good" routine. But the reacquaintances are reduced here to skeleton performances of about one minute each, after which women start bringing forth something that turns our crowd into a horde of hungry beasts: turtles stripped of their plastrons and roasted in their shells, smoked fish, and manioc cakes.

In a second, I'm on my ass in the clearing, ignoring bugs that promptly start crawling over my legs (they look like kitchen roaches except that they are twice as big). I grab with both hands several pieces of turtle meat, bite into the first one so hard that my teeth shake in their sockets, feel how an unchewed piece slides down my throat before I can even taste it. Oiled by its own juice, it just slips down, making a painful bulge in my oesophagus.

Never mind, I push it down with an unchewed jawful of manioc. My eyes goggle out, my brain loses its oxygen, I queasily hear the whole mess break into my stomach with an audible rumble. Never mind that either, I'm already tearing another mouthful, while a burp wells up from my stomach and whizzes out through my clenched jaws. Gulping, gobbling, gorging, I respond to a yell of *more! more! more!* echoing out of every cell of my body. I lick, suck, slurp, rend, chew, till my blood sugar, shooting back to a more adequate level, fogs up my eyes, and I feel drunk, drunk with food, drunk with momentary survival.

Then I get up and inspect the place. Youngsters notice my movement and start trailing me, carrying pieces of meat and biting and chewing as they follow me. When I look at them, they grin, their expressions greasily friendly. I see Barnacle eating on one of the conference logs where the men were reacquainted, biting and tearing with similar ferocity. Flies and mosquitoes are slapped off naked bodies by sticky fingers and clammy palms. Belches, gurgles, farts break the sloshy music of chewing and swallowing produced by the whole community. Right now, my brain still clouded up by hunger, my intellect silent, my sense of decorum canceled out, I'm one of them too, in no way different.

I've always liked turtle meat—and this time it is utterly delicious. Teddy Roosevelt, in his *Through the Brazilian Wilderness*, mentioned what "good eating" jaguars and pumas were and confessed his regret for not trying lions while in Africa. Maybe after sufficient starvation I can learn to like mashed bugs and rotten caiman eggs and other such gastronomic exotica. Hell, maybe I'm stuck with this tribe, maybe I'm over the line already.

A little later, I lean against one of the trees, fighting drowsiness. Amazing, but no one else seems sleepy yet, while I can't even stand up: my knees bend, my back skids along the tree trunk. The coarseness of the bark scratches my back delightfully: I enjoy it so much that I stagger up again and repeat the motion. Like a replete beast. I've stuffed myself, and now I'm scratching.

Then I sit, feel on my shoulders the sting of ants I collected rubbing against the bark, and just don't care. The shutters of my eyelids hang down, but under their soothing darkness I still see. I see men arriving from the bush, carrying armfuls of hacked vines, green ones. Not good to fuel the fire. What are they for, building extra huts? Too short, not sturdy enough. My thought gets tired, I don't care what they're for, I'll find out later or tomorrow—there is a tomorrow.

Close by, next to a good-sized fire, several women are chewing manioc mash. They rake their throats often, spitting blobs of manioc and saliva into big calabashes, sipping water from gourds when their throats go dry, squirting it out again into the drink. Gourds and calabashes are what's left of the round fruit of Crescentia trees. Nature's pottery. Fancier pots and drinking bowls are made of human skulls. If I die here, what part of me will be shaped into a useful tool by Indian hands? My skull, for a bowl? My forearm bones, cubitus, radius, long and lean, excellent as planting tools? My heel bone as a spear tip? These tribes find a use for every piece of the human skeleton. Even the vertebrae: strung together, they make heavy, noisy, appreciated necklaces.

I don't want to die here. I don't want any of us to die here, as part of a suicidal rite.

But we won't die without a party: these women are making *masato*, an indigenous beer. It will take their

saliva two to three days to ferment the manioc paste into
a milky inebriating drink, clumpy and sour and really
awful. There's still a little time. My eyes are almost closed.
The calabashes shake and rattle as the naked women
move among them to reach the empty ones. My eyes close,
open, close again. Under my eyelids the clearing stretches
in all directions; the canopy above me becomes a forest of
green stalactites. I'm in a cave, filled with statues of beasts
and people. Groping, crawling at random, I notice that
the statues come alive on my passage, then repetrify. That
strikes me as unspeakably meaningful. Light fills me
gently, blue, tender light, the light of revelations. I hear a
source, whispering nearby. I'm in the beginning.

When the howlers wake me, it's Dawn. Dawn of the next
day. Realizing that, I jump as sprightly as I can having
been awake two seconds, and inspect my clothes for
crawling creatures. Finding none, I breathe. I have slept
on the forest floor.

My body hurts from stiffness. Several Indians, all young
males, notice that I'm up and drift closer, but their
curiosity seems moderate. A friendly face breaks through
their loose circle, a warm smile puts me back in a world
of hope, and I exchange morning greetings with Câmbio,
in Portuguese — how wonderful to be able to share a
language! Câmbio saved me some breakfast in the shape
of a piece of beiju folded around a filling of fish, looking
like a coarse taco; as I'm about to bring it to my mouth,
smoke hits my bleary eyes, its odor abrades my nostrils
and throat, and a blast of heat slaps my face.

I open my eyes wide, fearing that the forest is on fire.
Muscular warriors are standing in the clearing around a
pulsating mass of flames shooting up from a pile of objects
shriveling and squirming in the blaze like penitents' bodies.
A broad blast of smoke thunders upward, and charred
fragments of canopy fall back over the fire and the shiny
ring of naked warriors.

The hours of rest were enough to restore to my body its

whole capacity for anxiety. Instantly I hum from it like a pinched string and search Câmbio's eyes, afraid to ask him what this is about, because now there will be no confusion in the answer. But Câmbio looks at my hand clutching the piece of beiju, seems concerned that I'm not eating it, and displays every sign of friendly normality.

"What's this?" I ask.

He looks at the fire. With some fascination, as if this was a rarely witnessed ceremony. And that's exactly what he calls it when he answers me. A *cerimónia*, over. I hold myself from landing my hands on his shoulders, to shake him, to snatch him over, across twenty thousand years of cultural distance, into my way of doing and understanding things. What sort of ceremony is he talking about? What is its meaning?

I feel like Barnacle's shadow, prehistoric, hirsute, has reoccupied my horizon.

"We're returning," he says, "over. These things die here, so we can return."

I'm transcribing the dialogue from memory. Filling in some words implied at the time, translating some lines unliterally, but on the whole certain of the general meaning. So they can return. I nod seriously, as if finding the notion neither outlandish nor comical. Return where? To a younger age, over, he responds, somewhat embarrassed—there is a civilizado level in him which he cannot share with me without divorcing himself from what we're witnessing. Yet what we're witnessing is so aggressively dramatic, so hard to mock or treat with skepticism, especially right now, while his fellow tribesmen are engaged in it.

"You mean you're going back in time?" I ask the question without any sense of ridicule.

He responds, no, not going back. Returning, over. He makes a circular gesture with his arm and uses a Portuguese expression, *ia e volta*, which means to go and turn back, and is used in airline lingo to signify round trip. So they are returning. To a time before they had those—he points at the utensils and weapons cracking in the blaze. But they could take those along, I protest—such things are useful? They are the wealth of the tribe; why destroy them? Because their spirits are stopping the tribe, over. They are stopping it from returning. All objects are inhabited by spirits, he explains, and these particular ones, being household spirits, are the strongest and most jealous—Câmbio describes them almost as an army of possessive, bigoted relatives. I stop him to clarify a notion which suddenly appears to me as terribly important: I thought that time, time itself, resided in those objects. Which made their destruction a prelaunch operation, so to speak, without which the tribe couldn't blast off into that free time, where neither direction nor duration were set or uniform.

That is too much of a pile of abstractions for him. He watches me, blinking. I simplify it as much as I can, and after some thinking and frowning he agrees that there is time in objects. Just like there are spirits in them. In that sort of coresidence he sees no contradiction. Anyway, in order to go and return in time (*"ia e volta no tempo"* is how he puts it) a tribe has to break its bond with its current life. Therefore, its valuables must be destroyed; the same with its huts and villages. Over and over. That operation of successive destructions, of repeated relocation, constitutes the voyage itself.

That at least explains what they were doing when I met them. They were sailing in time. Loosening bond after bond with each makeshift village they erected and then left behind. Getting freer and freer with every crop of tools and weapons they broke and put to the torch.

I ask Câmbio what will happen once the tribe reaches its destination. He grins and his open arms hug the clearing, the huts, the canopy, maybe even the sky beyond it.

"To hell with all this here, over." There is in his gesture and grin a feeling of deliverance, a wonderful hope that by going through with the ritual, this painful and complicated present will be shaken off.

Meanwhile, the fire wafts clouds of smoke at us. Câmbio's eyes smart and blink but he stays where he is, as if filling himself with the scene's symbolic power. I ask him where they expect to arrive at the end of their mysterious journey. After some groping for the right word, he tells me that their destination is the *nascente*. Which means "birthplace," or "beginning." Having gotten thus far, Câmbio studies my face, and his embarrassment seems allayed by my reaction: I display not the least bit of sarcasm.

If anything, I must be showing concern. I align in my mind what I've just heard with Barnacle's earlier message, and wonder whether I should test somehow the state of my own senses. Maybe do multiplication exercises on the little paper I have left. No, there's no time for that. I have Câmbio here, willing to talk. I have to pull out of him everything that can explain what I've experienced.

I convince Câmbio to step away with me, behind the huts and toward the trees. Maybe he understands why. He accompanies me without resistance.

I corner him into a triangle of low bushes closed on two sides by trees and on the third by an ugly, depthless view of the crude backs of two huts. Beyond them is the clearing's opening, the smoke rising from the immolation of those spirits residing in arrows, manioc graters, and pots, and the nation to whom Câmbio belongs.

I ask questions. I get answers.

Câmbio doesn't remember a time when the tribe was not on the move, which is why he knows that he was born on the river's Peruvian shore but not exactly where. Somewhere downstream. Always, the pattern was to migrate ahead of the spearhead of development. Anything predicting development was a signal for another cycle of nomadism. Six or seven years earlier, however—just before Câmbio's spell with that baptist mission—forest tribesmen in contact with acculturated Indians living downstream became aware of rumors of settlement. An invasion of impoverished farmers from the northeast states was predicted. Prospectors, road builders, and land agents were soon to rush in and secure bridgehead areas, accompanied by *pistoleiros* ready to shoot, just like the gunboats chugging upriver did, decades earlier.

The decision, apparently spontaneously made by several tribal groups, was a mass exodus upriver. That moment coincided with Câmbio's own flight into that baptist mission, so he confesses that he didn't witness how the decision for a mass exodus was made. The result, however, was that a number of tribal groups started upstream, apparently on both shores of the Javari, on trails distant enough so that massive movement would not be noticed from the air.

But Câmbio, I say, that kind of invasion is not happening here. It is happening in Mato Grosso and in Rondônia. But not upstream from Leticia, not on the Javari. There is modest settlement in progress at various points along the Javari's course, but no invasion yet, certainly not up here.

He listens attentively and shrugs. That was the rumor. Some tribal groups ignored it, and some decided not to take chances.

I ask him how many tribespeople were involved in that migration. He shrugs again—he doesn't know. He insists that some did meet settlers and clashes ensued. In one case, a group of Indians caught a party of settlers sailing up with their *pistoleiros*, their hired guns, over. They disarmed them, tied them to trees, over, smeared them with wild honey, over, and left them to the curiosity of army ants and other jungle creatures. Over and out.

Then came the exodus, during which certain groups lost so many members they were forced to blend with others, some even with traditional rivals. I know that a tribe falling below a head count of a hundred has a hard time surviving. They tried to replenish their population, Câmbio adds, by stealing people. Other Indians or mestizo river dwellers, children or girls grown enough to be mothers.

So that's what brought them here, over, he concludes, and opens his arms wide, justifying the smoky ceremony behind us. His expression is disarmingly peaceful, the expression of a human who never had in his conscious life an opportunity to resist or at least argue with the larger powers shaping his fate.

Câmbio, I say, all this is sad, very sad. But what your oldest headman is doing is not just leading his people upstream. He is leading them into something else, a ceremony that has all the appearances of a death rite.

Câmbio looks at me. He nods. Yes. That is what the old one is doing. Because there is nowhere left to go. I jump, point at the dense forest, this entangled rampart of life whose noise and restlessness, stimulated by the fire, attests to its vigor and size. Câmbio, I say, even if thousands of acres of rain forest were razed every day, there is enough wilderness left for this tribe to hide in for many, many years. The old one . . . the old one doesn't know. The old one might be crazy . . .

No, Câmbio answers. Even if the settlers are not coming now, they will be coming soon. And the prospectors and government agents will come too, with airplanes and guns and alcohol.

I have no choice but to link that expectation with what I've lived for the last two weeks. So what's left for them to retreat into? The beginning?

He nods, with the same disarming quality, of total lack of choice.

"What is the beginning, Câmbio?"

He narrows his eyes. His glance, direct and uncalculating, becomes opaque, as if turning to look inside. He seems reluctant to take me further, or maybe to picture for himself that beginning. I swallow nervously. I lean closer and pressure him. "What is that damn beginning, Câmbio?"

"You'll see," he mutters noncommittally. "You'll see,

Lowen, over."

Something makes me shiver, and I don't know whether it's his answer or my name—after so many days of not hearing it, the sound, just the sound of my own name has a hypnotic reality. Câmbio turns, ready to go back to his little nation, but I rush to block his way, overflowing with more questions. How does he know there is a beginning? Câmbio shrugs; he doesn't know, he just assumes. Who knows? The old one? Yes, the old one, confirms Câmbio, his body already leaning toward the space of the ritual, his features pulled down by a touch of reluctance, as if too much explaining amounted to a betrayal.

But I hammer on. "How does the old one know, Câmbio, has he been there?"

He hesitates, perhaps wondering how to answer, perhaps clearing up some notions in his own mind. He draws a breath, knots up his lips, almost defiantly, opens them again. No, he hasn't been there. None of them have. Yet the old one—

"The old one remembers, over," Câmbio announces.

Again he turns to go, but I'm not finished and I don't want to tread back into that clearing yet. I brought Câmbio out here so I could feel as free of the tribe's stimuli as possible (though I feel connected to them through a million thoughts). How does the old one remember something he's never visited?

He doesn't answer. I have no choice but to conclude that *remember* is used symbolically by the shaman with the radio talk, that what he's implying by it is some kind of magical knowledge. I take a breath and come to the core of my perplexity: I inform Câmbio that the old one told me about all this already.

Now I don't need to hold Câmbio here—he remains in my company of his own accord.

He shows some shock, though not a lot. I assure him that I speak no Mayoruna.

Maybe twenty seconds pass. Then Câmbio clears his

throat and opines that maybe Barnacle talked to me in the *outra língua*, the "other language." I make sure I understand what he is saying, and repeat that the old one talked to me without words, and Câmbio nods, that's the other language.

That's what Câmbio calls the beaming; the "other language." Here, however, Câmbio acts uninitiated. He doesn't speak the other language, though he knows that the elders do. *Língua velha*, he also calls it, the "old language," but when I ask whether it was prevalent at some earlier time in tribal history, he shrugs quietly. He doesn't know much about it at all, except that it's supposed to exist and be shared by the older tribesmen. I ask if the women share it, and he replies that he never heard of it being used or understood by women.

I ask him how the older men get their training in it, and about that Câmbio is at his vaguest. He finally opines that "they remember." He ponders for a long instant, as if trying to remember himself all he knows about this mode of communication, then repeats with somewhat more certainty: yes, that's it, they remember. But how they remember, he has no idea. The elders before them remembered too. I think about this, combine it with what else I know about tribal hierarchy; most experts report that there's not much of it, though they might be wrong. Tribal leadership roles are not hereditary; pretty much anyone can become a headman; any older male, if healthy and disposed to act as a knowledgeable busybody, will be treated as an elder.

I start wondering what *memory* means to this man, or to all these people. What special dignity or power does it confer to those carrying titles like "he who remembers."

The notion of the old one sharing his other vernacular with me has elevated me in Câmbio's eyes. Now he lingers with me, polite host, almost willing apprentice. And then . . . I get a sensation of message, though not from Câmbio. But it includes Câmbio. It seems to say that my reactions, my responses to these happenings are evidence that they are truly happening. I look at Câmbio, whose smile is at its friendliest, and feel like grabbing him and shaking him hard: What does that mean? What the hell have I become, the *proof* that their damn trip is taking place? And if so, why? Have they sensed a weakness on my part, an unwillingness to resist their nonsense? Have I suspended all my critical faculties? To what degree have I become impressionable?

Suddenly the strange silence of the sky above the canopy adds to my perplexity—am I unconsciously suppressing all the sounds of air traffic? The sounds I've been dying to hear for the last few days and yearned so much to differentiate among the jungle's howls and screeches that several times I took the gurgling of a distended bullfrog's throat as the turbulence of a rotor rattling above the canopy?

Again, the headman's primal shadow seems to reach toward me over the coarse crests of the huts, again I feel unfree and invaded.

At high speed, my mind goes over my experience, over the unexplained messages and the way I received them. Despite all my contradictory feelings I can't deny a sort of attachment to what I experienced. Resistant at first, I wondered whether I was losing my mind or having wakeful dreams. Yet I admitted the possibility of being contacted, and waited with increasing suspense for the next communication. I wanted to understand my captors, so I reached toward them with all my antennae deployed; the information had to come that way, since there was no other way. I learned to tolerate that amorphous background hum and discovered that the main source of the messages was Barnacle. That seemed more acceptable, though it put the contact on the unwanted terrain of hypnosis or telepathy, about which I know so little that I'd be hard-pressed to define them or even recognize their manifestations in other circumstances. Man being socially organized, being man before language as we know it, didn't seem so outlandish, though my common sense insisted that at such a level of development nonverbal messages had to be both very short and concretely focused on finding food, repulsing attacks from predators, finding shelter, mating. But the concepts that emerged through Barnacle's subsequent communications were sophisticated and lengthy. Time, a notion early man perhaps didn't harbor at all, except in the most restricted sense as awareness of one action happening before or after another, was presented to me as a flexible dimension, and despite the naive belief of its confinement in objects, it seemed to contain all the elements of a cosmogony; man's attempt to see himself in rapport with time was clearly the goal of Barnacle's most important and persistently pursued ritual manipulations. The concepts that were transmitted—which I worded in my mind in my own language, so the faults in translation were entirely mine— pointed not just to a community's painful transition, but to Barnacle's own dilemmas. His anxiety about the efficiency of his own magic. About not having room to maneuver, or fail. Meanwhile, the tribe actively acknowledged their belief about moving in time, toward the beginning. They severed their ties, repeatedly, with objects, abodes, locations. All these notions, one by one, became realities in my mind. And now . . . now . . .

Now what am I supposed to do—stay here and be their certificator? Again I feel like grabbing Câmbio and dragging him in front of that old man to voice my indignation, and even ridicule all this. So time comes in objects like milk in mothers, and if you smash objects you get rid of time—how sublimely concrete! And shuffling around in the bush over a hundred square miles is supposed to waltz us back across man's most puzzling riddle, time itself. Which would turn out to be nothing but a compliant mush of duration, ready to be kneaded at will by a few hundred Indians otherwise unwilling to undergo much less demanding changes, like putting on T-shirts and using matches to light fires!

Yet I feel invested in the situation, I have a responsibility regarding its outcome. Someone has to denounce the ritual and protest the hardships it imposes on these people, and if I'm to be the one, so be it. The trust Barnacle showed me is not the least of my problems. I gained something by going along. I felt closer to nature than ever before. I understood and felt and perceived with all of myself, in a wonderfully unspecialized manner. The promise of a disclosure has become so central to my emotions that I've delayed picking up any survival tools from those piles of smashed appliances. Instead, I've been hanging on, hoping for a revelation.

And now . . .

I make it clear to Câmbio that I want to be by myself. Though surprised by my brusqueness, he smiles and heads back into the clearing.

I need to be totally alone. I need to recapture the person I was just weeks ago, to identify that person through some familiar feature, a gesture, a thought, anything, no matter how trivial or foolish, so I can stop this invasion that started with my senses and is progressing now toward the loftiest seat of my being, my mind and its belief in my right to survive. I'm not a cell, not a molecule, not an ant in a column of blindly purposeful comrades, but a modern man.

If I am to survive, I must maintain and project a massively self-generated sense of who I am. I must pump out of the depth of my psyche all my residual energy, molding and compacting it like a weapon, so I can arm myself with it and stride back into that village, ready for a one-man insurrection.

I start the multiplication table in my mind, lose my focus, err, try again, give up. I rub my hands over my face and gather no particular impression of familiarity. I feel how the tribe sucks my mind away, the way the forest's ripe viridity absorbs my eyesight, melting it into a blur of color which is no longer color, no longer anything — except a triumph of this primal abundance, living and dying and living.

The Rio Javari, looking northwest along the boundary between Peru (left) and Brazil (right). It flows through mostly virgin flatland rain forest and is about as meandering and serpentine as a river can be.

Amazonia, the sea of green, from the air. Under the green mask of the foliage, travelers sought for El Dorado, or for mystery tribes like the Mayoruna.

Rivers are like jungle highways, and also form airport runways - landings must be made on infrequent estirones, straight stretches unencumbered by the trunks of fallen trees.

Lupuna, the "lighthouse tree," used as a landmark for navigation on rivers and for aircraft landings.

People living in rain forests rarely see "vistas" - the forest is a closed world where the clock of history stops.

The upper Apurímac near its source, where it is formed by converging brooks from the Cailloma basin.

McIntyre and a 500-year-old yareta plant, at 16,000 feet. These tough plants can repel an axe blade, and for more than a century have been excavated (sometimes with dynamite) for firewood. They are now rare except at extreme altitudes.

McIntyre at 18,383 feet, on Mismi's Choquecorao Ridge, atop the Continental Divide. The source was sighted from this spot.

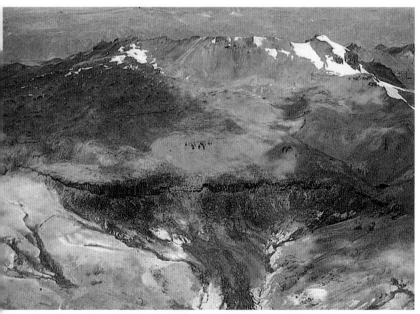

The Cailloma basin, whose rivulets feed the Apurímac. This was one of the driest years in history: the region is usually covered with snowfields. Laguna McIntyre is just below the ridge, to the right of centre.

Self-portrait: McIntyre drinking from the source.

A Mayoruna couple.

Mayoruna woman with
cat-whisker tattoos.

Canoes loaded to take McIntyre back to rendezvous with plane. Agent Silva accompanied McIntyre on the three-day trip hoping the pilot would spare him some gasoline. One canoe holds game: a deer and a howler monkey.

To recapture myself better, I face the forest.

The sensation that emerges in me as I stare at the green jumble of branches, stems, and creepers is gentle and carries no sadness or awareness of a fresh disaster. In fact, I only become aware of it when I realize that though I could flee into the forest right now, I have no interest in doing it. To encourage myself into action, I picture myself marching across to the closest tributary, a plan I've rehearsed in my mind, and then floating down to join the world I came from.

The action appears senseless: Escape from what? Into what? What lies ahead is made of the same rivers, of the same distances and forms of terrain filled with countless species of plants and animals, but it is empty of modern humankind. No one like me is out there. That doesn't mean that the civilizado world has disappeared. Simply that it hasn't appeared yet.

In my mind I mention Leticia and other names of river cities. They sound invented. Leticia isn't there. Leticia, Manaus, Belém, Brazil—they are nonexistent, their populations also nonexistent. They haven't happened yet. The Conquest itself hasn't happened yet. I am in the pre-Conquest time.

I stare at the forest. The pristine quality of leaf and stem grows, becomes overpowering. The forest's richness is vibrant and confident, as if backed up by unlimited space. The forest is back to what it was, its rustle so whole that I hear my blood charging up with it. But there are no humans. Barnacle's people returned, orbiting across time, to be the first humans in a territory of unthreatened, uncounted, and unnamed life-forms. And I went back with them.

The sensation lasts, then sinks to the depth of my mind and settles. Subdued, reconciled, like a memory.

3

Câmbio II

I step back into the clearing, undecided. Even if none of this were true, if these people's hope for deliverance were just folklore and nothing else, the beauty of that hope deserves protection. Who am I to unleash upon them a different truth?

The clearing seems so wide and full of people. Here some women are grating manioc; there men are erecting a string of little huts (smaller than family units; I wonder about their use). Right past those huts goes Tia—she is very thin, her vertebrae looking like a string of big, knotty beads hanging down her naked back. She passes Câmbio, who gives her no acknowledgment in the obvious fashion of civilizados, yet I know that he knows her and she knows him. All these people know each other. I spot Zonia in a group of girls her age. Her expression is still a little numb, but her gestures have recovered their vitality— a far cry from what she looked like the morning when I glimpsed her lover's body in that coffin of twined branches. I see a noisy, lively bunch of children gathered in the center of the clearing. A detail of women is busy rubbing the children's restless little bodies, already painted black with genipap, with a shiny oily substance, probably some resin. The resin makes the genipap paint shine brightly—some of those little arms, swinging around fussily, glitter and catch the light as if they were chromed. I must find out why those children are getting painted.

I step on something, and when I look down I see some fishhooks, carved out of wood and barbed menacingly with a big dark thorn affixed inside the hook's closure. There are three of them. They must have fallen out of a basket or out of someone's hand when the household possessions were being gathered during this morning's ceremony.

I sweep the clearing with my eyes, find no stares focused on me. As nimbly as I can, I kneel, clutch the fishhooks all three at once, one almost cutting my palm, and stuff them in my pocket. If I manage to escape downriver, these should be enough for my first few meals. I'll make other hooks with my knife, or use timbo if I manage to find it on the shores. It is a plant whose tendrils, crushed, secrete a drug which numbs fish without contaminating their meat. I was taught how to use it on the Xingu. I know how to fish with this one native narcotic. The Indians in both the Amazon and Orinoco basins are trained to use many varieties of such plants.

Minutes ago, I lived a strong sensation of being in pre-Conquest time. Now I feel that my own world exists again. That in itself is encouraging.

I rise, start moving again toward those children, and spot Barnacle coming in from the other side of the clearing. He looks so regal that at first I don't recognize him: he wears a great diadem of macaw feathers and one parrot feather in each nostril. He walks up to the children, stops and stands supervising the oiling of their bodies. A couple of girls arrive carrying shapeless little bales of kapok, the whitish fluff of the silk-cotton tree. They pluck tufts of kapok out of the bales, stick them on the kids' oily bodies, take more handfuls of kapok, throw them at the children again. The children laugh, scream, and kick, the girls and women laugh, and Barnacle looms over all of them, smiling with his obsidian teeth.

I know what he feels. And I know what it means, to smear children with resin and then decorate them with kapok fluff. These are puberty rites, though none of these children are pubertal. The age of the puberty rites has been lowered to pronounce them men and women now, not later. I know why. There is no later. I know all there is to know about this scene, attesting so joyfully, so proudly, to the endurance of tradition. We are in communication right now, the headman and I. His psyche has penetrated mine.

Barnacle hovers over the preparations to the rites. Among the children being smeared and feathered up is Tuti, who fusses and fights, displaying the privileged obnoxiousness of a royal son. Barnacle does nothing to discipline him, just grins. I feel a strong conviction that the two are in contact now, and not just by this smiling awareness of each other. Father and son are talking on the nonverbal track. About the continuity of their little nation, signified in such rituals. About time, which they have conquered. About Tuti's own obligation to pass on the rites and the *língua velha* which the old man is teaching him right this instant, while I target both with my rather jealous civilizado glance. Yes, all that makes sense. Barnacle is an able teacher and Tuti an enthusiastic student. They are surrounded by a community convinced of the power of its rituals. Raised in such hypnotic oneness, Tuti will be a strong upholder of the tradition.

The village is close to a waterway. I keep seeing people with calabashes traipsing forth and bringing them back filled with water. Some resupply the women who are still preparing the masato. Absorbed in their work, they masticate the manioc, spit out the resulting paste, take water in their mouths, spit it over that sour-smelling paste, gulp water again, squirt again, wiping clammy faces with hands sticky from that thick, nutritious glue.

I must bathe. Good for my brain, and against the oppressive heat.

*

A few minutes later I'm in the river.

On the bank, a *Bignonia unguis-cati*, in bloom, drapes a big tree in a robe of gold. The flowers are yellow like the plumage of canary birds, and shaped exquisitely: tiny trumpets, ending in petals like sweet little lobes. Underneath, pronged little supports cling to the bark. They look like cat claws. I see them, and they are *real*. I savor the sight, for once happy that I don't have my camera, that nothing is interfering between me and this moment.

I let the river run past me, feeling how its waters, divided by my body, rush to meet again, while there's a similar feeling in me—of streams coming together, of pieces falling into place. Otherwise I am weary, undernourished, my shoulders are cratered with broken pustules, I wince thinking of the state of my teeth. And I have no sense of the immediate or the distant future.

I get out of the water and wash my clothes, then spread them on the shore and sit by them while they dry. When they are halfway done, I dive back in for a final rinse.

"*Olá, Lowen!*"

I jump at the sound of my name. I whip around and see Câmbio on the shore, emerging statuesquely above the brush. The little shaman is armed: a spear rises from his right fist, slashing the air vertically.

Anywhere else in the world, an adversary of his size would make me smile. Here, he and his weapon sink an I.V. of alertness into my body. Yet his mouth is grinning, sending ripples of friendliness out across his face. And then I realize that what he is holding is not a spear, but a stick.

He drops his stick, gets in, and swims alongside me. Other Indians appear, mothers with children too young to have been included in the puberty rites. They trample into the water, start dousing themselves, swimming, playing. My pants and shirt are on the shore, unattended; I must get back to them before I find an Indian trying them on, offering me instead what he is wearing—a belt of river shells, or just a feather (such an exchange happened to me once, after I went swimming in Lake Ipavu with the Kamayura).

But I feel no urge to rush and check on my clothes. They don't matter anymore.

Câmbio swims athletically and yet smoothly, a skill he undoubtedly learned at the same time he learned to walk. He floats on his back, rises, and blows water out of one nostril, then the other, wades over to where I sit in two feet of almost cool water, and we spend a few moments talking. I ask about the children. Yes, the ones painted with genipap and adorned with kapok will receive their puberty rites. The little girls will be locked up in the huts I saw being built and will be kept there for about six months, fed through a passage in the wall and visited only by their mothers or aunts, who will give them an elementary sexual education. After six months they will step out to the light of the clearing again, bleary-eyed and unkempt, but schooled. Future husbands and wives will then line up and choose each other. I remark that they are not old enough to be husbands and wives, nor will they be in six months.

Câmbio knows that. He watches me with a warm, open stare and explains that the kids are receiving their rites so they can step prepared into the beginning.

I change the subject. I ask him if he knows of any dictionary of their language, previously compiled by missionaries or in the works right now. He remembers the mission's library but has never seen or heard of such a dictionary. Nor has he heard of the two Harriets' efforts to contact his fellow tribesmen. He calls his language Matse (I remember some authors interchangeably using the names Mayoruna and Matse) and is not aware of any other Indian lingo resembling it. In Matse, the Javari River is called *Ateahwah*. I remember Barnacle and his shamans prattling back and forth *"Ateahwah? Ateahwah?"* on the afternoon of my capture. So I was right; they *were* meaning the Javari River. I ask Câmbio about the source of the Javari. He's only seen it once. I should let him

describe it, but instead of doing that, I burst forth and ask
whether it cascades out of a mountain.

My strong reaction impresses him. He gives me a close
look, then confirms slowly that the source is in a
mountain. It's a waterfall, a few days upstream.

A waterfall.

The image of that twin jeweled jet, glittering preciously
down the green incline, is so vivid in my mind that it
makes me wonder about Câmbio's answer. Is he telling me
the truth? Is he agreeing with me just to humor me, as
Indians sometimes do when talking to civilizados?

He's probably wondering how I know about it, so I tell
him that I read descriptions of it. He seems to accept the
explanation. The moment passes, but I'm left inside with a
wonderful resonance. The fact that there was reality to
that moment when I sat looking at a spot known to just a
few humans gives me a unique sense of completion.

While all of this falls into place, we are still sitting in
the river.

It seems that the Mayoruna alphabet has under twenty
phonemes; I've been aware for a while of the repetitiveness
of their sounds, among which I hear nothing like our *f,g,*
or *r*. Instead, *b,p,sh,* and *ts* are frequent and salient, and
the vowels clear and elongated. The vowel/consonant
alternation is quite regular, giving the language a sort of
monotonous musicality. I ask the equivalents for the first
words that come to my mind. "Mother" is *tita*, "father"
papa(!), "son" *mado*, "brother" *utsi. Shubu* is "house." *Aca*
is "heron" and *isa* "porcupine." *Opa* means "dog."
Abukkid means "monkey." "Arrow" is *pia*.

I repeat the words, hoping to memorize them, promising
myself to jot them down later. In certain cases, like *pia*,
"arrow," I have a spontaneous and hard-to-explain sense
of the propriety of the term, of how fittingly the sounds
have been chosen to represent the object. Others strike me
as incredibly unexpected, the selection of their sounds
irregular and mysterious. Like *pucacunga*, a bird Câmbio

shows me fluttering under the low foliage; smallish, undistinguished except for a collar of red plumes. Why *pucacunga*? But what savant will ever be able to reconstruct the process of naming things?

The Mayoruna have a rich vocabulary, especially when it comes to flora and fauna. Câmbio rattles off plenty of names for species of birds and monkeys, which I forget right away. As for the trees, the varieties of palms alone are legion. I'm familiar with none of their names, just like the Mayoruna are totally ignorant of their Spanish or Portuguese equivalents. The huge *sumauma* tree, one of the best known species in the Amazon Basin, they call *uirapa*.

We climb ashore again, and among other little signs of friendliness Câmbio bends to help me pick up my clothes. Thank God that I'm quicker; I grab my pants and feel in their pocket the clawlike sharpness of the fishhooks. I pull my pants on guiltily, thankful that he isn't versed in the tribal ESP. How would he react if he guessed that I'm planning an escape?

Interesting question. I don't want to find out the answer.

When we get back to the village, there are more boys and girls in the middle of the clearing; they are contained there with some difficulty by a little army of women, this time unsupervised by Barnacle, whom I fail to locate anywhere.

I notice, however, that both women and children are acting with increased glee, as if the headman's momentary absence lifted an omen. The children are so excited that they wrestle and run constantly, showing off their vitality and readiness to enter adult life. The girls are even wilder than the boys. Not one of the girls has breasts yet. I see more women abandoning the cooking and joining the fun of painting and struggling with those slippery tarred and feathered bodies—Zonia and Tia are among them. They obviously enjoy the touching that the ceremony encourages. Zonia paints up one little boy after another, joking throughout with other women; there's a lot of laughter. They don't look like the depressed population they were yesterday. I wonder whether they could abandon themselves to such a celebration of existence and its joyful passages right before ending their lives.

Because as I watch the crowd I have the sense that this, these morning hours filled with excited shouts, are *it*: the expiration, the fall of the curtain.

Smoke is coming from the other side of the clearing; taking my eyes off the prancing and prating horde, I see warriors grouped there, smoking big cigars of green tobacco. Good. Maybe I'll get one; my palate, after so many days without spices, craves the pungency of anything, even reeky green tobacco. Some of those smoking warriors are the fathers of the boys and girls being tarred and feathered by their mothers and older sisters and cousins. They smoke and watch their flesh and blood get ready for the passage.

But the ceremony, as yet, isn't starting.

It's not starting, Câmbio enlightens me, because we are all going to be named again. We will receive brand-new names and symbols of our guiding spirits. That is a sign that we are very close to the beginning. One doesn't enter the beginning marked by one's old name.

"So we are close to the beginning?" I ask.

I breathe deeply, to calm the pounding in my chest.

"Very close, over."

"And how d'you know we're so close?"

"Didn't you notice? Time has *started to fall off.*"

He phrases it exactly that way, and I understand it so perfectly, I connect with that line so sincerely that I wish with all my heart that this was, this could be true. Time would start to *fall off.* Like a useless layer of clothes, like these rumpled, damp pants I'm wearing (I ought perhaps to take them off and fling them into the bush, letting some coatis nest in them).

And when did your time start to fall off? I ask. Yesterday morning, he replies with precision, when the tribe got rid of its belongings (I feel the fishhooks in my

pocket; like a testimony; and also like a secret but
desperate clinging to the concrete expressions of time).
When the canopy of leaves, singed by the hot breath of
the flames, filled up with howls and screeches and cackles
and other noises, and the noise of planes or any other
civilizado machinery wasn't one of them.

I point upward. What if we started hearing a plane,
right now?

"No," answers Câmbio simply. I blink, perplexed: No,
we won't? No, we've left planes and all other such vehicles
behind? The way we left behind those manioc grinders and
pots? Are we breathing the air of thousands of years ago,
when neither planes nor manioc grinders had yet occurred
to the human mind?

He refuses to elaborate. My certainty of the end, not of
the beginning, grows stronger. I have to make an effort to
keep speaking to him.

"What did they call you at that mission?" I ask him.

"The operator gave me a *nome português*, 'Portuguese
name,' over. He called me Tito."

"You could've stayed on at that mission, Tito, or moved
to Leticia or some other town. Why didn't you?"

He thinks, then answers that he couldn't get used to one
thing. The wavering *ca'ah*, or total lack of it, of the
chotac. *Chotac* is the term by which the Mayoruna
designate outsiders, particularly *civilizados*.

"What is *ca'ah*?"

He explains to me that everything and everyone has a
ca'ah, which is the first abstract Mayoruna notion I'm
faced with. *Ca'ah* means identity, but it contains a strong
element of intent, of purpose. I keep asking questions, he
gives me examples, and it becomes apparent that a man's
ca'ah is his direction in life. It is contained in his spirit,
which is mysterious, but it is controlled and corrected by
his conscious decisions. I think fleetingly of karma, which
is more than destiny. Of the Samoan mana, which is a
man's power, projected in his gestures and rooted in his
inner consistency.

Câmbio is nonplussed by the white people's contradictory, self-defeating *ca'ah*. "How can some of them behave so kindly, while others . . ." Missing the word, he swells his cheeks, then shoots a volley of air bullets, matching amazingly well the sound of an automatic rifle. Things like that convinced Câmbio that in the civilizados' contradictions lay a sort of curse. He tried to understand the regulating principle, the main jinx, so to speak, that ran the civilizados' lives. He couldn't, and he went back to his tribe.

He asks me what my *ca'ah* is. After some hesitation, I explain that "my *ca'ah* is to find things and photograph them." He wants to know what things. All sorts of things—I shrug—like the source of the big river that receives the flow of the Javari.

For source, I use the Portuguese word *nascente*—beginning, the same word he's been using for beginning of time. He doesn't seem confused by that. He narrows his eyes to daggers, as if checking an inward image of what I've said. Then he smiles, apparently appreciating my *ca'ah*. "*O nascente do rio, sim*," he mumbles, the beginning of the river. I draw a summary map of the river on the ground for him. With its mouth on the Atlantic coast, its main tributaries, and its Andean feedwaters, primary freshets formed by the snow of the peaks.

Halfway through, he shakes his head.

"The source is not where you think. It's up there, over."

And he points at the forest's canopy.

"In the trees?"

"In the sky, over."

"How do you know that, Tito?"

"The source has to be in the sky, over. Rain comes from the sky. Rain—that's what the river is."

I nod, remembering the twin waterfall and myself staggering toward it as if toward a hallucination. Those thundering, milky veins came from the sky. The other source, the one lost among the gelid crests of the Andes, comes also from the sky.

During this conversation, our faces have gotten as close as Indian etiquette allows. Câmbio talks to me, not at me, and his eyes and mine are in frequent contact. I ask him whether he knows any legends about the big river. He wrinkles his forehead, perhaps silently checking his vocabulary, then relates the following fable: Once upon a time, the big river flowed in the sky. Its whole valley was carried on clouds, fastened to the clouds with bulky liana ropes. Many people lived in the valley in the sky in perfect harmony. But one day a curious bunch of little girls untied one of the ropes. That was enough to undo the whole: rope upon rope snapped under the pressure, and the valley crashed onto earth. Thus the big river split into thousands of smaller rivers, and the sky, sad over the loss, cried its first rain.

Câmbio finishes the fable and I smile: this cosmology attributes the original catastrophe to the curiosity of women. Its moral is unconsciously modern: one snapped rope undid the balance, just like one ecological link, destroyed, could change the planet's fate. I feel overwhelmed that this anonymous tribesman sees the world as I do: so healthy in its functional design, but so vulnerable in its balance. But Câmbio's story is very logical, too logical and causative. Indian legends aren't usually like that. Most of them start with: There were three brothers and then there was a fourth and a fifth—for in the middle of the narration the storyteller often realizes that a fourth character is needed, and a fifth, and throws them in. That's how those stories are told, with interruptions and corrections, without regard for logic, because so many of them are spontaneously invented at the campfire. The storyteller doesn't narrate to make a moral point, but to share with the audience a sense of wonderment caused by a unique exploit. He introduces freely all sorts of new elements, often conflicting with the old ones—some are related to whatever is central to his psyche, but most are incidents or accidents recently occurred to him, to his kin, or to his friends. Often the audience identifies the familiar elements and laughs.

A lot of the charm of these stories lies in their irrationality: the jaguar, being widowed, decides he's had enough of singleness and marries no one else but the moon, who bears him a child in human shape. The child travels to earth, meets a big snake, and chops it up with his ax. The chopped-up pieces turn into manioc tubers. Or man is created as a result of a god's blunder. A deity, deciding to make himself a toy, fashions it from clay in the shape of a man, puts it in the oven, and forgets about it, and when he remembers to pull it out the clay has grown hard and dark and hot. The god burns his fingers, drops the effigy, and curses. From the hand of the god, the effigy falls to earth and becomes the first human. Lacking symmetry and logic, such myths nevertheless capture everyone's attention. They have a unique power to satisfy individual hopes and to dissolve traumatic lingerings from the daily encounters with danger and death. They teach the audience a sense of freedom to which imagination, luck, and an individual's own daring participate equally. Though I have heard and read many Indian legends, I have found in none the message of obedience of established religions.

We did it the same way, once. But then the official clergies stepped in, rewriting and regulating myths and ascribing to their scenes symbolic functions to be reenacted by an indoctrinated population. They engraved the myth on the tablet and kept it there. A body of priesthood with strong social purposes went at it most seriously, asking the congregations to believe, but above all to conform. Stories with clear beginnings, middles, and ends suggest manipulation of the audience, and I smell some of that in Câmbio's own story. It has lost the rough and shoddy feel of spontaneous inspiration. It is too round and moralistic. A father confessor stood by, straightening its meanderings and bringing its dramatics into the fold of message.

I breathe deeply. *"Os civilizados tem alguma coisa quê voce quer?"* I ask in a friendly voice, "Do civilizados have anything that you miss?"

"*Ouero, fósforos e doces*," Cambio says with a grin, "I miss matches and sweets."

Through the day, the explorer and the shaman talked. Directly or implicitly, Câmbio kept mentioning the spiritually regenerating function of the return to the beginning. He asked McIntyre questions, particularly about his reasons for wanting to return to the beginning of the big river. The explorer tried to explain that as yet he had never visited the beginning of the big river, but was actually hoping to discover it, to pin it down once and for all and then reveal its location to everybody else. Which puzzled Câmbio, since McIntyre seemed to know so well where to look for that beginning and had drawn the river's map on the ground with such assurance. And what was the purpose of pursuing that beginning, if it wasn't part of a return? The literalness of Câmbio's comparison between the tribespeople's ritual and their visitor's goal amused McIntyre. He knew he could clarify the difference; yet he refrained from doing it, feeling that the ostensible affinity between the tribespeople and himself brought him closer to Cambio and gave him a chance to share more intimately the tribe's immediate existence.

The sensation of beaming had by now become familiar enough to feel almost normal, and even somewhat discountable, like an obsessive thought after a while taken for granted. Alternating between believing and disbelieving it, McIntyre was aware of the fact that the communication, the nonlingual language that Cambio had called the "old language," was part of a tribal psychodrama of a vivid and explicit kind. The ritual he witnessed was, after all, not that obscure in its symbolism. Flexible time was a belief other tribes possessed and a concept McIntyre himself had once wondered about, just as it was a permanent topic for astrophysicists and philosophers focused on the nature of the universe. The universe's most mysterious dimension, time, was present in the minds of these Indians and was the subject of their rituals. Heisenberg's uncertainty principle was a theory that men like Câmbio or Barnacle would not find alien. What astrophysicists had speculated upon after observing the implosion of stars—that is, the reversibility of time—the Mayoruna were proposing also, though on a smaller scale. The temptation to accept was very great.

Meanwhile, McIntyre noted the total lack of airplane sounds above the canopy. All he heard was the rustling of the canopy itself, disturbed by no mechanical noise whatsoever. As if planes were staying away deliberately, to make Barnacle's claims credible.

McIntyre let his mind wander. Instead of questioning the beaming, this time he tried to build a case for its plausibility:

- The possibility that these tribespeople remembered a system of communication that predated language. Perhaps limited and rudimentary at that time, it had been brought to a certain refinement later, when language itself was available with its whole arsenal of abstractions.

- Quite likely, this system operated as the language of priesthood, and Barnacle, like a trained priest, had raised it to a personal perfection.

  That did not preclude the ability of the whole community to "transmit," no doubt aided by the fact that magical actions, rituals of consequence to the whole community, were frequent in tribal life. For Barnacle's people, the physical and mystical were fused in daily practice, and the beaming probably acted as a reserve of nervous energy which renewed itself simply by being used. Perhaps the reliance on the beaming would be lower at times less fraught with danger and momentous decision. But he had not met these people at such a time, and there was nothing he could do to bring them back to a peace they had not had for months or years, and as a nation for centuries.

As a footnote, he remembered that after years of linguistic research performed with the most advanced devices, an affiliation between the Amazonian Indian languages and any of those spoken in Asia or in the Pacific had not been substantiated. All over the Americas and particularly in Amazonia, tribes separated by just miles of territory, many in traditional and well-certified contact, spoke vastly divergent idioms developed, it seemed, *after* each tribe had settled in its own area of mountain or forest. There, finally, larynxes, tongues, and brains had found the respite necessary to produce systematized sounds all building together a vehicle for imagination and abstraction. But did that mean that the Indians' ancestors had no languages when they crossed the land bridge twenty thousand years ago? That seemed impossible. The human stock of Asia was organized in numerous self-sustainable, functional communities. McIntyre tried to picture them without languages and failed. But language was such a constant in man's assumptions about himself that it acted almost as a prejudice.

● The most intriguing thought was that what he had experienced facing the forest, that drifting of his mind into another age, was not a total fantasy. Had the tribe's memory, collective or crystalized in exceptional individuals like Barnacle, somehow become available to him? The sensation of being in the vanguard of a migrating humanity was strong and haunting.

He was coming thus to the most attractive speculation of his experience with the cat-people. Maybe a contact with earlier tribal memories was possible, and Barnacle and other tribesmen had mastered such a contact. That explained why they believed in moving about in time. Their time was not sequential, and it was in their power to visit the past, which for them was next door to the present.

As for time having behaved differently at an earlier stage

of the universe, whether in terms of pace or direction, no one could answer that question.

But whether one could answer it or not, McIntyre's sensation of active inner voyage was almost continuous now, and quite clearly the headman was his companion, if not his guide. Almost at all times, McIntyre felt the headman's psyche, enormous, oversized, rolling invisibly in the narrow space between the canopy and the surrounding thicket, suffusing, pervading, taking over with both calculation and candor the psyches of all the other tribesmen and tribeswomen, and that of their visitor.

He told himself that he could leave the tribe any time he wanted. He could escape the cat-people's fate whenever he chose, for freedom was there, half an hour's walk into the forest's green indifference. But he was incapable of just walking off into the trees. He was stopped by a feeling of futility as strong as it was absurd. He would be alone, alone forever.

He examined that feeling and wondered at its absurdity, without managing to get rid of it.

Meanwhile, in calabashes scattered around the clearing, the masato was brewing, releasing an acrid and festive aroma. The preparations for the puberty rites went on.

4

The Interview

At nightfall, I felt so tired that I could hardly keep my eyes open. I rigged up my hammock and slid in.

It seemed that I had dozed for exactly a minute when someone leaned against my hammock and wiggled it. I opened my eyes again and saw Câmbio's face. He beckoned at me palm down, Latin fashion, and whispered briefly, "*O chefe.*" The headman.

Suddenly awake, I threw my legs out of the hammock.

We had such a short distance to walk to reach Barnacle's hut that I had no chance to put my thoughts in order. It was cold and I fought a slight tremor by clenching my teeth. I was alone, surrounded by inscrutable strangers and on my way to meet a man whose intentions about me were unclear. Being summoned to him at night felt very different from the friendly relaxation I had shared with Câmbio.

Câmbio bent under the low entrance to Barnacle's hut. I stepped in after him and stopped short so as not to bump into a thick group of men sitting on the floor. Seven or eight of them filled the hut completely, with Barnacle sitting right in their midst. I recognized, in profile, one of the huacas. I looked around and saw that the others were also shamans, or at least elders. The thought of a tribunal made me clench my teeth harder.

But it wasn't a tribunal. There was a fire on the floor and a youngster stood by the back wall, holding a torch. Between them, these sources of light splashed their glow over Barnacle's face. With his eyes, he motioned me to sit down, then lowered his eyes again, as is the custom in polite Indian company.

I sat down by pushing against two other bodies. In the same way, Câmbio made room for himself on Barnacle's left. My other hosts sat expressionlessly, looking at the ground; their faces, compact masks of blankness, seemed made of unglazed terra-cotta.

Then, without looking up, Barnacle spoke briefly and Câmbio translated his words with a question: "You have come to us. Why?"

I remained silent, thinking of an answer while all the Indians kept their eyes down and waited. But I was almost physically aware of their attention; it felt like a concrete pull at my person. Then I answered carefully that I'd heard of their tribe and wanted to photograph it. I made a living by traveling and seeing things, and capturing them on film for others to see.

There was another silence. Then Barnacle asked whether I had encountered other Indian tribes, and I mentioned briefly my experiences on the Xingu (he had no idea where the Xingu was). Then Barnacle spoke longer, and Câmbio rambled somewhat in his translation. But the gist of it was that Barnacle wondered why I hadn't left the tribe.

I answered that I had chosen to stay because I wanted to witness their beginning.

That provoked some confusion. Câmbio started to translate, then stopped and turned to ask me whether I meant the beginning (*nascente*) of the river; to which I answered that I was interested in river sources, for I expected to learn something from visiting them, but this time I meant their *ritual*. While I spoke, Barnacle became intrigued enough to stare me fully in the face, and everybody else gave me fleeting glances.

I repeated that I was interested in their beginning.
I had never experienced anything like their
beginning.

As soon as Câmbio finished translating, the little crowd
reacted with something akin to pleased attention, or so I
inferred from the way they shifted their bodies on the
ground, as if becoming at ease with me and with the
situation. Barnacle stared at me repeatedly, and all of a
sudden I found a thought in my mind, completed and
clear, as if planted there: *My staying here made the ritual
good.* Which was essential for the survival of the tribe—yet
this last line was not part of the same thought, but rather
my own mind's commentary on the situation. In a flash, I
remembered the flies buzzing around Red Cheeks's dead
face and felt the menace of his rebellion on the little
community.

But that was not said out loud and translated. That
simply filled my mind while the Indians stared at me more
and more boldly. Then Barnacle looked at the ground
again, imitated by the others, and I looked at the ground
too, as if digesting what had been said.

I was aware of a thread of satisfaction connecting me
with Barnacle. And yet, though it felt like a sort of
comradeship, I wasn't reassured; their ritual didn't seem
more benign. In fact, what made a stranger's testimony so
important to them was their declared need to believe in
their ritual and go through with it.

Nevertheless, the ice was broken. From formal, Barnacle
became friendly, punctuating his talk with smiles dark
with obsidian teeth. As we talked, the others started to
interrupt and Câmbio struggled to keep up with the
vivacious conversation. Meanwhile, I thought to myself
that since I had become so useful, Barnacle would
probably keep an eye on me even more assiduously in the
near future—I didn't believe at all in his statement that I
could go free.

We talked, they in Mayoruna, I in Portuguese, about

their belief in moving about in time. Instead of transcribing the lines, rambling and interrupted and rendered even more confused by the shamans, who kept arguing among themselves, I shall record the general sense of the exchange. Both Barnacle and I struggled with notions neither had dealt with before, so I felt I was living a sort of prehistoric thought, which both of us shaped as we went along.

Intrigued by the length of my visit with the tribe's highest authority, a good crowd had gathered in front of the hut's entrance. To minimize the distraction Barnacle gave an order, and two men brought a sort of upright curtain of reeds. They sealed the entrance with it, to shield us from the eyes of the curious. Then someone lit one of those fifteen-inch cigars of green tobacco and passed it around: in a few minutes the narrow space was turned into a gas chamber. When my turn came, I puffed on it as briefly as possible, but I was already light-headed from the smoke filling the hut.

Through the smoke, I studied the headman. He is very unaffectedly regal, and his eyes have two expressions: shrewd when he ponders a question, and innocent when he asks one.

I ask him whether his people have sailed back in time before. The answer is negative. Barnacle never witnessed this type of ritual, but his father, a chief in his time, described it to him in detail. And how did his father learn about it? "He remembered," Barnacle replies. It isn't clear whether his father remembered the ritual, or the beginning itself. At any rate, nothing matches Barnacle's expression of confidence as he repeats to me, in Câmbio's translation: "We're going back to the beginning. We'll be there soon."

I cough from the green cigar's smoke, then manage to speak: "How soon?"

Barnacle talks, and Câmbio translates: "After tonight, and tomorrow, and another night."

"So where exactly is the beginning?" I ask. Barnacle

consults with the other shamans, then shrugs: "Here. All around us."

"Here? Right here?"

"Yes."

"If it's right here, why do we still have to go back to it? If it's right here, we're in the beginning already."

Not yet, he says. For that, I get no explanation. All I can do is assume that the beginning might be here, yet it will take some time before it starts to manifest itself as such. I suggest that explanation to Câmbio, who translates it. Barnacle and the others listen, neither approving nor disapproving. I choose another angle of attack. What if, I ask, we go back, only to find out that the beginning is over?

Barnacle blinks, perplexed, then starts laughing. The beginning *cannot* be over. Here follows a lengthy, halting conversation about the nature of the beginning, during which, with some help from the other shamans, it is revealed that the beginning has a duration of its own, unaffected by what follows after it. The beginning lies at the inception of time, populated by all the gods and models of all objects and beings.

But this inception of time seems to be something else than the world's first stretch of duration shooting forth into the future: someone interrupts again, arguing that though the beginning lies at the beginning of time, it is also present anywhere *along the course of time*. To convey this, Câmbio's Portuguese is put to some strenuous tests, while the experts disagree, and despite the narrowness of the hut two of them jump up and there's some explaining done with the hands, during which I follow as closely as I can, trying to guess what they're saying, fascinated with the unique spatiality of their concept of time.

Finally, it seems that though the beginning lies *at the beginning*, it is also present elsewhere; in fact, it is the companion of regular time and can be reached by any number of doorways, which are the rituals. While all this is explained, and also sketched with the hands in the air, Barnacle and the other shamans listen and seem to agree. I observe Barnacle: he listens attentively and each time someone comes up with another detail about the beginning he reacts with satisfaction, like a teacher listening to a bunch of students' creative efforts rather than to objective information. I suppose that the more the shamans improve on the concept, the more all of them feel that it is real.

But—I realize it and feel no particular shock or panic—I feel the same. Each improvement adds to the reality of this encounter. Which adds to the reality of the beginning. Whatever it is, it is getting more real by the minute. I stop listening, try to evaluate my own feelings about it, identify a core of anxiety—after all, these people might go through the stages of the ritual only to make themselves die at the end—but otherwise I want the beginning to be real. I do, as if I were one of them. I've been thinking about the beginning, I've been fantasizing about it in an abstract and obscure way, and now I find myself yearning like a tribesman for its purported trance and liberation.

I puff on the green cigar and feel high and crazy. My hosts are crazy too. We are crazy together.

So. It appears that the beginning has a double territory—*before* everything else happened, but also hovering mystically *everywhere*, in close proximity to regular time. So going back to the beginning is not really a return, but rather a form of *exiting* history proper, into the mythical time of renewal.

I ask questions about history proper, and the men debate among themselves, as if the flow of current events never occupied their powers of definition as much as the beginning did. That's pretty standard. Forest tribes, apart from lacking a written history, lack the institutions that would capitalize on historic development. They have no dynasties, keep no records of battles or other heroic deeds, and have no concept of research into the past. Everything they have is recent and perishable. There is no such thing as opening an ancestor's grave and peering into its accumulated darkness. And yet . . .

They may have no sense of history, but they must have a clear sense of the erosion, depletion, degradation that time and events create—otherwise why would they feel such a need for a renewal, for a "repair" of their very identity?

Finally, it seems that history proper is made of a succession of "darks" and "brights," like the days and the nights. The invasion of the river by settlers is a "dark." I ask them to repeat this, so I make sure that the dark periods mean strife, hardship, and retreat, and the bright ones relative peace and relaxation. Yes, the darks and the brights are their version of history's cycles.

"We can escape the dark," Barnacle explains and Câmbio translates, "by moving back to the beginning."

The atmosphere is friendly now, and speculative. I feel that I can discuss the tribe's predicament, so I point out carefully that these people have not been eating and that the ritual is hard on them, particularly on the old ones and the children. For some, each step closer to the beginning is a step closer to death. *And what if there's nothing in the beginning? No relief, no redemption?*

Whatever happens in Barnacle's mind, it steels up his gaze, and I get "beamed" by the same thoughts I received when he ran around the village plaza to undo my spell. There's no other way out: the old belief has to be proven true. I hear the warning in that, yet I persist: Some people will die. And maybe there isn't any beginning.

He frowns painfully, his most emotional pose so far.

"Yes, there is," he repeats. "Tomorrow morning you shall see the signs."

He uncrosses his ankles and suddenly springs up; I gawk at his athletic agility. He could send me to the beginning now, if he wanted to. All he would need is one of those short and heavily maced war clubs, studded with nasty wooden barbs, the hurling variety.

But there is no confrontation. Barnacle simply utters a

parting line, which Câmbio translates: "You'll see the signs."

The interview is over. I search Barnacle's face. He is expressionless, but not hostile. Câmbio moves toward the entrance, and I follow.

We step out of the hut into a mass of excited humanity. They smile and prattle when they see me. There are many children among them, dressed in their kapok fluff, looking like giant freshly hatched chicks.

Sophisticated concept, the beginning. Particularly the idea that time has two forms. One mobile, sequential, recordable, the other static, eternal. One like the earth, the other like heaven.

I know I can't escape now. I've become an essential ingredient in this passage. I walk to my hammock, stand examining it in the glow of several fires. It's a typical forest Indian hammock, very light and narrow, of cord spun from palm twine. Apart from what I wear and what I keep in my pockets, this is the only thing in the village I can call my own. The hammock's cords leave a pattern on my skin each time I use it, and their coarse mesh lets every passing bug sting me. But they would sting no matter what precautions I might take; jungle gnats and *piums* and fleas sting even through two layers of clothes, in their stubborn quest for sustenance and a place to lay eggs.

No one seems to want to go to sleep. The fires, richly supplied, blaze the darkness away, the children run around, enter the huts and reexit them, men and women walk in twos and threes, spark little conversations that sound inconsequential, move again. A state of trepidation has seized the village and won't let go of it.

Later.

I lie in my hammock and try to fall asleep. Finally I sleep fitfully for only a few minutes, it seems, then get stung hard on my arm by some unseen aggressor and jump up.

The fires are still high but the air is cold and has that fresh quality of predawn. The canopy is silent. Men sit and stand throughout the clearing, some leaning on trees, their faces carved with fatigue. I swing out of my hammock, convinced that some time has passed, at least a few hours.

I suddenly see a knot of bodies forming in the entrance of Barnacle's hut. It breaks, and the shamans who witnessed my interrogation drift out of it and across the clearing toward their own huts. I feel like I was asleep only a few minutes, but a relaxed sensation in my eyelids, which just before falling asleep felt irritated and tense, convinces me that I'm wrong, that some time has passed. So the shamans stayed on in Barnacle's hut until now. Doing what? Helping, no doubt, with the ritual. Helming our strange vessel along the unseen sea lanes of reversed time.

The population is still awake in the clearing fragments and recenters around each of the returning shamans. Then Câmbio appears, hands busy with something that turns out to be a calabash of paint. He spots me, smiles without stopping, and whispers two words: "*Agora, Lowen.*" Now. Loren. Now, what? I want to ask. Then I don't need to ask; I know. Câmbio flashes me another look, in which I discern nothing sad or ominous, and he repeats: "*Agora, Lowen. Câmbio.*"

Now, Loren. Over.

I see a compact front of warriors. Having coagulated somewhere between the most distant huts, it now breaks forward toward the center of the clearing. A piece of wood thrown in the fire behind me cracks so hard that I jump, but don't turn. My eyes are filled with the uneven landscape of the clearing's center, as if missing one second of that sight would make me miss some critical signal. Now, Loren. Now, Loren. *It was supposed to be for tomorrow night*, a voice mutters at the back of my mind, watching Câmbio lay down his calabash of paint next to other calabashes. *What about the night and then the day, and then the other night?* Indian stuff, the same voice mutters back there, they just saw something that changed their minds, or the chief smoked a pipe and received a revelation and now it's not tomorrow, it's now.

That's why they brought out the paint; most ceremonies start with applying paint to the bodies of the celebrants.

Now, Loren. Over.

5

Breakfast at the Dawn of Man

The warriors approach carrying more calabashes of red urucú and black genipap, and more sacks of kapok. Each one of them wears his cat whiskers. During ordinary activities those spines are sometimes worn and sometimes not, but this is a ceremony, so the cat-people must look as much like their ancestors as possible.

In less than a minute the village comes alive and starts buzzing with activity. The remaining adult males flock in from all directions, cluster in a disorderly group blocking the warriors' advance, then deploy in a long file, and I find myself in it. I lost Câmbio, my fragile link with the outer world. What outer world? Was it ever there?

Never mind; I spot Câmbio several naked bodies down, rush past other tribesmen, insert myself in the file right next to him. I shiver from the cold, and my elbow pokes him in the side. He turns with the friendliest smile and tells me something that gets lost. He stands on tiptoe to reach to my ear and shouts in it that we'll receive new names. I shiver and nod, unencouraged. That sounds like an initiation. But initiations precede many Indian passages, including death.

But we will dance first. Câmbio steps widely to the left, and the whole line steps left with him. I throw myself in that direction and instantly have to step forward—three small, minced steps—after which, with another two to the right and two more back, we close a sort of rectangle and come back to the departing point and everyone including me claps his hands once, hard. Again, the wide leftward step.

Câmbio swings his elbows, raises his small but muscular palms while his feet go again through the boxlike step, and brings his palms together as all of us step back to the initial position. From all the chests, a plaintive call rises, somewhat like this: "*Aah-tah-way, hey, tah, pakawah, eeh-eeh, ooh-ooh,*" and then again: "*Aah-tah-way, hey, tah, pakawah, eeh-eeh, ooh-ooh.*" Fitted almost exactly to the boxlike step. Again we go, again the call rises, monotonous but rigorously paced, and while some of the voices sound creaky and unnaturally high, the thud of naked soles and heels on the ground is regular, full, and masculine. "*Aah-tah-way, hey, tah, pakawah . . .*"

I'm fully integrated in the dancing formation. In the tribe. I miss not a beat, and my lips start mouthing the line of song, not knowing what it means. It probably doesn't mean anything, a serial sound used to regularize the dance movements. My hands rise now through exactly twelve syllables of song, clapping soundly on the last one. My feet have learned the step and follow it all by themselves. My voice is singing now, drowned by the other voices, while my eyes stare vacantly forward. I feel fatigue, but my body is obeying. "*Aah-tah-way, hey, tah, pakawah . . .*" We are here, thudding with bare feet (except for my battered, parched, half-dead sneakers), making a sound like a giant hand knocking on a door, the door to the beginning.

We shall step through that door. We shall receive new names.

We dance for a long time.

The sun explodes above the horizon, but we only learn about it when the undersurface of the canopy turns from black to misty grayish green. The glow of the fires dims and the night, romantic in its contrast of light and shadow, gives way to the many-shaded vulgarity of daylight. A cycle has ended, another is beginning, and I feel like we've been dancing all night.

I look around and see ashen faces, and miss a step. Câmbio has been thudding next to me, digging a small plot of footprints in the forest floor. So have the other dancers. I stand a few inches lower into the ground than when I started to dance. Câmbio's face, under the band of pounded tree bark tied around his forehead, shines with sweat; his eyes are almost closed, and he no longer mouths the dance song I have by now learned it so well that even when I stop whispering it I cannot switch it off—it ricochets around in my mind all by itself.

Most of the dancers are too hoarse to sing; they whisper just like me, while the whole line of cat whiskers droops about back and forth. Still shuffling about, Câmbio and I knock elbows, and his eyelids twitch open. I find my voice and ask about our new names. "We will get them soon, over," he whispers, and stops pacing and reels in place, unable to be completely still.

My neighbor on the left stops pacing too. Finally the whole column stops.

Our bodies cry with exhaustion.

Above us, the macaws start flitting in and out of the leaves, cawing and pairing up by color. I count several blue and yellow pairs. Nowhere in Amazonia have I seen so many macaws as in Mayoruna country.

Câmbio pokes me, and the whole line of cat-whiskered men looks left, to where Barnacle appears again, followed by most of last night's wise old men. His diadem of egret feathers sits proudly on his head, and I hear him answer a question from the ranks. His voice is thin and halting from the fasting.

I am so curious about the name I'll receive that some residue of excitement runs through my body. I wonder what sort of personality I evoke in this old cat-man's eyes.

Câmbio will translate it for me.

*

Disappointment. I'm supposed to select my own name. I realize it as I hear Barnacle, coming closer, asking a standard question, to which warrior after warrior responds with a different answer. Kiatoo. Axi. Sava. Upopai. They've chosen their own names and declaim them to the chief without any hesitation. Ekke. Nutushi. Barnacle repeats them seriously, as if he will remember each of them, and with a thumb so red it looks bloodied he puts a print of red urucú on each forehead he passes.

Behind Barnacle, several of the old men carry pots of genipap. It is a tree sap relatively clear when extracted, but quickly turning to black in contact with the oxygen in the air. The older men dip a hand into the pot, scoop out a palmful of genipap mixed with palm oil to make it more liquid, and paste it on the chest of the respective initiate. The initiate turns to his neighbor and lets him spread the paint on his body into some geometric or figurative design.

Barnacle stops before Câmbio, whose Christian name, given by the padres at the mission, is Tito. I expect Tito to open his mouth and propose some panoan-sounding appelative, like the others.

"Câmbio," my friend christens himself. And he winks at me. Barnacle mutters the name in confirmation, Câmbio, Aha. Splash comes the genipap. Tito—sorry, Câmbio—is officially registered into the beginning.

Barnacle moves over to me. I can't think of any other name but my own. I don't want to lose my name, even if it is just a memory. Yet I'm too aware of Câmbio, who's been calling me Lowen since my second day with the tribe. I wet my lips and mutter "McIntyre", embarrassed and hardly audible.

Barnacle is totally unphased. "*Mackin-tayah. Tayah, aha,*" he mutters, finding the contraction to his liking. Next to me, Câmbio mutters approvingly, "*Tayah, tayah.*" The bright red thumb stamps my forehead. And the cool, turpentine-smelling black paint slops down on my chest. I know that it is practically impossible to wash off genipap. Its stains peel off in about ten days, when the old skin cells start being replaced by new ones.

The chief steps past me, stops before the next man. More tribesmen, younger ones, are bringing additional calabashes of genipap and urucú, placing them on the ground for communal use, while others walk around with gourds, offering a beverage: the masato they've been preparing for the last few days.

I turn to Câmbio, and we paint each other. I still have my pants on, but I take off my shirt. I clumsily rub the black goo over Câmbio's pectorals, wondering what pattern to choose. He's much better at it than I am, and faster: his small hands (Câmbio must be five-two) have strong fingers, with robust little bones wrapped in taut muscles. They move over my chest in a quick, animal scurry, completing a starlike design, then turn me around with authority and continue on my back. I go for the easy solution: I'll draw the same starlike design on him.

A bowl of masato passes me; I take it and swallow a big mouthful. I haven't had water for most of the night and under this latitude one needs liquids continuously. I taste herbs, which the Indians often mix in the masato; nothing hallucinogenic, I hope. All around me, Indian men sip the masato and seem so candid to me, so pure. I hope there's no drug in that drink.

There is.

Half an hour later. I'm living a state of mild hallucination.

Two thousand miles to our east, the sun gilds Brazil's coast and shines on the mouth of the giant river. The day is ripe back there, but here it is still morning, a morning loaded with events as yet unhappened. One of those events might be our death.

I plunge ahead into a future that may never occur, travel to the green escarpment of the Andes, then climb to the source of the river. That primal raindrop or snowflake, those molecules of water seeping into the most distant tributary.

They'll never make it to the river's giant mouth, those molecules. They'll succumb to evaporation again and again, rise into stormy clouds, cry down again and be recycled again, back into steam and back into rain, over and over until their progeny so many times removed will reach the ocean.

It would be so adventurous to stand where the primal raindrop hits, where the primal snowflake whirls down.

I feel a numbing of my limbs, very pleasant, and also a slight pain in my bones. A strangely sweet pain: the only way I can describe it is, it feels like my bones are liquefying, a liquefaction suggesting a kind of birth. Very slowly, from skeleton hard, they're growing mellower, and sort of coming alive.

I see the bowl passing. I've always resisted taking drugs, though tribal people offer them at most major ceremonies (on the Orinoco, I've seen them being taken daily). This time, I take the bowl and sip again. The aroma is dulcet, faintly reminiscent of anise flowers, of which there are plenty in the bush, but there is no taste per se. What could it be? I feel less than inebriated, and yet more. I feel again like I could expand and contract distances at will. I'm slightly nervous, as I've always made it my principle to ingest nothing dubious in the forest, even when I could count on other civilizados' help—this time I obviously cannot.

Câmbio and I finish painting our bodies with black, and now is the time for the red dye, the urucú. I place a pattern of jaguar spots between his chin and the roots of his hair, and he draws long thin lines on my cheeks with his thumbnail. I become worried about having my lips and cheeks painted: what if these people decide to puncture my skin with a spine or an agouti tooth and leave me permanently tattooed?

But after having my face painted, no one rushes at me with a spine or tooth or any tattooing implement. A little later, I stare in the mirror of some liquid left in a pot, and like what I see: a stylized bird is stretching its wings, taking off from the middle of my face.

Câmbio motions me to follow him. We pass more bowls with the whitish drink. Chopped segments of vine litter the ground, next to abandoned graters and wooden dishes with sticks in them: coarse mortars and pestles. A pet macaw pecks awkwardly at the stuff left in a mortar, loses its balance, and collapses in the dust. Câmbio shows it to me, laughing: the bird is drunk, too.

The fires are being started again; I smell fish being fried, but I feel no hunger. The children, smeared with genipap and fluffed up with kapok, are running around, calling each other shrilly. I'm getting gradually more high just by standing here. Women sweep the chopped vine tips off the plaza ground, throw them in the fire, producing a sour smoke. They look like the ones I got high on alone in the forest, squeezing them for water. I wonder if they intensify the "beaming." Câmbio beckons me over with his palm down.

I follow him behind the huts, starting to hear a mighty croaking of frogs—though the little brook I bathed in is in the opposite direction.

Suddenly we come upon a group of about fifteen men, surrounding tightly several of the huacas, who are opening a sort of long box of bamboo. My whole being tenses up, expecting to see someone's sacrificed body, but as soon as the lid lifts, there is an indignant chorus of croaking and cawing, and an obese bulbous frog tries to jump out and lands in someone's hands. It is promptly pushed back in. Câmbio makes room for me in the little crowd, and I get to lean over the box and see that it is compartmented inside by little screens of bamboo and that the frogs are kept down by a sort of latticework of twigs, two or three to each enclosure. Through the latticework, little wood chips, leaves, even bare fingers are lowered to touch the frogs and spoon off their backs a teary semi-transparent secretion, which the huacas collect carefully, drop by drop, in wooden bowls.

I ask Câmbio if they are collecting poison for arrows. He explains that it isn't poison, it is something they take. To demonstrate it, he pulls a frog out and holds it for me. There are gross dark granulations on its back and legs, and even a few on its throbbing throat. A tear forms out of one of those lumps right before my eyes, streaks down along the animal's side, and Câmbio shoots out his tongue, and licks it.

"To see the beginning, over," he explains.

"See the beginning?"

"See the animals in it. Talk to them. See the *tigres* and talk to them."

The *tigres*—the jaguars. I remember that these men are jaguars. Other tribesmen are sipping from the wooden bowls, sticking the collecting wood chips in their mouths; a few even hold frogs and put their mouths directly on those bumps and pimples, which keep weeping quietly, like so many ulcers. Câmbio holds the frog in front of me, offering me a try. I shake my head. Meanwhile the animal kicks with its muscular hind legs, and its wide and grotesque mouth gapes at the morning air, stiflingly hot by now.

Huaca One raises a knife of chonta palm and I turn away so as not to see him slice a frog, but when I turn back I find him pulling the hard, sharp blade of wood away from his forearm and letting blood seep out of his torn skin. Immediately, two other huacas rush to take hold of his arm; they pull aside the lips of the bleeding wound, and liquid from a bowl of frog secretion is poured on it. Straight into the bloodstream, for a quicker and more lasting effect.

The chonta palm knife is passed around. Other huacas and some of the warriors open their skin to the drug. About half prefer the ingestion. When did they catch those frogs? How long did they keep them in that box, collecting their skin fluids? I was entirely unaware of the operation. How much is happening in this community at all times that I, more than just a guest now, am still not able to detect?

I may never know.

The men have finished taking the frog potion and pace around now with distracted expressions, as if inwardly focused. Now, according to Câmbio, they will start meeting the jaguars and other primal spirits. I keep asking whether the substance is poisonous, and he denies it but I'm not convinced. Animals secreting skin fluids do it to repel predators, and the stinging or burning sensations that make a jaguar or caiman quickly spit out such prey always come from a highly toxic content.

Growls, shrill caws, barks are suddenly heard from the clearing, and they are so real, so full of the jungle's primal panic. Câmbio turns and hurries around one of the huts, directly into the menacing sounds. Again I follow, and as we both step into the clearing we are confronted with another bunch of men, some of them quite old, behaving outlandishly. Right in front of me, one of them falls on all fours and barks and hisses, while another, staggering about, screeches like a macaw, so convincingly that his sounds and his catlike tattoo are in total contrast. Behind them, I glimpse a man putting a hollow reed about a foot long into another man's nostril and blowing into its opposite end. The recipient snorts noisily, then takes the reed out of his nostril and puffs out a tiny whitish cloud. He loads the reed from a pouch and blows the fresh content into the other man's nose, then both stride toward us. Their pupils appear very contracted, like dark dashes streaking their irises vertically. One of them opens his mouth and pants noisily, as if feeling terribly hot, then lets his tongue loll about like a dog's. His eyes meet mine. The tunnels in his pupils are a dark passage into something I'll never visit. With those dark tunnels he looks at me, looks at the clearing and at the man who just administered him the drug, and I can tell that he doesn't see us.

I jump when someone collapses to my right, then crawls sideways using only one arm, as if the rest of his body were disabled. Câmbio rushes up to the Indian with the pouch and the reed, dips one end of the reed directly into the pouch, and takes a mighty snort.

I have to ask questions quickly: I see Câmbio's forehead pearl up with sweat and realize that the drug will be working in him in seconds. What do they call this substance? He mumbles something sounding like *okawa*, or *okana*. How is it extracted? It's the bark of a tree, burned and then ground into a powder, but Câmbio calls both the tree and the frog extract by the same name, *okana* (or *okawa*). Confusedly, he tries to explain that frog and tree are of the same family, or lineage.

I press him about the effects of the drug, noticing that after inhaling it some Indians rush their hands up to their faces, as if having received a hard blow. Yes, one feels like one's face is exploding, one's tongue is on fire—sometimes to relieve the pain tribesmen bite their tongues hard, causing deep lacerations, even losing tips (Câmbio mimics the spitting of the tongue tips). The eyes fog up, the daylight dims, and one is in a *floresta*, a "forest." The forest of the beginning. Big snakes, jaguars, rodents, bats, and caimans appear. Plants grow "inside our bodies," claims Câmbio, touching his shoulders and rib cage with such conviction that I expect bromeliads, branches, tangles of creepers to push out through his skin.

At this point, most of the men are lying down or sitting with empty eyes, and some wriggle and writhe on the ground. Câmbio has to sit down too, and I sit next to him. He talks intermittently, smiling, with spit trickling out of the corners of his mouth. He explains that the *okana* is also called "hunting powder" because one earmarks, during such trips, some of the animals one will track and kill later, and one talks their spirits into not taking revenge by offering a deal of some kind. What sort of deal? Well, in sleep one can switch places with a hunted animal, protecting it from predators. The animal will not mind, later, to be bagged by the hunter who offered him protection. Câmbio keels over and sprawls on the ground.

I bring my face inches from his to ask him when the drug will wear off.

"*Uma hora*," he slurs. One hour.

His eyelids flutter, opening, closing. His chest is a mirror of sweat. All the men around are sweating; they are staining the clearing with the dripping of their foreheads, torsos, backs. I feel strange standing up alone, almost sober, over this throng of stumbling, crawling, growling men. I see the children in the clearing, their fluffy bodies no longer darting about: a task force of mothers is standing by vigilantly, seeing to it that the children don't disturb or mock the men's business.

I walk back around the huts, curious to find out what the other drug ceremony came to, and a pungent reek of vomit hits my nostrils. Plots of vomit and bowel content foul up the clearing floor, and it's obvious that these men's experience is far more taxing and deep than the snorters'. I move among them, feeling that I'm hallucinating. I cannot describe the effect of their stares when they touch me: it's as if something not human but looking like a human took in my whole person and saw in it something I'll never see. Some of them are shaking as if from malaria. Some sit in their own dirt, leaning against trees or against each other back to back. Their eyes are open, but they are staring inside. Every few seconds one of them titters or utters a feeble animal call, meeting that animal in the forest of the mind. They also hiccup, belch, cough, and slobber. A copious buzzing starts overpowering their noises as formations of bugs begin to attack the mounds of dirt and the celebrants' sticky bodies.

Though spectacular, this isn't too different from the shamans' standard method of "cleansing" someone: what they administer is a vegetal emetic or laxative, but the herbs they use are often hallucinogenic, so the accompanying effects, the dreams, the visions, become diagnostics of a spiritual sort. Fever is interpreted as the convulsions of the deity of the disease being expelled. Sweat or feces are collected and burned, since they were induced, it is believed, by a spell or a malevolent presence. If dreaming occurs during the cure, the patients share the dreams with their families after they recover and bathe. None of this is too unusual, except that what these men are visiting now is the beginning.

I see the box of frogs—thrown away to the side. The big ones tore out through the bamboo latticework, and the small ones are trickling out after them. A *collubrid* snake slinks down from a low branch, opens its mouth, and catches one of the frogs, inches from a collapsed tribesman's face.

It may have been an hour. I run away from the stench of the frog-potion drinkers and scuttle back and forth around the clearing.

A cough starts in a celebrant's chest, then in another's. Coughing and sneezing, the men stir, try to sit up and don't make it, fall down, doze off again, blink dizzily again, finally regain consciousness.

In a while, a few of them are able to stagger up. Câmbio himself stands up on the spot where he collapsed, and rubs his hands over his face. Then he sees me, lumbers over exhaustedly, and sits by me, next to one of the big trees in the middle of the clearing. In a while he is able to speak again. I ask him about what he saw in the beginning.

He met many magical animals in the beginning, he tells me, and saw magical plants. I ask him if he saw any humans. He thinks carefully; no, no humans. He is very tired now. They are all tired. But later in the day another part of the drug will kick in, and it will charge him with an amazing energy and acuity of his senses. He tells me that he will be able to go hunting that night because he will feel alert and rested and able to see in the dark.

That is why the *okana* is called "hunting powder." A number of hours after taking the hunting powder, the body not only recovers, but experiences a remarkable liberation of its unknown powers, which makes it ideally fit to go into the jungle and return with a great catch. The eyes see clearer and farther, the nose sniffs more accurately, the feet tread more firmly. To say nothing of the earmarking that happened during the drugged-up sleep. Even bad hunters, Câmbio says with a tired chuckle, bring in a great catch after taking hunting powder.

I ask about those who took the frog potion. They will be out of commission at least until tonight. But the effect of the frog potion, while more massive, is nonrecurrent, while the inhaled stuff, according to Câmbio, wakes up inside the body every few hours, offering a quick and semi-sober reliving of the initial plunge. It only wears off completely in a couple of days, which is why he prefers to inhale the hunting powder.

I nod, accepting all this as interesting and meaningful, and feel strange. Feel strange while drinking some water, feel strange while sharing some fried fish with Câmbio (during this snack, he has a two-minute-long relapse and sits zombielike, eyes open, irises narrowed, staring inside himself). Maybe it's just my imagination, but the air seems separated into tiny, flexible rivulets of oxygen. Like a delta of air. I close my eyes and try to visualize my own version of the beginning. I meet no fabulous beasts but people, people roaming into an uninhabited, pristine territory. They come in little groups and in long, loose hordes. They labor across a landscape looming fogged up and uncertain, intriguingly devoid of firm features, until I realize that the landscape is not territory, but time.

I see time.

It looks like a sort of fog, drifting evenly, uninterruptedly, from nowhere to nowhere. Its movement is beyond doubt, but its regularity is such that though time flows, its endlessness makes it fixed and still. Time flows but does not move. Instead, man moves about in time, in all directions, trying to cut paths into its facelessness, at first succeeding, then stopping in confusion as the paths vanish under him and he finds himself surrounded by the same persistent, even almighty fog, whose transience is as merciless as it is alien and inexplicable.

But he keeps moving. He advances and returns, crosses and recrosses his own steps, meets with himself in the fog but fails to recognize himself, and goes on, seeks on, obsessively.

I see man, exploring. I see time passing, and man exploring that passage.

Across the fog, a silhouette sails into view. I open my eyes and see Barnacle, who stops next to me and Câmbio and sizes me up with an interesting mixture of friendliness and hostility. The light under the canopy has begun to dim, making the fires brighter.

I acknowledge Barnacle's presence and point to the crowd. What will happen to them? I ask.

Câmbio's knowledge of Portuguese has been somewhat befuddled by the ceremony, but finally he gets a grip on himself and we all sit on the ground, the headman and I facing each other. Câmbio sits to one side, interpreting. Inside this triangle of sweaty faces and eyes filled with the fitful play of the fires, the future will be decided.

I explain that I would like to take a census of this village and of some other Mayoruna villages and collect enough data so I can prepare a document which might determine FUNAI to build a *pôsto* on the upper Javari. They would gradually make contact with the tribes, provide medical aid and some useful tools, help the tribes develop some more sophisticated agriculture.

While I speak my eyes roam the surface of Barnacle's face. Only a few inches of air separate us, but my glance seems to travel an immeasurable distance before it gets pulled in by the gravitational field of the drooping cheeks, of the nose cratered with big open pores, of the forehead. Dried up, the wrinkles on his forehead look like riverbeds sculpted once by free-flowing water. Above the face, under a compact forestation of black hair, I sense the brain: pulsating hotly, like a volcanic core.

"Why would you do that?" Barnacle asks.

I try to make an effort of concentration, but for an

instant I can't come up with a reason. Like my glance, my thoughts seem lost in the space between his face and mine. They will crash into some detail of that face and come to rest, in broken pieces, in an anonymous crater.

I gather myself, think about my reasons. All the thoughts I've had for the last few weeks, about tribal man, about the forest, about the properties of its plants and animals to which tribal man's knowledge is the key, they all knock about in my head. That backward clock, the clock of discovery. Our future, glimpsed in the vertiginous pit of the past. I cannot wrap them in words. I shrug, and glance at Câmbio. But Câmbio watches Barnacle.

"My people need help too," I say. "Your tribe could help them."

I wait what seems like a good five minutes. All of a sudden, sitting erect, his face like mahogany, Barnacle speaks, pauses for Câmbio to translate.

"The chief is sad," translates Câmbio, "that you won't be able to help each other."

Death. Death speaking to me through those lips pierced by labrets.

"But we are now in the beginning," pursues Câmbio. "You cannot return to your people anymore." Câmbio sympathetically adds a line of his own: "You wouldn't find your people, Lowen."

Barnacle speaks again; as he speaks he moves his hands in the air, and I feel that his gestures are wiping away whole sections of invisible reality. Câmbio translates: "The beginning is here, and we are here, over. Your people are not here, over. There's nothing we can do for them now, or they for us."

A bar of metal seems to hang across my forehead. Pressing back my brain, containing an army of thoughts which pound at it from inside, seeking expression. I feel like yelling that this doesn't apply to me: I'm not one of them, my reality is well in place, at the other end of a two-way radio if I had one. I look at Barnacle, find his stare opaque and sphinxlike.

I can't get up. I can't raise my voice either.

"When are we going to die?"

I'm not sure I ask the question that directly. I put myself across, though, because Câmbio jabbers fast to Barnacle. Barnacle says something in reply, then leans over to tap my arm with his open hand, which feels hard—like the hand of a statue.

"*Não. Não morrer,*" says Câmbio, "Not to die."

Not to die. The metal bar across my forehead lifts. I feel like a sack filled with air. I wouldn't be surprised if I started to float away, seated as I am, with my ankles crossed. Not to die.

Through a filter of weariness and incredulous relief, I hear Câmbio explain that it isn't necessary to die to reach the beginning. It used to be that people starved themselves to death to reach the beginning, but this time, though a number of them perished on the trek, the goal has been attained quickly. The beginning is here.

I don't understand what distinguishes this time from others. I don't even want to find out the difference. The cold wing of death has lifted, but it's still so close that I feel my hair prickling up on the back of my neck, fearing its return.

Zonia, Tuti, Tia, Câmbio. Barnacle, myself. Not to die.

"I'd like to sail downriver," I say. *Slow down, be reasonable.* I try to make my voice light, conversational: "To check out and see if there's really nothing back there."

Barnacle answers something.

"There is nothing back there, over," Câmbio translates irrefutably. "There's only us."

Barnacle asks something, Câmbio answers in Mayoruna, Barnacle nods, directs his eyes at me, and smiles in confirmation. I contemplate the possibility of being the only civilizado in the beginning—or in the world, for that matter. Surrounded by nothing but rain forest, long before the conquistadors. Landscape with a lone civilizado, in the beginning.

"I must go back and find out," I repeat.

In his personal tone of voice, Câmbio warns me: "Don't try, over. He won't let you do it."

"What's the matter?" I ask. "He doesn't want me to upset the spell?"

"Yes, over," answers Câmbio.

I breathe silently for a few seconds. And then, somehow, the notion becomes credible. Just like Barnacle undid my spell by running counterclockwise, I could undo their return. I could be the crack between here and there, the tunnel between this sphere and the outer sphere, whose survival, however, they deny. Or maybe I couldn't, but in their expressions I discern a healthy dose of prudence. Why take chances?

"Where is the beginning?" I hear myself ask. "I want to see it."

My voice is firm. Weighted with the strength of legitimacy.

Barnacle stands. He does it suddenly, making himself soar to the lower edge of an overhang of leaves, while the creases of skin on his once bulky body fall down in one energetic ripple, and I understand from this resolute motion that there is no way he would let me leave. He'd rather kill me.

He gestures for me to follow him.

I do, across a section of clearing littered with bodies, between two huts and into the trees.

I follow the brown slopes of his shoulders for about thirty steps.

The muddy tributary announces itself with an indifferent rustle of water, and Barnacle stands on the low bank and breaks a branch blocking his view. I stop next to him, smelling the water, cool, slightly putrescent from that heated mud, and the chief's body: after so much fasting, the last caches of fat are being consumed inside him, making his smell potent. All around us, the forest exudes aromas of hot midday and busy biotic transactions.

Barnacle whispers one word, and I think it means "look," because he points upstream. I look upstream. The murmuring vein of water enters the landscape some five hundred yards from where we are standing, gushing in between two higher banks, then easing into a succession of pools, a series of pockets of still water crossed lazily by the main current. An invisible change of lenses seems to occur, and my eyes tumble forward. The five hundred yards extend, while the sound of the water changes. It really isn't sound anymore, but a signal to all my senses, a *passing*, in which distance and time combine. I sense the distant mountains rising right behind that backdrop of trees. The beginning of the river is also there.

The source of the river.

Barnacle turns toward me. But before he can speak or gesture, my mind receives a message that comes from the source and is wordless but so gigantic that it breaks all boundaries. It fills all the space outside me and inside me and fuses the source and the beginning into one notion.

The beginning, beams Barnacle, and his message is a piece of the broader message. I nod, mesmerized, expecting the curtain of trees to part so that I see the gigantic beam, or hear it, or register it in some other familiar way. I see and hear nothing, but I feel how the beaming expands, ramifies and builds on itself. It has already engulfed everything. Unclearly, my mind tries to create some fictitious reality, just to get away, just to free itself. It finds the beaming there already.

Finally, time starts moving again. Barnacle and I face each other, and he explains, still without words, that he cannot allow me to leave. Not after I have been part of this.

So—you know, I whisper without words.

We know, he responds in the same fashion, and looks very naked and tired—in fact, he looks aged and vulnerable. He walks away, back toward the other naked, tired people of the forest.

*

I stare after him, while my body seems to lose its solid state; it somehow ripples toward the ground, and I find myself seated.

Whether what follows is reason derailed from its familiar tracks or a defense mechanism trying to make the extraordinary into ordinary, I don't know—but I review what I'm feeling and decide that after all it's not too abnormal. I am beginning to react like a man of the forest. Soon enough I will invest the trees and animals with supernatural powers. What I know about my old, rational self will visit me now and then, like my old obsession with the river's source. I'll discover that source here, in a ritual. I'll be who I was, except that I'll satisfy my ambitions and quests differently. That, after all, is the only way in which I'm different from these people.

I scratch my sprouting beard, feel the gauntness of my cheeks, and marvel at the strength and endurance of my own body. It is incredible that being under such strain I haven't broken down yet. I'm covered with sores, scratches, and pustules, but I assume I haven't developed any major infections, though many of those wouldn't declare themselves until later. Since my body's minerals wash out in my sweat like water through a porous soil, I'm tortured with hunger, horrible hunger barely relieved for minutes by a few mouthfuls of protein now and then, after which follows another obsessive wasteland of pangs and rumbles in the stomach, of empty swallowing and headaches—hunger, hunger. So badly I crave my minerals back that I feel I could eat zinc in its pure state.

Captive in the world's most humid land, I'm also thirsty, as if the water I keep drinking never reached my stomach, as if it evaporated on the way like the rain drenching the treetops but barely making it to the ground. I wonder if I caught intestinal worms by bathing in the river; or maybe that triumph of tropical insidiousness over the body's defenses, Leishman's disease transmitted by bloodsucking sand flies. The parasites the sand flies carry break into man's phagocytic cells, the very disease eaters which defend us from all alien invasions. Living inside man's defenses protects them from those very defenses! And what do they do to the human body? Well, from a few original ulcers they go on to reduce the white blood cells, bring on fever and chronic anemia, attack the liver and the spleen, wreak havoc on the body's inner balance, and if untreated eat away the nose, mouth, and pharynx. One variety kills in under two years.

But those symptoms wouldn't show up for a few months. And that kind of risk, under these latitudes, is the lot of the body.

I remain seated where I am and decide that I'm feeling better. In fact, I convince myself that I'm experiencing a wonderful easing of pressure. Until just hours ago I was a modern man, activated by the pressures of my civilization, increasingly more and more crowded inside its own limits. Barnacle and his tribe were pressured by the advance of my civilization even more effectively, for their only alternative was flight. Yet now the certainty that blooms in every leaf and blade of grass is that we are alone, alone completely, like those vanguard groups of Indians crossing the Arctic land bridge and encountering nothing before them except virgin space.

There is hunger in that virgin space, and there is risk and fear. But there is no pressure, no pressure at all.

I try to stop thinking, try just to be, so I can open myself completely to this transmitted memory, and I almost manage. I get a taste of something, an awareness that's frighteningly immediate and overfilled with sensorial stimuli. I try not to censor it, but I tense up as I'm trying and it vanishes, leaving me with just my capacity to reconstruct it mentally. It felt so unconstrained when it was genuine.

I give myself another task: to focus on one of my contemporary concerns. With an effort of detachment, I think about the source of the Amazon . . . It cannot be on Mount Huagra. The farthest source has to be at the farthest point on the Continental Divide where snow falls and melts into trickles that gather into brooks running into the highest headwaters. In that region of the Andes, the Continental Divide forms a loop open to the north, shaped more or less like a bight in a coastline. The ramparts of that loop are the farthest from the rest of the Amazon Basin and the river's mouth. One has to scrutinize every detail of that bight to determine the farthest source, and Mount Huagra is well short of it, some thirty miles, perhaps.

Yet the finding of the source seems now so inconsequential. Sadly and sweetly inconsequential. The river itself hasn't been discovered yet. The world itself hasn't. To get up from where I sit and walk back to this tribe, being still who I am, knowing still what I know, that's the job at hand. Life is global now, and my tasks as a man are global. There is no room for competitive achievement. All that matters is this tribe. Its unity, its cohesion, its survival in its forest home.

I hear voices, the tribe's voices. I turn and stagger away, my mind close to exploding.

I want to slip away, even for just a few minutes. Away from this loud communion, whose members never take time off for themselves, whose bodies never deviate from the merciless duties of *being*.

I pad broadly over flat leaves, divide a bush with my hands, start slipping across and get scratched on my thigh by the jagged bract of an unknown flower. Above me, the foliage is rustling. The rustling is musical, almost like a song. I feel absurdly that if I stopped I could distinguish a voice, but I'm too full of the last hour's shocks to stop, too filled with my old humanity, which is up in arms and screaming, sensing that this niche in the forest might well become its grave (and that is quite likely: if from now on I am to share the tribe's life, I shall also share its daily ration of dangers). So I pad noisily over huge palmated leaves, seeing before me only trees and branches and creepers and branches and trees. Palmations, striations, reticulations. Unexpectedly, I sneeze. My skin is stuffed with gooseflesh and the air feels strangely cold.

What's ahead? When's tomorrow?

"*Tayah!*" someone calls me by my new name. A real voice this time, a voice already familiar. I look over my shoulder, see Câmbio, whose stick looking like a spear plunges in and out of the thicket. He smiles, but in his eyes gleams the cool flame of the hunt.

I was walking away from the village, back toward the water.

I nod reassuringly and start retracing my steps, while the song of the forest rises, gaining in melody and richness. But since I'm walking noisily, I cannot relish the voice or make out the words. My prison, my wonderful prison, is singing.

6

The Rains

"In the beginning, there was a man-god, whose name was Time. He sired sons and daughters. When they grew up, they desired to see the world, and Time agreed to their wish.

"To allow them to travel, the man-god Time made a big river and taught them how to sail down on it. He planted a few stands of trees, providing the wood from which his sons and daughters built canoes. They started down, while their father waited, for on their return they had promised to bring him nuts and fruit and other good things to eat.

"But the sons and daughters saw that the world was wide and full of wondrous things, and forgetting about their obligation to their father tarried long enough to make him angry. He made the river overflow, and some of his sons and daughters drowned.

"Angry in their turn, they promised to sail back upstream and kill their father. To protect himself, the man-god Time filled the river with rapids, grew the *mata* on both shores, and threw many tree trunks in the river, to make it even harder for his sons and daughters to return . . ."

Using the Portuguese name for "forest," *mata*, and calling the strange creator "*homen-deus*," Câmbio kept recounting tribal cosmogonies to the explorer. Questioned, he insisted that they were part of the tribe's folklore, but the coherence of their metaphors made McIntyre suspect, like before, that the shaman had tampered with their initial candor and lack of causality.

Still, the myth of the man-god Time with whom the humans quarreled found resonance in McIntyre for a different reason. Whether these people moved in time or just believed that they did, time was the material of their experiment and it connected with the explorer's own fascination with it. Accompanying them in their ritual, he had traveled inside his own intimate time and found it as flexible as they claimed their sequential time to be. Concerning sequential time, he had made some discoveries which overlapped interestingly with the loss of his camera, his machine to capture the present. The civilizados had hardly any present. Splitting time through measuring it more and more accurately amounted not to a better grasp, but to a narrowing of it. The present got shrunk and if it kept shrinking into ever tinier fractions, then where was time, and what was it made of?

These tribespeople lived in a present of an entirely different nature. Despite the succession of mornings, afternoons, and evenings and the alternation of days and nights, their present was not momentary, but undefined and capacious. At virtually any moment it could be extended into a trip to the mythical time, where the tribespeople would linger as long as necessary for rest and replenishment. The unpressuring quality of such a time concept was conspicuous.

But wasn't that a proof of a sort that the beginning existed, and that in this corner of the forest time behaved differently? Wasn't that proof that analogies like "time equals river," "source of river equals beginning of time" were acceptable? In this ambience, they undoubtedly were. But in this ambience a civilizado's mind functioned differently. It mixed categories, reasoned by symbols, and ascribed a magical potential to what had been measurable, objective, and inanimate.

For such a dialogue, in which the categories shifted and the objective and subjective constantly mixed, Câmbio proved to be an excellent respondent. Asked whether time moved, the shaman answered seriously that time didn't move and never had. It was man who raced along its course, like the man-god's sons and daughters sailing up and down that river.

With the anxiety of an impending mass sacrifice now lifted, McIntyre spent several days after the ritual in Câmbio's company. The black genipap paint on his body was starting to peel. The kapok fluff had been washed off the children, while the little women of seven and eight had been locked in their little educational huts, where they were regularly visited and instructed by mothers and aunts. The tribe recuperated from its trials by hunger and treks through the jungle. Everyone basked in the friendly glow of the beginning, recharging themselves, in order to be able to go back and cope better.

With Câmbio's help, McIntyre's knowledge of the Mayoruna language was improving. Now he could identify words in the natives' dialect and even systematize the inflectional changes in a sort of rudimentary grammar. He noted that cases and tenses were indicated by adding suffixes and prefixes to root words. Derivatives were formed in the same way: thus "who" was *tsutsi*, and "with whom" *tsutsibed*; "what" was *totsi*, "which" *atotsi*, and "in which" *atontsin*. "How many" was *tedtsi*. It seemed that the common root *tsi* was remarkably strong, being perhaps one of the Mayoruna's first conscious articulations—it was also present in their name as a tribe, Matse. Another common root, *daed*, "two," supported a whole list of related units of meaning: *aid daed* meant "both," *aid daedi* "the same two," *daedpambo* "two at a time," and *daedpen* "many," in keeping with the primitive numeral concept treating everything over two or three as a multitude.

Along with his first steps into the Mayoruna language, McIntyre learned basics about the Mayoruna themselves. According to Câmbio, they conceived of three classes of humans: the *matses*, which meant the "people," or themselves; the *mayu*—"other Indians," or people similar to the

Mayoruna though not related to them; and the *chotac*—the "outsiders," which essentially designated civilizados, past and present, whether white or black or mestizo. Male *mayus* were captured in tribal wars and incorporated into Mayoruna tribes; so were *chotac* women, kidnapped and taken as wives to balance the tribal inbreeding through cross-cousin marriages. Yet McIntyre noticed no cases of lighter skin or blonder hair among his hosts; he concluded that this particular tribal branch had been isolated longer and exposed even less frequently to contacts with white outsiders.

He learned that there was a dual organization among the Mayoruna, according to which many Mayorunas were *bedi*, which meant "cat-humans"; specifically, *bedi* was the word for "jaguar." Yet some Mayoruna were not born jaguars and did not wear the traditional spines; those tribespeople were named *macu*, meaning "slug," or "worm," apparently without a deprecating content. Men could marry on either side of that distinction, and a mixed couple could produce full jaguars if the father was a jaguar. There was a certain pride in being a jaguar, but no curse in not being one, as if the two species recognized each other's proximity and codependency.

Also, McIntyre learned more about the tribe's regulations concerning marriage. He received no clear explanation as to why cross-cousin marriages were encouraged while those of parallel cousins were forbidden, but the rule seemed to embody a concern for health. Sameness of blood represented strength and solidarity of kin, but only if the parents of the newlyweds were of opposite sex. If they were of the same sex, brother and brother or sister and sister, the intermarriage of their children was forbidden, for that closeness was viewed as unhealthy (still, to counter inbreeding the defective children were strangled or thrown into animals' holes, while the capture of outside women ensured the replenishing of the genes).

The rule was codified by a terminology: *shanu* was the term applied to a marriageable female cousin, while *chido* and *bene* were the respective names for female and male fiancés on the safe side of cousinhood. Since in practice the parents of marriageable cousins might differ in age considerably—for example, a brother and his offspring could be ten years older than the baby sister and her respective offspring—there were many "assignments of marriage" between mature males and females not yet nubile, and sometimes not even born. As soon as the marriage was approved, the female cousin became *chido*, "wife," while the male was considered her *bene*, "husband." A *bene* could openly fondle his *chido*, even if she was a child, and often moved her into his home before she reached puberty. Before puberty a *bene* was not allowed to exert his husband's rights, but the *chido* was his charge, particularly if she had no other family. Thus very few women lived in Mayoruna society without some man being responsible for them, and it was undesirable for a girl to grow up without a male protector. However, sexual liaisons outside the *bene-chido* relationship were strongly disapproved of; if a pair of offenders were found out, the man was killed by the woman's family and the woman was beaten, often severely enough to induce the miscarriage of the unwanted offspring if she was pregnant.

Overall, the rule had a protective meaning not just for the individual but for the tribe as a whole. It made sure that older tribe members took care of the younger ones and held them in the close bond of recommended marriage. Between sameness of blood and renewal through the blood of strangers lay their concept of genetic health (women from outside were *shanu*, "marriageable," by definition). The limitations ensured a well-regulated sexual behavior, repressing the effects of nakedness and physical closeness more effectively than clothes. In fact, with the advent of acculturation, the introduction of clothes was often associated with a loosening of tribal morals.

During the following days, Barnacle and the explorer met often; the headman continued to act friendly, yet McIntyre sensed a subtle triumph in his attitude and a continued determination to keep his tribe safe from change. The weather, meanwhile, became surprisingly cool, as if a front of lowered temperature were crawling up from Patagonia into the steaming jungle.

On the night of November 9, or maybe 10 (the dates were to be established later, by backward counting), a storm shook the trees and rain lashed the canopy so violently that liquid columns of downpour started to pierce through, while the thunder crashed every other second. The darkness that reigned under the canopy, the roof of the jungle was lit repeatedly by flashes bathing the treetops in an apocalyptic blue light. The nearby tributary suddenly rose out of its bed and whipped with unexpected strength at the trees, swamping their roots, overflowing the forest floor, and starting to build an intraforest arm whose surge forced into action all the animals that couldn't count on the trees for protection. Many of them were good swimmers, ancestrally trained to survive a flood. The others headed for higher ground.

The relatively thicket-free spaces under the bigger trees, the trees depriving the forest floor of sunlight most successfully, were the first to fill up with water; the dark river broke into these areas, snatching up the rotting litter and mixing it into a dirty soup on which drifted insects and worms and little rodents and reptiles surprised by the flood. Fish liberated from the river darted among the trees, ready to snap up whatever prey the inundated forest floor offered them. The Amazonian rain season usually starts with squalls that raise the water levels gradually, but flash floods occur if the terrain is hilly, and the Mayoruna village lay close to the elevation McIntyre had climbed on the day of sighting the mysterious waterfall. The other reason for flash flooding is cold air sweeping in from as far south as Patagonia, and on that night the temperature, already unusually cool, dropped dramatically.

The river seemed to make a leap in volume. Hearing the cannonade of repeated thunder, the Mayoruna swung out of their hammocks and rushed confusedly to gather their belongings and children. Meanwhile, the bush was in an uproar: in the thick darkness, McIntyre imagined the animals fleeing randomly before the advance of the water, species bumping into species. Pig-sized capybaras, the world's largest rodents, traipsed on webbed feet, not alarmed since they spent half their lives in water; more inconvenienced, the jungle pygmy deer, the huge possums, the ocelots galloped, scurried, and jumped, stirring smaller mammals and birds and reptiles—all of a sudden, the bush seemed three times richer in animals. As if to reaffirm its mastery over creation, the river drowned a generation of life-forms only to secure, through the expansion of its wet matrix, the conditions for the birth of another.

What was happening around the little village of Indians would be happening in days or in hours to most of upper Amazonia. Hundreds of tributaries would flood their banks; brand-new lakes and backwaters would form and last for many moons; O Rio Mar, the River Sea, would start to fill up a swamp of thousands and thousands of square miles, literally making it into an inner sea planted with trees. From now through June and into July, tracts of Amazonia adding up to the size of England would be constantly underwater. And after the waters' retreat, hundreds of rivers would show new courses, with oxbows and loops unmarked on any charts.

Having rolled out of his hammock, McIntyre was almost knocked down by a panicked traffic of tribespeople. To get out of their way, he ran into the surrounding trees and found himself in water to his knees. The water was building up quickly and he was surprised by its swiftness and strength. He was nearly swept off his feet, then pushed against a tree trunk. He tried to wade back, was hit in one knee by a floating object, groped, and felt the shape of a drifting balsa, a raft of the simplest construction, made of two logs of lightweight wood lashed together with palm fiber. He fell across it without even thinking of clinging to it, and the current dragged them both into a screen of low branches; McIntyre felt the branches tearing at his flanks, then felt a tug that almost snatched him off the raft. Before he could realize what held him, there was another tug, at his waist, and the lanyard tying his Swiss army knife to his belt gave way, while the current pushed the balsa under the branches and beyond. He tried to stay flat on his stomach on the balsa, yet slipped into the water (noticing that it was warm compared to the chill air), and found himself bobbing in a much swifter and deeper vein of river. Suddenly shaken and tossed furiously, as if a new branch of the river was forcing its way through the forest, he flailed desperately, grabbed the balsa, and pulled himself afloat again.

He took some more hits from low branches as the balsa rotated directionlessly past flood-swept trees. Trying to steer it back by paddling with his hands, he realized that back was just the village, with nothing of his in it except for his hammock. He struggled to reach his reinforced pockets and found that he had lost one roll of film, while the other was still in his left pocket. The more ominous discovery was that the fishhooks he had saved so carefully were missing. His book and pen were also gone (or perhaps he had left them in his hammock), and he found it amazing that the water had robbed him so quickly and efficiently in just minutes. He floated past a screen of half-submerged bushes and heard louder thunderclaps and the lashing of rain on leaves. The air grew even chillier. The river's open expanse lay ahead, and the balsa no longer rotated but headed straight into it.

Behind him, he still heard the voices of the Indians.

The raft responded somewhat to paddling with his hands, harder to one side if he wanted to steer it in the other direction. He could try to return to his new family, but perhaps the confusion of the rainstorm was his opportunity to escape. He quickly weighed the risk of sailing off and being followed: in pursuit, the Indians could move through the trees much faster than any oar-powered craft down the river. But now that risk would be offset by the flood's giant distraction. With a knot of tension in his throat, his tired senses back on full alert, he realized he had already opted for escape.

Balsas are the commonest conveyance in river communities, whether tribal or civilizado, and Indian children often play with them. Their porous wood makes them unsinkable and their lightness prevents accidents. Holding on to the balsa, he would be all right as long as he could avoid snags or rapids. Immersion in the rain-swollen water would protect him from sunburn later, after the intermittent squalls gave way to sunshine, and the risk of piranhas and stringrays was reduced—they were mostly to be feared in shallow waters during the dry season. There were other dangers, like the presence of caimans, but McIntyre barely gave them a thought; other things were of greater concern, like traveling by day in order to spot his camp, which he estimated to be at least a couple of days downstream. He needed to find the camp, for he had no weapons to hunt with and couldn't rely on fishing in a rain-swollen river.

Still, of the thoughts tumbling around in his mind, one of his most anxious was about the headman. *Don't beam, Barnacle*, was more or less his mind's hurried prayer. *Don't beam, Barnacle*.

He hoped Barnacle was busy now with his own people's survival. The pilgrim tribe had to deal with its best ally and worst enemy, the weather.

Seconds later it seemed, the raft floated into the river, and the repeated lightning revealed a boiling, frothing, flooding purple stream, already several feet above the mudbanks and sand bars of the dry season, rushing between the trees on both sides and felling some as it went. Of the logs fallen across the river, some were submerged and others had been dislodged. The free ones were herded down by the water, and McIntyre realized it would be impossible to steer around them: the rushing water would bump and bob the balsa past them and all he could hope for, since returning now was impossible, was to escape battered but without major injuries.

There was constant illumination from the lightning, and the water bubbled with obstacles; half a dozen times in less than a minute the explorer almost collided with some dark mass. Then he passed a huge chunk of shore collapsing into the river like a giant slice of cake. Behind the fallen slice, a secondary flow came out of the swamped forest, joining the river in a frothy collision of waters. The river opened, growing twice as wide, the fallen trees starting to naturally range themselves against the tangle of forest on both sides. McIntyre and his balsa seemed almost to be driving freely on a raging highway of water.

As the peril of a collision diminished, McIntyre breathed and hugged the two balsa logs. He felt the cold lash of the rain over his whole body. The river's water, normally seventy to eighty degrees in the daytime, was receiving an invasion of cold water from the sky. The air itself, down to perhaps fifty degrees, felt freezing.

Farther downstream, the flow widened more and yet its speed increased. It still rained hard and the flashes of lightning and rumbles of thunder followed each other as if electronically programmed. McIntyre lay on his stomach, paddling with his hands.

The two logs under him, some eight inches in diameter and seven feet long, were well tied together. The balsa seemed new. McIntyre told himself that he had a chance with the river, but had to do his best to find the camp. It was marked by that *lupuna*, that lighthouse tree. But there were plenty of *lupunas* on both shores, and any tall tree would be a good target for the incessant lightning. In truth, his escape was heavy with risk, except that the harder it rained the more the river swelled; that decreased the risk of collision and guaranteed some speed to the current.

The morning came fast, the rain itself seeming to bring a grim gray mass of light down onto the frothing waters. Where the river had been only fifty feet wide, now it looked three times wider, and its waters rippled over fallen trunks, carrying the balsa along. Still he had to try to paddle away from snags and every so often disentangle himself from them. After an unmeasured time, he let the balsa get stuck and lay half on the balsa, half submerged in the water, for a few minutes of rest.

Scenes from his childhood paraded disconnectedly across his half-closed eyes, while his gaze, directed at the gray flow, seemed to liquefy into the river.

In the 1920s Seattle still smelled of the frontier. The beaches of Lake Washington were always littered with driftwood. Even before learning how to swim, Loren had paddled his favorite watersoaked log across a mile of open lake to Mercer Island. At twelve, he had built a boat; his sister and two brothers helped him launch it for a shake-down cruise on the lake. A sudden storm nearly drowned the little McIntyres, but their parents never knew.

Exhausted, he now watched childhood drift back. Then he fell asleep, dreamed of walking through the forest and meeting a swift and powerful river, which he dared not cross, as he could hear the giant crashing sound of a waterfall just a few hundred yards downstream. The foreboding of tumbling down with the waters terrified him, while the waterfall in his dream seemed to flash its own light at the world, the vast light of a chaotic curving, falling whiteness.

He decided not to risk the crossing, yet felt that his whole existence was governed by the river and by that majestic and terrible and final waterfall. He walked back into the forest, where a remembrance of Barnacle and of his cross-eyed little boy filled McIntyre with a strong but measured sadness. Barnacle had died, but in the Indian way, without truly disappearing. Without being destroyed, or defeated. In fact, death made him more present, more evenly distributed in everything he left behind him, more meaningfully remembered. Death was his last trick and ritual.

McIntyre awoke and found himself clinging tightly to the balsa raft. The clouds were low and black. The rain was hard and very cold.

Then he heard a splash and wondered if it was from a caiman. He looked at the water, thought he saw a pair of sculpted nostrils, wondered if fatigue and nervousness were playing tricks on his senses. There were many black caimans in the river; their larger variety was called *jacare-açu* by the Indians. Civilizado hunters nicknamed them after their size: watch straps, belts, magnums, and dragons. "Watch straps" were a couple of feet long, while "dragons" measured fifteen feet and over.

He let himself into the river's flow again.

He drifted at a speed he estimated at three knots, scanning the right bank for his camp, though by his calculations he was still a day's distance upstream. He saw no *lupuna* trees. He knew that the mudbank he'd landed on would now be underwater, but he counted on sighting his rubberized bags, wisely suspended some six feet above the ground.

A few hours later he drifted into a stretch so overloaded with debris that progress became exasperatingly slow. The advantage of the weather was that there was no oppressive midday heat. Hungry, he thought of detaching segments from the palm fibers tying up the balsa and weaving them into a fish trap. Then he discarded the idea, for the trap would quickly clog with debris, and at high water all good fishing spots were overwhelmed by the flood.

He visualized the map of the region. The Javari flowed some nine hundred miles. Almost two hundred miles downstream from its source, on the Peruvian side, lay Bolognesi, a hamlet named after a hero of Peru's war of 1879 with Chile. It was a military outpost primarily established to keep an eye on Rodrigues, a similarly diminutive settlement twelve miles downstream on the Brazilian side. Between the two hamlets the twisting river straightened in an *estiron* suitable for hydroplane landings. With luck, and using the increased speed of the floodwaters, it would take about three days of paddling to reach Bolognesi.

There were a couple of hamlets on the way, but he would probably find them deserted, as most Amazonian communities vacated their villages at flood time, retreating toward higher ground. There were also *purmas*, rubber tappers' settlements, some dating back to World War II or even to the turn of the century. The majority had been abandoned for years. But he might find in one of them a canoe or the remains of one, which would increase his chances of making it to a permanent settlement.

He was facing Amazonia's most challenging feature, its isolation. One could still get lost in it, for weeks or for a lifetime.

The rain stopped, and he continued to float. Dripping with rainwater, the jungle watched his passage.

In the afternoon, he let the raft ground itself on a sand bar built high and hairy with branches carried by the impetuous river. Hulks of drowned animals were stuck among the lower branches. A dead deer, swollen grotesquely, sailed by. Flapping their wet wings, vultures fought over the storm's casualties.

Lifting the raft above his head, McIntyre climbed the sand bar and settled under a tree where the soil had become as drenched as everything around it. He had been immersed in the water so long that the skin of his hands and feet resembled a prune's.

He slept.

It rained during the night, but the next morning the clouds broke and the sun appeared. McIntyre drank water gathered in the cups of big leaves, tasteless and cool, and felt an upsurge of energy, though he had eaten nothing in over thirty-six hours. To avoid sunburn, he tied his shirt around his head, then launched the balsa and floated beside it, holding on to the logs. The river refreshed him, and apart from the hunger he felt optimistic.

He kept glancing at one shore and then at the other, then again, obsessively, at the Brazilian shore.

No *lupuna* trees. Not a trace of the camp.

He kept rewriting his notes in his mind, occasionally losing the thread of the events and having to go back. He remembered details of his communications with the headman and wondered why he received no messages from him now. Did the absence of messages mean that Barnacle was dead? Or was the memory itself a message?

Toward the middle of the day, a glum conviction that Barnacle was dead seized him. The headman was gone, yet uneradicably present. Now there was no sadness to the thought, just a low, cool, quiet certainty.

It was late afternoon when McIntyre realized that he probably wouldn't sight what was left of his camp that day, and wondered whether he might find it at all. So that he wouldn't pass it in the night, he beached the raft again, so tired that just pulling the light logs ashore was a monumental exertion. He collapsed by the balsa and dozed off, and woke up surrounded by darkness and shivering from cold.

He decided that the camp had been totally destroyed by the rains, or, having been much closer to it than he thought, he had passed it on the first night, while drifting away from the village.

The next morning he set himself on a rigorous routine of drinking plenty of water to avoid any other unnecessary depletion, and looked for shrubs and leaves to eat but found nothing that didn't taste bitter. He finally pushed the raft into the water and let himself follow the river. Around noon he saw a big tree fallen in the water, branches sticking up. Among the branches . . .

He made an effort of concentration, painfully sharpened his senses to make sure he wasn't seeing a mirage, but the result of the strain was that he almost fainted. He fought his weakness desperately and came out of it shaking, heart pounding frightfully. What at first had looked like swollen corpses stuck among the branches became man-made shapes. He counted one, two, three of his rubberized bags.

He paddled the raft toward the tree, was nearly swept under and beyond it, but managed to cling to a branch. He lost his raft in the process, saw it float away and snag itself among driftwood, against a brand-new island of debris rising in the middle of the river.

Clambering around among the branches, he freed two bags strung together, but the rope snapped and the third bag crashed into the water with a dull rattle of canned goods, almost pulling him in with it. He let it go. Tattered remains from more bags hung limply from the exposed branches, pouches of empty rubber ripped by the current, with nothing left in them.

He could try to reach the island and recover the balsa by using the two bags as floats. He cast off, but one bag sank and he was considering letting it go too, when he stepped on a shallow bottom. The balsa was dead ahead, stuck in the wet debris surrounding the new island. He lifted the bags onto a mudbank, feeling more canned goods roll around inside one of them.

Minutes later he was opening the bag: it contained cans of vegetables and fruit, but no can opener. He finally found a can with a backwinding tab, filled with salty Brazilian-made corned beef.

In a daze, he sat in the mud of the riverbank and ate.

After finishing the corned beef, he took a can of peaches that required an opener and tried to break it by dashing it against a stub, but the stub was too soft, rotted with rain. He looked for another stub, tried again, finally punctured the can and ate the peaches, amazed at how sweet they tasted. He opened the other bag, hoping to find clothes, and took inventory of some camera accessories: batteries, filters, motor drives, and some flashguns, but no cameras or film. Since the flashguns could be fired manually, they might be useful for signaling to some friendly human being or to an aircraft. He decided to take them with him. He left the bags on the mudbank, limped over to the balsa and dragged it back to the bags, then sat down to rest between the balsa and the supplies. Later, seeing himself in a glassy puddle of rain water, he noticed that the genipap stains on his face and torso were beginning to fade.

He was alive.

He wondered about the tribe. How many of the people he knew were alive, and how many had been injured or lost in the flood.

He wondered whether the cross-eyed boy had survived. As for his father, he knew that Barnacle had been lost, knew it with a certainty that allowed no room for hope or doubt. Barnacle was dead and death made him uniquely present, not just in McIntyre's memory but also in everything that surrounded him. Dying, the headman had exited the daily, physical sequence of time, entering instead that space/time/mind continuum McIntyre had almost accepted as possible during his weeks with the Mayoruna.

Staring randomly at the rain-soaked wilderness, he told himself that in a number of months he might be able to return to these shores and find the vanishing tribe. With some approximation, the Indians would give him the date of Barnacle's death. In the unwritten history of a forest tribe, the beginning of a rainy season was a strong marker. If Barnacle's death was confirmed . . .

He felt deeply persuaded of the headman's death, as if Barnacle himself was making sure that the news reached him. As strong a proof of the beaming as he might ever get, he thought, though he couldn't present it as such to a group of skeptical scientists. He touched the remaining roll of film in his pocket. Then he sat on the mudbank, so close to the dead Indian that he felt Barnacle's features superimposed on his own, as if they were one person.

The time/space/mind continuum existed. They were traveling through it together.

Then the fantastic sensation, like others experienced recently, faded.

He remained seated on the mudbank for several hours, feeling sad, though his sadness was diffuse and diluted like the headman's presence in the surrounding landscape. He thought of the big river and of its ultimate source. Somehow the beginning, the *nascente* mentioned by Câmbio, had become part of his fascination with the ultimate source, strengthening a commitment to find it or at least to visit it. His stay with the Mayoruna had tied together a lot of incidents in his life, bringing forth memories from his childhood and youth, transfigured now and connected with his quest. *If I ever make it up there . . .* he caught himself thinking.

He tried to concentrate on something concrete and practical, but no matter what he focused on he couldn't erase the conviction that if he made it to the Amazon source, he would experience a discovery far more satisfying than just putting a trickle of water on the map.

Apart from that sense of connection, something else had changed for him, and that was time. Time had become a permanent ingredient of his thoughts. The Mayoruna's ritual had given him not a beginning of wisdom, but a puzzlement with time's own substance; that puzzlement allowed him to notice details and features of time he'd always known but never treated seriously. In the oppressiveness of the forest time had freedom and flexibility. In Lima or some other big city, its value per hour and minute was exasperatingly fixed and predictable. And now he was floating back toward predictable time, aware that if he survived, that predictability would once again become a constant in his life.

Just weeks before meeting Mercier in Iquitos and deciding to fly with him up the Javari, McIntyre had been in the Andes, photographing a live volcano: Ecuador's Sangay, wrapped in clouds like a holy of holies all the year round. During the rare lulls of clear skies, it looked like a twin of Fujiyama except for the deep green rain forest dressing its lower slopes. Glimpsing it clear of clouds one morning, McIntyre rushed to hire another frail Cessna, to fly over its crater and photograph its activity.

Right above the crater, McIntyre looked through his lenses into red rivers of molten magma rippling down the steep snowfields of the seventeen-thousand-foot cone, while the crater's bottom sputtered, ruptured, and hurled past the plane chunks of lava which froze and blackened before the explorer's eyes. The chunks hissed and trailed steam like shrapnel, then fell down gelled and black, back into the crater or onto the fresh snow covering the crater's rim.

The Andes, geologically young, still behaved the way they

had while the South American landmass was drifting into its current location. Pushed up the mountainsides by winds from the east, the steamy air of the jungle made it to altitudes where colossal condensation followed, resulting in some of the world's heaviest rainfall. The Rio Polara, an Amazonian subtributary, flowed eastward out of the base of Sangay like most Amazonian headwaters once did out of hot and magma-congested volcanic cones. Down there, a time span of seventy million years had not exhausted itself, while away in the cities a human race capable of imagining such durations was busy at grinding duration almost down to nought.

Since his meeting with the vanishing tribe, all this had acquired a new meaning.

He sat on the mudbank, feeling that he belonged simultaneously to several periods of time, to several windups of the planet's clock. He was circulating freely from one period to another, following the elusive yet unmistakable silhouette of the headman.

He finally found the strength to move and decided to push ahead downstream while the daylight lasted. He lashed the rubberized bags to the balsa logs, balancing them one to each side, lay down on the logs, and let the river take him.

He drifted, paddled with his hands, and kicked his feet the rest of the day.

Before dusk, he landed at an abandoned rubber tapper's settlement, a *purma*, whose hut was underwater except for the thatched roof and the top half of the door. Against a mango tree he saw a half-sunken dugout canoe, somehow not dragged away by the waters. Its hull was cracked in several places. In it, he found a paddle with almost half the blade broken off.

Wading in water up to his waist, McIntyre gathered bits of floating wood, tore thatch from the roof, and started pounding wooden plugs into the holes, and wedging fiber into the leaky seams of the canoe. He managed to make it float, bailed the remaining water out by splashing it overboard with the paddle Amazon style, then climbed in and paddled through the open door of the hut. Ducking his head, he floated into a darkness smelling of human occupation, though everything inside was under three feet of water. On a shelf he found an iron bracket with which he could pierce the top of his tin cans.

Soon he was paddling downriver, bailing the water out with his paddle.

The canoe was hardly big enough for a grown man, much less for the bags he had stuffed into it. It was insufferably cramped: if he knelt or squatted while paddling, his bones started aching, and if he sat on his bags the boat's center of gravity rose dangerously. Soon it capsized; McIntyre slipped out of it into the river, frantically grabbed the rope connecting his bags and the paddle, and let the canoe drift into a fallen tree and become enmeshed in the branches. He righted the canoe, piled the bags back in, climbed in, and launched himself down the river again. It tipped over several more times. He redistributed the weight of the bags and paddled and bailed, bailed and paddled, for endless hours.

He fell asleep and woke up sinking. Water-soaked, the wooden hull barely floated. He painfully pushed the canoe to a beach, bailed it out, started again.

Toward dawn he thought he sighted candlelight on the Peruvian shore, but the river was flowing fast and strong, and he couldn't stop the canoe. He shouted and gestured till the light, maybe a hallucination, disappeared.

He dozed off during the brief spell between predawn and first light, then woke up under oppressive clouds and heard the sound of an engine. He looked back, saw a long *estiron* behind him, and the ghostly shape of a plane taxiing for takeoff. Frenziedly, he tore at one of the rubber bags, pulled out a photo flashgun, and snapped it on, all the while wondering whether he was dreaming or hallucinating. He prayed that the flashgun's capacitor would charge before the plane disappeared, and his heart pounded wildly when the indicator glowed red. The plane's pontoons left the water but the plane rose only a few feet, to stay clear of the overcast. For once he was thankful for the clouds—they made it dark enough for the flash to be visible. He pressed the test button and fired the flash directly at the rising plane. Then he waved his arms frantically as the plane roared overhead, its tail painted with the vertical red and white bands of the Peruvian flag.

They didn't see me.

The flash recharged, the button glowed red again. In desperation, he fired a second time at the departing tail, a hundred yards ahead.

The plane held its course, dwindling in the distance and the mist.

They didn't see me. Hell, they wouldn't be looking for me. I never expected to see a plane this far upriver.

The sound of the engine faded.

For an eternity, all he could think of was that the pilot would soon be enjoying a warm meal in some place full of light and laughter.

Then the sound reemerged; the plane reappeared and steered right at him. He fired again, but the plane was already landing. As it taxied toward him, he read the letters ARMADA PERUANA on the fuselage.

A crewman in white stepped out on the float and tossed McIntyre a rope. He grabbed it, felt it in his hands, coarse and real, fastened the end around the knot of one of his lashed-together bags. The crewman pulled him onto the float. Right next to the plane, the canoe took on water, then began to sink. He hardly noticed.

As he clambered into the plane, an overpowering emotion seized him: strapped in his seat the pilot had turned to look at him, and he wore the familiar white fatigue of the Peruvian Navy. *Gracias a Dios*, McIntyre thought crazily, in Spanish. *I'm back in the navy. They have an air arm now. They didn't when I taught at the Escuela Naval at La Punta.*

He didn't know that he was thinking aloud till the pilot exclaimed: "You *what*? You taught at the Naval Academy?"

Then he snapped around in his seat to look ahead: the plane was drifting toward a tangle of fallen trees.

Having pulled in McIntyre's bags, the crewman closed the door. The pilot started the engine, then turned and taxied to the curve at the upper end of the *estiron*, all the while shouting back questions at the emaciated apparition who spoke Spanish with a slight accent and claimed to be a navy man. Had taught ordnance and gunnery at the Naval Academy after the war. What year did the pilot finish the Naval Academy?

"In '56," muttered the pilot, whose name was Luis Castro. He wrinkled his forehead in recollection: the main text in his gunnery course at the academy was *Armamento y Tiro Naval*. By L. A. McIntyre, *Capitan de Corbeta*, USN—a gringo instructor who left the navy and stayed on in Peru. The pilot's eyes glowed, and he suddenly addressed the apparition with the black stains on his face and neck (the genipap paint hadn't quite faded from McIntyre's skin) with the deferential tone reserved for navy superiors:

"*Comandante* McIntyre?"

7

Rescued

Having flown in supplies for the little navy garrison in Bolognesi, Lieutenant Commander Luis Castro had been held up there by the atrocious weather through his birthday ("Imagine, *Comandante*, my birthday in that hole, and without a drop of scotch!"). However, rescuing the amazing gringo compensated for the delay. Castro asked him his destination and McIntyre answered, "Iquitos, or any other place with a doctor and a post office."

"I'm flying back to Iquitos," answered Castro. Then he pulled a sandwich out of a bag and offered it to the gringo, who continued the conversation while eating it, starved but visibly trying to take his time chewing and swallowing. And who was the officer in charge at the naval base in Iquitos?

"Admiral Guillermo Faura Gaig." Behind the sandwich, Castro saw the stranger's face widen in a smile. "You know him?"

The stranger who looked like a *bichicoma* (Peruvian pronunciation for beachcomber) answered that of course he knew Admiral Faura—they were shipmates on the cruiser *Grau* in 1947, right after McIntyre's transfer. Then he mentioned other names, proving that he knew the whole Peruvian Navy top brass. He was good friends with Faura and they shared a passion for geography. Faura had written a six-hundred-page book about the rivers of Peruvian

Amazonia and was a member of the Geographic Society of Lima. All of which finally prompted the question, what was the *comandante* doing on the flooded river in command of a leaky canoe?

McIntyre, now sitting in the copilot's seat, answered carefully, aware that too many details might land Mercier in trouble. Meanwhile, the floatplane tooled along, a ninety-minute hop over solid green to Nauta, population four thousand, where the Marañón and the Ucayali entwined like embattled boa constrictors to form the Amazon's main stream.

At Nauta's floating dock, Lieutenant Castro lent McIntyre money to buy a cheap shirt and pants and sandals for his cut and swollen feet. McIntyre was waited on by a mestizo woman, who pulled back when he held her hand an instant too long.

They took off and flew again for another fifty miles. Castro radioed the Iquitos naval base; shortly thereafter, he put down the plane on the Nanay River, behind the city. A car from the *comandancia* of the river fleet was already waiting there; it picked up McIntyre and drove him to the same Hotel de Turistas where he had left some of his gear in storage before setting out with Mercier.

The familiarity of the place he had left just weeks before lent his adventure both credibility and a sense of unreality. He showered, soaping his body for a long time, trying to get rid of the last stains of genipap, which looked so strange glimpsed in a bathroom mirror. He shaved with a shaky hand, then put on clean civilian khakis and shoes that pinched his feet, swollen and tender from the long immersion in water.

When he was ready his driver reported that Admiral Faura had settled the hotel bill and invited him to transfer his lodging to the bachelor officers' quarters at the base. After recovering his film supply, locked in the hotel's refrigerator, McIntyre let himself be shuttled to the base.

The Amazon at Iquitos has a forty-foot annual rise and fall, and the harbor's floating docks accommodate ocean-going cargo vessels. McIntyre had first visited Iquitos in 1948 and strolled in a US Navy uniform across the Plaza de Armas with its obelisk to the native sons fallen in the 1879–83 war with Chile. The great bronze castings of the obelisk were designed in Italy by a sculptor who misread his instructions, understanding China for Chile, and portrayed the Peruvian troops repelling Chinese invaders dressed in mandarin robes and hats. In 1910, Iquitos had been the site of an investigation ordered by the British parliament, about the atrocities of a British-owned rubber company operating on the Putumayo River. The company worked the Witoto Indians to death, tortured them, crucified them head down, and even killed them for sport—the kind of treatment that forced the Mayoruna to vanish into the wild.

In 1948, Iquitos had been considered the Siberia of careers; now, in 1969, it was a booming port, it was a sought-after billet. The car pulled up in front of a well-scrubbed navy base, with prim silhouettes in white moving with purpose between the new buildings. Admiral Faura's quarters were freshly built from varnished hardwoods. Faura himself opened the door; well fed and friendly, he embraced McIntyre, calling him by a diminutive he had used in their navy days together:

"Ay, Mac-cito, it's really you! What the hell were you doing up on the Javari? The first time I cruised its upper reaches, we carried loaded pistols and shotguns!"

From a hi-fi set made in Japan flowed symphonic music recorded in Europe that Faura had bought in the United States. McIntyre eased into a leather sofa, far kinder to his spine than the coarse mesh of a hammock made of forest products. He was back in his world. The liquor in the pisco sour offered by Faura immediately went to his head, and he asked to sit outside on the veranda—he couldn't yet take the cool wind of the air-conditioning. He looked around at the furniture and appliances, proof of man's ingeniousness, and felt that he was appraising the Western world with a layered and enhanced understanding. He had only appraised it that way a couple of times before, once after reading Burckhardt's *Civilization of the Renaissance in Italy*.

*

He hesitated to tell Faura about the beaming; like most Peruvians, Faura probably felt culturally superior to the illiterate Indians. Cautiously, McIntyre described the first contact, some of the Mayoruna ritual, his solo trek through the forest. Faura listened intently. When McIntyre described the twin waterfall, Faura pulled from a shelf his book about the Peruvian Amazon tributaries and unfolded the map insert.

Faura's finger traced the eastern foothills of the Andes, then pointed a hundred miles beyond the foothills—there was the beginning of the Javari (*Yavari* in Spanish). The Javari flowed from a sudden and separate range, a lone mountainous vanguard lost in the jungled plains, for which it was called the Cordillera Ultra-Oriental, "Ultimate Eastern Range."

"It gushes from the northern slope," said Faura. "The Cachuela de Esperanza, the 'Waterfall of Hope.' It's a *doble catarata*, a 'twin waterfall.' Let's check its position."

With a pair of dividers, probably exercising his cartographic skills for the first time in years, he pinpointed the latitude and longitude: 7 degrees 8′ 47″ south and 73 degrees 46′ 9″ west. Deeming McIntyre's initial landing spot to be some twenty-five air miles below the waterfall, they tried to figure the explorer's route across the jungle. McIntyre looked at the map, while images from his walk through the jungle lit up in his mind.

So he *had* seen the waterfall. At the time, he'd wondered whether he was hallucinating.

But, Faura pointed out, while the waterfall had been no hallucination, maybe he'd been hallucinating, whether mildly or strongly, the rest of the time. "If those Indians were performing a ritual, they might've spiked the food with frog-skin toxins regularly," the admiral said with a smile.

"What?"

"They do that," Faura smiled on. "I know it from my years on the river gunboats, when we ate an Indian meal now and then, just to switch from the navy slop. And they don't use a lot to make it work, just a few drops. It's been demonstrated through experiments that a single one of those frogs stores enough venom to kill several adult men. That's why Indian shamans throw up when they have their visions."

Loren felt a brief tremor. Frog-skin toxins in the food? All through his stay with the Mayoruna, had he been on a diet of visions?

But then . . . the beaming?

His mind rebelled. If he was constantly intoxicated, being invaded by Barnacle's thoughts could be easily explained. But then everyone else's thoughts could be invaded as easily . . . . And yet . . . He was convinced that what he had witnessed was a powerful ritual, but not a case of collective hypnosis. Up to the initiation ceremony, everyone had behaved as if normal and sober. As for ingesting a quantity of drugs every day, except for one bout of loose bowels his stomach had adjusted to the diet perfectly well. No, no, there wasn't anything unusual in the beiju, in the fish paste, in the turtle meat. If there was something, it was more likely vaporized in the air, scattered in the whole scene, and brought to eloquence in the unique person of the headman.

He felt the same strong yet quiet conviction that Barnacle, though dead, was present. Not as a ghost but as a conduit. Simultaneously he had an impression of the cross-eyed boy, who seemed sanguine and safe in continuing his father's gift.

But he had left the village days before. Sailing down the river, there had been no chance whatsoever of continuing the intoxication.

Yet Barnacle had stayed with him, present and unambiguous. Therefore the beaming.

McIntyre shook his head and refocused on Faura. The admiral marveled aloud at how the Indians had discovered so many poisons and counterpoisons, cleansers and emetics, sedatives, sudorifics, painkillers, coagulants, hallucinogens and contraceptives, natural detergents, skin conditioners, even perfumes. Some were from animals; most were from the leaves and roots of unspectacular plants of which there were thousands of varieties in the forest, their properties totally unadvertised. Yet tribal man knew about them as if he'd spent his entire spell in the new world tearing shrubs and leaves and sampling them for effects on his organism.

"They're incredible," McIntyre replied with amazed simplicity. To which Guillermo Faura nodded, sharing the feeling.

McIntyre was examined by the doctor at the base, who opened his abscesses and cleaned them of parasites, then advised him to rest. As soon as he was alone, he collapsed and slept into the early evening. He woke up, put paper in the typewriter provided by Faura, and wrote brief letters to his wife in Arlington, Virginia, and his two sons in California. He put off a trip report to the *National Geographic* and started to reconstruct the notes he had lost in the flood. He worked well for about an hour, on sheets of official paper which reminded him of the reports he used to send to his naval mission chief twenty years before. Then he started stumbling and losing his concentration, nagged by an obscure feeling. Finally he took a fresh sheet of paper.

"*Cacique Barnacle,*" he typed at the top of the sheet, "*Tribu Matses, Cachoeira Esperanza, Ultra-Oriental Cordillera.*"

I'm slipping my cables, he thought. Plain old slipping my cables.

"Dear Barnacle," he typed in English to a man who spoke no English and couldn't read or write, who never knew that Barnacle had become his name and who was perhaps already dead.

> I don't expect this letter to reach you, since the postal service doesn't even reach Bolognesi, and if it did you couldn't read this without help from someone like Câmbio (hello, Câmbio). Still, writing it makes me feel that you're alive.
>
> I sailed down with the flood to return to my territory; soon I'm going to look for the beginning of

the mother of rivers, west of yours and up in the Andes. But I shall return someday to your beginning, with my pack full of knives and medicine. Together we'll perform acts of kinship no wild creatures ever perform: like sitting near a fire and sharing food, or making arrows, or simply thinking silently at each other, till our thoughts find a way to connect.

He stopped. There really wasn't anything at all to say, since his communication with Barnacle had never been verbal.

But he continued:

I wonder if you ever thought of the possibility of a time/space/mind continuum. But you probably didn't have to think about it, for you are an expression of that continuum. Dear Barnacle, you are a scientist in your way as I am in mine, and we both know that what makes science possible and scientific inspiration effective is attitude.

Your attitude is that everything around us is alive, and therefore reachable. Since everything is alive, there is nothing that is forbidden to human experience. That's why you can travel in time though you don't know what time is (but for that matter, do I?), and that's why you are present here and will somehow manage to learn the content of these notes.

I want to know about time, and about everything else. I want to know about earth, and foremost about the source of this big river and the natural world it sustains. For you, it is less important to know about all these things—what's important is what you do with them. You're doing something with time instead of agonizing about understanding it. So you've taught me a lesson.

I expect that you will give me further proof of the existence of the time/space/mind continuum, not because I was so important and you had nothing else to do, but because I arrived onto the confines of your mode of operation. And some of that mode of operation is becoming mine also.

I shall try to keep tabs on your tribe, although trips to your territory are almost impossible. And although I don't really have to. There are other territories I'm planning to visit where you'll be able to appear and share your information. One of them is my own memory. While reconstructing these notes, I expect to learn certain things about you which, busy as we both were at the time, we considered implied and self-understood. And you shall learn things about me. There will be a result to our association. Maybe more people will benefit from it, or maybe just you and I.

He was interrupted by a knock on the door. An orderly was here, with a report from the base photo lab that his last roll of film had been deteriorated by river water seeping inside it.

He thanked the orderly, waited for the door to close, then took a fresh sheet of paper. Slipping it into the typewriter, he was interrupted again, this time by a vision of Barnacle: wide-eyed, desperate, as a rush of water lifted him off the forest floor and he clutched a sapling vibrating in the flood.

Maybe he didn't know how to swim; some forest Indians didn't though they bathed in shallow rivers and pools every day.

He typed again:
Captain Loren Alexander McIntyre, USNR, Base Naval de Iquitos, Loreto, Peru
Muy perturbado señor comandante

You fluffed one of the prime purposes of your life. You failed to get the picture. *The picture.*

Ease up. It has happened many times before, and you got over it. Be glad you weren't born before photography, when explorers had to be able to sketch or to take along a landscape artist. Or even before that, when the way to describe a discovery was to raise your voice around a campfire.

The very first thing that Barnacle signaled to you was that "some of us are friends." How did he do it? Could it be that he carries a code in his genes that you and your peers do not? August Weismann, whose theory of the germ plasm is the basis of modern genetics, would've thought so. A century ago, after studying insect embryology, he speculated that germ plasm, an early concept for genes, governed the development of all organisms. Today, we accept that genes can also carry psychological states of great antiquity, like ancestral memories and so on. But how much of those psychological states do they carry? How much ancestral memory is transmitted to each of us, to be later erased or at least inhibited by the pressure of contemporary culture? The debate is open.

Anyway, Weismann strongly influenced a favorite author of your youth, Jack London. Who wrote *Before Adam*. Remember how spellbound by *Before Adam* you were when you read it in the hiring hall of the Sailors' Union, at 59 Clay Street in San Francisco? It happened just before you shipped out to South America in 1935.

You already noticed, *comandante*, how your trip to the Javari resembles the adventures of *Before Adam*'s hero: a city boy who roamed a territory of dreams, a vast forest where his other self was a remote ancestor called Big Tooth. In those dreams, time stopped being sequential and became capable of jumping and circling.

Well, you are luckier than the city boy, for you met your ancestor in the flesh, in the guise of a tribesman nicknamed Barnacle, whose mastery of circular and unsequential time appears real, despite the fact that it is not achieved with time machines, and that his only holographic tool is his mind.

But what about clairvoyance? Does Barnacle carry

some extrasensory code in his genes? Made of tribal memories, and of an understanding of nature as a whole so deep that it can be wordless?

Maybe you'll never learn the answer. Or maybe you will if you return to take pictures of your Mayoruna friends. Realizing though that what you most devoutly wish to discover can never be recorded on film.

Before that, *comandante*, go look for the beginning of the big river itself. That's something Barnacle would understand.

He finished the second letter with the dim sounds of Iquitos in the background, feeling them not as an intrusion but as necessary and related. He folded the letters and saved them in a pocket of the portfolio Faura had sent him along with the typewriter, then went back to rewriting his lost notes.

THE SOURCE

"The Lord Oracle—Apu-Rimac—is said to have foretold the coming of bearded men who would subvert the Inca Empire. Attended by a priestess of Inca lineage, the Lord Oracle dwelt in the Apurímac River gorge that split the realm just west of Cuzco."

LOREN McINTYRE, *The Incredible Incas and Their Timeless Land*

1

The Andes

Cerro de Pasco, two hundred miles northeast of Lima and over fourteen thousand feet up in the Cordillera, is an atypical mining town. It is a blight on the face of the earth, an open pit half a mile in diameter looking from the air like the cauterized eye of a Cyclops. Down inside the gory socket, humans and machinery crawl and wriggle like hungry grubs. Before the 1950s, Pasco was perched on top of a porous wasteland of hills riddled in all directions by mining tunnels. In earlier centuries, men had dug those tunnels looking for gold and silver. Now the product is copper, and some zinc and lead.

Eventually, the town became so undermined that whole blocks of houses fell into the galleries below. The Cerro de Pasco Copper Corporation, an international consortium, decided to move the entire population of thirty thousand onto a nearby hill. Then, with great power shovels, the company tore the crust off the collapsing honeycomb where the town had stood and hollowed out that cyclopian pit.

Other mines dot the hills and mountains of the region, as they do by the thousands throughout the Andes. Some distance south of Cerro de Pasco, near Lake Junín, lies the world's largest vanadium mine. North of Pasco, at Goyllar-isquizga, the world's highest coal mine puffed and whistled until 1973 (the Incas had called the site "the place where a star fell"). There are no active volcanoes within hundreds of miles of Pasco, but the soil's strata are underlaid with volcanic rocks millions of years old. Over unthinkable spans of time, water from the bowels of the earth seeped upward into the cracks of the crust and left rich deposits of minerals. Dribbles of ore washed down into the Amazon feedwaters and were panned by the Chimu and Inca. Their amazing goldsmiths fashioned countless adornments for their kings and noblemen. Then came the Spaniards, lured by tales of an empire with roads paved with gold. In the early days of their rule pits were dug in the mountainsides, and the veins of raw material were chiseled with gouges and plucked out with picks. Today, heavy machinery does the job of gouges and picks, and a large part of the Andean population is still toiling in the mines.

Meanwhile, on the jungled side of the continent, solitary adventurous men pan the Amazon feedwaters for alluvial gold washed down from the Brazil and Guyana shields; in comparison to Andean deposits that gold is ancient, some of the oldest on earth, for the shields were mountains long before the Andes rose some sixty million years ago. Under the rain forest roof, desperate to strike it rich in the very midst of natural richness, those men work thousands of holes in the ground called *garimpos*. The *garimpeiros* come from all levels of society, but many are uneducated and superstitious, and their very trade pushes them to violence. Most of the time they don't stake a claim to their respective holes, but if it proves rich, it is worth dying for. "Gold and lead attract each other"—so goes a saying born in the gold muds of Amazonia. Thus in a thousand places along the muddy Brazilian tributaries there's always a gold rush in progress, more primitive and unregulated than California's gold rush of 1849.

But around Pasco, in the high pampa of Junín and up farther in the hills and peaks, mining is a vast enterprise, run by corporations both Peruvian and foreign, where the little people are never admitted as tough adventurers, but only as employees. For hundreds of years before the arrival of the

Spaniards, the earth's richness of precious metals was known, and the locals candidly confirmed it to the conquistadors. Not content with alluvial gold, the conquistadors cut shafts and galleries as in Europe, found deposits for which they needed thousands and thousands of workers, and to satisfy their manpower needs they adopted the Inca *mita*, or tribute in labor. Armies of Andean Indians were sent to work in the mines. Mercury was used to draw gold and silver from the paydirt; the amalgam, heated in kilns to vaporize the mercury, gave out deadly fumes that killed the kiln workers. Adding mining to disease, warfare, and loss of will to live, a hundred years after the Spaniards' arrival the Andean population had fallen from six million to less than two million.

For the next two and a half centuries, the *mita* system gave the Spanish monarchy easy cash and condemned the Indians to a sinister bondage. They were born in the mine pits and died in them. The hopelessness of that arrangement, with its cycles of revolt and apathy, caused them to react to European presence in a manner not different from the Indians in the rain forest. They retreated. But having no forest to get lost into, they made apathy, suspicion, and hostility their escape.

Even today, that separation is visible; all Andean republics contain in their midst an island, whether big or small, of highland Indians who speak minimal Spanish, resist novelty and improvement, reveal little of themselves to outsiders, and barely trade with them— sizable parts of the high Andes are still outside the money economy. And whether the civilizado who comes to the Andes is a government official, a mining engineer, a priest, or a doctor, they distrust him and make him feel that he is an occupier.

Cerro de Pasco's giant, gaping pit is particularly shocking because of the stark beauty of the surrounding countryside. The pampa of Junín, where Bolívar's troops defeated the Spanish colonial army in 1824, has a strange, somber charm. From April to October the weather is clear; from November to March it is wet and the sky incessantly patrolled by heavy clouds. Lake Junín is home to countless birds. Odd rain-carved spires of shattered rock, thrusting out of the Continental Divide, seem enchanted; they are known locally as "stone forests." In the distance, the Andes' snow-clad peaks loom bluish from the clouds' reflection.

The mines of Cerro de Pasco were discovered in 1630 and promptly began producing millions of dollars' worth of ores. In 1851, an envoy of the U.S. Navy, Lieutenant William Lewis Herndon, crossed the Andes heading for the Amazon, with orders to sail its whole length and bring back to Washington a report on its economic potential. Herndon stopped in Cerro de Pasco.

> "I can compare it to nothing so fitly," he wrote, "as the looking from the broken and rugged edges of a volcano into the crater beneath. The traveller sees small houses, built without regard to regularity on small hills, with mounds of earth and deep cavities in their very midst; and mud chimneys of ancient furnaces, contrasting strikingly with the more grace-ful funnel of the modern steam engine . . . The hill of Sta. Catalina is penetrated in every direction; and I should not be surprised if it were to cave in any day, and bury many in its ruins."

A century later, his prediction was fulfilled. Herndon also noted that some mines were nicknamed *mata-gente*, or "people killers."

The altitude being well over fourteen thousand feet, Herndon suffered from the Andean mountain sickness known as soroche. The austerity of the place depressed him: human rapports were minimal and drink the only escape. "The lust for money-making seems to have swallowed up all the finer feelings of the heart . . . There are no ladies—at least I saw none in society; and the men meet to discuss the mines, the probable price of quicksilver, and to slander and abuse each other."

Traveling in July—winter in the southern hemisphere's

reversed calendar—Herndon found the temperatures so rigorous "that the hens do not hatch, nor the llamas procreate." Rain, snow, and hail brought the thermometer down to thirty degrees. The worst discomfort, however, was the air's low oxygen content, the hypoxia, accompanied by low pressure. Herndon took to bed, while in the pits men of Inca blood worked on. (They were not even the Andes' most tested workers; in Bolivia and Chile, mines operated at 20,000 feet. At 20,262 feet, almost four miles up in the air, McIntyre had watched the sulfur ore miners of Aucanquilcha climb every day 2,000 feet of snowy slopes on foot to reach the mine's gates; at the end of the day, they breathtakingly tobogganed home on sleds they had carried up with them in the morning.)

Herndon continued on to the Amazon Basin, which he defined as mankind's future breadbasket, ignorant as he was of its thinness of soil and dependency on biorecycling. A century after his visit, the mines of Pasco had been modernized, but the solitude was unchanged and the death rate still high. The engineers, both Peruvian and foreign, lived in a state of semi-exile. Acclimation to soroche was essential. Those who liked mountain climbing were lucky.

Richard Bradshaw, a metallurgist from Birmingham, England, under contract with the Cerro de Pasco Corporation, liked mountain climbing and spent most of his free time exploring the neighboring slopes and peaks. One morning in August 1971 the phone rang in his office at the mine and he was informed that an *americano* from out of town wanted to meet him; minutes later, Loren McIntyre made his way to Bradshaw's office, which was adorned with samples of rock, diagrams of the mines' output, and photographs of various metallurgical processes.

Bradshaw was in his late thirties, tall and slender, the unobviously muscular type. The American was in his early fifties and had hazel eyes and a sharply sculpted profile with a straight and well-defined nose. He packed a camera case. He looked fit, thin but muscular, and taller than his five-ten due to a quiet nimbleness in all his movements. Being an alpinist, Bradshaw appreciated athletic people and guessed that this one had been around the area; the quiet assurance with which he walked in, the appraised glance he gave to the memorabilia on Bradshaw's desk and on the walls made him seem anything but a tourist.

McIntyre introduced himself as a writer-photographer for the *National Geographic* and almost in the same breath told Bradshaw that the *Geographic* was sponsoring an expedition to the source of the Amazon River, which he, McIntyre, was in charge of organizing. Given the fact that the source lay in a region of high peaks, four thousand feet higher than Cerro de Pasco, a skilled alpinist would be useful to have along. After hearing in Pasco that this mining engineer was a particularly passionate climber, McIntyre had come to offer Richard Bradshaw a place on the team.

"I was here the first time in 1947," said McIntyre. "Drove over the divide in an old Packard that almost didn't make it. I spent the night in Pasco and woke up gasping for air every five minutes. It was my first time at such altitude."

"Why did you come this way?" asked Bradshaw.

"I wanted to drive on to Tingo María in the jungle and take pictures."

"Were you after the source in those days?"

"I was thinking about it, but it wasn't an active search."

Bradshaw, usually a reserved individual, was forced by McIntyre's straightforward manner into relative vivaciousness. He commented that as far as he knew the source had already been found. The American smiled and confirmed that yes, it had been found, not once but a number of times. It had been surely found by the Indians, men of Inca blood like the ones toiling beyond Bradshaw's office windows. Long before the arrival of the Spaniards, they had scaled most of the peaks in the southern Andes to build cairns of worship or offer sacrificial victims to their supreme god, the sun. Without knowing it, they had found the sources of all Amazonian feedwaters and given them Quechua names that never made it onto the Europeans' maps. After the Spanish conquest, the source had been found again a number of times, starting in 1707 when Father Samuel Fritz, a Jesuit missionary, had followed the Marañón upstream and found a superb lake in the Cordillera Huayhuash, known locally as Lauricocha (in a straight line, barely sixty miles northwest of Cerro de Pasco). Father Fritz had decreed Lake Lauricocha to be the Amazon's source, and that claim was still honored by a number of contemporary maps.

But though the Marañón was one of the largest headwaters in volume (after the Río Negro and the Madeira), it soon became doubtful that it was the longest, and Lake Lauricocha kept its claim of being the source more through inertia than conviction. In the nineteenth century, as further explorations added new details to the map of the Andes, geographers began to speculate that other rivers, booming in the gorges and defiles cutting perpendicularly through the mountain ranges, journeyed many miles more. The Marañón's source couldn't be *the* source simply because the Marañón didn't flow as long as other tributaries, chiefly the Apurímac-Ucayali, which originated three hundred miles farther south in the gelid Andean heights.

"Bit of a puzzle, isn't it, that kind of source," opined Bradshaw, with the type of British understatement that said it wasn't a bit of a puzzle, but really quite a big one.

The explorer nodded calmly. He mentioned the sources of the Amazon that were right in that area. The Huallaga, beginning near Cerro de Pasco, was an Andean headwater of considerable length; even longer was the Mantaro, flowing out of Lake Junín, some twenty-five miles to the south.

"When it comes to the Amazon, everything is a source," McIntyre said with a smile. "Even the Orinoco, if you will. The link through the Casiquiare makes part of the Orinoco flow go into the Amazon, so technically the Amazon also originates in the Orinoco headwaters. But then, all the Amazon's sources are in the sky, in the sense that it's the rains and snows up there that start the river."

It had been hailing and snowing that week. The river in the sky had been pouring all over Bradshaw's office building and into the open pit of the mine.

The tranquil competence of the American had begun to appeal to Bradshaw. He felt as if he were talking to a living encyclopedia of the region; the issue of the Amazon's source, which he hadn't given much thought to before, suddenly acquired some mystery and importance.

"There is the problem of soroche," he said, jumping to the heart of the matter. "How many of the expedition's members are experienced mountain climbers?"

"Well, for one, I'm not really experienced. I've done plenty of climbing around here and in Ecuador and Colombia, but recently I've spent most of my time in the Brazilian forests. In fact, I just got back from the Xingu. Now, we're going to have with us Victor Tupa, who is the chief of classification of the Inter-American Geodetic Survey Office in Lima." McIntyre's voice warmed up; he was obviously talking of a friend. "Victor is in charge of validating place names on maps, so he's essential because whatever we find has to be authenticated by someone with the authority to do so. But he hasn't been on a field trip in a year or two, and his job is pretty sedentary."

"What about the others?"

"I'd like to keep it down to just me and Tupa. With you, we'd have a three-man team."

Bradshaw wrinkled his forehead. He was beginning to realize that the expedition was in front of him, all in the taut person of the gringo on the other side of his desk. Meanwhile, McIntyre explained that if Bradshaw was interested in joining, the *National Geographic* would pay all his costs. The Inter-American Geodetic Survey Office in Lima was contributing the vehicle to drive to whatever altitude they could reach before continuing on foot. The expedition would provide the food and the altimeters, orientation devices, maps, and everything else required.

"You don't have to worry about tent and gear. I would bring my own," muttered Bradshaw.

"You mean you're joining us?" asked McIntyre. It had been merely a half hour since he'd entered Bradshaw's office.

Bradshaw drew a big breath, though he was superbly

conditioned for this altitude. He felt that something meaningful, even history-making, had been put in front of him; a centuries-long process of search might begin to be resolved here, in his office.

"Tell me more about the source," he said.

The explorer reached into a side pocket of his camera case. From it he extracted two maps so carefully folded that they looked like shut Japanese fans, and deployed them. They were compiled by the Instituto Geografico Militar of Lima, also home to Victor Tupa's IAGS office. The first map's scale was 1:1,000,000. McIntyre fanned it out on Bradshaw's desk and showed him a region some 450 miles southeast of Pasco. Above Arequipa, between Cordillera de Vilcanota and Cordillera de Chilca, the mountain ranges did not look like chains arranged north to south as in most of Ecuador and northern Peru, but like broken bones in a trampled-on skeleton. Tall peaks alternated with round slopes and deep canyons in which the thin threads of mountain rivers wriggled like uncertain trails. Arequipa itself, Peru's second largest city, lay south of Cordillera de Chilca, at the foot of El Misti, a volcano 19,100 feet tall.

"We can drive to Arequipa and then on to Cailloma," explained McIntyre, pointing his finger at a diminutive dot. Bradshaw reacted to the latter name with familiarity: Cailloma was a mining village. "Depending on the state of the road, of course. But we plan to do this in October, the last month of the dry season, so the roads should be in pretty good condition."

McIntyre unfolded the other map, containing only the district of Cailloma. Its scale was 1:100,000. Detailed shapes of mountains, lakes, and rivers sprang up before Bradshaw's eyes.

"From Cailloma, we'll start south toward the source area," pursued the explorer. "We'll be at over fourteen thousand feet, so we might have to spend a little time in Cailloma, to let Victor adjust to the altitude. Anyway, there are no decent roads directly south of Cailloma." He gave Bradshaw a quick little smile. "We can take our chances with the trails, but we'll pretty soon have to leave the vehicle, find some llama pack train to carry our gear, and continue on foot."

Bradshaw didn't comment. He looked at the map and saw a maze of threadlike little rivers, snaking about in a catchbasin walled in by mountains, around the little dot of Cailloma. All meandered finally into the area's single substantial flow, highlighted on the map with dashes of marshes and tufts of grassland floating among them: RIO APURÍMAC said the map, in characters twice as large as in the other names.

Glancing from one map to another and then to a big map of Peru hanging on the wall, Bradshaw's eyes followed the flow of the Apurímac: it coursed north and then northwest, received the Mantaro, changed its name to Ene, twisted east and then west, changing its name again to Tambo, and finally became the Ucayali. Flowing now across the green, jungled eastern half of Peru, the Ucayali became the Amazon above Iquitos, after uniting with the Marañón.

Bradshaw's eyes jumped back and forth between the tortuousness of the Marañón and that of the Ucayali.

"The Apurímac-Ucayali looks definitely longer than the Marañón," he muttered finally, and whipped around to look at the explorer. "There was something in the *Peruvian Times* last October, about another expedition to the source."

"The British Ridgway-Asheshov expedition," confirmed McIntyre. "They claim the farthest source is on Mount Minaspata, while in '69 Helen and Frank Schreider declared it to be on Mount Huagra. Both are on the rim of the Cailloma catchbasin. But what puzzles me"—he tapped pensively on the map—"is why they ignored the headwaters more to the south, coming out of the Continental Divide. Those ought to originate thirty miles farther away than the Schreiders' and at least five miles farther than Ridgway-Asheshov's." He paused. "There might be another explanation. According to Nick Asheshov's own report in the *Peruvian Times*, all their people were downed by soroche. They were able to walk only a little beyond their vehicle, and they returned to Cailloma the same day they set out. So they never made a comprehensive check."

"In your opinion, what's the altitude of the most distant source?"

"Between seventeen and eighteen thousand feet," answered McIntyre without hesitation.

Bradshaw frowned. At fourteen thousand feet, most people begin to show some symptoms of soroche. At eighteen thousand, air pressure falls to half of what it is at sea level. Breathing draws in only half the normal amount of oxygen. Undersupplied, the brain starts to produce faulty judgments precisely at a time when alertness, resolve, and sound reasoning are critical. Vomiting, feverishness, acute fatigue and muscular pains, hallucinations, drowsiness, even fits of paranoia have been reported, sometimes by experienced climbers. Climbing too fast may result in cerebral edema or even death. The mountain gods, according to an Indian folk tale, begin to play with the mortals' minds; the ones they like, they steal.

"So let's go there." McIntyre smiled as if in conclusion to Bradshaw's thoughts; for an instant, Bradshaw glimpsed in that smile a character he didn't know yet: a youngster, almost a boy. Eager for challenge after having read exploration stories up in the attic.

"With only a three-man team?"

"It's not Annapurna." McIntyre smiled wider.

"It's eight thousand feet lower," replied Bradshaw, who knew his peaks. "But still, we can find plenty of trouble at eighteen thousand feet."

There was an instant of silence. Outside, the hoot and clang of the mines went on. In the rarefied air, lamps in domes of wire secured to every corner of the buildings burned on against the full daylight; there was no shortage of power here.

"The company would probably let me go," Bradshaw pondered out loud. "And with a day of acclimatization somewhere along the way for you and Victor. It will be fun," he decided suddenly, looking directly at McIntyre.

McIntyre rose, and Bradshaw reached for a pen to jot down the explorer's phone number and address in Lima. Not much more was said, since in the wilderness, whether mountains or jungle, the same rules apply. If two strangers meet to discuss an enterprise and agree that it is of common interest, trust is automatically implied. McIntyre would do his best with his knowledge of the area, and Bradshaw with his alpinistic stamina and experience. Nothing much had changed from the conquistadors' times, when men like Francisco de Orellana or Pedro Teixeira wagered life and the outcome of their thrusts into the unknown on instant choices of partners.

Walking McIntyre to the door, Bradshaw inquired about his stay in the Xingu; the American explained that he had visited the Waura and Kamayura natives, among whom he had old friends. Learning that over the last twenty years McIntyre had spent time with some thirty tribes, Bradshaw realized that the pursuit of the source was part of a much larger experience. It would be interesting, he reflected, to share some *alpinismo* with such a character.

They shook hands, and the explorer stepped out into the throb of the mine. Giant machinery made the earth quiver, while clangs, strained voices, and steam whistles raised a chant of purpose toward the sky.

2

The Phone Call

The Schreider expedition had drunk from the icy waters of the Huaraco, the timid mountain spring trickling from the side of Mount Huagra, in the summer of 1968. The surrounding area contained nothing except windswept plateaus, snowcapped peaks, thin streams of water often vanishing underground, a few scattered hamlets of Indian herders, and the village of Cailloma, undistinguished except for its nearby mine. The herders grazed llamas and alpacas on the ascetic shrubs and bunchgrass of the plateaus. As in Inca times, they lived outside the money economy, slaughtering their animals for food, making clothes from their wool, and using their dried dung for fuel.

Traditionally at this altitude the transportation was by llama packtrain. The plateaus averaged twelve thousand feet, near the limit of permanent human habitation, while the peaks rose to seventeen thousand feet and more. Nature was majestic, the roads bad, and the accommodations nonexistent. For an outsider, the peril of soroche, the dreaded Andean mountain sickness, of getting lost, or even of freezing to death was constant.

In December 1969, weeks after being plucked from his leaky canoe on the flooded Javari, McIntyre was still pondering the Schreiders' choice of Huagra as the site for the ultimate source. The only mention of Huagra he had found in the Biblioteca Nacional de Lima, Peru's most comprehensive library, was in a 1955 *Boletin de la Sociedad Geografica de Lima, Tomo LXXII*. In a two-page article, Colonel Dianderas, the geodetic surveyor, described his triangulation work of 1934 covering the provinces of Espinar and Cailloma and established two things: that the source was not in Lake Vilafro, a modest lake in the Cailloma Basin from which water was piped to serve a mine, and that the most likely headwater was the Huaraco, issuing from Huagra, whose exact latitude and longitude he noted, as well as its height of 5,239 meters (16,765 feet). The claim of the source being in Laguna Vilafro was easy to refute: its insignificant *chorrito de agua*, or "threadlet of water," ran into a stream already in existence, the Huaraco, which meandered by hamlets and mining camps named Huaraco, Vilafro, Bateas and Flor del Mundo, before it joined the Apurímac. In a final paragraph, Dianderas even argued that the source might be not the Huaraco, but an even less spectacular *riachuelo*, or "rivulet," the Monigote, whose course was longer than the Huaraco's; but Dianderas noted that the Monigote was formed by a series of *pântanos*, or "bogs," all more or less at the same altitude, and that there was no settlement of importance anywhere near it. Thus mixing in an unexpected demographical criterion, Dianderas himself dismissed the Monigote. The article, published two years after Perrin's expedition, no doubt responded to an increased interest in the ultimate source absent at the time of the 1934 triangulations.

The Schreiders, McIntyre was fairly convinced, did not know about Dianderas. But Perrin quite likely did; in 1934 the results of Dianderas's triangulations had been communicated to a regular session of the Sociedad Geografica. Dianderas was a lifelong member of the Sociedad Geografica and had been director of the Instituto Geografico del Ejercito ("Army Geographic Institute," later known as Instituto Geografico Militar), where the records of all Andean expeditions were kept while their details were worked into Peru's maps. Though almost unknown to American experts, Dianderas was a heavy. His assumptions were hydrographically based, his tone prudent, and his self-effacing attitude the clear mark of a worker uninterested in stunts. Dianderas was perhaps wrong about the Huaraco, for in his time there was no aerial photography to speak of. But his emphasis on the Cailloma catchbasin seemed unchallengeable.

After rereading Dianderas's article, McIntyre decided to act. From Lima's downtown telephone office, he made a call to the *National Geographic*'s map division. He waited two hours to use a relay of land lines and radio lines that ate up one word out of three, and after the connection was established, he asked for one of the map division's forty employees, an expert with bright red hair named Russell Fritz.

Fritz came on the line. To McIntyre's question as to how he was occupying his time, Fritz replied that he'd been ordered by Associate Chief Athos Grazzini to verify Helen and Frank Schreider's claim that the Amazon as measured from *their* source beat the Nile not just in flow and other parameters, but also in length. So he was verifying, concluded Russell Fritz. And so far, he didn't think they had it.

"The source?" McIntyre asked.

"No, not the source. The length. It's a tall one, to claim that the Amazon is longer than the Nile, so it's got everyone buzzing, and Gil Grosvenor [the *Geographic*'s vice president and associate editor] is pressing me for the numbers."

The issue of which river was longest had impassioned the experts for centuries; despite occasional challenges to the Nile's preeminence, there had always been a strong "Nilist" party among geographers, meeting challenges with hostility and making triumphant noises after the challenges were proven wrong. Around the turn of the century, measurements of the Mississippi-Missouri by the U.S. Army Corps of Engineers had provoked considerable excitement, as they seemed to prove the superiority of the American giant. But the corps finally reported that from source to mouth the Mississippi-Missouri stretched 3,891 miles *only*. In its last survey, the Nile had polled 4,145. The "Nilist" party reinstated the old champion.

"Anyway, the Schreiders say the Amazon is four thousand one hundred and ninety-five miles long. That makes the Nile second by fifty miles. But all I can find is some thirty nine hundred," said Fritz.

"You must be measuring the main channel, north of the delta. That's the shortest way to the mouth," remarked McIntyre.

"Well, it's hard to pick a place to say, 'This is the mouth,'" countered Fritz. "This river just keeps widening and widening until it becomes the ocean. But the north channel is the established way to measure, so that's how I'm measuring."

McIntyre nodded to himself. Conservative geographers denied the Amazon a part of its flow, that of the Para River, which marked the southern edge of the Amazon Delta. It was argued that since most of the Para's water came from the lower reach of the Tocantins, a separate river system, the length of the Amazon should be measured the shorter way, north around the island of Marajó—as big as Switzerland and lodged like a giant green olive between the Amazon's lips. On the other hand, many geographers and hydrologists, especially in Brazil, considered the Tocantins to be the easternmost Amazon tributary, thereby adding to the Amazon two hundred miles of navigable channels winding behind Marajó, and on out to sea beyond Belem. There was really no good reason to exclude the Tocantins from the Amazon's system. But length was not what interested McIntyre.

"You know, Russell," he declared across thousands of miles of relay, "I don't think the source is on Mount Huagra."

"Why?" asked Russell Fritz.

"Look at the maps," answered McIntyre.

"That's what I'm looking at all day."

"Then look again. Look at the most detailed map, the

one-to-a-hundred-thousand scale, and you'll see that the source isn't on Mount Huagra. It cannot be on Mount Huagra. There are other tributaries in the area, and they come from farther away."

There was a pause, and then a low little chuckle. The expert at M Street in Washington, D.C., found the challenge attractive.

"I'll look," promised Russell Fritz.

"Thank you. I'll call you back in a few weeks."

They hung up simultaneously. Fritz, who had spent several years with the Army Map Service, was a hard worker and a fanatic for precise measurements. Exactly the kind of expert McIntyre needed. Now the expert was going to set himself to it with road gauge and ruler and bigger and smaller maps, and the manic silent patience that had earned him his reputation.

3

How the River Got Its Name

As far as McIntyre knew, there was no record showing that the Incas were preoccupied with the source of the Amazon, although they had three-dimensional topographic maps made of clay and they were clearly geography conscious. Their empire was known in Quechua as Tahuatinsuyu, which meant the four quarters of the world, and their network of roads, radiated from Cuzco's central square, which was deemed to be the navel of the world. An empire as far-reaching as the Romans' and as tightly organized could not function without a sound knowledge of territory.

Of the largest formative waters of the Amazon, a good number stem from Inca territory. Some originate in the snowbound plateaus and peaks, while others start in the sloping, jungled *montana* to the east of the Andes. On a map, the latter are visibly shorter than the Andean ones, but encountered in the wild none give any indication of their length. The Incas possibly knew that to the east of their empire there was yet another river, biggest of all, sucking all tributaries into its monster bed. There is some archaeo-logical evidence as well as uncertain references by chroniclers that Inca parties made it downriver as far as present-day Manaus.

But if that eastward push occurred, it is doubtful that it resulted in some comprehensive map of Amazonia.

Meanwhile, over on the Atlantic Coast and inside the forest, the local tribes explored their own environment. Most of the tribes occupied defined territories, well known to their neighbors; even the itinerant ones orbited inside boundaries determined by the pressure of other tribes. When they moved, tribes followed the courses of the local rivers; whether they occupied a territory or just visited it, they gave it a name and exchanged that information with other tribes. Thus it came that during the conquistadors' trips inland, friendly Indian tribes provided the strangers with substantial facts about the adjoining regions and populations.

But that kind of knowledge was never organized into an overall picture. There was no conception of exploration per se, and the indigenous explorers, whether forest Indians or Incas, never garnered rewards for their discoveries, or a place in the public record.

Thus the first conquistadors arrived to find a total lack of cartographic information in the European sense of the term. Had they guessed the size of the world to be mapped, they might have been intimidated, for it was twice as large as Europe and thirty-five times larger than Spain. In the west it was embossed with the world's longest mountain range, the Andes; between the Andes and the Atlantic, a unique network of fifty thousand miles of navigable river irrigated about 2.7 million square miles of lush, humid savanna, matted scrub, and forty-odd varieties of tropical rain forest. At flood time, perhaps a seventh of that basin was rivers, lakes, and inundated lands. At high water, the rivers poured in and out of lakes and old arms and flooded plains with the ease of blood cells coursing through the veins of a healthy body. Together they formed the Amazon river system, a broad, majestic main stream flowing west across an enormous landscape, and the innumerable tributaries emptying into that main stream.

It was not known then that three of the river's major tributaries were more than a thousand miles long, or that eight of the big tributaries could match volume for volume the earth's next eight largest rivers, which included the

Congo, the Yangtze, the Ganges and the Mississippi. Yet it was clear from the beginning that the whole was one of the world's biggest, if least explored, flowing masses of water.

Almost everywhere along the fifty thousand miles of waterways, the natives had named the water, usually by capturing the most salient physical feature of a particular stretch. Place of quiet flow, place of rising river, place of bubbling rapids, of many fishes, of fallen logs, of fierce mosquitoes were frequent translations of mysterious names in the Quechua and Ge, Carib and Tupi languages. Sometimes the names were personifications, like Apurímac, meaning "the lord orator" or "the great speaker." Often, the same river bore a succession of names because its aspect kept changing or because neighboring tribes contributed a name each.

Thus when the Spaniards and the Portuguese landed in South America they found the vast territory named. To the lack of maps was added the confusion of a multitude of names, all alien-sounding and secret. Though European toponymy stepped in with its usual array of saints, kings, and other heroic patrons, the Indian names were simply too many and they remained the majority. To this day, ninety percent of the names in Peru are Quechua, just like seventy percent of the names in Brazil are Carib, Ge, Tupi-Guarani, or Panoan. The more detailed the map one looks at, the more overwhelming the native symphony; because everything nameable, whether field or valley, hillside or crest, bog, creek, grassland, forest, meeting of streams, gorge, plateau, or peak was named long ago by an Indian community who lived nearby. All the European topographer could contribute was to adapt the native name to the Spanish or Portuguese alphabet.

Yet at one time or another the big river was bound to become known to the world by one name. As it happened, that name was based on a fantasy, if not a lie, but it fulfilled its function of wrapping a new territory in an unforgettable resonance. Something romantic was perceived in that name, imposing it over others, older and more legitimate. The explorers who ventured into the maze of waterways and islands within the giant river's delta called it Maranhão or Marañón (in both Portuguese and Spanish it means "big tangle" or "maze"). Then the region south of the Amazon's mouth, first a Portuguese captaincy and then a Brazilian state, was baptized Maranhão, while the name Marañón migrated west and was applied to the major tributary starting in Lake Lauricocha, though its layout is not a maze—yet the idea of a maze had a strong hold on the explorers' imaginations, illustrating their anxiety about getting lost in that water world.

However, the name Amazonas was imposed upon the river as a whole as the result of a tale told by members of Francisco de Orellana's expedition. They were the first to sail the river from the eastern slopes of the Andes to the Atlantic, and reported being attacked by fierce women warriors, reminiscent of the Amazons in Greek mythology. It soon became clear that there were no such warriors on the river; the story was ridiculed by contemporaries, and seemed destined for oblivion. Yet Amazon is the name by which we know the river today, and we find that name replete with strength and evocativeness.

Who were the original Amazons? They were a fictional creation, a fabulous nation of female warriors said to raid the ancient Greeks' borders—like most early cultures, the Greeks had their own version of a fabled barbaric land adjoining their own, a land where customs are strange and reversed. Thus the Amazons, though female, had chosen the male occupation of waging war. The name Amazon meant "breastless," for each she-warrior supposedly cut off her right breast so it would not interfere with shooting a bow or hurling a spear. Since they and their realm were pure invention, the Amazons' habitat was moved about by the Greek storytellers as their knowledge of real world geography improved. In *The Iliad* they lived in Phrygia and Lycia; later they were to be found on the Black Sea. When the Black Sea was colonized, they migrated even farther—one can actually trace the development of Greek geographic knowledge by the increasingly remote locations assigned to the Amazons. Nonetheless, their mystery and purported threat remained intact. Like the half humans, half beasts of exotic latitudes, their cultural function was to maintain the interest in adventure and exploration.

Myth in the new world had the same function. Columbus never gave up the fiction of the Indies. El Dorado and La Canela and other dreams of riches beckoned to Europe's best navigators, cartographers, and administrators, and they eagerly responded.

Looking for spices and mintable metals, the Europeans approached the new world with a specialized attention, and the biggest river wasn't their object at all. It was just a roadway the conquistadors deemed useful to follow in their attempts to find El Dorado and La Canela, both rumored to lie right by the Andes' eastern ramparts. That was the myth, and to materialize it the conquistadors couldn't overrun the Incas fast enough. In 1541, the enterprising Gonzalo Pizarro, half-brother of Francisco, the conqueror of Peru, raised a huge expedition of 220 knights and four thousand Indian baggage carriers and led them across the cordillera in search of gold and cinnamon. They carried with them small cannon, harquebuses, horses, war dogs trained to fight hostile tribes, and whole herds of pigs to eat—a larger and better-equipped force than that used by Francisco Pizarro to defeat the Incas.

The expedition was a disaster, but from that disaster resulted the river's first major exploration. The Spaniards descended the Andes and entered a steaming jungle where the first victims were their baggage carriers, highland Indians unused to the heat and humidity. Gonzalo Pizarro's lieutenant was a certain Francisco de Orellana, who had crossed the ocean at sixteen and lost an eye fighting the Incas. Neither anticipated the rigors of jungle traveling. Apart from the heat and the demise of the baggage carriers, the major shock of the quest for El Dorado was starvation in a natural paradise. Though the local Indians found the bush full of tubers, fruits, fish, and game, the Spaniards neither hunted nor fished successfully and had to eat their dogs and horses. The daily rains rotted the knights' shirts beneath their coats of mail. And there seemed to be no El Dorado here (the expedition was stuck on the upper course of the Napo), or it was always beyond the next tangle of forest, beyond the next curve of the river, or in the next unfriendly tribe's territory—Gonzalo Pizarro's men, too frustrated to deal with natives intelligently, raided villages for food and shot their inhabitants.

The only thoroughfare across the wild was the river, so Gonzalo, a hot-tempered but otherwise resilient leader, ordered his men to build a brigantine. According to the chronicle of Garcilaso Inca de la Vega, Gonzalo rolled up his sleeves and "was the first to cut the wood, forge the iron, burn the charcoal, and employ himself in any other office, so as to give an example to the rest . . ." The brigantine was secured with nails and rivets "made from the shoes of horses killed as food for the sick." But even the brigantine did not sufficiently speed up the pace, as it was too small to carry everyone and part of the force trailed behind on the jungled shore. Finally, Orellana suggested that they divide the force and that he and fifty others sail ahead in the brigantine, looking for food and for natives who could be trusted as allies and guides. As soon as those were found, his party was to return to Gonzalo's camp.

Gonzalo agreed, and the two parties took leave of each other on Christmas day. They had already roamed eleven months without finding a single cinnamon tree or lump of gold.

From here on, the character of the expedition changed. Instead of groping, Orellana determinedly voyaged downriver and, whether or not he still believed in finding El Dorado, he behaved as if the Atlantic Coast was his destination. Having learned a smattering of Indian idioms, Orellana negotiated with several encountered tribes and initially his party was received hospitably. During one such stop they built a second, larger boat and lingered for a month to give Gonzalo a chance to catch up—but by this time Gonzalo was convinced of Orellana's treason and was making preparations to return to Quito. (Arriving home after another ordeal, Gonzalo rebelled against the king of Spain and became absolute ruler of Peru; four years later, he was defeated in battle and beheaded by loyalists.)

For his part, Orellana had to weigh the chances of being charged with insubordination against the lure of sailing the river in its entirety. He reasoned that they couldn't return to Gonzalo's camp by force of oars anyway, for the river irresistibly tugged them downstream, and he decided to continue east. But to acquire some legitimacy, he denounced obedience to Gonzalo and proclaimed himself a captain of His Majesty, taking possession of everything he saw and drifted past in the monarch's name. His choice is easy to understand: behind him lay a failed enterprise and potential conflict with his commanding officer. Ahead lay the Atlantic (the Spaniards had some idea of the contours of the continent), and before he reached it there was practically no limit to the wonders he would see, touch, describe in his log, or bring back in samples or in a story to be told to the whole world. His captive audience would include all Christendom, starting with the pope and Europe's kings. What decision could he possibly make but to press on?

He pressed on. He and his men were the conquerors of the wilderness and also its prisoners. For many weeks they saw little more than a narrow segment of the river; their boat seemed pinned to an almighty monotony of brown water, broken only by junctions with other rivers. Orellana's downstream voyage lasted eight months; during most of it, the feverish eyes of his men probed the luxuriance of the shores with a unique mixture of wonderment and suspicion. In June (they'd been away from Quito for fifteen months) they passed a river whose waters were black as ink; this was the Río Negro, whose dark injection ran side by side with the main stream's silty café au lait for more than ten miles.

Gradually the giant flow became an inland sea. Storms requiring the Spaniards' seasoned seamanship threw onto their decks huge flying insects, birds and bats, drippings from a hellishly teeming bush. In the water there were big turtles, caimans, manatees, the pink Amazon dolphins, the *botos*, and countless kinds of fish. It was beginning to dawn on everybody that this land's richness was not so quickly exploitable, though it was beyond calculation. Wood, nuts, dyes, hides, and above all new subjects loomed as the true gems in this exotic crown.

Of the Amazon's breathtaking statistics, none were known at the time. Orellana and his men sailed down *one fifth of the continental runoff of all the world's rivers combined* (yet what they floated on was only a fifth of that fifth, since evaporation along thousands of miles of network took out the other four fifths and kept them at all times suspended somewhere between steaming upward and raining back down—a process that would take several centuries to understand). The river mouth Orellana's party was headed for, had God moved it to Spain, would have stretched from Madrid to Valencia, half of Spain's width or the entire distance from New York to Washington, D.C. The sediment the river discharged into the ocean each year averaged a billion tons—were it limestone, that volume could build the pyramid of Cheops one hundred and seventy times.

What lived in the river and on its banks was as superlative as the river: the snakes and caimans were the longest yet encountered, anacondas nearly thirty feet, black caimans over fifteen; some insects were seven inches long; the abundance of species, both flora and fauna, defied computation and still does, and the multitude of tribes was astounding. For a solid year, Orellana's men noticed novel flowers blooming and withering in the jungle, where it is always spring for some species. All that, uncounted, unexamined, unclassified, was forced upon the visitors, who only had their overworked senses to absorb it. The fierce soldiers and top explorers of their time were awed like a gaggle of children.

But having shot and hung a few Indians, Orellana's soldiers were preceded by news of their cruelty, and for the last two thousand miles of their voyage they met with clouds of arrows and fierce surprise attacks. The Spaniards were no puppies—the wars with the Moors had trained them for sieges, ambushes, and hand-to-hand combat which they could sustain for hours, while the Indians preferred quick strikes and quick retreats. Still, according to Garcilaso the Indians were "very fierce, and in some parts the women came out to fight with their husbands. On this account, and to make his voyage the more wonderful, he [Orellana] said that it was a land of Amazons, and besought His Majesty for a commission to conquer them."

So here they are, the Amazons, as usual prowling on the border of known civilization. Orellana's own chronicler, Friar Gaspar de Carvajal, mentioned female "captains" and archers (he was injured by one of their arrows himself); they were tall and fair-skinned, "robust," "naked but with their privates covered," each fighting as fiercely as ten native men. Further in his chronicle Carvajal inserted other reports from local Indians, not of wives fighting next to their husbands, but of unassisted she-warriors, a veritable military matriarchy to whom other tribes swore allegiance.

From time to time the Amazons were said to capture men from other tribes for the purpose of insemination. When they were done with them they sent the fathers home. Of the children, they killed the baby boys but lovingly raised the girls.

As expected, the tale about the Amazons, the juiciest part of Orellana's account of his trip, reached many noble ears, starting with the king of Spain's. Whether the Amazons were the detail that prompted the royal commission, as Garcilaso seemed to insinuate, is impossible to tell, but Orellana was empowered to explore the Amazon again, this time from the mouth up. Meanwhile a noisy controversy started regarding the veracity of his report about the Amazons. Many contemporaries openly laughed at Orellana's invention, yet for the next fifty years, until Garcilaso wrote his *Royal Commentaries*, the story was much repeated. Of course, the she-warriors were never seen on the river again, though occasionally women were observed fighting in the ranks of this or that tribal population.

The endurance of the story is interesting. After Orellana's

voyage, fresh maps of the continent were drawn, containing a simplified but reasonably correct sketch of the river. On those maps the names of tribes were noted, and that of the Amazonas was marked east of the main stream's junction with the Río Negro, where the encounter allegedly took place. While there was no general name of the river (on some maps it was called Río de Orellana), the name of the she-warriors was more easily remembered than any other. In a matter of a few decades, it was applied to the river itself.

The myth of the fighting matriarchy was in character with the image of a lush and deadly realm. But what exactly had reminded Orellana of the legendary breastless she-warriors? Neither he nor his men had a classical education. Could it be that in the heat of the battle the Spaniards had mistaken some long-haired Indian men for women? Even so, then why the name Amazons instead of some other name? Puzzled by the obscure motivation, McIntyre had read and reread the chroniclers, looking for a clue. While posted in Lima, he paid a visit to San Marcos University and began to dig up dusty tomes in the university library. He came upon an interesting possible explanation in one of the *novelas de cavaleria*, the chivalric novels churned out after 1490 by Europe's newly invented printing presses. At the time of the early conquest, while the Inquisition put out the *Malleus Maleficarum* to assist Christians in their fight against the devil, the Iberian population devoured a different class of literature. Their hero was Amadis of Gaula, the knight who single-handedly defeated thousands of Moors and Saracens across twenty volumes of blood-soaked adventures of all kinds (including an aerial combat between a winged dragon and a knight riding a griffin).

In Book V of his saga, Amadis fought the "black Amazons of Californie." Those were a more likely inspiration to Orellana and his chronicler Carvajal than the Greeks' breathless furies! And it's interesting that "Californie" also found a new life in the new world, as California. The conquistadors were devotees of chivalric tales, and those who couldn't read could hear them in their native

Spain and even in America, declaimed by balladeers. Young soldiers sizzling with ego and ambition, they meant to equal their superheroes. Whether Orellana and Carvajal's invention was spontaneous and even ambiguously sincere, it was inspired by the current culture and struck the right chord in the audience: a familiar fantasy was being acted out in an exotic new environment.

The name remained. *Amazones* became *El Rio Amazonas*, the River of the Amazons. The myth was alive and well.

Meanwhile, in his readings about the Mayoruna, McIntyre had found some other connections with the myth.

Eighteen months after starting from Quito, Orellana made it to the Spanish Main, rounding Brazil's and Guiana's coasts without charts or a compass. After the news of his feat raced around the civilized world, he won royal backing to reexplore the river from the mouth up. That second expedition led to his grave.

Other Spaniards were already pushing in his footsteps. In 1560, Pedro de Ursúa and Lope de Aguirre took 370 Spaniards, almost twice the Pizarro-Orellana force, plus two thousand Indian carriers across the Andes and to the banks of the Huallaga, where, better prepared than their predecessors, they used some prebuilt material to make two brigantines and seven large flat-bottomed boats. Their objective was a somewhat less fantastic paradise, the kingdom of the Omagua. Ursúa planned to explore the little rivers one by one; stashed between them, he was sure to come across the kingdom of the Omagua with its huge tanks for raising turtles which had so impressed the preceding traveler, Orellana.

But though his plan was good, Ursúa was an unbusinesslike leader who had brought his mistress with him, a Spanish aristocrat who made him neglect the duties of leadership. His men raided the neighboring tribes including the Mayoruna, first mentioned by name in a civilizado chronicle. Eventually Lope de Aguirre murdered Ursúa, installed a puppet leader he manipulated, and pushed the expedition downstream. He planned to reach the Spanish Main, trekking across land if he had to, thinking himself powerful enough to invade it and wrench it away from the Spanish crown.

Gradually, Aguirre developed into a regular Richard III of the jungle, his suspicion of conspiracy causing him to kill freely. He forced the remaining Spaniards to sail the length of the Amazon, keeping up the pace by forbidding landings along the way. While plundering the Spanish Main, he composed arrogant letters to the Spanish crown; in one he estimated the river at two thousand leagues—six thousand statute miles—and declared that a hundred thousand armed Spaniards would still find their deaths on it. Before being executed by troops hurrying in from Peru, he killed his own sixteen-year-old daughter, who had accompanied him all the way from Quito and witnessed a year of his dementia.

During Aguirre's macabre voyage some of his soldiers deserted, choosing the cannibal-infested bush over loyalty to their leader. The Mayoruna reportedly admitted some Spanish stragglers into their tribe. This report, like the tale of the Amazon women, worked its way deeply into the record. A chronicler some years later suggested that the whole Mayoruna nation was "descended from Spanish soldiers of Ursúa's expedition." Serious travelers began to describe them as lighter than other Indians, taller, sometimes having thick beards. Whether the light-skinned tall Indians were Mayoruna or some other elusive tribe is hard to establish. But this story endured—as late as 1835, the British Smyth-Lowe expedition noted the Mayoruna's specialness: "They are of a light olive complexion, taller than most of the other tribes, and go perfectly naked. . . . The poison they make is esteemed the most powerful of any. . . . They are well formed, the women particularly so in their hands and feet; with rather straight noses and small lips. . . . Their cleanliness is remarkable, a quality for which this tribe alone is distinguished."

Light complexion, taller stature, straight noses and small

lips, cleanliness.... Nonchalantly bigoted, those notions argued for the European lineage. But the mythical qualities were the same as in the case of the Amazon women: oddity, and secretiveness. Instead of the conflicts with other tribes or the odd character of their own culture, the Mayoruna's elusiveness seemed explained by their racial mix, which was described as stable and of long date. There was an implication that their option for hiding had to do with their unusualness.

And yet, precious little was known about these people. In 1851, W. L. Herndon, sent by the U.S. Congress to estimate the economic potential of the Amazon, wrote that "little is known of this tribe, as they attack any person who goes into their territory and boatmen are careful not to encamp on their side of the Ucayali." The Mayoruna seemed to always lurk just beyond the reach of major expeditions, becoming a long-term Amazon mystery.

Many tales were deliberately reinforced by the Indians themselves, who were quick to learn what sort of truths the civilizados wanted to hear. No civilizado ever saw the Amazon women again, but at least one important traveler was informed of their existence almost a century after Orellana. Out of their strongholds by the Amazon's mouth, the Portuguese had ventured more slowly and more coolheadedly than the Spanish. Instead of El Dorado, they were after good practical goals like red wood and Indian slaves. Rowing west from Belém in 1637, Pedro Teixeira led seventy soldiers and more than a thousand Indians upstream, and after eight months and two thousand miles he met the Omagua and the Mayoruna (who were at war with each other), ascended the Quijos tributary, which the Spaniards had sailed down, climbed the Andes, and entered Quito, the base camp of most Spanish expeditions. Portugal's claim to a Brazil extending to its present western limit was thus stated.

Along his route Teixeira left forts, sites for future missions, and even treaties with tribal chieftains—by the day's standards his treatment of the natives was exemplary.

Advancing upriver, he had to choose several times which headwater to follow. The notion that all led to sources, some more distant than others, no doubt crossed his mind.

Perhaps telling him what he wanted to hear, the Tupinamba Indians confirmed to Teixeira the existence of the Amazon she-warriors. However, their residence was not on the Amazon anymore, but in Serra Tumucumaque, the densely forested region on the border of today's French Guiana. Just like the Amazons of the Greeks, these fantastic creatures seemed to be migrating away from civilization. The Indians described the juicy sexual mores of the Amazons, who once a year invited men into their villages to orgiastically assist them in procreation. And naturally, there were more stories of tall, European-looking native tribes.

While the myth survived and adapted, the river now existed both on maps and in people's minds. Amazonia had entered the human psyche as a permanent fixture, and among its novelties the Indians commanded a good deal of attention, much of it from European missionaries. The missionary orders became energetic vanguards of both Portugal's and Spain's advance and pushed on their own beyond the agreed-upon boundaries. In 1697 the Portuguese Carmelites forced their way up the Solimões River (the Brazilian name of the Amazon above Manaus) and were met with strong resistance from Bohemia-born Father Samuel Fritz, a Jesuit in charge of all Spanish missions in Amazonia; they included Nuestra Señora de Guadelupe, across the river from today's Leticia, which boasted the acculturation of some Mayorunas. In the ensuing military operations, the Omagua and other tribes were forced to swear allegiance to both sides, to supply troops, and to bear the brunt of the fighting. The Mayoruna, as usual, took to the bush. The war of the missions was fought like most colonial wars, with troops from the subjugated colonies.

The controversial Father Fritz had sailed the whole length of the Amazon to Belém, protesting the increasing Portuguese slave trade. But when the Omagua tried to benefit from the war's confusion and overthrow the Spanish rule, he had their chiefs flogged and their idols burned in a jungle auto-da-fé Europe would have been proud of. The war lasted almost half a century. In 1750, the Treaty of Madrid agreed to the Portuguese claim and the new border was fixed where it is today, along the Javari River, which cuts right through Mayoruna territory.

In 1707, the indefatigable Father Fritz, in his fifties and suffering from recurrent malaria, explored the upper course of the Marañón. He reached the Cordillera Huayhuash and found that the Marañón headwaters seeped out of a lake four miles long, an irregularly shaped amethyst cupped against steep twenty-one-thousand foot tower of ice. This was Lake Lauricocha, which, Father Fritz concluded, was the source of the Marañón and of the whole big river. Why Father Fritz ignored the southern Andean tributaries, which aerial photography would eventually reveal as longer, is easy to explain. The Marañón rushed down with a mighty flow, more impressive than the Ucayali and other headwaters, and the good father reasoned that more flow meant more length. This was a mistake in a region where river flow depended so heavily on daily rainfall and seasonal snowmelt. But Father Fritz had the limitations of his era. Amazonian hydrology was an incipient science; water volume was estimated by the naked eye and its variations not monitored.

The Amazon had one ultimate source now, though not everyone agreed on it. Up until 1978, most reputable maps noted Lake Lauricocha as the source. But there were other candidates. In the fifties, Loren McIntyre found five different sources cited on various maps. The confusion didn't seem to bother anybody; the verification of *the* ultimate source became a loud issue only in 1953, when Michel Perrin declared that it lay not up the Marañón, but up another headwater, the Ucayali. He also claimed the Amazon's total length to be longer than the Nile's, which upset members of the geographic community and led to some expectation of a race to the Amazon's source, like in the days of Burton and Speke, the Nile's heroes.

There had in fact been other quests for the ultimate source

since Father Fritz's pronouncement, but they had drawn little attention. In 1864, American archaeologist E. George Squier retraced the mythical journey of Manco Capac, founder of the Inca dynasty, from Lake Titicaca to Cuzco. He found that from the mountain lake of La Raya trickled the Rio Vilcanota, which changed its name to Urubamba before joining the Ucayali. Squier estimatd that the Ucayali started three hundred river miles farther from the Amazon's mouth than the Marañón, and suggested the ultimate source to be Lake La Raya. He was right about the Ucayali being the longest tributary, but not about the Vilcanota being the headwater. Instead of the Vilcanota, the headwater would turn out to be the Apurímac.

The Vilcanota flowed some seventy miles northeast of the village of Cailloma. It was as if exploration, like the tip of a giant finger, was groping around that side of the Andes, probing one mountain range after another and not quite locating the right one. But Squier had brought the finger closer, moving it to the Ucayali. In 1914, another American, Captain J. Campbell Besley, reached the place explored by Squier and captured it on motion picture film; he also discovered "a lost Inca city" and "the skeleton of a human eight feet tall." By that time, Peruvian maps were citing Lake Vilafro as the ultimate source; a trickle of water channeled away to serve a mine flowed from it into the Apurímac right past Cailloma.

It seems amazing that it took almost sixty more years to finally pinpoint the source. But there is a logical explanation: there were no detailed local maps, not until the 1950s, when U.S. mapping planes started taking shots of the area from above, adding to cartography the essential tool of aerial photography.

4

A Source of Sources

I saw that old father Nile without any doubt rises in the Victoria N'yanza, and as I had foretold, that lake is the great source of the holy river which cradled the first expounder of our religious belief [Moses]. I mourned, however, when I thought how much I had lost by the delays in the journey having deprived me of the pleasure of going to look at the northeast corner of the N'yanza to see what connection there was, by the strait so often spoken of, with it and the other lake where the Waganda went to get their salt, and from which another river flowed to the north . . .

Thus had John Hanning Speke described, in a style meandering more than the Nile, his moment of triumph, when he stood at Ripon Falls with cheeks roseate with pride, facing the Nile's source. He was thankful that his sponsor, the Royal Geographical Society, "had seized the enlightened view that such a discovery should not be lost to the glory of England." The sight itself left him a tad disappointed: "the scene was not exactly what I expected . . . the Wasoga and Waganda fishermen coming out in boats and taking post on all the rocks with rod and hook, hippopotami and crocodiles lying sleepily on the water, the ferry at work above the falls, and cattle driven down to drink." He had led two hundred men overland from Zanzibar, rounding lakes and crossing rivers steadily until he reached Uganda and was kept several months as an unwilling guest by the local king Mtesa. Mtesa regularly beheaded the women from his harem, and occasionally the visitors he disliked. In the course of his trek, Speke had suffered heat and illness, hunger and even captivity, yet he found the source in a land well peopled and developed. It isn't surprising that he wanted his triumph more dramatic.

For the next seventy years, the issue of which was the world's longest river kept flaring up: Was it the Nile? The Amazon? The Mississippi-Missouri? By the mid-1930s, more than a century after measurements were started by the U.S. Corps of Engineers, it was formerly declared that the Mississippi-Missouri system (the concept of a river as a system was now accepted, though not understood in its ecological implications) totaled 3,891 miles from the Missouri's remotest source to the Mississippi's mouth at the gulf of Mexico. So the Nile was king after all. Still, as late as 1969 the *Encyclopedia Britannica* noted that there was "reason to think that the Amazon is more than 4,000 mi. long, but its length is taken from maps on a scale of 1:1,000,000, while the Nile has been measured from maps on scales ranging from 1:100,000 to 1:250,000. More detailed maps of the Amazon on a larger scale would be likely to increase its estimated length because of the effect of sinuosity." The difference in the maps' scale reflects the fact that Africa had never been forbidden to explorers by its type of terrain or vegetation. Its vast open spaces easily allowed the drawing of detailed maps. Amazonia, impossibly unyielding, only gained its first complete maps with the advent of aerial photography.

The Nile flows through a desert, mostly along a single obvious channel without tributaries for the final twelve hundred miles. The Amazon flows along thousands of channels through dense forest; at high water many of the channels blur into confused lakes. The Nile is fed by three rivers; the only possible confusion regarding its ultimate source is that it might lie up the rather short Blue Nile, whose feedwaters are in Ethiopia. Though short, the Blue Nile is fed by so many little affluents receiving the comparatively rich rains of the Ethiopian mountains that it provides seventy percent of the famous Nile flood. Still, the ancients were always convinced that the source was far to the south, at the beginning of the White Nile, for merchants and travelers always brought back the story of distant lakes forming a big long river. Livingstone, shortly before dying in Africa, noted that Ptolemy had long ago made an accurate guess about the Nile's headwaters.

The task was always to march to the Nile's source rather than to figure it out. As for the society encountered on its shores, there were numerous black kingdoms, agricultural and stable, some benevolent, others warlike. None belonged to the Stone Age. No density of biota comparable to the Amazon crowded the shores of the Nile, which were also relatively clean of parasites and pests. The local civilizations had rubbed against the white world since times immemorial. In contrast, South America greeted explorers with an abundance of obstacles.

About the location of the Amazon's source, the 1969 *Britannica* was circumspect, noting only that the Amazon's "main stream rises in a chain of glacier-fed lakes near the western edge of the Andes in central Peru." Despite that vagueness, it put the length at thirty-nine hundred miles. Those estimations were not new—the *Britannica* is a yearly update of earlier editions, perpetrating much truth and also some error. By putting the source in "the Andes of central Peru," the *Britannica* left open the possibility of a longer tributary than the Marañón. But as it was eventually discovered, that tributary starts in southern rather than central Peru.

Developed in the 1920s, aerial photography only came into its own as an offshoot of World War II. It was introduced into South America by the United States, the country that won the war by treating it as a technological challenge. The United States provided the planes, the pilots, and even the film on which those pictures were taken—vast repeated surveys of Peru and Bolivia, Ecuador and Brazil. Such an intimate perusal by specialists from another nation would be unthinkable today, but those were the fifties, the time of the Good Neighbor Policy. In less than two decades, strategic secrecy became a moot point anyway. Today, satellites swirling around the world at all angles have made the United States the biggest custodian of earth information, and anyone can buy government satellite photographs, paying $10 for a 7.3 inch black and white shot.

But it was that initial postwar aerial survey that allowed geographers to clear up all manner of residual confusions. It became instantly obvious that the Río Negro and other tributaries that began on the plains could not compete in length with the Andean headwaters, and the debate about the source was narrowed down to the high Andes. In 1953, Michel Perrin announced his plan to canoe down the whole length of the Amazon, starting from a brook running into the Apurímac right outside Cailloma. Perrin knew his hydrography: following the Apurímac to the Ucayali, then on to the main stream and ultimately to its mouth, would allow him to prove that the Amazon was longer than the Nile.

Alas, Perrin's fellow canoeist gave his life to the Apurímac's roaring waters, and the expedition was aborted. From aerial photographs and the measurements Perrin had managed to make, an agreed-upon length of the Amazon was adjusted to thirty-nine hundred miles. The figure matched the one quoted by the *Britannica*.

Peru and Brazil, the countries who might have been the most interested in championing the Amazon as the longest river, were quiet. On the outskirts of Lima, the Instituto Geografico Militar kept gathering and sifting new data from both the Peruvian Air Force and the U.S. Army Corps of Engineers, eventually incorporating them into the best maps of the Peruvian Andes yet available. The data were verified by ground teams sent out by the office of the IAGS, under the direction of its *jefe de clasificacion*, Victor Tupa. Tupa, whose family name recalled that of Tupa Inca, emperor when the Incas were at their greatest geographic expansion, had the final word on identifying and naming any dot, line, or curve on the map, past and present.

Victor Tupa and Loren McIntyre were friends. For years, McIntyre had obtained his detailed maps from the Instituto Geografico Militar. For years he and Tupa had carried on an oft-interrupted and always resumed dialogue about the source.

Recently they had analyzed the aerial photographs of that catchbasin around Cailloma from which the Apurímac drew its waters. It was crisscrossed with rivulets like the bottom of a cracked bowl, all issuing from nearby heights.

Loren had flown more than once above those peaks, leaning as usual toward the open doorway of the plane, camera in hand. At twenty thousand feet the cold air bit his hands so fiercely that he could barely click his camera. His eye teared into the eyepiece. A sudden swoop of the plane through a thin air pocket combined with a defective seat belt could catapult him out into the abyss. Despite the danger, he froze in his seat, peering into the depth as if for a fateful answer.

Though perilous, those flights were familiar. He'd hovered repeatedly above the jungle-camouflaged headwaters of the Amazon's Brazilian tributaries. And he had dared the frozen sky above the beginnings of the Putumayo, the Napo, the Mantaro, the Marañón, the Vilcanota and the Choqueyapu, all trickling from Inca peaks in what were now Colombia, Ecuador, Peru, and Bolivia. Though his official purpose was photography, the flights added up to a headwaters' map in his mind. It was there, to pore over and ponder anytime the issue of the ultimate source came up. And speculating about the source was a solitary exercise, the way guessing the location of El Dorado had been for some conquistadors.

What he saw when flying above the high Andes was a jumble of mountaintops with glaciers and snowfields, and tiny streams issued from them that were visible only as dark threads. If the sun was out and the hour was early, orientation was easier, but if it was overcast only the compass could tell him where the cardinal points were, and he needed them to correlate what he saw below with the maps in the next seat of the little plane. With his eyes on the ground and then back squinting at the maps, ruffling their cold paper with frozen fingers (every so often a map was sucked out of the plane), his movements rendered more awkward by his oxygen mask, he studied how different the peaks and crests below looked from the aerial photographs and maps.

And they were different. They were so much richer in outlines and details. Those traillike, zigzagging lines were rivers. At midyear those rivers often vanished, sucked into the barren Andean ground. In spring they gushed, rich from the snowmelt, temporarily swamping their banks and giving the valleys an unfamiliar appearance of humidity. Then the dryness choked them again, and then the snow covered their beds again, equalizing them under thick layers of pure whiteness. Fierce winds carved the snow, snatching off long strands and pulverizing them into the frigid air. And when the winter blizzards howled, there was nothing to be seen down there but a witch's brew of gray-white swirling fumes in which the hunched peaks looked like penitents on a mournful pilgrimage.

That was the cycle of fresh water at such altitudes. And those were the high Andes of Peru, in summer a smooth palette of green and brown, in winter a deathscape of hundred-knot storms, snowfalls, earthquakes, and frightening avalanches.

The chains of mountain ridges called the cordilleras were crossed by shorter formations, like giant vertebrae. In winter, the spaces in-between were smoothed by arctic tablelands of snow. Under the snow or just inches under the bone-dry soil, human remains were buried on many peaks and passes. In the passes, they belonged mostly to Spanish expeditions that had once crossed east toward La Canela or El Dorado. On the peaks, they were the bodies of Inca subjects sacrificed to the sun.

Practically every peak in the Peruvian Andes had been climbed by the Incas. Two types of huacas, or Inca shrines, stood guard on the peaks and sometimes at the source of high-altitude streams. One was the *apachetas*, the cairns of stone dedicated to the whole pantheon of Andean deities. These were built simply by picking up a stone and throwing it on top of other stones, followed by more stones added by more passersby, until a crude nonfigurative monument rose among nature's own stone piles. Each Inca subject performing the stone-dropping ritual also offered prayers, adding a piece of his spirit to the surrounding universe.

After the worshipers left, blizzards and gales slapped the cairns and snow and seeping water carved them. But since to the Incas the spirit was undying, an inexhaustible fuel to the universe, the *apachetas*, even broken or collapsed, never lost their magic. Other worshipers came and added to the shrines. Whether deserted or visited regularly, the shrines remained sacred, and during religious festivals the mountains themselves became giant huacas.

By using stones, the Incas built a relationship not just with the soil, giver of food and of healing herbs, but with stone itself. Stones were considered ancestors by many Andean tribes. Stones had turned to warriors to assist Inca Pachacuti in his war with the Chancas. Stones were not lifeless. The innumerable huacas comprised temples, tombs, battlefields, caves, forts, quarries, and of course stones, stones, stones. Stones and springs were supposed to constitute half of the empire's huacas. Buildings, palaces, houses, bridges, and certain public meeting places were the other half, most of them also made of stone.

The other class of shrines on the peaks were the remains of humans sacrificed to the sun, another key ritual in the Inca religion. Annually, each Inca province provided boys or girls to be sacrificed as a form of taxation. They had to be physically perfect, without marks or infirmities, the boys about ten years old, the girls between ten and fifteen. Sometimes they were strangled with a cord, but most often they were just stripped naked, daubed with red paint, and allowed to chew coca leaves while squatting on a frozen peak, arms hugging their knees. Facing toward Cuzco, the imperial capital, they stared at the snowcapped peaks while the cold put them to sleep.

The sites of river sources were also considered huacas. Like the Incas long before them, Father Fritz, Dianderas, Perrin, and the Schreiders had followed the tiny mountain brooks up into the world's highest temple.

In 1969, Loren had flown over the source area twice; in September, right before meeting Mercier in Iquitos and deciding to undertake the Mayoruna contact, and at the end of November, less than three weeks after leaving Barnacle's tribe.

In September, the peaks and slopes were dry and full of color. Surveying them was part of Loren's assignment to get more pictures for the Schreiders' book. He also felt compelled by a sort of intellectual obligation: the whole couldn't be understood without the beginning.

A hundred miles straight south from Cuzco, he found himself above a valley whose southern rim was the Cordillera de Chilca, with the Huagra massif in the valley's northwest corner. Slightly southeast from Huagra, just seven to eight miles away, lay Cailloma, the Schreiders' base. From Cailloma, they had advanced by truck and then climbed up on foot, following a rivulet called the Santiago, whose own little headwater was the Huaraco.

The Huaraco-Santiago, barely visible from the air, trickled down until it joined the Apurímac, or "Lord Oracle," as the Incas called it. The Lord Oracle, whose roaring voice echoed in the tall Andean canyons, was said to have predicted the arrival of bearded men who would conquer the Inca Empire. The Apurímac River gorge divided the Inca realm just west of Cuzco, and the Lord Oracle dwelt in it, attended by a priestess of Inca lineage. The oracle's effigy was a tree trunk girthed with a belt of gold one palm wide, ritually splashed with human blood.

When the Spaniards rode into the area, it was said that the priestess threw herself into the gorge, calling on her god Apurímac.

Once freed from the Cailloma Basin, on its way to meeting the main stream, the Apurímac kept changing its name as it received other feedwaters. It became the Ene, the Tambo, and finally the Ucayali, a river so big that at Pucallpa, four days of boating from Iquitos, it was half a mile wide and throbbed with the trade of latex cured into huge balls and of lumber cut from the dense jungle.

The Schreiders had used the results of aerial photography ingeniously: they had pieced together charts and photos of the Huaraco-Apurímac-Ucayali-Amazon's zigzagging route and then stretched them next to each other along two hundred feet of corridor in the *National Geographic* building. With rulers and road gauges they had measured that uninterrupted flow all the way to the delta. The result, the whole, most recently surveyed length of the Amazon was a monster course of 4,007 miles by the Amazon delta's northern channel, and of 4,195 by its southern channel. Thus the southern route proved to be fifty miles longer than the Nile. The Schreiders found it geographically and hydrologically correct that the delta's southern channel should be included in the reckoning. There was no reason for the Nile to retain a title simply because the world was used to it.

As for identifying the true farthest source, Loren felt that the job had to be done in two steps. Step one was to analyze all the data provided by aerial photography and decide which area of the Andes was the most remote from the Amazon's mouth. Step two was to physically travel to that area, identify the longest tributary's original feedwater, and then ascend it to its inception, making sure that no earthquake or other whim of nature had interrupted it or significantly shortened its course.

As he flew over the source area in November, Loren found it under a cloak of early snow. Plumes of white were whipped off mountaintops by fierce gales, and fresh moldings of snow broke and slid down like overloaded cake toppings. In the east, a snowstorm was just forming: the wind whipped white powder across the slopes like a cavalry of ghosts galloping to meet the plane's shadow.

The basin held some scattered houses and corrals, a couple of hamlets, several mining camps, and one tiny village, Cailloma. There were lakes down there—Loren counted at least a dozen. There was the Apurímac, bubbling between snow-covered banks into its narrow and twisting gorge, once bridged with some of the longest, finest spans of vegetal rope ever suspended between two heights. And there was also Mount Huagra, a modest-looking peak rising northwest of Cailloma.

He was horribly airsick from the movement of the small plane. The atmosphere above the Andean peaks is calmer in the morning, but he had arrived late in Cuzco and insisted on flying above the peaks after midday, against howling gusts of wind. With the sound of the engine boring at his temples, he gritted his teeth and tried to review in his mind the lower half of the Cailloma Basin, now under snow.

The valley's southern end was closed by the Continental Divide, rising some twenty miles south of Cailloma, perhaps thirty from Mount Huagra. One rampart of the divide looped from west to east, making up a bight from which other brooks descended northward, toward Cailloma and the Apurímac.

In September, those brooks had seemed longer than the one starting on Mount Huagra. The slopes from which they issued crested up now into a bulky snowbound massif which the explorer, after squinting at the map, decided was the Mismi massif. Mismi was part of the Continental Divide; behind it was the Colca River, which plunged abruptly a few miles farther into a gorge ten thousand feet deep. The Colca flowed into the Pacific. It became part of a system of irrigation that made some agriculture possible on Peru's dry west coast.

Why had the little streams and brooks seeping out of Mismi not been included in the Schreiders' survey? Or had they?

He couldn't answer the question. But there seemed to be a lot of sources there.

The episode with the Mayoruna lay silently in Loren's memory like a text between two covers—his two flights over the source in September and now. The Mayoruna had nothing to do with this beginning of the river. Yet some connection between their quest and his came alive inside him. As if the flight had stirred up images of lush jungle, mixing them absurdly into the landscape of white valleys and peaks.

The source is in the sky, over. Rain, that's what the source is.

He heard the voice in his mind. He waited, in a state of lucid daze, pictured Câmbio, and heard his voice again.

The source is in the sky, over. Rain, that's what the source is.

Of course. What fell on the Andes, as rain, as snow, could only flow down one side of the Continental Divide or the other. Before that, what would become snow was just pregnant clouds tattered by the jagged spine of the Continental Divide. It was in that divide, in its curves and twists, that the farthest area from the mouth had to be found.

The divide was now right under him. The pocket inside that bight south of Cailloma was the area farthest from the mouth that could be considered, of that he was convinced. And whatever flowed out of it was longer than the Huaraco—it had to be.

Loren remembered the trickles coming out of that bight. He had seen them. In September.

He couldn't see them now because of the snow. Anxiety gripped his chest. The whims of seasons and the peculiarities of the terrain were factors. Increased snowfall created new streams, some fated to last just weeks. Trickles and rivulets sank into the ground, or their glaciers and snowfields of origin shifted, moving the trickles' fragile courses from one level of altitude to another. What Loren had seen from above had to be continuous and perennial, otherwise it had no relevance. The point was not to challenge past discoveries, but to offer something real and geographically valid. Farthest source had to really mean farthest source.

It had to be as close to the Continental Divide as possible, almost on top of it.

He looked at the rich snow and felt reassured that there must be something under it. Right by the continent's crest. A stream, a frozen pond. A body of water somehow cupped up there. Right there where the snowflakes from the river in the sky turned into a river on earth.

The source is in the sky, over.

You're right, Câmbio, my friend. The source is in the sky. Where the sky touches the divide.

That was the concept.

5

Wisdom and Panic

After meeting Richard Bradshaw in Cerro de Pasco, McIntyre returned to Lima. No longer the hospitable colonial capital of his youth, Lima was now a hybrid, impatient giant, loud and disoriented by its own growth. Its heart was still in the elegant Plaza de Armas, where on the founding day Pizarro had deeded to his lieutenants 117 of the as yet unerected city blocks. But its body, now harboring a third of Peru's urban population, was infected with squalor, political unrest, and drug trafficking. The city McIntyre had first walked into in 1947 wearing his smart U.S. Navy uniform was more and more becoming just a base camp for his expeditions. And like a base camp it was messy and cramped, and it pulled his attention in a dozen directions at once.

Two years had passed, yet the weeks spent with the Mayoruna were singularly etched in his memory. He kept visiting other tribes, and if they lived in the forest he found himself comparing them mentally to the cat-people. In the Xingu, he had mentioned the Mayoruna to the Villas Boas brothers, founders of the Xingu National Indian Park. Orlando and Claudio Villas Boas had spent most of their adult lives among forest tribes. They were the high priests of Indian culture observed and recorded, and their opinions on any related matters had considerable weight.

The Villas Boas brothers listened to his disclosures, finding them neither impossible nor utterly inexplicable; they were what they were, the experiences of a single civilizado surrounded by an uncontacted tribe, neither speaking the other's language. McIntyre had witnessed the cat-people's attempt to reach another reality. Pressured by the fear of an invasion (an unfounded fear, since the Javari was still largely undeveloped, but understandable in light of the Mayoruna's history), the tribe had resorted to its ultimate ritual of survival: flight through time. They believed in time travel not as a deregulation of chronology, as in a science fiction story, but as a way of reaching a special area of time, where they were to be the only people present.

But where was that special area of time located? In their minds only? In some part of objective reality?

The hold that his experience with the Mayoruna had on McIntyre's mind seemed stronger whenever he worked on the question of the Amazon's source. He'd been aware of it as he flew over the source area in November 1969. He was aware of it now, returning to Lima after adding a new member to the expedition.

Instead of going to his hotel, he decided to sort out his thoughts. He took a taxi to San Isidro and got off at the Olivar, the long olive grove with walks of red bricks, boats for hire, lovers lying on the grass, and children herded about by nannies. He wandered through the Olivar, sifting through the bizarre connections in his mind, nostalgically aware that he had lived ten years with his wife and two sons just at the edge of that olive grove, at Avenida de Los Incas, 465. At the other edge, at Avenida de la Republica, 740, stood the building he had chosen as a film studio in 1952. He was walking between them now, and between the Amazon source to the southeast and the Javari River across the mountains to the northeast, as if between the cardinal points of his life.

The Indians, time, the source. Three notions whose connection he couldn't understand, unless he was satisfied to be that connection himself.

He sat in the grass under an olive tree, telling himself that to seek an answer was more foolish than to pursue a first trickle of water among fifteen thousand. Concerning time, it was the least understood of reality's dimensions. There was no objective time, although there was evidence of its passage and awareness of its moments. Otherwise, despite historic remains scattered across the world, it was as if time didn't exist at all: people felt its effects in the transience of things, but never felt time itself. And the main feature of time by Western definition was its *passage*.

The cat-people, however, challenged the notion of time's passage, or rather accepted it only if that passage suited them. They had strong ideas about the direction of that passage and how it could be modified. In a sense, they had cleared man's most enduring perplexity, the one regarding the nature and material of time, for they were the material of time themselves. They were what moved time forward or back, or what kept it still. Through them, time expressed itself and found its direction; it acquired utility and even a sort of moral character instead of remaining the monotonous, faceless, merciless *passage* of more evolved cultures.

For the Mayoruna time was at once mobile and static, abstract and yet concrete. They saw man as something of a master of time, as if both community and individuals owned their time and carried it around with them, like an extra layer of existence. Time moved with man, stopped with him, advanced and retreated with him. Time was not the implacable judge, condemning man to a tragically brief life. Time was a shelter. An escape into safety and regeneration. A repository whose chief function was not piling up the past, intact yet dead, but rather keeping the past alive and available. At certain moments the tribespeople called on that past, to assist them with an alternative to a menacing present.

But was there, as a scientifically minded Westerner would ask, any objective reality to all that? The "beginning" sounded fine as tribal folklore. It was convincing as subjective reality, whether collective or individual. But what about it being *true* in the Western sense of the term? Which meant objectifiable, quantifiable, and observable under lab conditions?

To that, McIntyre had no answer. He was doubly at a disadvantage being neither a psychologist nor a physicist and having been imbued since childhood with the healthy old Scottish conviction that whatever exists in this world must be both real and concrete. And yet . . .

And yet he had seen those Indians taking action and had found their action disturbingly convincing. He appreciated their courage in dealing with man's most perplexing query. From quantum mechanics to parapsychology, much of human inquiry was focused on time, and so far all had failed to define its nature otherwise than as an abstract of everything. Instead of thinking of time as an abstract, the Indians attacked its unreality directly and with vigor, by the method most comfortable to them, which was ritual. They starved and exhausted themselves, brought themselves almost to the brink of collective disaster, yet once at that suspenseful threshold they exploded into joyful antics and declared themselves redeemed, admitted into the beginning, and safe.

Sitting in the Olivar, McIntyre thought about his tribal friends. Two years had passed, but maybe they still believed that they were in the beginning. They would abide there as long as necessary till they felt they could unleash themselves upon the present again, confident in their renewed chance of survival.

Maybe their whole tribal history was made of such dilations and contractions. Time was that tribe's heartbeat.

On his return from the Javari, McIntyre had recontacted the linguists in Yarinacocha and asked about their search for the Mayoruna. Still buzzing around in small planes, the missionaries had achieved some contacts but no stable cultural exchange with the cat-people. McIntyre told them of the existence of a branch of the tribe living close to the Javari's source. Through officials of FUNAI in Brasília (there were no FUNAI agents posted on the course of the Javari), Loren tried to assemble the latest data about the Mayoruna southeast of the Peru-Brazil border. The responses on the Brazilian side were disappointing: Indians with labrets had been sighted now and then from boats and planes, by pilots and prospectors and other Indians. In the absence of regular exchanges, their territory remained elusive.

Or maybe, in spite of how fantastic that sounded, there was another kind of territory down there, a secret territory? A sanctuary in which the Mayoruna could hide effectively and reappear when convenient? The existence of a Shangri-La on the Javari would account for the blanks in their history. But the notion was as charming as it was incredible.

Where was Barnacle now, and what was happening to his tribespeople? Were they still celebrating, still dancing and taking vision-inducing drugs in that magical space they called the beginning?

Not Barnacle. McIntyre felt certain that the headman had perished during the flood. But did that mean that Barnacle was truly gone? The beginning, as explained by Câmbio, was the locker where the models, the molds, the originals of everything and everyone were kept. Even dead, Barnacle could not lose his place in the beginning any more than McIntyre could, assuming that the *chotac*—the non-Mayoruna, the "others"—also had originals and that the Mayoruna had allotted them room in their magical locker.

Meanwhile, another expedition to the upper Javari was neither cheap nor easy to arrange, and there was the daily business of making a living. In the last eighteen months, McIntyre had shot film footage for an eighty-minute *National Geographic* documentary on Colombia, visited the salt-gathering Indians of the Guajira Peninsula, and made several trips to the Xingu, and made several trips back to the United States. To hurriedly return to the upper Javari in-between, without coordinated planning and sound rescue arrangements, meant to take a foolish risk.

Besides, he was preparing an expedition to the source.

*

The last week before Christmas 1969, McIntyre had waited every hour for a call from Russell Fritz. Finally he gave up and phoned Fritz in Washington.

"Just getting ready to call you," said Fritz.

They spread maps at their respective ends of the line, McIntyre in a narrow phone booth at Lima's central telephone office and Fritz in the comfortable Cartographic Division of the *National Geographic*. Fritz confirmed that a tributary did flow right out of the Continental Divide, and it was called the Rio Lloqueta. The Lloqueta continued down into the Challamayo, which gathered strength and flow and became the Rio Hornillos. The Hornillos veered east and then north again, and coursed down a long range of hillsides till it threw itself into the Apurímac.

"So it's longer than the Huaraco?" asked McIntyre.

"Yes. By about thirty miles."

McIntyre nodded. "I see some brooks running into the Lloqueta," he said, squinting at some threads twisting out of the southernmost rampart of the Continental Divide.

"Yes, they are the Lloqueta's feedwaters, five of them. The Calomoroca, the Apacheta, and the Carhuasanta are the longest."

"So the most distant source must be up one of them."

"Seems that way, but you'd have to climb up there to be sure."

"Are any of those brooks strictly seasonal?"

"From what I hear, almost everything's seasonal up there," said Fritz. "So if you really plan to go and check it out, I suggest you go during the dry season. That way you won't take some freak little flush water for a tributary."

"Good point," agreed McIntyre.

"Planning to do it soon?"

"Yes, but . . ." He felt invaded by the same quiet, lucid daze he had experienced flying over the snowbound catch-basin. "I need someone of authority to take with me, a real credible authenticator. I'd also like the *Geographic* involved, but right now they're still hung up with Mount Huagra and that longer-than-the-Nile business. But that's okay; if the

Lloqueta is the real thing, it will be there."

"I guess you're right. Let me know if I can help."

They said good-bye and hung up.

Now he had to wait. The wet season had already started, spreading the cloak of snow over the entire source area. Besides, he had to finish his documentary on Colombia. In any case, an expedition of this sort was unthinkable without scientific sponsorship. He discussed the issue with Victor Tupa; Tupa saw the merits of a verification of the source and suggested they call on Lieutenant Colonel James Hawks, U.S. Army Corps of Engineers, liaison to the IAGS office in Washington and one of Tupa's superiors. They went armed with piles of maps and photographs, spread them on Hawks's desk and floor, and convinced him to write letters of support if necessary. McIntyre caught himself smiling; his plan was beginning to come alive.

Days later he was jolted from his growing confidence by an article in the *Peruvian Times*. A British expedition had just driven to Cailloma, roamed around Lake Vilafro, then pushed as far south as their guide could move his truck, and declared the true source to be on Mount Minaspata, a peak on the Continental Divide but slightly northwest of the semicircular rampart targeted by McIntyre. According to the article itself, the expedition members had been too sick with soroche to climb the peak; about the location of the source, they took the word of a certain Dick Knapp, manager of Cailloma's Huayllacho Mine.

McIntyre read the article in a badly lit Lima cutting room, taking a break from assembling film footage on Colombia. Half an hour later he was at the telephone office. Two hours later he was talking long distance to Russell Fritz.

"I see what they did," said Fritz over thousands of miles of relay. "They drove southwest, up the Ancollagua, instead of south, up the Lloqueta. They still missed some five and a half miles of flow. The Lloqueta's feedwaters are longer."

"Are you sure?" asked McIntyre, huddled in the old-fashioned telephone booth, exhausted after two hours of waiting, nervously fingering IGM maps 31S and 16g, made from stereoscopic photographs.

"That's what my road gauge tells me. They probably took that local's word that the source was up Minaspata. Whatever dribbled up there, they called it the source."

McIntyre breathed, then glanced at his maps, hoping that Russell's road gauge was not mistaken. But if it was, then it was wrong about the Ancollagua too, and about all the other features of the area.

"You're all right, Loren," said Fritz, "but they came awful close."

They discussed the error of the British expedition and agreed that the attempt had merit. The valley was crawling with tributaries bewilderingly seeping in from all directions. No expedition would have the energy to follow each one, battling snow and soroche.

Meanwhile, the Britons were the talk of Lima, and the talk was *trés chic*. One, the son-in-law of a lord, was planning to start a school of adventure for the world's elite; another was a former ski champion who had competed in the Olympic games. They seemed cut of such a different cloth from McIntyre, this gringo who had roamed the continent bunking with *garimpeiros* and lepers, piloting riverboats for their drunken captains, flying with snakebitten Indians to bush hospitals, and eating beiju with denizens of the forest. Amazingly, those sophisticates had gone up without a thorough cartographic analysis of the area, stared at a peak from Dick Knapp's truck, and then rolled back down.

"You gotta do it, Loren. You gotta go up there," concluded Russell Fritz.

McIntyre expected time to drag, but instead it started to race. He flew back to Washington to lay the music and sound track onto the Colombia film at the *Geographic*'s film laboratory. The film was completed and screened at Constitution Hall in March 1971, for audiences totalling twelve thousand viewers. The *National Geographic* Society's president and board of trustees were in the audience. Virgilio Barco, ambassador and soon-to-be president of Colombia, gave McIntyre a bear hug backstage and told him with Latin excitement that "Colombia is yours." The *Geographic*'s editor told McIntyre that the Amazon was his, both text and pictures, the entire region, to cover for the magazine as soon as he was ready: "Go wherever you like, take as long as you want, just come back with the Amazon in your bag. Fifty million readers must feel that they're making the expedition with you."

By assigning him to paint such a broad portrait of the river, the *Geographic* was both officializing and funding the expedition. The source and area of the source were to form a distinct chapter of the story. McIntyre and Fritz pored over the maps and aerial photos one last time, laughing shoulder to shoulder instead of catching every third word over a wretched intercontinental phone connection. The *National Geographic*'s Travel Department issued McIntyre the airline tickets he asked for, while Accounting provided thousands of dollars in cash and travelers' checks. A long way from drifting alone, half naked and hungry, on a raft down a rain-swollen tributary.

McIntyre called Tupa in Lima. Tupa enthusiastically agreed to join the expedition. Tupa's boss, Colonel Hawks, offered to provide the vehicle, a 1970 all-terrain Ford Bronco. Thus the trip up became a joint *National Geographic*–IAGS effort.

Tupa and McIntyre set out from Lima on October 9, 1971. Two years had passed since the Apollo 11 astronauts had walked on the moon and McIntyre had paddled a leaky canoe downriver to civilization. This time, in two days, McIntyre and Tupa were to drive more than seven hundred miles down the Pan American Highway, across one of the world's driest deserts, and then head east into the high sierra. They were to spend the first night in Nazca, near the mysterious lines on the desert, and the second in Arequipa. There Bradshaw would rendezvous with them after flying in from Cerro de Pasco. On the third night, the expedition was scheduled to reach Cailloma, base camp to the assault on the source.

6

Into the Dream

Victor Tupa took the wheel of the Bronco, while McIntyre huddled in the front seat next to him. Carrying only portable stoves, a Bishop Ultimate tent for four, cooking utensils, food—mostly dehydrated, medicine, ice axes, ropes, and crampons, the ATV looked spacious and the expedition undersupplied. Packed in cases were cameras, eighty rolls of 35mm film, compasses, and altimeters—so minimal, it seemed, for attacking the Cordillera. There were also two small folded flags, one Peruvian and one American (Bradshaw was bringing his own miniature Union Jack), a tiny *National Geographic* banner, and a circular plaque of the IAGS, with a map of the Western Hemisphere inscribed in a triangle of azure blue stamped with a castle (symbol of the U.S. Army Corps of Engineers). The flags and plaque seemed frail and unlasting. In fact, in the dank chill of the Lima predawn nothing in this enterprise seemed safe or glorious. With the words "Off to the source," Tupa swung the Bronco from the potholed pavement of the suburbs on to the dark asphalt of the Pan American. Immediately, beyond its windows began a vision of stern timelessness.

The desert south of Lima is one of the earth's driest, making North American deserts look like bustling green-houses. Vast dunes, their crests disheveled by the wind, rolled back, alternating with valleys of graveled stone. The Pan

American is an asphalt highway, lunar with holes made by the heavy truck traffic. Every so often, mostly on the curves, rise clusters of crosses marking fatal collisions. The landscape is as barren and stark as Amazonia is lush and verdant.

They drove along that narrow strip of desert, with the ocean on the right and the mountains on the left. They followed the wrinkle forced on the continent's brow as South America drifted away from Pangaia, overriding the tectonic plates ahead and forcing them to respond to pressure with pressure. That clash built the towering Andes. The giant river existed already, but it had flowed from east to west until the Andes rose in its way and stopped its flow. As a result, a huge lake had been formed in the middle of South America. Next to the simmering dough of the rising Andes, the water started to evaporate, adding to the bursting rain clouds of an era more hot and humid than ours. The clouds rained down on the Andes in sea-sized volumes, and maybe that stirred the giant lake, pushing the captive waters eastward, until they burst through ancient highlands — the Brazilian and Guiana Shields — and flowed into the Atlantic. In comparison to the ages these processes took, man's antiquity was a blink. *Homo erectus*, a tribesman like Barnacle, and Loren McIntyre were absolute contemporaries.

Tupa broke McIntyre's train of thought. He was a voluble, optimistic individual of medium height and true Andean build, round and muscular. His eyes were deep brown, his face fleshy, and his lustrously black hair struck with some grayness. Thanks to his sedentary job he had gained weight, and he joked about it. "You don't *really* expect me to climb to the source, with my waistline. Seventeen thousand feet is well beyond the call of duty."

"It's above seventeen thousand, and we'll do it slowly," McIntyre reassured him. He was staring through the Bronco's windshield at the somber sierra. So insect-free was the desert air that the windshield showed not one speck from a squashed bug.

He remembered some lines by Kipling: "Something hidden. Go and find it/ Go and look behind the Ranges/ Something lost behind the Ranges/ Lost and waiting for you. Go!" Strong, simple lines of unselfconscious vitality. Born under the tropics' extreme stars, Kipling had lived like McIntyre, at the edge of a mysterious world. "Lost and waiting for you. Go!" Soon there would be nothing lost behind the ranges.

"You look very philosophical." Victor smiled, glancing away from the road.

"I was thinking," replied McIntyre, "about that MACON irrigation project to dam the upper Apurímac."

Just as the Incas had diverted rivers to water their potato-growing terraces, a consortium financed by Peru, Spain, South Africa, Britain, Canada, and Sweden was currently excavating canals to catch various headwaters on the Pacific side of the Continental Divide and divert them into the Colca River. Eventually, a 43-mile-long tunnel through the divide would also bring Apurímac headwaters into the Colca, to triple its volume and irrigate one hundred thousand square miles of Peru's rainless coast. The project was already behind schedule and running into colossal unforeseen expenses.

"I'm concerned that if they dam the Apurímac or throw some grid in the way of the Lloqueta, some people might say that the Apurímac is no longer a valid headwater for the source," mused McIntyre.

"That's ridiculous." Tupa laughed. "After the *sovieticos* dammed the Nile, did anyone suggest that its source had been moved down to Aswan?"

"I know. But if *all* the Apurímac headwaters from the Cailloma basin are directed to the Pacific, none of them can be the source . . ."

Victor scratched the short hairs on his temple, their straight dark fibers confirming his Inca ancestry, then turned his fleshy face toward the *americanô:* "Don't worry, Loren. You just said the key word: *All* the waters. Unless a hundred percent of the flow is sent through the tunnel, some of the source waters we're going to see will still feed the Amazon."

"And if not, prepare to start looking for another source," the explorer said with a laugh.

He looked at the sierra again, and Tupa guessed his thought: time had changed the sierra so slowly. Man could change it so disastrously fast.

By five P.M. the Bronco was driving into Nazca, past the puzzling lines left by a civilization otherwise unknown. In a dry wasteland with almost no fauna, the ancient Nazca Indians drew an orgy of animal forms: a monkey, a whale, a giant spider, and eighteen bird figures, some extremely complicated. A huge hummingbird stretched six-feathered wings on each side of its body, a five-feathered tail at the back, the whole drawn with a single line that never crossed itself. Abstract shapes accompanied the animals, some made of faultlessly straight lines. Tupa commented with professional appreciation on the Nazca's surveying excellence. They had moved millions of rocks to clear the lighter ground underneath and then laid out the rocks in absolutely straight rows, or along perfect figurative contours.

After having supper with Loren's old friend Maria Reiche, doyen of the Nazca lines, the two men decided to go to bed early, to stock up on energy for the strain of high altitude. Yet after dinner McIntyre walked out of Nazca's state-run hotel and stood under the sharp glitter of the Andean stars trying to sum up the day's thoughts. Why had such noted civilizations as the Nazca and Inca flourished here? Why would people decide to live in a strip of desert, with their backs to a hostile mountain chain? Particularly if behind it spread the vastness of Amazonia, warm and teeming with wildlife, a hunter-gatherer's paradise?

He knew some of the answers. The desert coast, when watered, was surprisingly good for agriculture. The ocean next to the desert was swarming with fish. The mountains proved livable up to fifteen thousand feet and on their terraces the cultivation of corn and potatoes became a yearly miracle. Stockpiling food allowed the formation of cities, the maintenance of armies and engineering forces, the invention of systems of accounting and legislation, and the creation of official mythologies. The temple-building cultures became possible, but their armies lacked the horse, and the Spaniards' technology, which led to such easy defeat.

But why had other ancient populations remained hunter-gatherers, like Barnacle and his people? Had they never been exposed to agriculture and fixed settlement during thousands of years of wandering in the New World, after crossing over from what is now northern China? All American aborigines were not truly aborigines but had reached the Americas by the same route: a land bridge one thousand miles wide that linked Siberia with Alaska during the last two glaciations. Barnacle's ancestors crossed that bridge along its southern edge, which was sufficiently free of ice to permit hunting on the shore and fishing in the ocean. To their north towered masses of ice perhaps two miles thick, but they found enough passage to keep straggling south.

They left the glaciers behind and hunted the virgin lands into Mexico. They dripped down the funnel of Central America and found the Andean highlands before them. Southward along the coast stretched the inhospitable desert.

The desert was too hostile. Even in Inca times, there was little traffic along the coast itself. The early travelers would advance up one of the short rivers that flowed into the Pacific, reach the highlands where the climate was less extreme and game was plentiful, then descend again farther south, along another river valley. The coast was thus settled, by small communities arriving in successive spurts, until they coagulated into more populous cultures.

Others kept moving, on to the next horizon, and the next. McIntyre imagined Barnacle's forebears following the rivers up, keeping to highland meadows, finding passages across the Andes, which could only be other river valleys. Now the rivers ran east. Down those rivers, into the forest. Long before the temple-building days, Barnacle's forebears were already settled in the forest.

The forest forced them to a different course of development. Innumerable barriers of growth like so many green frontiers kept the communities small. Contacts with others were restricted. Hundreds of tribal languages developed in Amazonia, reciprocally unintelligible, all seemingly unrelated to their Asiatic counterparts. In the forest, food could not be stockpiled; it would rot. Building materials were abundant but unlasting. Everything was at hand but the horizon was oppressively near. There was no need for exploration beyond the extension of hunting trails or the trading of one tribe's feathers against another's pottery.

In that ambience, time was not a social stimulator, as there was no hurry to produce, and there was no history of kings, battles, or dramatic triumphs over the environment. There was no achievement beyond a village, a federation of tribes, an undisputed territory. Tribes became numerous as a result of successful hunting and gathering of tubers during periods of minimal warfare. Otherwise, time stood still. Had McIntyre visited the Mayoruna five thousand years earlier, he probably would have found them at a similar stage of development, minus some knowledge of the forest plants' utilitarian properties.

But they had surely descended into the forest carrying some atavistic memories of their trek south.

He wondered what memories of that trek they were carrying. Surviving that huge expanse of ice. Slogging along its edges. Then climbing into the highlands. Getting hallucinatorily close to a sky they deemed filled with gods, while in fact it was full of radiation from the formation of other worlds.

Nothing ahead but pristine space. Trekking, trekking, absorbed by the emptiness ahead. Along that passage, did they speak a language? A host of languages? Was that passage so prolonged that at the end their languages had changed beyond recognition? Or was language a late acquisition, a development started in the open spaces and completed in the forest? In which case, the beaming might have been an earlier way of communication. The continuation of an old tribal practice, rather than a recent shamanistic technique.

Moving along, aware of just a few generations of ancestors, how much memory from the odyssey of a race was carried by individuals? How much of it was clear, how much fogged-up and hesitant, and flexible like a campfire tale? McIntyre had no way of knowing, but assumed the existence of tales, of oral traditions, for they were part of any tribe's heritage. Trekking on. Time passed. Peeking behind the horizon took centuries. This was exploration of the most tentative kind, in search of game and edible roots.

Moving from ice to brush, sierra, and forest. Carrying now memories of extreme antiquity, some of them perhaps genetically fixed. Did those memories result in the ritual of "the beginning"? Was the beginning a metaphor for that sense of pristine, unpeopled space?

He had no answers to those questions.

Except for this: Barnacle's ancestors had survived the ice, passed along the highlands, then followed the rivers across the mountains. Watched by the same stars, witnessed by the same snowcapped peaks. Toward the forest where time stopped.

After streaking southeast along the coast, the Pan American Highway veers inland at Camaná, toward the high sierra, and quickly climbs through rainless sands to seventy-five hundred feet elevation. At sunset on October 10, as the last rays of sun gilded the summit of El Misti Volcano, the Bronco neared the "white city" of Arequipa, second-largest in Peru, lying at the volcano's base. Its older districts were built of a compacted white volcanic ash called *sillar*. After a day of hard driving, the Bronco rolled into Arequipa and across the downtown sections as if reviewing their history. Around the Plaza de Armas, the faded pearl-white *sillar* still glittered in the walls of churches and palaces. Cobbled lanes zigzagged between massive walls, and clocks tolled in church towers. Then the Bronco sped through the new Arequipa, industrial and noisy. Aggressive traffic, modern supermarkets, the giant Leche Gloria condensed milk plant (there was some of that milk in the expedition's supplies), and the rapidly expanding slums overwhelmed the poetry of colonial days. Broken neon signs blinked over shops and bars, political posters poxed the walls, and the Indian faces in the streets looked blank in their ready-made clothes. Above both the old and the new presided a congregation of snow-clad volcanoes, barely visible in the fading light: saddle-peaked Nevado de Chachani, cone-shaped El Misti, and lopsided Pichu Pichu off to the right.

They found Richard Bradshaw in the dining room of the Hotel de Turistas, seated facing a window overlooking the garden, where a pet vicuña chomped the grass. "Keeping the lawn cut," explained the hotel manager. Bradshaw had flown down wearing knickers, woolen stockings, and British hiking boots. When he rose to greet McIntyre and Tupa, the energy of his tall body seemed to put the expedition instantly into focus.

This being their last civilizado dinner for a while, they all ordered beefsteak. On the road to Cailloma they would eat canned products, and once on the trail they would be restricted to lightweight, high-energy foods like candy bars, condensed milk, and soups. Bradshaw promised to cook Indian meals, for which he had acquired a taste: *chuño*, frozen dehydrated potatoes; *charqui*, strips of sheep or llama meat crisp-dried in the sun, softened by dunking in a rancid soup; and coarse flour pancakes. Nutritious and unrefined, Indian food was like the sierra, solid, incapable of pretense.

After dinner, in McIntyre's hotel room, they took another look at the map. Up to Cailloma they would follow Road 109, into the Andes and over the Continental Divide. From Cailloma, smaller roads connected the mining camps to the surrounding villages, but no drivable ones south of Cailloma reached the divide.

Over the whole fate of the expedition hung the question of the weather. The hotel manager, as good an expert as any in a country without weather forecasts, claimed that 1971 had been an exceptionally dry year. On the way in,

McIntyre had noticed that not a speck of snow whitened the nineteen-thousand-foot cone of El Misti. But that could be reversed at any time in less than an hour by winds pushing over a steely buildup of clouds, pelting the earth with a peculiar fine hail, like a white sandstorm. If repeated snowfalls caught them on their way up to the Continental Divide, the expedition could be seriously imperiled.

As for the road to Cailloma, it was poorer than an untended county road in Utah, being just a flattened bed of crushed rock and gravel traveled by an occasional bus or mining truck. The distance from Arequipa was only some seventy miles by air, but by car it took a good long day of attentive driving, often slowing down to ten miles per hour to avoid tire damage. The road ran almost straight north along a dour altiplano, crossing the Continental Divide some thirty miles east of Mismi. Then it squirmed into the Cailloma Basin, a harsh, swampy plateau watered by innumerable rivulets. Not long before reaching the tiny village of Angostura, the road started following the lower course of the Hornillos River, fed by the waters of the Lloqueta. At Angostura the Hornillos joined the Apurímac and the road veered west toward Cailloma, where the expedition was to spend its third night.

On the fourth day they planned to start south toward the Continental Divide. McIntyre estimated that at most they might drive two hours out of Cailloma before all trails disappeared. The map indicated rolling hills with lakes and bogs. They would have to park the Bronco, load their gear onto a couple of dollar-a-day llamas, and head for the heights.

"That's where the fun starts," predicted Bradshaw.

But the fun started as soon as they left Arequipa. Before running straight north, Road 109 wound steeply uphill through old ashfall from the volanoes El Misti and Chachani; a chill wind started to blow between the two giant peaks, making the brand-new Bronco feel as penetrable as a screen door. The ashfall made the road hard to follow. Local trucks had ignored the switchbacks of the road and frequently descended straight down the slopes. Tired of the winding, Victor Tupa tried to go straight up in their tracks and found himself on an incline too steep for the Bronco's four-wheel drive.

They made it back to the gravel top, the Bronco springing and bucking. The wind kept blowing and the team took the rough ride as best they could, teeth chattering from both the wild tossing and the cold. Despite the discomfort, it was impossible not to admire the landscape's frigid majesty. Thin clouds whipped over dramatic crags, and when their shadows rippled down, the dark ramparts seemed to be dripping silent music. The barrenness was total; the eye searched in vain for anything green rising to a person's height. Deep against the sierra, a pair of *huallata* geese flapped slowly from one patch of green to another. Mated for life, those dedicated creatures evoked the area's loneliness and lack of choice.

They eventually rolled out onto the flat high plateau behind Chachani, encountering no traffic except a llama pack train with two drovers. At fourteen thousand feet elevation they had to stop, as Tupa was stricken with a piercing headache. He stepped outside to breathe the cold thin air, and McIntyre followed him. The wind yowled down the frozen road; when standing sheltered behind the Bronco, the mere lack of wind felt like a radiation of warmth.

They were following the route of an ancient Inca road. Imperial postmen, *chasquis*, raced it once, thinly clothed, with nothing but the godly sky above them.

Even sick, Tupa had a good sense of humor. He forbade the others to worry about him and joked about the IAGS mandarin they'd been forced to drag along just to have their find authenticated. A few minutes later he felt better and urged McIntyre to get back behind the wheel. Inside the Bronco, things felt reassuringly small and familiar. Used to the heights, Bradshaw was patiently silent.

Tupa's headache was just a warning; farther up they might

encounter real soroche, the kind that played with your mind.

Then the landscape turned a little greener, the air warmed up, and they stopped for Loren to photograph grazing llamas and alpacas. The growth along the road was mostly *ttola*, an aromatic scrub used for domestic fuel. Its stalks and twigs were tough, yet flexible enough to stuff into a car tire if it went flat. In the distance they saw big mounds of yareta, a type of giant moss that grew in five hundred years from a clump the size of a mushroom to diameters of thirty feet and heights up to three. Through five centuries the mounds of yareta kept growing, rain or shine, in blinding sunlight, under snow, against winds and storms, till their organisms, depleted, finally shriveled. Dead, the yaretas looked stagnant and dull. At peak size it was so difficult to uproot them that miners searching for fuel sometimes blew them apart with dynamite.

The region was like the yareta: slow, enduring, resilient. There was a profession unique to the high Andes, that of the *yaretero*—the man who gathers yareta, dries it up, and sells it for fuel, representative of how directly dependent the Andean civilization is on its environment. And yet that severe locale allowed the Incas to grow to a population of six million in a land equal in length to the Roman Empire from Britannia to Persia.

They passed Pulpera, a few stone houses with thatched roofs. Callalli followed. At little markets, they glimpsed Indians buying and selling, hats bobbing above their faces. The women's clothes were carefully embroidered, their designs differing by region and sometimes by village, while the men universally wore ill-fitting Western pants and jackets. But the hands of all were bare, their feet were bare, and every inch of exposed skin, even the faces of infants, was severely chapped by the dry air and mercilessly unfiltered sunlight. Dryness was so prevalent here that dirt itself didn't seem dirty; it was clear and unfermented, large-grained and cracked.

At Sibayo, 147 kilometers from Arequipa, they crossed the

upper reaches of the Colca River. Another 64 kilometers to Cailloma. They passed the Continental Divide almost imperceptibly, while a cloud spat a sprinkling of snow at the windshield. A brook appeared, first running on one side of the road and then the other, and Tupa identified it as the Hornillos. Late in the afternoon, they came to the village of Angostura, which appropriately meant "narrowing." Pitifully small, it looked like a prop. Suddenly the marshy bed of the Hornillos joined what looked against the general dryness like a genuine, legitimate river. It was the Apurímac.

Excited, they stopped the Bronco and rushed out onto a spongy plateau dotted with yareta mounds. Here was the Apurímac: just a flat little flow in a bed maybe thirty feet wide, not nearly filled. Its spongy yellow shores, tufted with bunchgrass called *ichu*, meandered like an overgrown old trench with a rocky bottom. The absorbent terrain slowed some of the flow in marshes and captured it in little pockets spottily reflecting the darkening sky.

This was the Apurímac, the Lord Oracle, the Great Speaker. Silent now, it would fall into the canyons of the eastern Cordillera with a raging bellow, turning into the unfordable stream that killed Michel Perrin's companion. The Incas dared cross it only on suspension bridges of another type of bunchgrass named *kkolla*, repaired and rededicated every year to the river god's favor. Its course was the natural boundary of the original Inca kingdom before that kingdom grew into an empire, and it was the matrix of a mythology still alive in the Andes' Quechua-speaking strongholds. This was the link between the tears of the moon and the earth. This was the Apurímac.

They contemplated it for a few minutes, commenting on the sponginess of the terrain in spite of the season's exceptional dryness. This was an indication of the original flow's energy. The soil's porousness hid much of the water, which traveled underground, surfacing at lower altitudes. The Amazon was robustly alive and flowing literally under their feet.

They packed back into the Bronco and drove west,

following the headwater upstream. The peaks behind them were washed with the coral pink of dying sunlight, while the slopes below turned to cold turquoise, then to menacing black. They crossed the Apurímac on a Spanish bridge of thick masonry, arch-shaped, with low parapet tops curving out into chipped lips of stone. It was dated 1879, but looked like an apparition from Pizarro's time.

The bridge was just outside Cailloma. An ore-processing plant slid into view, its sheet-metal roofs stepping down the mountainside, lit by naked bulbs set on tall urban poles. Cailloma itself was almost nonexistent, a low flock of houses with a single church steeple. There was no one in the streets. In corrals of stone or sod, llamas chewed placidly, the woolly bangs on their foreheads still wet with the afternoon's snow flurry.

There was no inn in Cailloma, and it was too late to try to find lodging at the mining camps. Catching an owner locking up a bodega, a combination cafe/grocery store, McIntyre bargained for an area of floor to sleep on, and they were allowed to stretch their sleeping bags inside. For safety, the owner locked them inside, promising to return early next morning.

Tupa was recovered and in good spirits. "I hope there's some wilderness left up there," he quipped, sitting with his back against a pyramid of cans of cooking oil.

"Not after Sunday," Bradshaw cracked back. "We'll put that source in the schoolbooks, and then there'll be no more explorations, just stunts."

They were ready to turn in; but this being the airless roof of the Andes, a touch of the absurd was in order. A truck roared to a stop outside the door, a key ground in the lock, lights came on, and men delivering a shipment of food and domestic supplies stamped in and requested the very floor space the expedition had taken. They had the choice of arguing or moving out and camping under the stars.

They chose camping under the stars. In the dark, Cailloma looked squashed into the frozen Inca earth. Aware of how hard he was breathing, McIntyre helped the others to stow their gear back into the Bronco and they rumbled off along the Apurímac's shore till they found a flat little plateau shielded by a slope. Bradshaw pitched his little one-man blue tent, McIntyre his four-person red Bishop Ultimate for Victor and himself.

They spread mattress pads under their bodies, mercilessly battered by the day's rough ride. Even so, the frozen earth felt like steel. "Here's your wilderness, Victor," joked McIntyre, pulling out an altimeter to take a reading.

They were at 14,100 feet. Beyond the splutter of the narrow headwater, the silence was galactic.

7

Into the Dream II

October 12, 1971

Up at six. Daylight. I crawl out of the tent; instantly a column of warm vapor builds above my face, from my mouth and nostrils. The mountains seem turgid with inner power, like a warning waiting to find expression. I hope it won't be in an earthquake. Last year in May, on a Sunday afternoon, a quake shook down the northern peak of Huascarán, Peru's highest mountain, entombing the town of Yungay with its eighteen thousand people, killing fifty thousand more elsewhere in central Peru.

I'm not alone. Bradshaw is up, squatting in front of his tent, already cooking porridge over his tiny stove. He is unshaven and wears a brown zipper jacket and a felt hat. He hums, cheerfully self-sufficient, the embodiment of all the sons of Europe who built such fires and ate such meals on distant shores.

I know I've chosen right—for Bradshaw, so superbly conditioned, the climb will be a romp. Not so for this jungle boy here, who's also almost two decades older.

He reads my mind. He asks me again about the peaks I've climbed. I mention Cristóbal Colón and Cotopaxi, both about nineteen thousand feet. Starting in 1957, I lived five years at twelve thousand feet in La Paz, Bolivia, becoming reasonably well acclimated to oxygen shortage. But since 1962 my lungs have been retrained to the lowlands, sorting out the fumes of swamp and thicket.

Bradshaw thinks that Tupa will manage; he's in his mid-forties and strong. I tell him that I'm worried about something else: soroche's effect on our judgment. We will be wandering on a moonscape of peaks and saddlebacks all looking alike, with little trickles squiggling down similar brown slopes, each appearing and disappearing into the frozen earth, each barely crevicing the cheek of the divide, and most of them pointing in the same direction, north. I don't want to miss one that might not be on the map. I don't want to mistake one for another. I'll take constant compass and altimeter readings and try to photograph as many salient details of terrain as I can to document not just the climb but also each of the Lloqueta's five forming brooks.

Otherwise, despite our exhaustive cartographic preparations, we could end up as wrong as those before us—whose lack of thoroughness, seen from up here, seems far more excusable. There are a hundred sources in the area and they're almost impossible to distinguish. But we're here to find a particular one. The farthest one, and no other.

Up here you can lose a river. It may go into the ground and reappear farther down. It may come into being from a single snowfall and trickle down, looking legitimate and convincing—but it won't be here next spring, or even next week. I don't want us to be fooled by such impostors and hope that the weather will stay the same—bone dry. Yesterday, the man at the bodega where we didn't spend the night confirmed the report we got from the hotel manager in Arequipa: this is the driest season in decades. That helps us, as some temporary freshets have dried up, but what if the drought has temporarily concealed a genuine, continual feedwater?

How can we know? The catchbasin ahead suddenly appears to me like a maze of potential deceptions.

We need rigorous observation. For that we need clear minds, which soroche wipes out, and Tupa and I are quite likely to experience soroche. We must eat right, but if we can't hire llamas to carry our gear and provisions we will have to carry them ourselves, which will severely limit our supplies. We'll eat liquid and semi-liquid foods, easiest to digest, and drink water from freshets and melting ice. But altitude sickness makes one reject food and drink. Lack of food added to lack of oxygen impairs judgment; thus impaired, one can forget about the impairment itself, because the next thing that goes is memory.

Most people climbing such heights experience the classic effects—headaches, nausea, cramps, dizziness, even fever. The heart starts thumping scarily, breathing gets raspy, the sensation of never being able to fill one's lungs leads to panic—the last thing you need while making scientific observations. I remember in Ecuador, right under Cotopaxi's summit crater, how I had to fight a sudden sensation of AMS (acute mountain sickness). I don't remember the specific discomfort other than headache, but I remember not being able to explain to myself why I was there. I knew where I was, my name, the time, but not *why I was there*, which resulted in a momentary fantasy of being someone else, a stranger with mysterious motivations. Luckily, the whole thing quickly passed.

I'm not worried about survival. There are three of us and even if we have to rope up we won't encounter treacherous icefalls or avalanches. But I don't want exhaustion or hypoxia to stop us short of the ultimate source, whatever it turns out to be. Or to cause us to come back with unverifiable results.

Tupa crawls out of the Bishop like a bear out of his lair. He doesn't look well rested, but true to his nature he's cheerful.

A little later I propose breakfast. Not hungry, says Tupa. An altitude symptom, or just coincidence? I'll get him to eat.

I want to take pictures of the mines, so we drive back into Cailloma and then follow a well-traveled road winding around a mountain west of town. Within ten miles we're up at 15,800 feet and begin to pass mining camps called Flower of the World, Water Trough, The Devil, Saint Christopher, Knife Slash. I wonder how they acquired their names; unfortunately, we have no time for local folklore. The camps are not at all photogenic, so I settle for an Indian mother and her baby boy. Francesca Chavez is the mother's name, while her baby's is Angel Caohuana. I promise to send her prints of the pictures through a mine superintendent.

Minutes later, something in the lighting changes and the landscape acquires a fierce beauty. Even the steam pouring from the mines, the puffing of industrial stacks in the perilously thin atmosphere, seem brave and ingenious. In the brief streets, among adobe homes and sheet-metal mine buildings, the sun begins to reach with warm red fingers. Boys are already out, in their knit chullos with earflaps, noses running, feet bare. Truckloads of miners rumble up and down the slopes. Men and women stride through the streets with the vital ungainliness of montagnards everywhere. Some are chewing coca leaves, the ancient Inca panacea.

In Cailloma we buy fresh bread. As for llamas, no one wants to rent us even one; a burro is also out of the question. Maybe we'll be lucky enough to meet an empty llama train and strike a deal with the drovers. There must be plenty of them around. Cheeks swollen with coca leaves, the Indians cross the divide back and forth all the time, over ancient passes; they barter, visit, wed, and maybe pursude a vendetta on the other side.

Daylight makes the Apurímac look smaller: it's really just a ditch, shallow and full of stones as if someone had purposefully gathered them off the barren sierra and thrown them in the river. Among the stones, a cold stream shoals down against clumps of puna grass growing in the riverbed. They bog down the water into unkempt puddles, creating one of the world's higher little swamps.

It is amazing that this "little stream of llama piss," as I heard someone at the IGM in Lima describe it, becomes in just a few miles a powerful river. Ten thousand feet lower it boils and roars in rock gorges that are crowded on both sides by a jungle of trees and creepers clawing their way up the spurs of the Andes. The plants use every inch of ledge, every palmful of dust tossed by the wind onto the granite flanks and moistened by the rain into a thin layer of soil. They stab roots and limbs into that soil, reach the rock underneath, split it and settle in, flying their green banners above as if over a conquered kingdom. It's exciting to see life so driven by its own desire to exist, so capable of using anything that will help it prevail.

Farther downstream, beyond those thundering gorges, the banks of the Apurímac are just endless life and lushness.

So it's time to prowl the pampa of Cailloma, pushing the Bronco as close as possible to the southernmost curve of the Continental Divide. We'll cross rivers and rivulets and eventually reach the Lloqueta, seeping down from the divide. Then up again, surely on foot by now, along the Lloqueta, which is made up of five brooks: the Ccaccansa, the Calomoroca, the Apacheta, the Sillanque, formed by two other little trickles, and the Carhuasanta. By Russell Fritz's reckoning, all five might be longer than the rivulet found last year on Minaspata. The Carhuasanta certainly is, by at least five miles.

But what I'd like to find is not the metric proof that those brooks are longer. I'd like to find a *body of water*, something fluid of a certain volume and direction, absolutely real and stuck on the Continental Divide, practically on top of it. Something obviously not caused by a climatic whim. Someplace from which a flow begins. Amazon-bound yet so close to the sky that it illustrates how the snow becomes the beginning of the river.

The beginning. *The* nascente, *eh, Câmbio? Eh, Barnacle? You're gonna be with me on this one, Barnacle, my friend. So you better brace yourself for the cold.*

O nascente. *The source.*

Here we go, out of Cailloma, jostling and jouncing southeast.

The basin outside Cailloma is laced with service trails to maintain the canals and tunnels supplying water to the mines and processing plants. One such tunnel is a mile and a half long, and I wouldn't walk far into it for all the gold of the Incas. This is a region of frequent earthquakes. Just recently, engineers of the MACON project cutting a tunnel near Ampato Volcano were caught deep within their galleries by a mighty rumble and shaken witless.

We pass a man-made lake, Huarhuarco, equipped with controlled floodgates and some natural ponds. Approaching one, I see a flock of Andean flamingos stalking the shallows. I rush out of the Bronco with a telephoto lens. Before I can shoot, they take off, wings brushing the sky with strokes of black and red.

So much for that. To make the Bronco's engine run better at this altitude, I had advanced the sparks several degrees in Arequipa. Still, our brave little vehicle is beginning to sound like an angry jaguar, growling, catching its breath, growling.

Sedulously, we drive into the empty basin. Mount Huagra is now clearly behind us; on its left flank there is the wide, slanting trail left by a vanished glacier. It's pretty clear that between Huagra behind us and the divide ahead (we're still too far: what I can see of its battlements looks flat and insignificant), there is a good distance. At least thirty miles. Thirty miles that make or break a world record.

Late Afternoon

Now there's no road at all. We are driving past a lake, not sure whether it is Lake Huarhuarco or Lake Carhuasanta. At any rate, its left shore becomes a swamp into which we sink axle deep. I'm at the wheel. I reverse, shooting salvos of mud, and force the Bronco back onto dry land. What to do? Try to circle the lake on its other side? We'll probably encounter the same type of terrain.

We have to start hiking sometime. But the day is almost over. I decide that we'll pitch camp here and continue tomorrow on foot, leaving the Bronco by the lake.

Since we have no llamas, we have to cut down our loads to the minimum necessary. Bradshaw wants to take his own stove and tent, though he could use our stove and there's room left in the Bishop. But preferences of that sort matter to an experienced climber, so I agree. We'll leave behind the heaviest food, the cans, and take just enough supplies for three days.

We crawl into our tents and prepare for the night. While Tupa turns his back to me to go to sleep, I lift myself on my elbows, flick on a forehead lamp, and open my diary. It is October 12, 1971, 479 years to the day since Columbus landed in America.

I can't write. My eyes burn, while my ears are freezing. I flick off the lamp and listen to Victor, gasping in his sleep.

October 13, Morning

We wake up to a brilliant sight of the lake, impeccably still and seeming much wider than yesterday. Bradshaw whips up breakfast for all of us.

Soon, our silhouettes swollen by our supplies, we are ready. I lock the Bronco's doors and back hatch. Then we walk single file ahead, Bradshaw first, I in the middle, and Tupa behind me, already sucking air loud and fast. By contrast, Bradshaw practically dances against the brown landscape. Remembering some classic altitude tests, I try whistling. I can whistle just fine.

All we need is three days of dry weather.

8

The Apacheta Trail

Finally walking—the good old essential workout of any expedition—we approach the divide from the north, beginning to sense its shape and size, that of an ascending arch more than thirty miles across, laid out like a giant amphitheater. We are advancing into the amphitheater; we've entered down front into the orchestra pit and will climb up this aisle or that to reach the top row. Beyond that top row, which is the upper edge of the divide, there's a sheer drop of ten thousand feet into the Colca River gorge that leads to the Pacific Coast.

As in all explorations, the feeling of the place starts to invade us. It's impossible to avoid the thought that there's someone on that crest, watching us, waiting for us. If there be gods, they are sitting in their thrones seeing far beyond the slopes we labor on, to where the curvature of the earth shuts off their gaze. Supreme among them is the Inca's Sun God, who could behold the entire earth at once, for the Incas believed that the planet's sunless underside was all water. Not so far wrong, considering the size of the Pacific Ocean.

This might be the last act of a work of exploration started long before us, so I feel a certain sense of mission; I'm sure that Tupa and Bradshaw feel it too. The source is there to be found and witnessed in the utter normalcy of its appearance, unique for just an instant, that of its discovery. Then it will pass into the history of exploration, which is a chronicle of transience. No matter how fiercely pursued, each discovery's effect on man is to push him to look someplace else.

So that is our role: to pierce the mystery, remove the obstacle, and help redirect the energies of explorers to other targets. Is that enough? Is that worthwhile? It must be useful in some way; witness the three of us panting along on these slopes.

I've met many an Amazon traveler. I once met Commander George M. Dyott, Royal Navy, Fellow of the Royal Geographic Society, a serious and passionate wanderer and writer, more famous for trying to find the extravagant Colonel Percy H. Fawcett than for his own expeditions. Dyott welcomed me on the doorstep of a farm he'd carved out of a piece of jungle in Ecuador, and talked to me from that doorstep without asking me inside. I saw a man with a long nose rooted between narrowly set eyes that had a disturbing fixedness, a dry face with the skin of its chin hanging, a drooping mustache. The picture of a widower who hadn't seen himself in a mirror in weeks. He wore a gardener's outfit and a battered straw hat.

The year was 1966, and I carried with me a copy of my first story in the *National Geographic*; I had just read one of his in a 1929 issue, about the volcanoes of Ecuador. G. M. Dyott, not looking his eighty-six years, stood in his doorway leaning on a hoe sticky with garden dirt, and told me a slightly demented story. He was growing coca trees; to quicken their development he had wired them up for electric shocks, for he put a lot of faith in electrification of plants and soil as the basis of a brand-new agriculture. He lived alone. While away to collect his mail from the British consulate in Quito, his house had been robbed of books and travel souvenirs, including a sword mounted with rubies presented to him by an Arabian prince. Though he spent almost an hour with me and while standing there read some of my Bolivia story in the *National Geographic*, I felt he never quite trusted that I wasn't one of the robbers. I photographed him at his gate, sent him the pictures later, and never heard from him.

He died in the jungle of Ecuador, at ninety. I was haunted by the memory of our encounter, by its taste of loneliness and waste. He died forgotten, while Fawcett was never found; yet in their prime they were both pointmen in that alert and inquisitive vanguard, exploration.

In Dyott's books I caught glimpses of what I discovered exploration to be: the most solitary and hard-earned pleasure. Enjoying a place at its last moment of mystery. But there is more than that. There is that unique emotion when a human, limited and ephemeral as we all are, feels overpowered not with what he has found, but with the world he left behind, without which his find would be valueless. There is a seed of selflessness in that moment, curiously synchronous with the triumph and confirmation.

All that makes up the motivation and reward of explorers. Why else would they give up love and family, and all the other fulfillments one leaves behind by going it alone?

Looking for something lost behind the ranges. What kind of world will it be, when everything behind the ranges has been found?

Bradshaw signals a stop for a drink and a snack.

Amazing how tired I already am. I carry a fifty-pound pack and so does Tupa, while Bradshaw's is about seventy-five. Even the ultralight tent weighs eight pounds. Sleeping bags, blankets, food, pots, ice axes, ropes, all pull at the straps, sinking them into our shoulders, while the added weight buries our footfalls into the boggy soil. In addition, there are the cameras. Against my right shoulder blade I feel the pressure of a tripod. All the things I couldn't bear to part with now quicken my breath and slow my steps.

Ten minutes pass like seconds. "Let's go," calls

Bradshaw, hefting his pack.

Gotta husband my energy. Inhale, exhale.

Tupa is wheezing. Paying for a year of greasy Lima meals.

They advanced around the lake until the abandoned Bronco dropped out of sight, then continued south, passing several other small lakes, one of which Loren couldn't find on the map at all. Victor made a note for a future survey team to check if it was seasonal; if it was not, as *jefe de clasificacion* he had to find out its local name or give it one.

They moved under searing sunlight; farther up, the snow's glare would force them to wear snow goggles. McIntyre was wearing gloves to protect his hands from sunburn, but his lips were already split and his throat so raw from breathing through his mouth that he had to clear it each time he spoke. Even for the dry season, the terrain's aridity was exceptional. He kept scanning the barrenness of the slopes, comparing them to aerial photographs he had examined over the years, remembering them shiny with ice fields and glaciers.

"Where the hell are the glaciers, Victor?"

"I don't know. It's been a long hot summer."

"I know that. But glaciers don't melt in a single summer."

One of those little things the earth did, without informing the humans. McIntyre drew a dry painful breath and walked on, now scanning the landscape for llamas or alpacas. He saw none. As they hiked on, Mount Minaspata, tagged as the source site by last year's Amazon expedition, drew closer. It looked dry and easy to climb, with a small glacier right under the summit.

"Let's climb it," suggested Bradshaw, "so that no earlier expedition can object that we haven't duplicated their feat."

We'll see you on the rope tomorrow, you fire eater, thought Loren. "What's the point?" he countered. "Tomorrow we'll follow the Apacheta; after a few hours we'll be farther into the source area than anyone else."

"Maybe it's time you unveiled your strategy," Bradshaw grinned.

"Well . . ."

This was as good a time as any. All three of them stopped. Feeling a pleasant throb in his chest, McIntyre deployed the IGM map, put his finger on the junction of the Apacheta and Carhuasanta, trickling in from that farthest rampart of the divide and combining to form the Lloqueta.

That farthest rampart had been so much on McIntyre's mind that he could draw its thread on the map blindfolded. Quehuisha, a steep little peak, normally snowbound, rose at its westernmost end, its snows giving birth to the Apacheta. Halfway between its beginning and its junction with the Carhuasanta, the Apacheta also collected the trickles of the other three minuscule subtributaries. From Quehuisha, the Continental Divide curved eastward some five miles toward its highest point, which was the summit of the Mismi massif. The Carhuasanta, marshy and hesitant, trickled out of Mismi's slopes. After Mismi, the divide wound east another four or five miles, dropping toward a lower peak, Puma Chiri. Puma Chiri was the limit McIntyre had set to their investigation.

"We'll go up the Apacheta to the top of the divide," he announced. He glanced swiftly at the other two, noted the concentration in their faces, cleared his throat. "We'll climb Quehuisha, then walk the whole crest of the divide, at least nine miles—"

"Forgive me; if we go along the crest, it's going to be more like twelve," predicted Bradshaw.

"Whatever." Was it excitement or just the high altitude? He couldn't catch his breath. He cleared his throat again. "We'll walk twelve miles, covering every snowfield up there. Every snowfield or accumulation of ice, or any other body of water no matter in what state. Those are the farthest bodies of water in all Amazonia, so that's where the farthest source is."

He smiled at Richard Bradshaw: "If there's any sort of monopoly on the source area, that's the way to get it."

There was a silence, then the two others nodded. "Clever," Bradshaw commented briefly.

"Sounds almost easy," reinforced Tupa.

"We'll see how easy it is. We should set a base camp somewhere along the Lloqueta, and then go up, photographing every snowfield of significance. The Apacheta will probably take us all of tomorrow. The day after tomorrow, we'll attack the crest itself."

There was an instant of unspectacular excitement. Staring at the map, each of them saw that farthest rampart in his mind's eye.

Then Loren folded the map. Inhale, exhale. The expedition marched forward again.

They reached the Lloqueta in the afternoon and followed it up to the junction of the first two brooks, the Apacheta and the Carhuasanta. They pitched camp on a narrow plot of bunchgrass, between a granite ledge and the trickling flow of the Lloqueta. Loren measured the altitude: 15,748 feet, exactly half a mile less than the summit of Mismi.

Victor wasn't wheezing anymore; in fact, claiming to be *tan fuerte como un caballo de carrera*, "as strong as a racehorse," he decided to climb along the Apacheta and maybe check some of the smaller brooks. Richard and Loren exchanged a glance. It sometimes happened that people's bodies caught up with the altitude, and from a gasping casualty Victor was turning into a fearless athlete.

Without a pack, he went off almost nimbly. He returned after an hour and told them that he had branched off to the right to follow the Ccaccansa and then the Calomoroca. He was stopped by steep rock walls with great boulders, deposited there long before by a glacier. That was as far as he could advance, and the length of the two brooks, as expected, was insignificant.

"Makes the Apacheta more suspenseful," joked Richard. Loren saw him pull out of his pack a covered pot. He carried it to the Lloqueta, immersed it into the ice-cold water, and weighted it with a rock.

"What the hell is that?" asked Loren.

"The makings of a spell. You'll see the results tomorrow

341

night," the Englishman said with a grin.

Along with the sun, all warmth left the plateau and arctic puffs started shooting out of the three men's mouths and nostrils.

As they crawled into the tents that night, Loren turned on his forehead lamp and made his notes, then turned it off and lay in the dark, thinking about the weather's exceptional dryness. There was a dusting of snow on the crest of the divide, visible from here, and its melt had to go someplace. But what if it all percolated directly into the dry soil? What if its connection to the Lloqueta's brooks could not be seen? In that case, the search would be far less conclusive. Also, it was in the nature of a long spell of dry weather to be reversed by a sudden snowfall. If snow fell tonight, it might hide critical features of the terrain.

He tried to tell himself that none of that really mattered. His targeted piece of the divide was the farthest from the Amazon's mouth, and the snow on its crest was the farthest source. It was as simple as that. Yet a body of water would feel like the natural crowning of the search, rewarding the trek and the years preceding it.

He lay awake a while, then groped in the dark for a bottle of aspirin. The fatigue and the altitude had given him a piercing headache.

October 14

In the morning, I see no fresh snow on the ground.

To brush our teeth, we have to break the crust of ice at the edge of the Lloqueta. We wash our faces, but shaving is out of the question. We eat a breakfast of cereal and crackers, cheese from Lima and dry fruit, and review our strategy. Up the Apacheta to the divide; we'll climb Quehuisha and find a spot to stash food and gear for tomorrow's trek along the crest. This will be a day of serious picture-taking, for which I'll lug my tripod, a full set of lenses, and at least twenty rolls of film. Richard is planning to collect some mineral samples. Tupa wants to verify features by checking them with the map. Sounds like a pleasantly intellectual day, except that we'll spend it above the limit of human habitation, in high soroche land.

Bradshaw's pot is still in the river. I ask him about the results of his spell. "You'll see them tonight," he grins.

The pack straps, with the weight of two days' supplies plus equipment, sink into shoulders sore from yesterday's march.

The climb proves steep and the sunlight hard, forcing us down to sweaters and for a while just to shirts.

Unexpectedly, an Indian on horseback materializes in the landscape, driving two pack mules ahead of him. As he sees us, his eyes roll in his head. He pauses and greets us in Quechua and then in Spanish. He's coming from the other side of the divide, from the village of Madrigal, down in the Colca River gorge. His mules carry sacks of flour and sugar, a brick of salt, a can of cottonseed cooking oil.

The mules continue down the trail unattended, while Tupa breaks out the map and shows it to him; I don't think he's ever seen a map before, yet he confirms the names of most of the local features. With some difficulty he understands that we are headed for Mismi, and points out the tallest peak in its long crest, Choquecorao, which means "Golden Sling." Puma Chiri, far at the end of the rampart, means "Frozen Mountain Lion."

Tupa finds them on the map. The Indian himself has never climbed Choquecorao or Puma Chiri, but noticing the ice axes strapped to our packs, he offers some free advice: "*Alla no hay ni oro ni plata.*"

Which means, "There's neither gold nor silver up there."

Tupa tries to explain that we're not after gold or silver. The Indian canters after his mules, puzzling out the meaning of three city gentlemen carrying their own burdens up the trail. A little later Bradshaw points back down the valley. The lone horseman is a moving speck of color, driving his mules toward a *ranchito* somewhere on a mountain's flank.

We go on. Inhale, exhale. Step after step. Measuring the weight of our footsteps by their echoes in our temples. Wiping the dryness of lips with raspy, bitter-tasting tongues. The divide's crest is now visible, and it's white. The sight of the snow is encouraging. At least the top of the divide isn't dry.

We are scorched by the sun but whipped coldly by a wind that meets no trees or anything flexible to ruffle and announce its presence. We hear its empty moans changing direction. My lips are very chapped and the palms of my hands feel like parchment. I take off my woolen cap and my hair crackles with electrified dryness.

We are now higher than ninety-nine percent of the earth's living things, and half of the earth's protective atmosphere is below us. Therefore we are exposed to an increased electromagnetic bombardment from beyond the blue dome of the sky. I remember my visits to the Cosmic Ray Laboratory on Mount Chacaltaya, in Bolivia. Just above the lab was the ski lift that carried visitors up over perpetual snows, only ninety minutes from my home in La Paz. Lab technicians had rigged detectors on the whole mountainside around the lab. They measured the impact of gamma rays from cosmic explosions light-years beyond our solar system.

Those incredibly tiny particles arrive very infrequently, but when they come, usually in showers, they pierce our internal organs, our hearts, our brains, and they drill hundreds of feet into the earth. Radiation is thought to effect genetic changes. Highlanders are exposed to more radiation than lowlanders. Do they evolve more quickly?

My mind wanders. Best thing to do to forget the fatigue, the pain of the straps on my shoulders, the thirst. I suppose I'm thinking like an Indian now, allowing everything in the universe to become connected. The most fantastic connections seem both ingenious and plausible.

World and mind are one.

As I ponder what genetic impact the cosmic rain has on the people living up here, I stumble. Tired, or do I lack a gene programming my feet to step high enough to avoid tripping? I guess it's easier to blame a galactic beam than to admit that a fifty-four-year-old body can falter.

The Apacheta's bed, two feet wide with a wet dribble running down the middle, seems to scream for rain. We find that it dribbles out of a spread of gravelly banks, above which the divide's crest is visible. Runoff from snow on the crest seeps under the gravelly banks and reappears as a little brook. There's nothing much to photograph except some crags with icicles hanging above the gravel. Some icicles are ten feet long. I snap Tupa's picture next to one, with the IAGS shield at his feet.

"You can call this an ultimate body of water," he jokes.

We reach the crest and there's the *apacheta*, a pyramidal pile of votive stones over six feet tall, with a crude wooden cross leaning out of kilter at the top. Almost every high pass in the Andes has an *apacheta*, and many are ancient. A tally of the good-luck stones would give a minimum count of those who climbed up here. Not all worshipers add stones. Less enduring offerings include candles, halved cigarettes, wads of chewed coca leaves, or hairs plucked from eyebrows.

Each of us adds a big rock to the pile—we need all the luck we can get. A vicious wind starts blowing up from the Colca Gorge, so we sit in the lee of the *apacheta* to eat lunch and rest. Then, without packs, Bradshaw and I scale the Quehuisha summit, he cantering ahead with my tripod, I following wearily with camera and lenses.

From the summit, we peer down thousands of feet into the Colca Valley. Beyond it we sight El Misti, the cone looming over Arequipa, it's hard to believe it is only sixty miles south. Then we look northwest, and locate Minaspata. "We're so much farther upstream," says Richard excitedly.

Then we look eastward, along the crest we plan to walk tomorrow. It is brightened by slanting snowfields.

It's hard to describe what I feel. That snow runs off into the Lloqueta's brooks. I see the source already. All the white I see over there is part of the Amazon's source. Measured from here to the mouth beyond Belém, the river would total just under forty-two hundred miles.

We rope down from the top, back to the *apacheta*, where we left Tupa. We still have time to push eastward a little, so we do it, breathing hard.

My mental acuity is low but I keep snapping pictures, bracketing exposures to make sure I'll end up with some decent shots. Finally we come to a crag where vanished snow or some secret spring has nourished a pair of enormous icicles, ten and twenty feet long. They pour in stop motion down the black face of the rock.

A vision of the twin waterfall at the source of the Javari brushes my mind; for an instant I get that magical feeling that everything is connected.

Victor tries to break a piece of those giant tears of ice, and gives up. The old icicles are hard like granite. "Here's your most distant body of water, solid," he jokes again, and again I snap his picture with the IAGS shield at his feet.

The sun begins to sink. We find a crevice under a large boulder, where we leave the equipment, the rope, and some food. Without packs, we start down and Bradshaw, though loaded with samples of rock, soon leaves us behind.

Later

Victor and I reach the camp in two hours.

We find Richard boiling something over the blue flames of his propane stove. I ask what he is cooking; he ignores my question, but as I step away I see the pot he's been hiding in the river. Although the sense of smell barely functions at this altitude, Tupa sniffs some ancestral aroma, for he gets down on all fours to be closer to the pot. "An Inca banquet!" he announces.

In minutes, Richard ladles onto our plates the meat and potatoes meal thousands of highlanders are cooking or eating right now all over the Andes. "Beats dinner at Buckingham Palace," he says with a laugh, and raises a cup full of a thick hot drink called *api*.

Api is brewed from *kaniwa*, one of the most nutritious of all grains (it contains eighteen percent protein). *Kaniwa* grows on rocky soils up to fifteen thousand feet, survives pests, frosts, and snowfalls, and even reseeds itself. When crops fail, it is the Andean farmer's survival. The meat and potatoes are *charqui*, dried llama shank, and *chuño*, dehydrated potatoes dried in the sun after the moisture is squeezed from them. I'm not a *chuño* enthusiast, but in the dark of this naked highland, where the only sounds are the splashing of the Amazon's farthest feeder and the crackle of ice forming and breaking again along its edge, this meal is perfect. I eat and feel as close to the essence of things as I did in the jungle with the Mayoruna.

I sum up in my mind our accomplishment to date. We went up the Apacheta to its source, not to speak of the shorter brooks, which were already checked by Victor. The other feedwater worth checking is the Carhuasanta; we'll explore it by descending to it from the divide, since it starts under Mismi's crest. This afternoon, up on Quehuisha, we were already farther from the Amazon's mouth than the previous expeditions, but for a thorough overview of the source area we still have to hike those twelve miles along the divide.

A tough hike. We must go to bed early.

What a wonderful thought this is. *Tomorrow.*

9

The Lake

October 15, 1971

He was awakened by the boom of cannon. Gasping for breath, he sat bolt upright and felt the deck of the USS *Charleston* shuddering under him. He was directing the salvos of her six-inch main battery, hurling 105-pound shells at the Japanese holed up in Chichagoff Harbor, during the Battle of Attu. They would soon pour forth in a suicide charge, a thousand men screaming, "Japanese drink blood like wine." Yet his sleeping bag was wrapped around him, and despite the cannonade he heard gentler sounds, like the bubbling of the Lloqueta. Sailor Tupa rose in his bunk, not in uniform but in McIntyre's spare parka, and a red ray of light transformed from a reflection of the battle to the beam of Richard's flashlight against the tent's red fabric.

"*Temblor!*" McIntyre yelled loud in Spanish.

"*Mas que temblor; es un señor terremoto!*" yelled Tupa, "This is more than a shaker, it's a regular earthquake!" Both of them heard another deep grumble, then felt it coming from the north, rippling down as if the divide were its conduit. There were two extreme tremors, so hard that McIntyre was almost knocked back onto his sleeping bag.

"Come on out," Bradshaw called matter-of-factly. "Better stay clear of the overhang of the ledge."

They gathered themselves and crawled out into the icy darkness. There were several other tremors, though feebler.

348

Loren thought of the disaster that cracked off the north peak of Huascarán. Millions of tons of ice and granite smashing at two hundred miles an hour on top of the city of Yungay. Hundreds of landslides all over central Peru. Tens of thousands of victims.

They stood surrounded by the mountains, waiting for the earth's decision. And there were no more rumbles. "That's it," said Bradshaw. Loren looked at his watch: its luminescent hands read three thirty-four in the morning. He turned toward Tupa: wrested out of darkness by the flashlight's beam, his face looked even more Incan.

"Want to go back to sleep?"

"What sleep?" mumbled Tupa. "Let's go. The gods have spoken."

They were ready in two hours, fast for this altitude and for making their preparations in almost total darkness. From their modest food supplies they made breakfast, which McIntyre felt unable to eat; he had a mug of hot liquid Jell-O. Then they zipped up their tents and set off, McIntyre first, Bradshaw last, Tupa in the middle.

Halfway up the Apacheta it was still dark, but having climbed the trail the day before helped. The dry ground creaked and crunched under their feet, like the crust of a frozen planet. They were to follow the trail up to about seventeen thousand feet, then veer left, attacking the divide itself.

The Andean dawn came with its characteristic layering of peaks outlined against other peaks. Like an injection of energy, the sunlight transfigured the landscape, turning the snowfields from blue to pink in an instant. At seventeen thousand feet, the three men's lungs had to work double time to ensure the normal amount of oxygen. They climbed past more icicles. Then past a curtain of ice hanging across a vertical cleft in a crag. Inside the cleft, feeding off the ice curtain's humidity, dark moss wrapped the wall with a somber luxuriance. Tupa stood before it in a conquistador pose, and Loren clicked his camera.

There was little snow except for the summits, yet wherever

they looked ice laced every fissure in the rocks. On their faces, the sunlight was already harsh, but in the shade the air was freezing cold. Exactly three hours after leaving the base camp, they came at last to the small pinnacle marking the crack where they had left the rope, food, and cameras.

Altogether, they had been up and active for five hours, but the day's work was still wholly ahead of them.

Victor and Richard broke out a trail lunch, if one could call it that at ten to nine in the morning. Loren tried to eat and still couldn't. He picked up his cameras and pushed on along the crest, thankful for sunlight and taking picture after picture. Clouds might darken the afternoon. He finally stood leaning on his ice ax, panting, till Victor and Richard caught up with him.

They started toward Mismi in the same formation, Loren first, Victor in the middle, Richard bringing up the rear. There was very little snow to their left, but whatever the amount, its melt was Amazon-bound. As he advanced, McIntyre kept looking for more snowfields ahead; they were paltry and few, yet enough to throw a tattered cape on the highest peaks; some lay right on top of the divide, like saddle blankets. Through their midst ran a gravitational border more real than the unseen equator. What slanted to the left would end up in the Amazon; what slanted to the right would end up in the Pacific.

To the east, beyond the closest snowfields, McIntyre saw other crests and peaks and snowfields and snowcaps, making the divide easily distinguishable. No clouds hovered over it anywhere. The sky was cobalt, the wind came in rapid bursts, and the scene's bright vitality inebriated him as much as the height.

The glare of the sunlight was becoming mercilessly harsh. He slipped on his dark goggles. Now all they had to do was walk twelve miles along the divide, and a few more descending the marshy trickle of the Carhuasanta.

With so little snow, they didn't have to bother using the rope, but the picture-taking slowed them down considerably. Every time Loren stopped, the others had to stop too.

Enjoying the few instants of respite, Loren clicked his cameras, then moved on with painful effort. Richard used the stops to pick up stones, sometimes chipping off samples with his ice ax. Tupa, less exuberant than two days earlier, seemed thankful for every lull. The maps, constantly spread and refolded, were tearing along the creases. Step by step, inch by inch, the terrain rolled back under their feet, and under their meticulous survey not a patch of snow was discounted.

Bradshaw, ever the most energetic, tried to joke about the source: "This'll teach people it's not a shower head gushing from between two rocks."

Loren found the energy to smile. He was burning roll after roll of film, while his forehead itched, his lips bled, and the bridge of his nose felt raw from three days of Andean glare. His tongue swept incessantly at his parched palate. Instead of leaving footprints on the snow, his boots were scraping rock and he had to be careful not to slash his ankles against their harsh edges. Since the rope wasn't needed, the formation had loosened. Bradshaw finally called for a halt, then pointed out that it was past eleven and most of the traverse was still ahead of them.

"I'm sorry that the pictures are taking so long, but they're not negotiable," answered McIntyre. "No one's taken pictures of this stretch of the divide before."

"Then let's bypass Mismi on the Colca side to reach Puma Chiri, and return on the Amazon side," suggested the Englishman. "That way we won't have to go around Mismi twice. We'll climb it anyway when we come back."

"That's a good idea," said Tupa. "We can rest on Puma Chiri, then trek back on the Amazon side the way we did so far, step by step and not missing a single snowflake."

His face was wrinkled with fatigue. McIntyre suppressed a pang of anxiety: as the expedition's official authenticator, Tupa had to be in shape to validate any new feature they might find. He nodded.

The expedition stumbled around the Colca side of Mismi, and suddenly came in sight of what looked like a spread of

World War II tank traps, executed in glaring white ice.

"*Penitentes*," muttered Tupa from behind Loren.

Loren had seen *penitentes* only once before, in the Andes of Argentina. They looked like huge worshipers in white shrouds, standing between four and twelve feet tall. Carved by the winds, they were hard to cut even with ice axes. The expedition advanced by squeezing between their hooded silhouettes. The good thing was that it was impossible to slip and tumble down a slope studded with *penitentes*, and most were too old to break away in avalanches.

Passing an almost five-foot specimen, Loren tried unsuccessfully to chip off its spike with his ice ax, to suck on it and assuage his thirst. However, what he felt was not really thirst but rather a command from the brain not to ignore the body's vital needs, now that its survival signals were scrambled by hypoxia. Eight hours after that single cup of Jell-O he still felt no hunger. He had a chocolate bar in one of his pockets and kept delaying, more and more dangerously, the moment he would eat it. The insides of his nostrils felt so parched that his inhalations stung. His shoulders were masses of bruised muscle and tissue. The glare was such that even behind sun goggles he squinted. Each time they switched from the relative protection of a rampart to the openness of a ridge, the wind was bitingly cold.

Tired but uncomplaining, Tupa lagged behind. Still loaded with the team's heaviest pack, Bradshaw monitored his companions' performance. Being concerned with Tupa eased McIntyre's concern about himself; but even Richard was moving slower now. They were three weary men strained by height and hunger, and still not in sight of what they were looking for. Step, step, step, they went on. Step, step, step.

Slowly, Puma Chiri, the "Frozen Mountain Lion," started to raise its head before them. It suffered their footfalls as they climbed its frozen nape, then held them on its frozen crown for some fifteen minutes of rest.

Only then they realized how exhausted they were—even Bradshaw seemed to welcome the rest. Loren sat down, looked at the surrounding peaks, and they appeared strange and meaningless. He sat in a daze, not able to tell what he was thinking about, remembered several things of some importance and instantly forgot them, finally strained his memory and brought back the chocolate bar. It might help to eat it right now. But he instantly forgot it again, for his hand didn't go to his pocket to bring it out, and he made no decision as to what to do to prevent forgetting about it anymore. He sat on, wondering vaguely about the Inca youngsters who once sat just like him, their brains boxes of vapor, till the cold put them to sleep. Then he made an effort of willpower and managed to concentrate on Tupa speaking with Bradshaw.

"Exhaustion alone can provoke hallucinations," Tupa was saying in response to a line from Bradshaw.

Bradshaw agreed, then commented that since none of them had been hit with serious soroche, there was a good chance that their bodies had adjusted successfully, though with every additional hour they had to fear the effects of exhaustion per se. Then he mentioned climbers seeing trees and roadways on barren peaks, or heavy machinery where no helicopter could have lifted it, for the air was too thin for whirling blades. McIntyre tried to remain awake but drifted off open-eyed. He woke up again thinking of a big flood of light, remembered he had read about it in an account by a nineteenth-century French balloonist, the only survivor from a three-man team that was hit by severe hypoxia at twenty-five thousand feet. The man had experienced extraordinary numbness, but otherwise he didn't suffer; on the contrary, he felt great inner joy, the result, he said, of a big, inundating flood of light. He would have come down a cold corpse like the two others in the balloon's gondola, but some reflex enabled him to move his hands and evacuate some of the balloon's hydrogen, causing it to descend slowly all the way to the ground.

In those days, people knew nothing about the effects of lack of oxygen on the brain, and that was how they learned. Cerebral edema, swelling of the brain, started with an unspectacular symptom, headache. Loren remembered the chocolate bar, and the fact that they were at eighteen thousand feet of altitude. Soroche was possible at any moment, but instant death unlikely. His senses back in focus, he looked around, saw Tupa's face, which was thinned by strain and lack of food, and then Richard's profile: the Englishman stared into the wind, a strand of hair ruffled against his forehead under the brim of his felt hat.

Just fatigue, McIntyre told himself. No vomiting, violent palpitations, anxiety, asphyxia. He decided to eat the chocolate later, resisted the desire to take his own pulse, and stood up just as Richard called, "Let's go."

They descended the frozen mountain lion and headed back, keeping the catchbasin to their right, at all times visible.

The Amazon side had fewer *penitentes*; it welcomed the explorers instead with pinnacles of fragile yellow rock, far more treacherous, for they crumbled easily and could lead to a frightful fall. Step, step, step, they approached the Mismi, an impressive massif with the peak of Choquecorao sitting on it like a dark face on a set of broad shoulders. Thin snowfields like long swatches of white hung on its sides.

They started climbing Mismi around two-thirty. Seventeen thousand eight hundred feet. Eighteen thousand. Loren felt his heart dilating in his chest. No nausea, though. Plenty of panting, but they were climbing and climbing fast for this altitude. No vertigo, no throbbing of the temples. Eighteen thousand fifty feet. He looked up at Tupa's back. It lumbered ahead of him, a thick piece of human presence against the dark mountainside streaked with snow. Drawing on his deepest, least often used resources, and doing it well. *Hang in there, big Inca*, he thought affectionately.

He was light-headed again. One instant his body felt like a leaden cast pulling him down, the next he did not feel his body at all. Eighteen thousand one hundred feet. Less than half the pressure at sea level. He'd been at higher altitudes. Back in 1963, air force doctors at the Wright-Patterson base in Dayton, Ohio, had checked his adaptation after five years of living at twelve thousand feet in La Paz, Bolivia. He was put in a chamber whose air was gradually pumped out to simulate increasing altitude, and while he was "going skyward" he was asked to write an account of his travels on a yellow pad. Things seemed to go well, then . . .

"Take him down," a command rang on the intercom.

"What?" He had stared at the yellow pad. "Wait, I'm doing just fine."

Air hissed back into the chamber. The doctors came in. He had gone rigid at a simulated altitude of twenty-six thousand feet, his pencil stopped in midword, his eyes wide open, seeing nothing. But when had it happened? He had no recall whatever of losing consciousness and regaining it as instantly.

"You were headed for a swift death," a doctor said. "We take pilots up to unconsciousness like this, to drive it through their skulls that fainting from hypoxia strikes without warning. Pilots who fly without oxygen gear above twelve thousand feet blank out without knowing it. The lucky ones snap out before the planes crash. The unlucky ones feel no pain."

The years in La Paz had been good training. La Paz was the world's highest capital. It had a fire department whose main activity was marching in holiday parades, since it was hard to keep even a match burning in such oxygen-poor air.

He looked behind. The catchbasin seemed infinitely distant. Ahead, Tupa and Bradshaw obstinately crept upward. Harsh gusts of wind struck now and then, and it seemed amazing that they didn't flip those frail human silhouettes backward into the void.

He kept thinking of how he had blanked out in Dayton, vanishing into a secret pocket of time, then returning. Time without awareness. But that's what human time was, awareness. That sounded like a very meaningful reflection.

It felt as if they would never reach the summit.

They finally stepped on a ridge so high that it seemed to look down on all the rest of the world. They were atop the Golden Sling.

Loren sat on a rock, his boots scratching the top of a long and narrow snowfield. Looking north, he saw a superb panorama of peaks and ridges cradling the Cailloma Basin in the middle. The brooks running into the Lloqueta looked like long dark smudges on the yellowish plateau, but he knew that they were there, real, permanent. Mount Huagra loomed far to the northwest, like a mammoth too slow to catch up with its own herd. Minaspata rose closer, but still a good distance away. The impression of size was imperial.

He pictured what lay beyond the mountains. He saw the crash of the headwaters in the emerald canyons, the sprawling of floods onto the lascivious plains, and the advance of the sediment-charged main stream, its humid breath sucking the sky down and making it the Amazon's own mask of oxygen and suspended vapor. Of the ever-jumping count of the earth's species, at least half of the million-plus fauna lived down there, amid perhaps as many kinds of plants. On the wing, in the ground, drilling into bark, making cysts in roots, swimming, burrowing, sporing in soil, air, and water, cocooning, sprouting, fungating, the river became life in all possible expressions. It was also death laying in ambush in countless forms, from the quickest and cleanest to the most gruesome. And at its beginning lay a patchwork of snowfields, and next to it he sat now, imagining the river ahead, flowing, raining, rippling, flooding, begetting, beaming.

He felt not disappointment, but a sudden blank, a voidance of expectation. After so much thinking about this moment, it was what he had anticipated and what he had dreamed, and less, and more. Then he felt joy, of a quiet, humble sort.

Beside him, Richard and Victor compared altimeters and took the mean. "Eighteen thousand three hundred," said Tupa. "More than half a mile higher than the Matterhorn," Bradshaw said with a laugh, "but an easier climb, eh, Loren?"

Loren didn't find the strength to let Bradshaw know that he'd never climbed the Matterhorn. Drained, he reflected that he was only eight years older than when they had tested him at the air force altitude lab.

Richard mounted to the pinnacle's very top to hoist a Union Jack nine inches tall. On a slightly safer foothold, Loren and Victor unfolded their miniature Stars and Stripes and Peruvian red-white-red.

Flag flaunting is a ritual mountain climbers are much given to, but it lasts mere instants, as the flag wavers are usually utterly exhausted. Now for the pictures. Tupa brought out the IAGS shield, stood it against boulders by Loren's feet, and Richard photographed Loren. Then Loren photographed Richard and Victor. Now for shots of the location. He set up his tripod and piled rocks around its legs to steady them, feeling their throb against the gusts of wind. He had a splitting headache. He mounted his shortest lens, a 20mm encompassing one fourth of the horizon, to try to take in the entire Cailloma Basin. All the trickles from innumerable icicles merged down there, forming the Apurímac. He put his eye to the viewfinder, saw the barren basin, the white summit of Huagra in the distance, barely visible, and noticed a sparkle in the lens.

He blinked, expecting the vision to disappear, but it held. He squinted hard at what was down there, at the bottom of the lens and dead ahead: the valley of the longest brook, the Carhuasanta.

Then he saw it, about a thousand feet below him, almost hidden in a field of *penitentes*. A pond, a mountain lake. A body of water, *liquid water*, the first since leaving the camp this morning.

He looked again, worried that it might be a hallucination. But the little lake appeared utterly real. A snowbank was draped around its southeastern edge, the one closest to him, and beyond it was the marshy thread of the Carhuasanta. The lake sat right on top of it.

Had they not traversed part of the divide on the Colca

side, they would have seen it earlier.

He checked the shot again, cleared his raw throat, and spoke in the most unassuming voice possible:

"I think we've found what we've been looking for."

10

The Source

No one gets training for such a moment.

It was October 15, 1971, shortly after three P.M. The expedition stood near the top of Mismi and stared down in silence at the little lake. Then Richard said something about the ultimate source, and Loren remembered that two months earlier those words had held little meaning for the young Englishman. Now he sounded so involved and excited. Loren's next thought was: the maps.

Victor unfolded the 1:200,000 first and found no lake on the northern slopes of Mismi. Then he unfolded the 1:100,000 and couldn't find the lake on the more detailed map either. He broke out the aerial photographs and all three huddled over them. At first they found nothing that looked like a lake right under the crest of the divide. Then Victor located a dark spot on a nine-by-nine-inch. They compared it with the terrain, and the locations matched—the dark spot was the lake. "This shot was taken back in 1955," said Victor carefully, "so it is a permanent lake; I guess this is the source."

After an instant, Victor added that if it had no local name, which needed to be verified, it should be named. As all three kept staring from the photos back down the mountainside, Victor pointed suddenly: "Look at that," he exclaimed.

Below the little lake, some two thousand feet down from

where they were standing, the meandering trail of the Carhuasanta dipped into another, larger mirror of water cupped between slopes. "Another lake," said Richard. The frozen fingers rushed again to deploy the tattered maps and the aerial photographs.

"Not named either," concluded Tupa after a moment. Then he turned toward Loren and commented that they had discovered a regular source system: the snowfield hanging down the slope abutted in the first lake, whose water filtered out into the Carhuasanta, which meandered down, fed a second lake, then continued on down, into the Lloqueta and the Apurímac. "The higher one, though"—somewhat solemnly, Victor pointed at the one Loren had glimpsed through the lens—"that's the ultimate source." And suddenly, as if his body had been programmed to endure only till they found the source, Tupa complained that he was feeling rotten. His lips were blue, his eyes unfocused. "I'm going to go down to look at it and then head for the camp," he announced. "I know you need pictures, Loren, but I gotta find some air to breathe."

In retrospect, Bradshaw, the veteran alpinist, should have stopped him right there and held the team together. But Bradshaw was too overpowered with the moment. Loren didn't think about it either. Both he and Bradshaw watched Victor start down, slipping and sliding on the loose brown scree left by dried-up snow. A while later, they saw him pause by the lake, then walk around it, examining it. Later he was to tell the others that at first he saw no overflow of the lake's water, then noticed the Carhuasanta brook emerging from the scree right below the lake. Satisfied by the connection, he started to follow the Carhuasanta toward the base camp.

Richard picked up his rope, his ice ax, his souvenir minerals: "Better head for the barn, want me to carry your tripod? We haven't had a decent thing to eat all day."

Later, Loren remembered responding just as brainlessly: "No reason to slow down for me; you'll have a meal ready by the time I catch up."

He handed Bradshaw the tripod and the camera case and was thus left alone on the slope, two hours before sundown, to document the find by taking pictures. He started by snapping Richard, running down the scree with giant skidding strides. Within ten minutes Richard reached the lake, stopped to look, then bent to drink from it. Then he hurried on down, hopping from rock to rock and keeping ahead of the minor landslides he stirred up. Loren was suddenly alone, still sitting on the frozen, windy height.

He wrapped his camera in a sweater and stuffed it into his pack, to protect it in case he slipped on the loose scree. Then he grabbed his ice ax and started down. With every step, the lake grew bigger and more real. A fairly wide rim of stones and gravel surrounded it, varying in color from brown to black and contrasting sharply with the snow. Finally he trampled over a heap of snow and found himself on the rocks forming the rim, where he checked the altimeter: 17,200 feet. In the middle of the rocks, the water was faultlessly blue, reflecting a faultlessly blue sky.

It was a small mountain lake, a tarn, almost ovoid in shape, its sharp end aimed north toward the Carhuasanta. It was only some two hundred feet long and a little over a hundred wide, flanked by short *penitentes* reflected in the water. The stones around its rim were of varying sizes, many quite small and rounded by water erosion, which confirmed that the lake was permanent and old. Loren could see the bottom at a depth of several feet. The wind rippled the surface in little waves which lapped away toward the northern end, the one aimed at the valley.

He looked up from the lake toward Choquecorao, trying to imagine a glacier that had shrunk and retreated over years and years. As for snow, the next snowfall would cover the top of the *penitentes*, hiding them and making the slope above the lake a continuous cushion of white all the way up to the top of Mismi.

He circled around toward the lake's northern point and knelt to examine the moraine that closed it up, a small moraine, without an overflow. Less dark than the rest of the rim, it looked discolored. A track of moisture meandered down from it, pointing into the Carhuasanta. The moraine looked thick and even, as if the percolation of the water had long found its truce with the gravel it filtered through. Altogether, none of what Loren saw seemed improvised by the whim of a recent season.

It was four-fifteen P.M. Exhausted but eager to enjoy the moment, McIntyre dropped on all fours, put his face in the lake, and drank the ice-cold water. Of the feelings he was aware of, one grew by the instant: how beautiful the source was, how appropriately located, how distinctly connected to the flow below and the snow above. And it was here, and he was here, surrounded by utter reality.

He remembered what he had to do and fought fatigue by giving himself precise instruction. *Need pictures by lake.* Drinking from its water, against the shiny surface and the *penitentes* on the other side, would be good. He picked out a flat-topped boulder near the western edge of the water, put the camera on it, and armed the self-timer. He triggered it, then rushed to stretch by the water, in the prone position. He had ten seconds and didn't make it, tried again, was not sure of the results, repeated the shot till he was too winded to make another attempt.

He sat on the boulder to change the film, but his fingers had gotten wet and were cold and clumsy. He dropped the exposed film cassette and it fell into a jumble of rocks under him, rattling out of reach.

Dammit. He couldn't afford to lose this one.

To find it, he had to move those rocks. One by one, he lifted the lighter ones and rolled the heavier ones this way and that, slowly, anxious not to dislodge the cassette or damage it. The loose rocks around the lake might be piled more than five feet deep, and he couldn't afford to let the pictures tumble out of sight. With numb fingers, he poked around carefully, noticing how much the light had diminished. The sun was slipping behind the mountains. Soon it would be entirely gone.

He finally got his fingers on the cassette. He was just rising with it, pushing it into a pocket of his parka, when he lost his balance. The universe swirled. The sun was turned off. He sank.

He saw walls of ice. High-altitude glaciers. Small humanoid shapes advanced through passes below the glaciers, following meadows and high ridges.

Then he saw them closer because he was one of them. They wore animal skins but stepped barefoot on patches of thawing snow, from whose tattered ends water trilled and dribbled away, into brown plateaus. An extreme sensation of cold in his feet warned him that he was barefoot too. He was walking barefoot on a high ridge. Under cold Andean sunshine, like a vast cosmic bombardment of light from the high dome of the sky.

They carried spears. The passage of their column, through landscape so sparse, warned all creatures that a new species was entering their habitat.

He was walking with them, following them into a majestic landscape of river sources. The feeling of limitless space was so overpowering that he looked at his closest companions, wishing to share the feeling.

He felt it was shared, and recognized his companions.

The men, women, and children trekked in winter, when the snow was falling, and in summer when the passes were bare and they could easily chase animals. They kept to the sierras and high ridges, but now and again some strayed into the hot, forested lowlands, where the heat made them throw away their animal skins.

They were Barnacle's ancestors. Trekking over the high sierras, past the trickling beginning of rivers, under the incredibly bright dome of the sky.

He resurfaced.

An upswell of almost indignant rationality seized him as soon as he could formulate a thought. It couldn't be. That the cat-men had trekked down from the mountains was quite probable, but they would have come down much farther north, not here. More likely they came down the Napo instead of the Apurímac, as their original territory was right by the main stream. But then, there or here— frozen and dizzy, he tried to sit up and couldn't—there or here, the landscape was the same: snowcapped peaks and glaciers, high ridges, source waters . . .

He drew himself up on one elbow and looked around. The sunset sky was laying an orange gloom over the snow and the lake. Gripping his ice ax with numb fingers, he staggered to his feet, but felt so weak that he sat down abruptly on a flat rock. *Well, Barnacle, now you know what it's like to make it all the way to the source. You freeze your ass off.*

His head felt like it was being hammered with rocks. He had fallen down, but luckily he felt no bruises or broken bones. Trying hard to get a grip on himself, he focused his thoughts desperately: *Don't do anything. Not in this extreme condition. Wait for it to pass.*

He breathed deeply and looked around. He saw only the barren slopes, the peaks, the lake. He was alone at over seventeen thousand feet, after an exhausting day, deprived of anything to attract attention to his plight. The daylight was gone. The wind was up and whipping the water. The lake looked like a gloomy chasm, wider now and totally without reflection.

Meaninglessly, he kept going back to his own imprudence and to Bradshaw's lack of foresight.

Then he felt a second upswell, of anger, and it was warm and welcome. The cold was hardly enough to kill a drunk lying in an alley, and he was dressed in a goose-down parka. It was the ataxia that was the problem, the inability to coordinate voluntary muscular movements. He felt incapable of getting up from his rock and placing one foot before the other. He had to vanquish the ataxia before cerebral edema swelled his brain, completely scrambling his mind. People died every year of cerebral edema caused by exertion and lack of oxygen above ten thousand feet, and McIntyre was sitting in the windy darkness nearly twice that high. Cerebral edema strikes athletes as eagerly as sedentary persons. He was already gritting his teeth from its commonest symptom, that splitting headache. Next came hallucinations, visual or verbal. Drowsiness, coma, and death followed quickly. The only known treatment was hasty descent.

He couldn't descend as yet. He was in no condition to move, let alone descend with any speed. And where was the Carhuasanta? He could distinguish neither the outline of the slope nor the headwater's boggy course.

Detached, foggy, he thought of this last battle of his body, which was to be fought in the dark, next to his lonely discovery.

His hope lay in pumping more oxygen to his brain.

He forced himself to breathe regularly and deeply. He ordered himself to think rationally, and came up with: *There are no trees around here, none whatsoever, not even a shrub in sight. Not a spine to pick your teeth with, or stick into a hole in your nostril. So where are you going to find your spines, Barnacle, my friend, to stick them in your nose and assert your status as head cat-man?*

The spines came later, beamed Barnacle.

What the hell did that mean, later?

There was a pause. Then he received the answer. A clear, wordless message that the custom of wearing spines came after the Mayoruna had descended from the mountains and were settled in the forest.

He was neither asking in words nor receiving his answers in words, while on his mind's word track another part of him commented: *Hallucination. Last thing going through your brain before it freezes. Very well. Let's see what else can be dredged from the subconscious before rigor mortis sets in.*

He looked up toward Choquecorao and almost didn't see it. Clouds blew in from the divide, starting to shut off those Andean stars, so clear that one could tell their colors with the naked eye.

He didn't try to fight what was happening to him. On the

contrary, he felt that if he went through with it, his chances of survival were better.

The message came, as faint as if Barnacle had beamed it from the Cordillera Ultra-Oriental. *Think heat. Think how hot it was on the upper Javari. Think of being bathed in sweat—hallucination, he kept repeating to himself, its acuity and consistency are no proof of its reality—think of running through the forest, following the hunters, hardly keeping up. Think of Red Cheeks's treachery, of stumbling into a dark thicket of spines, and of wandering in the jungle for days and nights. Think of the airless heat at midday, think of the fire beside the hammock at night, not in words but in feelings—*

He remembered how he used to "think scared" before running the two-mile for the University of California: that got his adrenaline up and left no room for any other thoughts. Now he had to think *I'll get out of this fix* and leave room for nothing else, and then get up and do it. For otherwise he would fall asleep and sleep forever, freezing to death at the beginning of the world's greatest tropical river—

With a boost from Barnacle, he beamed himself down the Apurímac, down the Ucayali, down the main stream to the mouth of the Javari, just after midday when the heat was insufferable (*I'm hallucinating about a dead Indian, but never mind*) he beamed himself upstream, past the tiny settlements and savage shores, to the warm source of the snagged-up little river, to a meadow at the foot of the Cordillera Ultra-Oriental. He reached it, fell down on the grass, lay in the sun, and hoped that Barnacle would beam a message full of warmth, and the Mayoruna would find him—

He was expecting to see the headman. He didn't see him, but there was suddenly an ether full of fractured juvenile beaming, and sure enough here came Tuti, the headman's cross-eyed son, with some other children. They started shooting toy arrows, without hurting him, and he jumped up and chased them, shouting at them without words. He pursued them but couldn't catch Tuti, who glanced back beaming laughter. Loren ran out of breath, stopped, heart pounding, while the boys fled along familiar white sands at the water's edge, where once he had sat watching the glistening Waterfall of Hope—

He managed to stagger up slowly and began to stamp his feet—they hurt, so they were not frozen. He took off his mittens, clapped his hands, and his fingertips began to tingle. He pulled down the knitted wool of his cap over his nose and mouth and breathed into it to warm up the air around his face.

Tuti and his friends had disappeared into the forest, and Loren was now gazing at the starless sky above the divide, not seeing anything, not knowing which way to head for camp except that down was down.

He always carried a flashlight, yet this time he had left it in the camera case he'd asked Richard to carry back to the camp. Dumb. As dumb as splitting up the team. He groped in his pocket, found the chocolate bar, and made himself eat it slowly. It had no smell at this altitude, but he was amazed at its good taste. The first nourishment to pass his lips since that predawn cup of Jell-O.

He shouldered his almost empty pack, started down, remembered the camera. He climbed back and couldn't find his resting place in the dark. Never mind; he had the film, far more important than the camera now. He pulled on his gloves and started working his way down, bending to touch his fingertips to boulders, careful not to injure his shins. All he saw in any direction were black mountains looming against a sky slightly less black; as a minimal orientation, he tried to keep the mass of Mismi behind him.

Then he realized that this combination of spongy little hummocks and shallow rills and brooklets was the Carhuasanta's boggy course. A broad, boggy booby trap. He advanced slowly, stepping into the rills and brooklets, loudly cracking their ice, ever thicker as the night wore on and the cold increased. His socks were dangerously wet, yet he couldn't hurry: if he broke a leg, Richard and Victor might not find him until daylight, and even if he were still alive they would have a terrible time carrying him back to camp at this altitude.

Slipping off an edge of frozen grass, he fell into a bog, splashing into ice water up to his waist. A quick stab with the ice ax kept him from tumbling in over his head. Clawing at the slippery edge, he pulled himself out, drenched with ice water.

This could be the end. If the cold made him unable to move his legs, he'd be good for the museum by morning, like those sacrificed Inca boys and girls. He tried to run just to get his circulation going, ran out of wind in seconds, stumbled into another bog. *Think about the hours of wading in the Javari. Skin wrinkled as a prune. Think hot, think hot, dammit, come on, Barnacle, give me a hand. Anything to stay conscious. Try a nursery rhyme. Dick and Vic ran down so quick/ And Mac came tumbling after . . .*

A star came out, as yellow as Mars. Then he realized that it was too large to be a star, and it was moving.

It was a flashlight held high by Richard, who was climbing back up toward him. Loren tried to call, but his vocal cords refused to obey.

Richard grabbed his wet sleeve, started to pull him along, faster, faster. In the sky ahead, another light started blinking, signaling SOS, of all things!

"That's Victor, on that high ledge that didn't break during the earthquake," explained Richard.

By the time they reached the tents, Victor had come down from the ledge and was stirring a potful of something thick, his smile lit by the blue flame of the burner. It was past ten P.M. Loren had been alone on the frozen slopes only six hours.

Victor lifted hot fluids to Loren's mouth and gave him aspirin to quell his headache. Richard helped him change into dry clothing scavenged from all three backpacks. Loren protested the attention, but he was still too weak and ataxic to help himself. He crawled into his sleeping bag with the dry clothes on. After a while he stopped shivering and fell asleep.

*

Sometime in the night, he snapped awake, gasping for air. Next to him, Tupa was snoring noisily in short, quick gasps, then not breathing at all for as long as a minute at a time.

Feeling the hard frozen earth under his sleeping bag, Loren wished for the comfort of a jungle hammock. The Mayoruna would be sleeping now, the way tribesmen slept, in shifts. He imagined the fires by their hammocks, burned down to coals. If his hammock were slung among theirs, he would be picking up a few scattered thoughts. How far did their beaming reach? Did its intensity decrease with the square of the distance, as with electromagnetic waves?

He thought: *I'm lying now like a chrysalis in the cocoon of my sleeping bag, and I think I know the secret of the beaming. It's in the genes. When Barnacle's ancestors trekked over from Asia, most of the terrain was covered a mile deep with continental ice. When they traveled south, generation after generation, the ice and then the mountains of South America forced them to stay high, exposed to that increased cosmic bombardment. Sometime during their ten-thousand-year trek, a shower of gamma rays from the explosion of a supernova struck and altered a gene in one of Barnacle's forebears. That happened at a moment of great emergency, when the people were too widely scattered to communicate by voice or gestures, yet their need for communication was most acute. So the beaming was born of extreme need. And so it came to pass that a few Amerindians possessed a special gift, conferred on them by a catastrophic event in a far-off galaxy.*

In time they wandered or were driven into the lowland forest, but their genes held an urge to return to that high landscape of mountain ridges and river sources.

Everything seemed to fall into place. If he accepted the beaming. And if he credited the Mayoruna with somehow spurring him to recover from his collapse by the source and making him increase his temperature by sheer will.

He followed Barnacle's ancestors coming down the Andes, camping in one mountain meadow after another, passing a hundred headwaters. When they descended into the eastern forest, they carried with them their origin myth, the source/

beginning, and the power of nonverbal communication.

He liked the idea of the beaming being an incidental cosmic gift. *I've been saved from freezing*, he thought, *by a series of events that began with the death of a distant star*.

Victor and Richard let him sleep until sunup, when they leisurely cooked breakfast and broke camp.

The fine weather was still holding. The expedition retraced its steps to the vehicle, and then to Cailloma, then back to Arequipa and Lima.

Two weeks later, at twenty thousand feet of altitude, a plane of the Peruvian Air Force circled the Cailloma Basin, verifying the source. Loren McIntyre was in the plane, photographing through the open doorway, buffeted by the icy air, and retching with airsickness. No snow had yet fallen and the entire terrain looked drier than ever. The little lake, the source that McIntyre had somehow shared with his Mayoruna friends, was clearly visible at the start of the Carhuasanta brook. He took its picture from aloft.

In July 1972, Loren received a copy of a letter on IAGS stationery from Victor Tupa, Nomenclature Supervisor, to Warren L. Ashworth, Chief of Engineers, USA IAGS Project Peru. Subject: Report on the Expedition to Determine the True Source of the Amazon River.

Tupa started his report by stating that "during the first fortnight of October 1971, the various controversies that existed about the true source of the Amazon River came to an end." He described how the expedition, "having determined by cartographic studies the probable point of origin of the River Amazonas," traveled from Lima to Cailloma, then

> continued by vehicle toward the south, following a trail negotiable by car. After reaching the end of it, we continued cross-country, making use of four-wheel drive as far as possible. After abandoning the car at the northern border of Lake Carhuacocha, we continued on foot in a southerly direction until we

arrived at our destination. There stood the peaks Hueracahua and Mismi, still without ice as of that date. Farther on, framed by savage beauty, stood out the snowpeak Choquecorao, covered with pedestals of ice in the form of stalagmites that gave the appearance of a white forest, created by the action of "fronts" of winds striking from both sides; they caused us serious difficulties during the climb.

In the accumulation of runoff at 5,200 meters (17,060 feet) elevation, on the north face of the mentioned snowpeak appears the first small lake, which I have named "Laguna McIntyre" in homage to the American friend, the indefatigable dreamer about nature. Another kilometer farther north from there appears a slightly larger lake, at a lower elevation of 5,000 meters. . . .

The aforementioned waters are the most remote that give the true origin of the Apurímac River and consequently of the Amazon River. . . . So it is that, if the remoteness of the origin is the determining factor of the source of a river, then the Amazon River is born of the source situated on the north face of the snows of Choquecorao at 5,200 meters elevation and at 15° 31′ 00″ latitude and 71° 41′ 40″ longitude, at the head of the Carhuasanta ravine in the province of Cailloma in the Department of Arequipa. In this place, as always occurs with rainwater, it filters into the ground, then emerges by capillary attraction to the surface in the form of springs and lakes. To these waters are joined those that come from the melting of masses of snow and then flow by gravity through countless subterranean channels to the bed of the Carhuasanta, where they reappear anew.

Then followed a description of the feedwater system created by the Carhuasanta, Sillanque, Apacheta, and Ccaccansa, all flowing into the Lloqueta, which ultimately joined the Apurímac. The report concluded that

The lakes mentioned earlier (Lake McIntyre and the lower one) are more distant than Mount Huagra by 45.5 kilometers, than Lake Vilafro by 39 kilometers, and than the Mount Minaspata source by 21 kilometers.

The *National Geographic* carried the Lake McIntyre source on its maps from 1972 onward, while the Smithsonian and the German publications accepted it only in 1977. The other geographic/cartographic institutions followed, their conservatism gradually defeated by documentation from the *National Geographic*, the IAGS, and the U.S. Defense Mapping Agency. In the following years, the find was verified by several expeditions, including one led by Jean-Michel Cousteau. But McIntyre's feat was noted in the *Guinness Book of Records* only after the Amazon Source-to-Sea Expedition of 1985 ran the monster's course again, in rubber rafts and kayaks, from near Lake McIntyre to the Atlantic. Only two members of that eleven-man expedition, Piotr Chmielinski and Joe Kane, traveled the entire 4,150 miles. Kane reported finding more snow in the source area than McIntyre had and noted that some of the Lloqueta's forming brooks appeared increased in both flow and length. He also confirmed that Lake McIntyre was there above all of them, its link with the snowfields on the divide and the rivulets below clearly permanent.

In that same year, 1985, five members of the Adventurers Club of Los Angeles, California, erected at the source a seventy-six-pound iron cross with a bronze plaque inscribed with the words: "*En honor de LOREN McINTYRE, descubridor del origen del Río Amazonas.*"

Above the inscription, a stylized drawing of a river showed the Amazon flowing from between snowcapped peaks down to a wavy line, the ocean, while the whole scene was lit by the Incas' father, the sun.

EPILOGUE

"Civilization must advance, though it tread on the neck of the savage, or even trample him out of existence."

LIEUTENANT W. L. HERNDON, U.S. NAVY,
in a report to the Congress about Amazonia's potential, 1854

In September 1976, a shocking story found its way into the world's leading newspapers. It originated with a FUNAI agent who reported to Brazil's *O Globo* that on the Javari River, the boundary between Brazil and Peru, the Mayoruna Indians were killing their children. Following *O Globo*, on 23 September 1976, the *Washington Post* ran a story under the headline A TRIBE DECIDING TO DIE, describing the natives' motives as despair and a sense of having "no place to go." The *Post* interviewed anthropologists who opined that in the general context of developmental pressure on tribes the news didn't seem farfetched. From 1972 to 1974, Petrobras, Brazil's state-run oil giant, had prospected sites along the Javari. To avoid losing advance teams to Indian attacks, the oilmen had been accompanied by units of the Brazilian Army. Their presence on the river was brief, however, since oil was not found and Petrobras discontinued its quest.

When the story about the Mayoruna infanticide broke, McIntyre was in Goiânia, capital of Goiás state, a guest in the house of Jesco von Puttkamer, an expert on Indians and a *National Geographic* contributor. McIntyre was located there by phone by Dieter Steiner, photo editor of the German magazine *Der Stern*. Steiner told McIntyre about the purported killings, characterizing them as racial suicide, since the tribe was scuttling its own ability to survive. *Der*

Stern wanted McIntyre to accept an assignment to find the Mayoruna, verify the story, and get photographs.

This looked to McIntyre like the long-awaited opportunity to revisit Mayoruna country, and he reacted with interest, though he doubted the story was true—the reporting agent (whose name was Paulo Lucena) might have been confused by the Mayoruna's custom of getting rid of offspring born with deformities, and sometimes of "excess" baby girls. McIntyre discussed the story with Puttkamer, who had good contacts with the FUNAI bureaucracy. With Puttkamer's help, McIntyre found out that Lucena, after working as *delegado regional* of FUNAI in Benjamin Constant, across the river from Leticia, had been fired by the agency. Now he was a critic of its policies, accusing FUNAI of ethnocentricity, paternalism and complicity in tribal genocide. Both McIntyre and Puttkamer recognized "ethnocentricity" as a buzzword used by some anthropologists in their polemics against state-run agencies. Lucena's complaints seemed likely to be exaggerated, since no aggressive settlement was being pursued on the Javari.

McIntyre learned that there was now one FUNAI station on the middle Javari—Pôsto Lobo, a two-hour flight out of Leticia, in an area of snagged riverflow as hard to land on as the upper course, where he and Mercier had attempted a first contact. He could make Pôsto Lobo the base for his investigation. This time he would have the backing of a major magazine, which believed that infanticide made good copy. The problem was a FUNAI permit to visit the area—such permits were always hard to get.

But like most expeditions, this one was easier to plan than to execute. While the notion of infanticide was kept simmering by the Brazilian and the international press, McIntyre had to satisfy other obligations, the main one being research for a book on Alexander von Humboldt's travels through the Americas. Finally, as 1977 arrived, McIntyre called *Der Stern* and told them that he was ready to go. The infanticide rumor was still alive, and also *Der Stern*'s interest in it. McIntyre was skeptical about acquiring a FUNAI permit, but he took the first step of flying to Brasília. To his surprise, he discovered that the director of FUNAI, General Ismarth de Araujo Oliveira, was convinced that the infanticide story had been faked by a disgruntled employee. Ismarth urged McIntyre to go and form his own opinion, hoping that what he would find would offset the negative publicity.

Equipped with the permit, McIntyre flew to Manaus, to set out for the Javari by way of Leticia, Tabatinga, and Benjamin Constant.

On the way to Manaus, he could see from the plane how new settlements were spreading along the Trans-Amazon Highway. Columns of smoke from slash-and-burn operations rose from both sides of the road. The government had offered plots to relieve population pressures in the dry northeast, but many of the migrants had little knowledge of how to farm land cleared from tropical forests. Deforestation of Amazonia was beginning to be a concern, a serious threat to both life-forms and native tribes. McIntyre's portrait-of-the-Amazon story in *National Geographic*, including his account of finding the source, had been published in October 1972. The issue's cover was one of his photographs, a close-up of a Txukahamei girl whose forest home had been bisected by a strip of rutted red earth, another "highway of progress."

Despite the concern of the scientific communities, the Brazilian popular press and some politicians fanned the fear that if Brazil didn't colonize its wild lands, then the Chinese or the Japanese would. Meanwhile, Brazilians marched into the forest, convinced that they were repeating the westward thrust that built the United States into a great nation. However, from the natives' point of view, it was a continuation of the march of the conquistadors, eating away at their world and undermining their independence.

Understandably, McIntyre felt a responsibility about investigating the reports of Mayoruna suicide. From his experience with the Mayoruna, he didn't believe that they would deliberately kill their own children. Yet he couldn't be sure. He had participated in a Mayoruna "ritual of exit." Could it be that they had moved on to a more drastic version?

In Leticia, he hired a floatplane for two round trips to Pôsto Lobo, where he would contact FUNAI agent Isidro Bautista Silva. Before taking off, he boated across the river to Benjamin Constant, to interview Paulo Lucena, the source for the original story. They met in a lumberyard, where Lucena reaffirmed that the Mayoruna had been killing all baby girls, plus, more recently, all male children and all their sick and crippled, irrespective of age. FUNAI, Lucena said, was trying to quash the truth, as they felt it reflected negatively on them. Lucena stated that of fifteen hundred Mayoruna on the Brazilian shore before Petrobras's incursion, twelve hundred had died from common cold, dysentery and gonorrhea. Lucena couldn't explain where the figure of fifteen hundred had come from, though—he admitted that it didn't come from a census. He estimated the Mayoruna in Peru at ten thousand. McIntyre remembered that the missionaries in Yarinacocha put the number at seven hundred. Lucena considered himself an anthropologist, yet had no precise information of village locations and had kept no maps from his service with the agency. McIntyre found him contentious and well versed in buzzwords. Somewhat relieved that the source for the grim reports didn't seem too dependable, he boated back to Leticia. Hours later, he was flying over the ocean of forest again.

As before, it was the dry season and the river's flow was choked with fallen tree trunks—finding an *estirón* on which to land was going to be a pulse-quickening adventure. After two hours in the air the pilot flew over Pôsto Lobo, waggling wings. A man came out of a cabin and stared up at the plane. On the second turn above the compound, McIntyre leaned from the doorway and pointed emphatically downstream.

Minutes below the station but days from it by canoe, the

pilot put down on a stretch of free flow, next to a muddy beach. McIntyre helped the pilot empty four *bidones* of gasoline into the aircraft's wing tanks, and the plane took off. McIntyre waded ashore. With a feeling of déjà vu, he slung his hammock between two trees and prepared to wait.

He expected that Silva had understood his signal from the plane and would send a canoe to pick him up.

Remembering from his first contact that the Mayoruna showed great need for needles and thread, spoons and pots, fishhooks and fishing line and medicine, McIntyre had brought such supplies in quantity. He also carried a Polaroid camera and film, to demonstrate the harmlessness of photography and win friends. Two sacks bulged with gifts. His other cameras were packed in Halliburton cases to protect them from marauding pets.

Now he was on the shore, alone, waiting. He was several hundred miles downstream from where he had landed in 1969, but the locations looked strikingly familiar. There were even *lupunas* here, lighthouse trees, one of them not too far from where he had waded ashore. As for the brown murmuring river, its sound was as familiar as if time had returned full circle, picking up exactly where it had been interrupted when the cold rain had begun to fall, leading McIntyre to his escape.

Eight years had passed and he had fulfilled a lifelong dream in the interim.

He didn't notice exactly when he started thinking about the beaming. He went through the operations of slinging his hammock, securing his gear for the night, making a fire, and cooking a meal in a distractedly automatic way, helped by routine and paying little attention to what he was doing. He was aware of the loneliness of the place in an unusual way, as if expecting from it a message or a confirmation. He felt no anxiety, but was so filled with excitement and suspense that the empty hours of waiting passed astonishingly quickly: suddenly the light was fading and the bush started to stir with the tense animation of the night.

He expected it would take Silva, or the men he was

sending, at least two days to get down here.

He slept calmly and woke up a little before dawn. Lingering between sleep and full awareness, he remembered the night he had discovered the source—not the bizarre and frightening hours by the little lake, but that later awakening in the tent. He thought again of Barnacle's ancestors crossing the Andes along access routes cut through the mountains by the sourcewaters, under a cosmic bombardment from the sky, and the birth of the beaming in some desperate moment on that high passage.

In the coolness of predawn, surrounded by the forest, these things seemed possible. Eventually the Mayoruna forebears had reached the forest and lost themselves in it. As they became involved with the forest creatures and admired their vitality and power, their memories of the high passage faded. Eventually they identified with the jaguars as totem ancestors. But their extraordinary gift remained, now ensconced in ritual.

He got up unhurriedly, knowing that he had at least another day to wait before anyone would show up.

Through the day, he took some photographs of nearby vegetation and of some macaws flying in pairs under the canopy, repacked his camera, prepared meals, ate, and rested, thinking about the beaming so often that he finally abandoned all attempt to think of anything else. Was McIntyre's elaborate construct about the ancestors' high passage pure fantasy, or had he truly received some of it from Barnacle? He remembered the strength of that sensation of archaic memory experienced next to the source lake. That memory felt like it was "shared," as if he and the headman had talked, so to speak, memory to memory.

He went to sleep the second night so keyed up he almost expected a boatload of Mayoruna to pull up on the muddy shore, guided to the location by his thoughts.

The third morning in the wilderness came misty and cool. He had finished breakfast and was turning around to throw from his cup the last drops of condensed milk made liquid with river water, when he saw a dugout canoe hardly two yards away. From it, three Indian men stared at him. They were young. Their faces bristled with cat whiskers that seemed longer than any he'd seen before.

He uttered his name, assuming that the men had been sent by Silva to pick him up.

"Lowen?" one of them asked back, as if in confirmation.

He nodded, starting. He hadn't even suspected their presence until they were almost close enough to touch him.

One of the Indians confirmed in minimal Portuguese that the agent at Pôsto Lobo had sent them for him. It would take three days of paddling to reach the station; going against the current explained the extra day.

"What's your name?" McIntyre asked him, expecting the standard *"Não tem"* ("Don't have one"); fearing spells, Indians considered it taboo to disclose their real names to strangers. But the Indian said that his name was For God's Sake ("Por Amor de Deus" in Portuguese). McIntyre was about to smile when another Indian also said his name:

"Câmbio."

Câmbio?

What did he mean, "Câmbio?" How did he come to be called that? McIntyre knew that Indians often interchanged names with relatives or friends, particularly the kind of names they confessed to civilizados. Was this Câmbio related to "his" Câmbio? He stared at the young Mayoruna, then realized that too much interest was the best way to inhibit any further explanation, so he turned away, heart pounding, to untie his hammock, roll it up, and gather his gear.

His mind was a storm of conjecture and hope. Câmbio, *Câmbio!* A coincidence was possible, but he didn't believe it. Both this new Câmbio and his friend For God's Sake seemed to have picked their nicknames from radio talk—but it was extremely unlikely they had ever been near a radio. Had they met the other Câmbio? Had they listened to his story?

They helped him lift his bags into the canoe. Climbing in, he sat on a narrow thwart of wood with his feet in two fingers of water. The three healthy young men lifted their paddles and slapped the river with them, and the shores rolled back.

On both sides of their advance, the jungle sprawled undisturbed. The notion of racial suicide seemed as out of place now as that of an alien invasion.

Câmbio. Was the tribesman close? Was he expecting the explorer, perhaps waiting up at the FUNAI station? What had happened to him all these years? Was he still the man McIntyre had known—that winning mixture of native friendliness, direct and expressive curiosity, and stubborn belief in rituals? McIntyre remembered him in vivid detail, and certainly Câmbio would remember the *chotac* photographer too. The visits of outsiders are always events, even to contacted tribes. And now Câmbio was near, perhaps. And wasn't it possible then that Barnacle was near as well?

A bizarre thought presented itself suddenly, as McIntyre panted his way into the midmorning heat. He had not received any beaming—but the coincidence itself, the fact that this man's name was also Câmbio—wasn't that somehow proof of the beaming?

I'm thinking like an Indian! Nothing is happenstance, and everything is connected and magical!

No, that was no proof. It was just coincidence.

Still, he was so buoyed up and cheerfully certain that he would be meeting his old friends that he almost started to tell his boatmen a story about Câmbio, the *other* Câmbio. He refrained, then tried to strike a conversation with the Câmbio who sat near him. The man did not respond, but concentrated on his paddling. His skin was somewhat lighter than his companions'; he also seemed to be the least conversant in Portuguese, so McIntyre decided not to press. When they got to the station he could ask Silva if he knew of an older headman with crusty warts on his legs. But it didn't seem likely. The station was several hundred river miles from the source of the Javari.

Then again, the Mayoruna were semi-nomadic and could have migrated that far over a period of eight years.

There were two shotguns in the boat, proof that these men had traded with the civilizados and learned to use their tools. Sometime after midday, they fired at a macaw flying overhead, not to eat it but hoping to wound it just enough to capture it and keep it as a pet. The great red bird crashed into the jungle. The Indians pulled alongside a tree fallen into the river and used it for a ramp to climb the high mudbank and go after their prey.

Eager to take pictures, McIntyre tried to climb along the trunk after them, but the branch he grabbed to steady himself broke, and he fell backward into the river with both his cameras around his neck.

That suddenly put his mind on a completely different track. For hours after the Indians came back with the bird and resumed paddling upstream, he sat in the canoe holding his opened cameras in the sun to dry them, worrying silently whether his mission for *Der Stern* would be a failure because of damage to his equipment. But the accident gave him an excuse for conversation. He told the paddlers that he'd visited the Javari before, when there wasn't a FUNAI station on its middle course. He asked about Lucena, and they said that they knew no one by that name. He didn't ask about the reports of infanticide. Indians who wouldn't give out their tribal names were not going to volunteer information about such a practice, if it existed.

Two hours later, they suddenly stopped on the riverbank by a patch of banana trees, whose disheveled shadows concealed a little hut. The three young Indians beached the canoe and headed for the hut, which was lopsided and had no door. After an instant of hesitation McIntyre followed them inside.

His eyes adjusted to the semi-darkness. Before he could figure out what exactly was happening, a bundle of rags stirred in an old, tattered hammock; a ghostly face turned toward the visitors, and McIntyre saw a swelling the size of a small melon on an old woman's emaciated neck.

The apparition clamped a skeletal hand over the swelling

to hold it in place, and said something. One of the youngsters responded with a greeting in which McIntyre identified *tita*, "mother," one of the few words he knew in the Matse language. Still holding the monstrous swelling, the apparition squeaked something back in which he distinguished *mado*, "son." He realized he must be watching a family reunion.

One of the Indians lifted the human bundle, so easily that McIntyre guessed she weighed no more than sixty pounds. Legs like sticks jutted out of her tattered dress, which was not gray but simply worn past color. The son moved the mother out into the sunlight between the trees and seated her on a log. Her gray hair looked like moss, one eye was sunk in its socket, but the other found the visitor and stared at him with concentration, as if trying to remember if she had seen him before.

McIntyre noticed a similarity between her wrinkled face and those of the three young men. She was light-skinned, but perhaps her pallor was due to ailment and age. One of the men informed McIntyre that their mother, Sally *Doña* Perez ("lady" was oddly placed between the two nouns), spoke Spanish.

"Where are you from, *Doña* Sally?" managed McIntyre.

In the opening of her dress, a limp lobe dangled, a one-time breast that had nursed these muscular men. Apart from goiter and cataracts and probably bad arthritis, *Doña* Sally looked as if she'd suffered months, perhaps years of malnutrition.

Her mouth corners crumbled into a doily of wrinkles, and a diffuse bluish tincture showed inside the wrinkles: defeating time, a Mayoruna tattoo persisted. But no sound was heard. "Were you born a Mayoruna?" McIntyre tried again.

A series of coughs and squeaks were heard, like from a deflated doll uttering flaccid sounds. Miraculously the squeaks became a voice thin like a thread of cobweb, speaking in fine Spanish. "I was born in Tarapoto, in Peru." She paused, took a breath, squeaked again: "My stepfather sold me and my sister to a river trader." Another pause, more squeaks: "When I was six."

McIntyre was silent, dumbfounded. The bright light of the sun outside the shade of the banana trees seemed to deny the absurd scene being played here.

"Then we were kidnapped by the Mayoruna, and I was separated from my sister." *Doña* Sally found a residue of energy in her deflated doll's body, and talked a little louder and faster. "We grew up in different villages. I don't know how old I was, maybe twelve, when a headman named Siní pierced my nose, tattooed me, and married me. I gave him three *mado* ("sons") and two *champi* ("daughters")."

McIntyre listened, transfixed. Sun rays pierced through the banana trees' foliage, and the apparition, warmed up, became almost vivacious.

"It was a hard life, but I got along with Siní. Then another headman named Kacuá killed Siní and married me, and we had six more children. These *con mado*, my sons" —her live eye glinted at the muscular boys— "are the last three."

"You never," he couldn't help asking the question, "you never tried to run away?"

The goiter went up, in sync with a shrug of the discarnate shoulders. "Where to? They would have caught me. And by the time I had children, what civilizado would have married me? But they are good people, the Mayoruna," she added hastily, as if concerned for the Mayoruna's reputation.

The explorer leaned closer to her live eye. He asked her if the Mayoruna ever killed their children. To which she answered categorically: Only if they were born crippled.

Then her eye fogged up and she seemed lost in a sort of wakeful sleep.

The explorer stepped back and gestured to the sons for permission to photograph. They agreed and he clicked his camera, then asked the sons about their father. They told him that Kacuá, *Doña* Sally's last husband, had moved years before to Caxias, a town way downriver, and maybe still lived there. He had changed his name and pretended not to be a Mayoruna.

He nodded, helpless to express what he really felt.

"*Adiós, Doña Sally*," he said.

"*Adiós, mí caballero*," she said with comatose elegance. He stepped back and watched as the sons said goodbye to *tita*, then all four men returned to their canoe and headed upriver.

They paddled till after dark, pulling ashore at a one-hut settlement on the bank where an Indian McIntyre could barely make out in the dark offered him his bed of straw to sleep in. Waking up the next morning, McIntyre saw his host's face and torso, and jumped: red pustules seemed to have exploded from every inch of the man's skin, over chest, shoulders, arms, neck, cheeks, and forehead.

It looked like smallpox. There was nothing McIntyre could do but take Polaroid pictures of the man's face, chest, and back, and later send them to the World Health Organization for diagnosis.

Boca de Lobo (the Wolf's Mouth) was the point at which an *igarape*, a flooded back arm once part of the main stream, opened into a luxurious creeper-packed swamp on the Brazilian side of the river, with a well-built Indian house on stilts at the confluence. Several hours up the tree-cluttered *igarapé*, on a bank forty feet high, well above maximum flood level, stood a cluster of wooden buildings—Pôsto Lobo, the FUNAI station.

The FUNAI agent, Isidro Bautista Silva, stood on the bank eagerly awaiting McIntyre's arrival, for he was expecting supplies he'd asked for and not received in fourteen months—mainly gasoline. He was crestfallen when he found that McIntyre had brought none. The explorer was equally upset that he had not been informed of Silva's needs—the agent obviously had little use for the wristwatch McIntyre had brought him as a welcoming gift. The Indians lounging around the station wore battered army shorts instead of the native *guayucos* (G-strings with tassels of vegetal fibers hanging over their genitals); they also gave thumbs-up or army-style salutes, which they had seen the oilmen and soldiers do. McIntyre noticed several Indians with lighter skin and almost European features, clear signs of mixed ancestry, but they wore in their faces the spines of the Mayoruna and seemed to speak nothing but Matse.

Questioning Silva, McIntyre learned that the Indians in the surrounding villages grew bananas, manioc, and corn. Most still hunted with spears and bows and arrows, but some owned shotguns; those who did loaded their own shells and prized ammunition as much as salt, medicine, or knives. They had little to offer in trade except fresh meat and a slight crop surplus, and their markets were many days or weeks downriver. Therefore, unsurprisingly, they had become very dependent on the help of FUNAI. But apart from not supplying Silva in fourteen months, FUNAI bureaucrats in Brasília had also not paid his wages, and the man was seriously thinking of leaving the station, though he knew that he wouldn't be immediately replaced. His charges would have to learn how to look after themselves again, or seek another patron. Concerned but powerless, Silva predicted that they would probably drift downriver and enter society at its lowest level, in Benjamin Constant or some other little port.

Right now, however, these Indians seemed comfortable with their compromise and had no notion that Silva might leave. Some had relatives upstream and visited or received visits from the "wild" villages. Unlike Lucena, Silva seemed the enduring type who liked his work and kept good records of the villages' locations, of elders' names, and of the supplies distributed. On his one-man effort rested the health and amicableness of the surrounding community. Silva was also fairly typical: FUNAI employed as agents in the field not city idealists or experts writing theses, but people themselves part Indian, rivermen for whom bush life was not a distant reality.

Silva said the area was quiet. Both army and oilmen had retreated after 1974. At the notion of infanticide his eyes widened. McIntyre pulled out several press clippings, which Silva read with a deep wrinkle on his forehead, then answered that, had he had any local reports, he would have alerted the central office in Brasília. "And probably gotten a reply next year," he added with a chuckle. He was positive that there was no infanticide around here unless in cases of deformed offspring. The Petrobras intrusion had sent some Mayoruna deeper into the wild, that was true, but not to kill themselves; as for the communities upstream, the farther away they were, the less one knew about them, but still he was skeptical. He could ask some Indians who had just come down from the Javari headwaters.

"Câmbio!" Silva called, getting up and waving at some natives camping outside.

Câmbio!

McIntyre found himself on his feet, rushing past Silva. From among several squatting brown bodies, a man with a headband of pounded bark rose and came forward, limping slightly. He displayed the Mayoruna tattoo and the little holes in his lips, though his labrets were missing. He seemed smaller, and his stomach had swollen a little. He raised a hand in a semi-civilizado salute, and in a flash the explorer remembered the feel of those muscle-packed palms, the knowledgeable scurry of those fingers, as they spread the black paint over his naked torso on a morning eight years earlier, under the untouched canopy, in the beginning.

Câmbio instantly recognized the explorer. He stopped dead, looked at him with eyes like black bullets, so intensely that McIntyre felt that the little shaman was casting a spell—but only for an instant. Then Câmbio threw himself forward again, limping even worse from the sudden movement. His small strong palm grabbed the civilizado's hand. They stared at each other, then both of them broke into clumsy, faltering salutations—*Olá, Câmbio; Olá, Lowen*—and the weight of feeling that McIntyre had carried with him for the last few days seemed suddenly to find its release. Without any grandiose or emotional gesture, he simply held Câmbio's hand until Câmbio pulled his hand back but remained where he was, radiating attention, while McIntyre stared back at him with the same focused intensity.

Then they heard Silva's footsteps. The FUNAI agent was walking up to them, intrigued by their unusual greeting.

Briefly, McIntyre explained to Silva his contact of 1969 and the fact that he'd met Câmbio then. Surprised, Silva digested the information, then turned to ask Câmbio whether he'd heard of any en masse killings of Mayoruna babies. Câmbio knitted his eyebrows, then answered no, he knew of no such killings. Meanwhile, McIntyre examined his long-lost friend: Câmbio had aged little, but his expression was quite different from the one McIntyre remembered. Instead of that liveliness and lack of reserve, the man before him seemed subdued, almost passive. Apart from the headband, he wore no native adornments: a pair of old swimming trunks wrapped his body where once his genitals had dangled freely or swung tied with the ritual cord. McIntyre mentioned that he'd been paddled up to the station by another native named Câmbio, to which Câmbio answered with a silent little shrug, as if the recurrence of such a name meant nothing special.

Instinctively realizing that an unguarded exchange between them would only happen without witnesses, McIntyre steered the conversation to the idea of taking a census of the neighboring Mayoruna villages. They could do it the next day, suggested Silva. Silva then asked Câmbio if he would serve as guide and interpreter. Câmbio agreed. Then he politely said, "*Até amanhã*," "See you tomorrow," and turned away quickly to join the other tribesmen. McIntyre saw him enter their little group; instants later, several of them, including Câmbio, grabbed arrows and bows and climbed into a canoe, obviously to go fishing.

Why had he turned away so quickly? Was he afraid? Was he embarrassed? McIntyre finally told himself that there was nothing unusual in that behavior. Quite simply, eight years had passed. He'd get his chance to talk to Câmbio tomorrow.

Silva explained that half a day of paddling up the *igarape* (a minute by plane) there were several Mayoruna hamlets. Their population had never been counted, and it was Silva's opinion that regional delegate Lucena had never gotten that far upstream. McIntyre was impressed by the friendliness of the Mayoruna he had seen around the post. In this area, Silva confirmed, they had been willing to try a little of the white man's ways, a fairly novel attitude. He didn't know what exactly prompted it. Perhaps a change in the younger tribespeople's impression of the *chotac*, the "outsiders." Perhaps the recent intrusion of the oilmen; events on the river were discussed now in terms of before and after that intrusion.

During that conversation, Silva commented that McIntyre knew more about the cat-people than some missionaries who had pursued them for years. *There is so much more to know*, McIntyre reflected silently.

The next morning, he was awakened by the howler monkeys bugling the arrival of a new day, then by some Indians beyond the station's wall swallowing river water and throwing it up, a native method of cleansing their stomachs. While the vomiting sounds went on, Silva woke up too and invited McIntyre to a breakfast of manioc pancakes and papaya.

Over breakfast, they discussed the population threshold below which a tribe could not be expected to survive in the wild. The accepted number was one hundred, but Silva did not believe that to be a firm figure. Unless colds or other germs from the outside overran them, even smaller communities had a good chance if they secured stable fishing and hunting grounds. On the other hand, with fewer than one hundred people their will to continue the inherited way often failed. Joining other tribes or the civilizados' way were then the only options, and if there were civilizados nearby, the Indians usually chose acculturation, which offered free food, medicine, and gadgets.

An hour later, they were following Câmbio through the bush toward the closest Mayoruna hamlet, where they were met by a quietly friendly population. Among the hosts, McIntyre saw a handsome youngster, lips traditionally tattooed, who looked part white. His right arm ended in a shriveled infant-sized hand, but he had obviously not been earmarked for execution. And there were plenty of baby girls.

No one here spoke Portuguese; Silva and Câmbio interpreted. The population understood fairly easily the notion of census and agreed to cluster in front of their respective huts. With a pencil on a brown bag, Silva marked the huts with a cross, the males and females in them with X and Y symbols, and the children with a unisex dash. McIntyre photographed a mother with an enormous tumor on the right side of her belly; eight of her eleven children were boys.

They passed a locked hut and Silva told McIntyre that a slave lived in it, a river woman who had been kidnapped from Peru. Letting Silva walk ahead with Câmbio and a crowd of tribespeople, McIntyre waited till there was no one around, then slipped the latch and peered inside. He saw a naked girl on a hammock slung so low that it nearly touched the ground. In her arms, an infant not yet a year old was reaching up to her necklace of red beads. Both were light-skinned, though it took the explorer an instant to realize it because of the film of dirt that covered them.

The prisoner looked up dazedly, but otherwise paid no attention to the intruder. McIntyre raised his camera, hoping that the hut's dim light would do justice to her unmoving eyes and her hands, which he found beautiful; she had long fingers, narrow palms, and delicate wrists. Then he stepped away and the latch sealed the door again.

Câmbio explained that this village was made of the splinters of three others. The original villages had disintegrated after skirmishes with the oilmen.

McIntyre asked the villagers about Paulo Lucena; no one here seemed to know him.

Silva's head count on the brown bag totaled 117 villagers. Sixty-six were children. The rest seemed evenly divided between men and women of various ages. The old were the fewest, but that proved nothing. Câmbio announced that the next village was his own; before sundown, they visited it and tallied its population at 102. They were invited to spend the night and offered roasted fish, and Câmbio introduced his family to Silva and McIntyre.

The moment when they could be alone came after photographing Câmbio's family. McIntyre stepped toward the water's edge, and Câmbio spontaneously moved along with him. McIntyre looked at Câmbio, who responded with a brief but calm glance. McIntyre breathed deeply to slow down his pounding heart and started by asking about Câmbio's leg.

Câmbio explained that he had broken his ankle hunting, a little before the oilmen's appearance on the river. Now he couldn't track game or teach hunting skills to his children as effectively. So he was planning to paddle downstream to that mission, over, where he had lived before meeting the explorer the first time. He wanted to learn how to be a radio operator, over. He would take along his wife and children.

Then, as if reading McIntyre's thoughts, Câmbio mentioned the old village. The flood was a disaster, over. Several people drowned, over, and the tribe broke up. The *bedi* ("jaguar") moiety separated from the *macu* ("worm") moiety. Some families, like his own, decided to raft down toward the settled parts. Among the flood's victims was the headman, who couldn't swim.

He couldn't swim?

Despite the fact that he felt both convinced of Barnacle's death and certain of his mysterious continued presence, the information struck McIntyre with the impact of tragic news. Barnacle drowned? The image of the healthy, muscular headman just didn't fit into that kind of death. Did he really drown? Was Câmbio sure?

"Yes, he drowned, over. He died trying to save his children." Câmbio's words seemed to be tiny bubbles of oxygen, which McIntyre rushed to catch, to inhale. Barnacle had saved some of his children; yes, as far as Câmbio remembered, the little cross-eyed boy had survived.

Tuti! Tuti had survived!

McIntyre felt thankfully happy. He controlled himself. They had reached the shore.

*

Now he was listening to Câmbio clarifying events and circumstances of seven years ago. Yes, Red Cheeks had been a chronic rebel, but he was mainly punished for impregnating Zonia out of wedlock; she had been pledged to someone else. Zonia was now remarried. And what about the *língua velha*, asked McIntyre, the old way of speaking, of flashing thoughts into people's minds? Was it still spoken?

"*Sim, se fala*," Câmbio responded, "Yes, it is spoken."

He added that it was taught to some of the youngsters. McIntyre asked how it was taught and Câmbio responded that a young apprentice would stay at all times very close to an elder, hunting and fishing with him, helping to build his hut. The closeness itself seemed to be the method of teaching. Finally, Câmbio came back to his own plans for the future. He had decided that if he wasn't accepted at the mission he would, *com certeza* ("surely") paddle back upstream to join the uncontacted Mayoruna.

McIntyre nodded, then told Câmbio how he had managed to climb to the *nascente* of the big river. He described the windswept peaks guarded by *penitentes*. The sourcewaters trickling across that high realm where there was almost no life, except for tough bunchgrass and fleeing flocks of vicuñas. Câmbio listened with the same fierce attention he had shown when first meeting the explorer the day before.

As McIntyre finished his tale, Câmbio was claimed back by two of his noisy children. A little later other tribesmen wordlessly helped the visitors rig their hammocks for the night.

McIntyre delayed going to sleep and lingered by the river. He sat down, challenged by the sight of the water, so dark and homogenous under the canopy that it looked like a flow of tar.

Although Barnacle's death was not a surprise, he felt more than sadness about it—he felt *saudade*, a Portuguese word infinitely more vibrant and powerful, implying affectionate nostalgia, and yearning, and remembrance, and lost love. For all of his certainty, he had hoped to find out that the headman was not dead. He had hoped to meet Barnacle again and to tell him the story of finding the source. Eight years earlier they had confessed to each other their hopes and confusions, their anguish and frailty. They had shared each other's plans and compared more intimately than in words their very reasons for being who they were.

Barnacle was dead now, with all he meant as custodian of the river and forest, and priest of the past. And the world was changing—witness these Mayorunas' emergence from hiding, their willingness to be counted, talked to, known, and guided, whether rapidly or slowly, toward becoming something else.

McIntyre realized how deeply connected the cat-man was, not only to what McIntyre had lived eight years earlier, but to everything he'd learned from it. To his sense of time, to his worries about the future. To the merits and risks of discovery. To mysteries being as valuable an inheritance as knowledge. To what he had achieved, before finding the source and since. He felt permeated by the headman's persona. The certainty of Barnacle's death clashed with an almost physical sensation of his presence, and of their mutual, continuing companionship. And the beaming . . .

"*Se fala*," Câmbio had said, "It is spoken."

The next day the census was extended to two more villages.

At the end of the day, back at Pôsto Lobo, McIntyre added up the final figures—325 Mayoruna, of whom almost 200 were children—and documented them with pictures. There was no truth in the infanticide report; by making up the story, Lucena had turned the international press into a forum for his resentment.

McIntyre sent his findings to FUNAI's main office in Brasília, and a letter with a pouch of Polaroid prints to Dieter Steiner in Germany, explaining what he had found and why he still thought it a story worth telling. Then he flew home. Weeks later, in Arlington, Virginia, when his Kodachromes came back from the lab, the 35mm slides of Sally *Doña* Perez and of the canoe trip to Pôsto Lobo showed a strange purplish tint. He remembered falling into the river with his loaded cameras around his neck—his picture-taking among the Mayoruna seemed to be forever jinxed. He also received an answer from the World Health Organization. The Indian in whose bed he had slept had chicken pox—smallpox, to which so many Indians had fallen victims, had been recently eradicated.

Months afterward, the Polaroid prints came back from Germany, with a note from Dieter Steiner: "They are interesting, but not what *Der Stern* had in mind." But if any evidence of infanticide was ever uncovered, *Der Stern* wanted to be the first to know.

Early in 1990, Loren McIntyre got what seemed to be a lucky break, a chance to return to the Javari and look for his Mayoruna friends. Especially Tuti. Barnacle's son would be now about twenty-eight years old, a hunter, perhaps a shaman, surely a father. The *National Geographic* had assigned McIntyre to search the upper Amazon region for data useful in planning articles for 1992, the five hundredth anniversary of the Europeans' arrival in the New World. One thing they wanted was the latest estimate on the rate of deforestation.

In Brazil, he learned both good news and bad. Based on ground, air, and satellite surveys, the good news was that in Brazil less than ten percent of the original tropical rain forest had been destroyed by use of the land for man's own purposes. The bad news was that the rate of destruction was increasing, particularly in the western states of Rondônia and Acre. One reason for it was the growth in Brazil's population: it had expanded fivefold in McIntyre's lifetime.

Trying to include the Javari's source area in his survey, McIntyre ran into some unexpected obstacles. Small planes were not to be found, even at the premium price McIntyre offered—$300 an hour, double the usual rate. The problem was that hundreds of planes had already been hired at shocking prices by the gold prospectors of Roraima. Meanwhile, through the whole month of March, the headquarters of FUNAI, providers of permits and information, were shut down: pending the inauguration of the new president of Brazil, no one opened doors or answered phones in the capital. McIntyre was certain that the Mayoruna were still in the upper Javari region, simply staying out of sight, as usual. Yet without adequate time and funding and a plane and reliable information there was no way to find them.

The most discouraging data for his survey came from Peru, which was struggling with an absurd inflation rate of ten percent a day, caused in part by a full-fledged drug war. Trees were being felled and burned all along the Andes' eastern slopes, including part of the Javari's lower course—not to make room for farms or cattle ranches, but for planting coca bushes, the ultimate source of cocaine and crack. What an incongruity, thought McIntyre, that Amazonia's tremendous botanical pharmaceutical resources were being destroyed in order to grow plants used to poison humans around the world. "Every time someone snorts in Miami or Los Angeles, another tree goes down," said a river fleet officer whose father was one of McIntyre's old navy friends. "Coca is by far the best-paying plant in the region, and it will grow anywhere." The officer pointed to the map. "In this wild space between the Ucayali and the Javari, coca fields are sprouting. It's easy to spot them from the air; they're a lighter shade of green."

A hundred years earlier, rubber tappers had gathered latex in that part of the forest. They killed or chased away the Indians, but left the trees alone. After the rubber boom collapsed they withdrew and the Indians had the forest back to themselves. In the new invasion, the *narcotraficantes* paid coca farmers to move into Indian territory, and there was not enough army and navy to chase them out. The riverbank trees once used to moor ships were being replaced by shrubs four feet tall.

The Mayoruna would meet this latest invasion somewhat prepared for it by their history. That was less true of other tribes.

The lack of planes for hire generated a string of delays, and in the end there was no time to whip together even a hasty expedition to the upper Javari. McIntyre flew from Iquitos back to Tabatinga, Brazil, next door to Leticia, his old stomping ground. In Tabatinga he booked a seat on the weekly commercial flight to Cruzeiro do Sul, Brazil's westernmost town and the terminus point of BR-364, the Trans-Amazon Highway.

He carried under his arm a copy of the December 1988 *National Geographic*, a hundredth-anniversary issue with a holographic cover picturing the Earth: tilted under overhead light, the three-dimensional globe shattered, symbolizing the planet's fragility. McIntyre slipped a business card into the magazine at the page where his article started ("The End of Innocence," about the doomed Indians of Rondônia) and asked the flight attendant to pass it to the pilot. "Tell him I would like to join him up front."

Within a minute, camera around his neck, he was in the flight compartment, telling the captain how he had once been marooned on the Javari, which ran roughly parallel to their flight line. The pilot obliged by staying under the high overcast so McIntyre could shoot pictures of the Javari if they sighted it.

Suddenly the airliner smashed into a wall of turbulence, unusual in this area at eight in the morning. The plane shuddered. The noise of the thunderstorm resembled a succession of auto crashes. A massive overcast blacked out the world. Glancing at the compass, McIntyre saw that the pilot had changed the course to get out of the storm. A few degrees to the west, closer to the Javari. And then, as quickly as it had begun, the storm ended. The plane flashed into a cloudless sky and gained altitude. Beneath its wings the forest stretched seemingly to eternity. Off to the right a small and solitary mountain range rose green above the forest. It was the Cordillera Ultra-Oriental.

McIntyre gazed at the highest peak as it fell astern, while the plane turned and began its descent to Cruzeiro do Sul, only sixty or seventy miles away. He did not expect to see the waterfall, for its milk-white double gush would be hidden by trees. But his mind was a jumble—so close to the

Mayoruna, yet so far away. Tuti may be standing on a riverbank shooting arrows at fish, maybe looking up at the plane. No, it was too far away. *Would Tuti even remember me?* McIntyre mumbled thanks to the pilot and copilot and went back to his cabin seat for the landing.

He pulled a sheet of paper out of his briefcase and wrote the date. He headed the page with his name, Lowen, and the place, Southern Cross (for Cruzeiro do Sul):

Tribu Matses, Cachoeira Esperanza
Cordillera Ultra-Oriental
March 24 (my God, my birthday).

Dear Tuti,

I don't expect this letter to reach you, since the postal service surely doesn't reach the Waterfall of Hope as yet, and even if it did you couldn't read this without help from someone like Câmbio (*olá, Câmbio*). Still, writing it makes me feel that you're alive.

Maybe I'm writing to you only to get my thoughts in order and try to reach you without a mailman. If only with a passing thought, Tuti, if I think of you in a thunderstorm and you think of me at a frog-poison ceremony, could we become aware of one another? Could you someday, somehow, pick up a living remembrance of me? Before it is too late?

The plane landed and the door opened for the passengers disembarking at Cruzeiro do Sul. Hot and humid jungle air washed through the cabin. McIntyre was still hunched in his seat. He would go back to find them, he thought, even if he had to live as long as G.M. Dyott. Then he continued writing. Writing and thinking, as in a dream, about the people who defied time, in the forests at the foot of the Ultimate Eastern Range.

Index